NEW DEMONS

Cultural Memory

in

the

Present

Hent de Vries, Editor

NEW DEMONS

Rethinking Power and Evil Today

Simona Forti

Translated by Zakiya Hanafi

STANFORD UNIVERSITY PRESS

STANFORD, CALIFORNIA

Stanford University Press
Stanford, California

First published as *I nuovi demoni* in March 2012 by Giangiacomo Feltrinelli Editore, Milan, Italy. Copyright © Giangiacomo Feltrinelli Editore, 2012.

The translation of this work has been funded by SEPS
SEGRETARIATO EUROPEO PER LE PUBBLICAZIONI SCIENTIFICHE

Via Val d'Aposa 7 - 40123 Bologna - Italy
seps@seps.it - www.seps.it

Library of Congress Cataloging-in-Publication Data

Forti, Simona, author.
  [Nuovi demoni. English]
  New demons : rethinking power and evil today / Simona Forti ; translated by Zakiya Hanafi.
       pages cm--(Cultural memory in the present)
  "First published as I nuovi demoni in March 2012 by Giangiacomo Feltrinelli Editore, Milan, Italy."
  Includes bibliographical references and index.
  ISBN 978-0-8047-8624-9 (cloth : alk. paper)--
  ISBN 978-0-8047-9295-0 (pbk. : alk. paper)
  1. Good and evil. 2. Power (Philosophy) 3. Ethics, Modern--19th century.
  4. Ethics, Modern--20th century. 5. Political science--Philosophy. I. Title.
  II. Series: Cultural memory in the present.
  BJ1404.F6713 2014
  170--dc23

                         2014025922
  ISBN 978-0-8047-9298-1 (electronic)

Typeset by Bruce Lundquist in 11/13.5 Adobe Garamond

In memory of Linda.

To the unpredictable with Marco and Pietro.

*Everything that isn't autobiographical
is plagiarism.*

PEDRO ALMODÓVAR

Contents

Acknowledgments

The writing of this book kept me occupied for at least five years, and in half a decade the debts that mount up are likely to become incalculable. I hope that throughout the text there are evident signs of my gratitude to many authors with whom the exchange has been more like an agonistic friendship than a transmission of information.

Nevertheless, there are people whose names I cannot help but mention: first Annalisa Ceron and Andrea Lanza, for having read and reread the manuscript with me.

I especially thank Giorgio Barberis, Laura Bazzicalupo, Richard Bernstein, Gian Mario Bravo, Barbara Carnevali, Adriana Cavarero, Simona Cerutti, Roberto Esposito, Carlo Galli, Olivia Guaraldo, Maurilio Guasco, Agnes Heller, Samantha Novello, Pier Paolo Portinaro, Marco Revelli, Luca Savarino, Luca Scuccimarra, Gabriella Silvestrini, Mauro Simonazzi, Zoltan Szankay (even if my thanks come too late), Domenico Taranto, Davide Tarizzo, Angelo Torre, Francesco Tuccari, Miguel Vatter, and Gustavo Zagrebelsky, for having encouraged me in various ways and on many occasions: listening to me or advising me, putting pressure on me or reproaching me, suggesting readings or helping me to avoid mistakes.

Finally, there are people I have to thank for putting up with me during this period: Susi Bigarelli, who countered my black moods with her affection and irony like no one else; and Manuela Ceretta, with whom I shared endless days of confinement at the National Library in Paris. Knowing that in the evenings we would go back to exchanging words, comments, and laughter turned those days into some of the best memories I have of those years. I owe special thanks to Grazie Cassarà, who believed in this work even when my constant delays might have made its very existence doubtful. Her grace and intelligence allowed me to continue pursuing the project. I am also very grateful to Donatella Berasi and Albertine Cerutti for their patience and expertise.

Thanks, finally, to Marco Geuna, because without his perfectionist rigor this book would have been finished earlier, but without his help and his infinite understanding there would have been no book at all.

For the American edition I must thank Chiara Bottici, Giunia Gatta, Emily-Jane Cohen, Paul Kottman, Alessia Ricciardi and, especially, Zakiya Hanafi.

Turin, December 2013

NEW DEMONS

Introduction

This book is the result of a compromise. A compromise between the desire, or need, to continue reflecting on evil, and the awareness that many of the concepts used to think about it are no longer usable; between the conviction that in relations of power there must circulate an ethical instance, and the certainty that the way to political moralizing has been barred to us forever. What approach can we take to the question of evil as it relates to power today, if the assumptions behind all claims to promoting the good—especially the political good—have been progressively delegitimized? Perhaps the first, unavoidable step is to declare that the dialectical relationship between good and evil has been broken once and for all. Hence, even if we are no longer able to believe that the good is fully realizable, we cannot and should not stop talking about evil.

A lot, if not everything, rides on the problem of suffering. Or more accurately, everything depends on whether suffering continues to be a *problem* for us, and in what way. In philosophical terms, it all depends on what significance we attribute to that ultimate phenomenological given—*the fact of pain and suffering*—which, even after its various stratifications of meaning have been deconstructed, remains before our eyes. This is not a question of the inescapable reality that inherently accompanies the finitude and vulnerability of our lives but, rather, what Emmanuel Levinas calls "useless suffering," which is *produced* out of human relations, and which propagates with varying intensity and range on the basis of the social and political context.

Although it is true that evil has been spoken of in many ways—as numerous as the explanations or justifications offered by philosophy in response to the dismay caused by pain, suffering, and death—there is no doubt that its meaning has swung back and forth between two recurring alternatives that cut across the different historical periods of thought. It is as if the same dilemma constantly presented itself: either evil does not exist, because suffering is "innocent," or, if suffering is viewed as the sign of some "guilt," evil risks being transformed into an independent substance. Either, as we would say today, evil is a cultural prejudice, dismantled as soon as it is observed from the perspective of the whole, from the Platonic One to the Deleuzian "multiple-One"; or it is a reality at war with being, from ancient Gnosticism to the "theoconservatism" of our day. This ontological alternative has often assumed an unfortunate form in political thought: either the pain of individuals caused by violence and oppression is viewed as a necessary and negligible contribution to the success of the final "project" or it is the confirmatory sign of an advancing, destructive nihilism.

What direction are we to take, then, if we share the premises of critical and deconstructive thought but also believe that the problem of evil—whatever name we choose to give it, even that of the idea of evil itself—is not only still relevant but also, first and foremost, the *a priori* in the human animal's search for meaning? What stance can we take if we do not feel aligned or comfortable with the abstractions of a normative political philosophy that believes it can overcome the negative by invoking the "you must"; and if we feel equally remote from the "euphoric" currents of an ontological, political immanence for which evil is simply the cumbersome legacy of a theological and metaphysical conception of the world? It is hardly a trivial problem if what is referred to as "continental philosophy" seems to be increasingly polarized between two distinct blocks of opinion: on the one hand, an emphatic revival—both religious and post-Kantian—of a notion of "radical evil" made to serve as a negative rule from which to derive, by contrast, the tables of the new categorical imperatives; and on the other hand, the mocking shrug that claims to follow the immanent power of life beyond moral prejudices, "beyond good and evil."

· · ·

To redefine the contemporary relevance of the question of political evil, I therefore chose to take the byways, so to speak, offered by the genealogical approach. I put it to myself to examine the relationship be-

tween evil and power, focusing on the political repercussions of the different philosophical presuppositions. I attempted to recreate the conditions
that made it possible to conceive of political evil starting from late modernity, in order to understand how the concepts that have defined it may be
kept, reformulated, or discarded.

The point of departure for a journey of this kind can only be Kantian.
Immanuel Kant's essay on "Religion Within the Limits of Reason Alone,"
in which he returns to the problem of "radical evil," is truly a watershed
with respect to the previous philosophical tradition. The definitive distinction that Kant established between physical evil, metaphysical evil, and
moral evil allowed the purely theological and metaphysical question of
"Where does evil come from?" to be replaced by the ethical, anthropological, and historical question of "Why do we commit evil deeds?" Thus, for
the German philosopher, moral evil is no longer a substance, but neither
is it a nonbeing. It is an act: an act that has to do with freedom. However,
although Kant makes it possible to reflect on the complicated interplay between evil and freedom, by his own admission he is pulled up short by the
"inscrutability" of the root of this connection. The possibility of evil actions
that *intentionally* violate the moral law is unthinkable for him; the existence
of human beings who pursue evil for the sake of evil is unacceptable.

To push beyond what Kant leaves "unspoken," to plumb the "diabolical abysses" of freedom, was the goal of later philosophical thought, which
continued to seek out the "root" of evil. From Schelling to Heidegger,
from Nietzsche to Levinas, from Freud to Lacan—to name only the main
figures whose works I will examine—a path can be traced that radicalizes
Kant's discovery to the point of overturning it, until transgressing the law,
whether divine law or the imperative of reason, became identified as the
main objective of evil.

In the philosophical thinking of the nineteenth and twentieth centuries, although appearing in radically different versions, the concepts of
nihilism, the will to death, and the will to nothingness defined the horizon of understanding of the "new demons." Thought of as a disease of the
will or as an instinctual drive, as the delirium of reason or as a passion for
the absolute, evil in any case always involved the forces of transgression
and disorder: in a word, *the power of death*. An eloquent, exemplary synthesis of this cluster of concepts appears in what I have decided to call the
"Dostoevsky paradigm." Not so much because the literary equivalent of a

specific post-Kantian idea of evil is to be found in the pages of the great Russian writer—particularly in *Demons* and *The Brothers Karamazov*—but because Dostoevsky's protagonists embody a set of insights, ideas, and concepts whose relationship, although changing, tends toward a clearly identifiable nexus. The schema that takes shape, not always directly and explicitly, starting from Stavrogin and his friends—*pars pro toto*—was for a long time the established condition of conceivability for evil. This paradigm, which I reconstruct, was one that Nietzsche and Freud participated in as well as Heidegger and Levinas (although their contributions to it differed). The works of these thinkers more than any others were turning points in a possible history of the contemporary idea of evil. However, we should perhaps note that this paradigm partly owes its existence to a "simple" way of reading these authors. As I show in the sections devoted to these thinkers, I am convinced that another perspective opens up from some of their writings, one that can easily merge into another, alternative genealogy.

There is no doubt in my mind that the expressive power with which the Russian genius gives life to his nihilistic, destructive demons not only definitively names the "secret" of radical evil that Kant had failed to reveal, but it also clarifies its conditions of possibility, placing evil in relation to the question of power. Maybe what looms up for the first time in *Demons* is the distinction between wickedness and evil, between a subject's way of being and the "systemic" outcome of the interaction between subjects. If wickedness has to do with the structure of the individual conscience, evil is a mode of the expression of power. Or, rather, it is the occurrence of a wicked situation in history, so to speak, that is the effect of a collective interaction between trespassing freedoms. All the characters misuse their free will in individual ways. But it is certain that for Dostoevsky the various demons, which correspond to the various ways in which evil makes itself visible, share the same absolute desire: to take the place of God and his infinite freedom. However, as finite creatures, since they are incapable of creating, they can only destroy. This is how evil comes into the world, for Dostoevsky and for all those who follow in his tracks. Evil enters the world as a diabolical disease of power; a power that, because it exceeds all limits, can only be the pure energy of oppression and domination, an inexhaustible source of suffering and death.

Nihilism, evil, and power: these form a conceptual triangulation within which, in a kind of secularization of the theological assumptions, many of the philosophers of the twentieth century believed it was possible to circumscribe the tragedies of their history. Will, omnipotence, and nothingness: although no longer framed in Dostoevsky's religious outlook, the correlation between these three terms was taken up and reworked by later philosophers, who continued to think of evil as a result of the perversion of the will in omnipotence, as the result of a sovereign subject—whether collective or individual makes no difference—that by raising itself up to the All creates Nothingness. This is a "simple," unidirectional vision of power that remains faithful to the model of sovereign and subjects, whose demonic cypher, also masterfully illustrated by the Russian writer, is depicted most forcefully in the relationship between victim and perpetrator. In other words, on the one hand there stands an omnipotent subject, bearer of death, and on the other, a subject reduced to a mere object, because he or she has been made totally passive by the other's violence. The same polarized view extends to the collective dimension and allows it to be modeled according to a similar, dualistic structure: on the one hand, a cynical leader who exploits the weaknesses of others, and on the other, the weak masses who are utterly incapable of resistance. The hermeneutic capacity of this schema has been expanded—as part of the nihilistic hypothesis that supports it—to include the key experiences of the twentieth century: total war, planetary, destructive technology, repeated genocides, and above all, Auschwitz. These are the new phenomena by which evil manifests itself in history, and for which there seems to be no better explanation than "a pure unleashing of the will to death."

· · ·

There is no doubt that focusing the gaze on the "accursed share," on the abyss of the subject and "being," has helped to go beyond the Kantian "prohibition." However, this way of thinking about evil and power, as well as about their relationship, is likely to rigidify our understanding of reality into overly schematic, unilateral categories. In the end, even in the most developed thinking on the topic, the emphasis is always given exclusively to the dark, transgressive face of a subjectivity that is avid for destruction. Inevitably, this leads to a return of the dualistic schema, which obscures the complex phenomenology of power and, equally, that of the scenes of evil.

The time has come, I believe, *to let go of the Dostoevsky paradigm*. We must leave it behind in order to understand the "black heart" of the twentieth century, and, even more urgently, to be able to contend with the concerns of today. Our present times no longer allow power to be represented as the simple frontal relation between the state and individual bearers of rights. At the same time, political evil—even the political evil that lurks in our Western democracies—can no longer be purely understood as the result of an unleashing of wickedness. The scene of evil is a complex scene where the will to nothingness and death do not reign supreme. Political philosophy has been stuck for too long in this paradigm, so that it never completely rids itself of a conception of domination linked to this "grandiose" idea of evil. In other words, it has continued to think of the relationship of power, which becomes an event of evil, along the binary lines of a dualistic, rigidly polarized conception, as if the eternal Dostoevskian scene of the violation of children—the quintessential innocent victims— were to repeat itself throughout history. Political tragedies, the grimmest events, have been analyzed according to this topology: *wicked demons* on the one side and *absolute victims* on the other.

There evidently exists a metaphysical and theological *a priori* that continues to affect us, often unconsciously. It is almost as if we refuse to look deeply into the intricate web of political relations and do not want to become aware of what happens before arriving at that final scene of domination, where, it is true, the most absolute asymmetry does indeed reign. We therefore need to dismantle this demonological vision of power and rely instead on an analytical model that no longer attributes evil exclusively to the desire for and will to death.

This change of perspective received a significant boost from Hannah Arendt's thought, and above all from that of Michel Foucault, clearing the way to contemporary reflection on biopolitics and biopower, among other things. In the middle part of this book, after reexamining their contributions, I look into several interesting discussions that have emerged from the reappraisal of their legacy. From historical studies on genocides to research on the theory of race, thought on biopolitics has contributed greatly to shifting the focus from the power of putting to death to strategies for maximizing life. It has directed our attention to how making life a unique, undisputed value has paradoxically fostered the mass production of death. An entire field of investigation and thought has thus changed its vantage point on evil, without explicitly discussing it, now focusing less on the omnipotent will of the perpetrators and more on the condition of the victims, who are transformed into waste material in the name of the absolutization of life.

There is no doubt that any attempt to rethink the relationship between evil and power cannot help but return to the historical scene epitomized by Auschwitz, and to how it has been interpreted. Myriad unanswered questions remain, however. What does the status of "absolute victim" mean in relation to the scientific and ideological obsession for enhancing life? If we start from the premise—now a commonplace among historians—that for a genocide to take place there must first be *a process of dehumanization and de-subjectification of the future victim*, we must nevertheless look more closely into how this process takes place. Is it really arrived at through the unleashing of a supposedly "naturalistic" nihilism that goes "beyond good and evil"? These are the questions I ask myself when revisiting some Nazi texts on racial theory, following a double thread that runs through them: the image of the parasite and the relationship between Soul, Body, and Type. Is it really true, as claimed by many interpreters of biopower—from historians of genocide to post-Foucauldian thinkers—that in the racist discourse the body of the future victim of extermination is emptied of human and moral meaning? Rather, is it not saturated with a "hypermoral" meaning that claims to know how to go about separating death from life? I believe that the supposed neutrality of a knowledge that was believed to be scientific, far from foundering in a nihilistic drift, has continued to exert a powerful influence through the traditional dichotomy of good and evil.

· · ·

In short, how does one exit permanently from both the dualistic culture that nurtures the scenes of evil and the often unconscious, although opposite, dualism of the many interpreters who judge those scenes? I certainly do not want to come to the discovery that the perpetrators do not exist, or that they are innocent, and that the victims are guilty. But I think we should break down these logical dichotomies to transform them into a field of forces and tensions, in which the antinomies lose their substantial identity. This is not to oppose the Dostoevsky paradigm to a contrary, specular way of thinking, but to place alongside it another paradigmatic set of concepts that integrates, at the same time as it unblocks, the geometry that is rigidly fixed on the separation between absolute subjects and objects of domination. A different genealogy of the relationship between evil and power can thus be brought to light: a genealogy that finally puts into question the inextricable, recurrent link between transgression, power, and death. This is the approach that was first taken in the third chapter of Genesis, which ever since has continued to conceive of evil as the action of a creature that is essentially rebellious, because deep down it seeks to equal divine omnipotence. I believe that, for a long time now, this anthropological figure is not the one whose dangers we need to guard ourselves from anymore. I think that today, more than ever, what needs to be questioned instead is the desire for rules and conformity that cements our lives in irresponsibility and indifference, a desire that philosophy, apart from a few exceptions, has not wanted or known how to take on.

The second and final part of the book thus seeks to tie the threads together so as to outline a different way of thinking about the hendiadys of evil and power and to propose a new paradigm: that of "mediocre demons" or "the normalcy of evil." My intellectual debt toward Arendt's famous work *Eichmann in Jerusalem: A Report on the Banality of Evil* is evident. Her book successfully transformed a particular occurrence into an event that was emblematic of an era, transposing Adolf Eichmann's trial into a general historical and theoretical redefinition of many political problems. However, because she passed away before completing *The Life of the Mind*, Arendt did not have time to develop the set of ideas that connect evil to an absence of judgment and to conformity. And rather than provide a reasoned argument on this association, she tied its conception to an expression, one that in my opinion is not entirely convincing—"the banality of evil"—which has left us with a long list of unanswered questions.

Now, there have been many ways to continue and elaborate on Arendt's legacy. The historical disciplines and some currents of social psychology were the first to try to overturn the equation between evil and transgression, investigating between the folds of so-called crimes of obedience. I give a quick overview of these, also pointing out the limits of these approaches from a philosophical point of view. To say that evil is systemic, as they do, that it does not stem from an innate "disposition" of the perpetrators, however, cannot be restricted to meaning that evil is the result of the outcome of an authoritarian context. True: evil is a system, in the sense of a tangle of subjectivities, a network of relations, whose threads knit together thanks to the perfect complementarity between (a few) wicked actors and originators, (a few) zealous, committed agents, and (many) acquiescent, not simply indifferent, spectators. But why do these cogs and wheels fit together so well?

Thinking within the paradigm of mediocre demons means primarily putting into question the exclusive role of the will to and desire for death, and instead viewing the scenes of evil as powerfully inhabited by the will to life, as the result of an attempt to maximize life itself. It also means focusing less on the "guilt" of the transgression and more on the devious normativity of nonjudgment, endorsed and celebrated by the morality that has so often taught us that judging is a sign of pride, that it is the shadow of that first sin committed by our first parents: the sin of disobedience.

Mediocre demons do not replace "absolute demons," of course. This is not what I mean by my work. Absolute demons exist, and still exist today; but if their efforts are successful it is because they seamlessly integrate into the desire of all those who, being too occupied with consolidating their life opportunities, adapt without reacting. For this reason, today, rather than pursuing the impossible goal of saying goodbye to the subject—an act that implicitly continues to adopt the subject as a synonym of violence and arrogance—it is important to ask how power and subjectivity constitute each other and are mutually reinforcing; to question not so much why we become wicked subjects but rather, above all, how we become obedient subjects. We need to understand what sort of delusion inspires our omnipotence; but even more we need to try and explain what desire motivates our anxiety to conform.

A genealogy of mediocre demons—and indirectly of pastoral power—must weave together the philosophical contributions of texts that, perhaps not always explicitly, have asked themselves these very questions. Accordingly, I track down the passages in Nietzsche's thought in which the critique of democracy, passivity, and conformism is not "simple" in the least, and in which the will to life plays an extremely ambivalent role. I have focused on the continuity detected between Christianity and the modern world in order to emphasize, and use, the complexity with which Nietzsche describes the process of subjectification that made the human animal docile and controllable, manipulable and obedient, bringing us one of the first and most powerful investigations into the link between subjectivity and power. I then search the work of Foucault, his personal continuation of the Nietzschean genealogy, for the possibility of naming political evil and of locating it at the highest point of subjective dependency, in those "states of domination" that suppressed the play or the movement between freedom and power. I draw arguments from his writings on governmentality and pastoral power, and even more from the lectures of his later years devoted to the "care of the self" and *parrhesia*, to try to formulate some partial answers to the questions that are key to the paradigm of mediocre devils. First of all: How is a relationship of subordination cemented? What kind of subjectification was introduced in the Christian West so as to make the relationship of care and protection a perfect mechanism for the production of generalized dependency? And also: How are the conditions of possibility for resistance to political evil to be conceived? Why was an entire field of experience, from the "care of the self" to *parrhesia*, removed from the spectrum of examples on which to model our ethical and political conduct? In a word, does another way of becoming subjects exist?

If so, it can only stem from an ethos that changes the perception of life and death and of their relationship; from a "way of life" that never silences its inner duality and that does not reify it into an internal essence of the good and an external substance of evil. What I seek to demonstrate is that these questions and their possible answers are not only significant for individual ethics, they can also be directly transposed onto the political and collective planes. This is what I try to show by reconstructing the theoretical ties that Foucauldian thought has forged with what has been called the philosophy of dissent from Central and Eastern Europe, especially with several Prague thinkers—from Jan Patočka to Václav Havel—who were engaged in the Charter 77 experience. In some ways it is easier to reexamine the philosophical and political contribution of the "dissidents" today than it was in the past: many of the allegations of anticommunism and philocapitalism that were directed against them have lost all meaning. However, my interest does not lie so much in rehabilitating an important chapter of European culture, one that is often overlooked, as it does in finding a "testing ground," so to speak, of the revolutionary character of an ethos that always confronts itself anew with the infinite and unsolvable problem of the meaning of a "life in truth." Because in actuality, living in truth—a prerequisite for the practice of *parrhesia*—is simply the witnessing of a life that ruthlessly questions itself on its own internal conflicts, and for this reason decides to make "inner anarchy" the terrain on which to cultivate a different political virtue, with the hope that this can be transmitted, by contagion, to the collective dimension. This is with all due respect to Fyodor Dostoevsky, who, in accordance with the most authoritative theological and metaphysical convictions on evil, was convinced that the subversive force of demons could be extinguished only by reining the two back into the One.

Ultimately, what Primo Levi also courageously examined were the political repercussions of a fatal, dualistic opposition between life and death. Perhaps it is no coincidence that he never really warmed to Dostoevsky. Everything in Levi's last work, *The Drowned and the Saved*, can be read as a refutation of *Demons* and the legend of the Grand Inquisitor, of that Manichean conception of power that opens up an abysmal distance between the feverish will of the wicked for power and death, and the passive obedience of the masses. Everything in *The Drowned and the Saved* forces us to take note of the normal, and yet at the same time perverse, functioning of the gray zone, which, unfortunately, does not only connect the opposite poles of the fence at Auschwitz. To think about the muted colors of the link between evil and power, above all from the point of view of the desire for life, is the difficult task bequeathed to us by Levi's last words, which were certainly not aimed exclusively at analyzing the circumstances of the death camp. Even in far less "extreme" situations, the gesture that separates life from death, absolutizing them in their opposition, always runs the risk of bringing along with it the conditions of evil. Or at least this is how I think *The Drowned and the Saved* should be read.

PART I

ABSOLUTE DEMONS: THE POWER OF NOTHINGNESS

The Dostoevsky Paradigm

Stavrogin's Ghost

He was a very handsome young man, about twenty-five years old, and I confess I found him striking. I expected to see some dirty ragamuffin, wasted away from depravity and stinking of vodka. On the contrary, this was the most elegant gentleman of any I had ever happened to meet[. . . .] I was also struck by his face: his hair was somehow too black, his light eyes were somehow too calm and clear, his complexion was somehow too delicate and white, his color somehow too bright and clean, his teeth like pearls, his lips like coral—the very image of beauty, it would seem, and at the same time repulsive, as it were.[1]

The analogy that Dostoevsky implicitly suggests in this presentation is difficult to miss. The resemblance between Stavrogin and Lucifer is only too obvious. Like the highest fallen angel, Stavrogin is endowed with all the contrasting qualities that make him not only the greatest of the damned, but also the most magnificent. Dazzling and statuesque, even his beauty hides the power of a demonic charm that attracts and repels at the same time. Too full of himself to love anyone else, too smart to be a fanatic, too disillusioned not to be aware of his own faults, everything about him is hallmarked by excess. And, as many Dostoevsky critics have suggested, with Stavrogin what barges in is more than just the most disturbing protagonist of the novel. Along with him comes the ghost of the next century: the specter of nihilism makes its appearance, in all its multiple facets. In Dostoevsky's view, nihilism was the last era of humanity when Nothingness insinuated itself into history to take the place of God, whose place had already been usurped by man, deified in his turn by positivist optimism.

With this young man who grew up without roots, with no father and no fatherland, the writer dramatizes the extreme consequences of what he saw as the ultimate fate stemming from the loss of meaning. Conceived by Dostoevsky as the main character of the novel, he is the point toward which all the other characters converge and, at the same time, the hub from which the force of negation radiates out along all its possible trajectories. His reason has gone beyond all bounds and touched on nothingness; his senses have run the gamut of excesses and plumbed the void. Stavrogin is not, therefore, simply a well-crafted synthesis of Dostoevsky's remarkable psychological acuity. The writer's intention is much more ambitious: to condense a philosophical vision into a credible phenomenology of the human subject. Indeed, he already knows what Nietzsche would later make clear: nihilism goes far beyond the suppression of traditional moral values and their religious foundation.[2] For this reason, Dostoevsky's writing also seeks to come to terms with the ontological rupture that has imprinted itself on the human realm and history. Beginning with *Notes from Underground*[3] (whose protagonist he develops and puts into action as Stavrogin), all of Dostoevsky's characters bear the signs of a "revolution of the spirit."

Now, this is not to take sides in the age-old debate on the philosophical status of the work of Fyodor Dostoevsky: that is, whether it represents, for philosophy as well, the final victory of a profound, authentic form of Christianity over the persistence of sin and guilt; or whether his work is instead perpetually dominated by an irrevocably tragic vision.[4] Nor am I interested in taking sides for or against those who, from Lev Shestov to Sergio Givone, through the masterful interpretation of Luigi Pareyson,[5] see the Russian author as the great thinker who anticipated Nietzsche, in some ways even "bypassing him" and successfully avoiding Heidegger's deviations. It suffices to recall in this connection that the young Georg Lukács had already noted "the smallness of Nietzsche" compared to the stature of Stavrogin.[6] What the Hungarian critic saw in this character, and in *Demons* generally, was a decisive step without which the West would never have gained full self-awareness. All this is to say that there are many influential thinkers who have shared, and continue to share, the emphatic view expressed by Nicolas Berdyaev: "We now philosophize about the *last* things under the aegis of Dostoevsky. Philosophizing about the *next-to-last* things alone is the task of traditional philosophy."[7]

But even leaving these questions open for discussion, without getting caught up in the interpretative conundrums about Dostoevsky's work that challenge its most philosophically demanding readers, there is no doubt that it marks a crucial change. Precisely for this reason, I think it legitimate to transpose the literary fictions that it has given voice to into philosophical categories, categories that, I believe, helped to reformulate the question of evil in European culture by linking it in two ways to the problem of nihilism. Going well beyond the traditional conception of the doctrine of original sin, Dostoevsky's radical position not only made an impact on ethics and religion, it also "ontologically" tied together evil and nothingness, freedom and will, into a single node. This is why "Stavrogin's ghost," *pars pro toto*, continued to waft around philosophy for a long time. Even today, it continues to inspire evocative, albeit impressionistic, interpretations of Islamic terrorism in the vein of *Demons*.[8]

In the second part of this book, I will explain why we need to let go of the one-sidedness of this approach in order to understand our present times; why, as a hermeneutic lens, in some ways it is still too dependent on a theological vision of the relationship between evil and freedom. For now, however, let us stick to one of its truths that can hardly be disputed: the figures that allowed philosophy, from Nietzsche on, to venture into the unexplored territory of evil took form from Nikolai Vsevolodovich Stavrogin, his thoughts, his actions, and his "friends." When expressed as concepts, these figures formed the horizon in which much of the philosophical culture of the twentieth century believed it could reveal something about the idea of evil in its connection with power that the earlier tradition had passed over. For this reason I believe that we can talk quite confidently of a genuine Dostoevsky paradigm: that is, an arrangement of concepts, a relation between categories, aligned according to a clear nexus, that for a long time was established as a condition of conceivability for evil—though never directly and explicitly. It is a paradigm that Nietzsche and Freud participated in no less than Heidegger, although in different ways: these are the thinkers who, more than anyone else, marked a contemporary turning point in a possible genealogical history of the idea of evil. But, to be more accurate, we should say that only specific aspects of the thought of Nietzsche, Freud, and Heidegger are pertinent to this paradigm, because, as we shall see, I am convinced that there often opens up an alternative perspective from their writings from which to view the question.

Let us start, then, by asking: What does Stavrogin personify? What is he emblematic of, along with Stepan and Pyotr Verkhovensky, Kirillov, and Shatov? But also, what about the three Brothers Karamazov, who are so glaringly "livid" in comparison to the disarming "glow" of Alyosha—what do they tell us? What are we to make of all these demons? What philosophical understanding are we led to by their lives, which even today represent one of the most monumental phenomenologies of evil? First of all, the expressive power of their roles dug up the ground in which the traditional philosophical and theological concepts had been rooted. Their characters played an exemplary, paradigmatic role. But although they have a name and a surname and their individuality is deeply anchored in the narrative context, the moment their complete uniqueness is expressed, a human typology becomes visible that can be transposed into a theoretical matrix. Each character corresponds to a mode of being that evil may assume, fitting together to form a complex phenomenology that can be broken down into its separate parts and yet also reassembled into a coherent, structured whole.

In a nutshell, evil can be expressed in many ways for Dostoevsky,[9] but all these ways fall under the same paradigm, whose structure, I would argue, he himself suggests to us. Although subsequent philosophers were able to reframe the question of evil as a question of nihilism—in the inextricable link that he posited between freedom and nothingness—in order to work within this paradigm those who followed did not need to share the same beliefs and aims as the Russian writer, and even less his religious, Christian Orthodox leaning. Embarking on the path opened up by *Demons*, before defining any content, meant breaking with the strategies that had served philosophy up to that point. It meant, first, sealing off access to any sort of naïvely dualistic, metaphysical resubstantialization; and, second, opposing all possible versions of the Platonic schema of the nonexistence of evil. It meant rejecting both theological and philosophical theodicy. And most importantly, it meant leaving behind the strategies that modern rationality had tried to use to circumvent or neutralize this question. We could go so far as to summarize Shestov's thesis—for whom "the true Critique of Reason" was performed not by Immanuel Kant but by Fyodor Dostoevsky[10]—with the claim that the genuine "radicality of evil" was conceived not in the arguments put forward in *Religion Within the Limits of Reason Alone* but rather in the plot of *Demons*.[11]

What Kant Dared Not Think About: Kant and Schelling

Perhaps it would be truer to say that Dostoevsky radicalized Kant's notion so far as to take Kant well beyond himself—or, rather, against himself. There is no doubt that, in the tortuous path along which philosophy attempted to think about evil, eventually restoring it to the freedom of the subject, the author of the *Three Critiques* marked a milestone.

Paul Ricoeur maintains that by naming evil, myths were the first instrument of symbolic and linguistic mediation to define and objectify the sense of a fear-inducing, confused, and speechless experience.[12] If this is true, what sort of activity did philosophical reason perform? How did it go about leaving behind that primary, naïve sort of "spontaneous Manichaeism" that separates an experience of the good from an experience of evil by rigidly opposing them? The idea that Being is coextensive with the Good, thus relegating Evil to Non-Being, was introduced by Plato, as we know, and developed by Augustine. It proved to be the most tenacious response put forward by metaphysics: a relation of identity that would hold firm in the face of many lexical and conceptual changes. However, there is an obvious danger associated with deconstructing dualistic substantialism: such a powerful downplaying of evil can turn the force of the negative into something that exists purely to serve the positive. Poised perpetually on the brink of this double risk—of a "realist" dualism on the one hand, and of an idealist or historicist reductionism on the other—philosophy tenaciously sought to avert the danger at several key moments. It did so by resorting to a "revolutionary" force, so to speak: one that posits a close relationship between evil and freedom, going so far as to make evil the very condition of freedom. Except that, when faced with the "absurdity" of Being and God that such a prospect seemed to invite, on every occasion it retreated in fright to return to its ranks, as it were. This is the alternation that the question of evil continued to repeat, both in theology and metaphysics, until the end of the modern era. It oscillated constantly between dualism and its neutralization, between a vision of evil as a substance and a vision that denied its reality. Only occasionally did philosophy escape from this alternation, by arguing for a moral evil that implies an irreducible freedom.

In his own personal journey, Augustine seems to have foreseen how the possible future solutions would play out. As we know, in the battle against the Manichaeism of his past—against a temptation that was perhaps never completely put to rest—he accepted the legacy of Plotinus in order to give a sense to evil that was also logically consistent.[13] Because thought about Being is equivalent to thought about the One—and therefore, to thought about the Good—evil cannot be a substance.[14] In addition to this perspective, in Augustine there appeared a new notion of "nothingness"—the nothingness associated with creation *ex nihilo* that is connected to the idea of an absolute origin. This sets up negativity as a sign of the distance between creator and creature, and marks the ontological deficiency of creation as such.[15] So alongside the belief that metaphysical evil is an error of the perspective from which human beings judge the world, due to our finitude, comes the idea that moral evil is the result of guilt, sin, or a perversion that deviates the upright will. Along with the Apostle Paul, Augustine knew that human beings have the ability to transgress or disturb the order of being.[16] And he knew that once we are opened up to that order, when we participate in the reality of God, the fullness of our own being that we experience can only make the return to our normal state seem like a lack. This is the first sign that nothingness—out of which human beings were brought into being—leaves imprinted on the creature. Though the ontological approach of the *privatio boni* (the privation of good) and the moral approach of a subjective perspective were still logically indistinguishable at this point, in the modern era they began to gradually separate.[17]

It was Kant who took the decisive step of restoring moral evil to human freedom. Under the blows to rational theology, which considered theodicy a "transcendental illusion," the Kantian critique laid down the first, foundational cornerstones for the deconstruction of onto-theology. From then on, it would be very difficult to go back to talking about evil in and of itself. The term had previously embraced a diverse set of phenomena and concepts—from natural disasters to suffering, from a metaphysical principle to individual death—but starting with Kant, moral evil achieved its own philosophical autonomy. As Richard Bernstein points out,[18] Kant's thought created the schism that made it possible to begin distinguishing clearly between physical evil, metaphysical evil, and moral evil. Consequently, the problem ceased to be purely a theological and metaphysical concern, while the relevant question shifted from "Where does evil come from?" to "Why do we commit evil deeds?"

For some, Kant's "radical evil" was a step backward with respect to his critical perspectives, while for others it was a coherent and innovative development.[19] Either way, the concept laid down the foundations for modern and postmetaphysical thought on the question. Ricoeur is right in suggesting that the problem of evil has always functioned as a theoretical device for reforming philosophical systems. In other words, philosophy has used the appearance of a new question about evil as a tool to undermine the coherence of the previous philosophical system, in a cat-and-mouse game of structuring and destructuring. However, with Kant there came about a decisive transformation: although both the concept of *malum metaphysicum* (metaphysical evil) and the idea of *privatio boni* negate personal responsibility and imputability, for him the doctrine of original sin also restricts exploration of the link between freedom and evil.

In effect, the notion of the "radicality of evil" as conceived in *Religion Within the Limits of Reason Alone* is at odds with more than just theodicy. In addition to going against the justification offered by the theological and teleological conception of history—opposed by Kant even in its rationalist, Enlightenment version—along with Augustine and Leibniz's visions, it sought to leave behind the very idea of an "original sin." The principle of evil cannot in any way be originary; it cannot be transmitted "by necessity" to the entire human race. The evil implicit in the concept of a *natura lapsa* (fallen nature) that can be redeemed only by divine will, in Kant's eyes, is likely to take on an overwhelming force, with a power the moral law would be helpless to counter. The essence of the doctrine of original sin—it is obvious that Kant particularly had in mind the Lutheran version of sin, which grants the possibility of good deeds only to grace and, hence, denies free will—not only assumes that human nature is bad, but also assumes that human efforts alone cannot redeem actions or gain the upper hand over inclinations arising from original evil.

How can it be argued, then, using reason alone, that evil exists and that it is inherent to human nature, without this natural character jeopardizing human freedom and imputability in the form of guilt? Evil should be thought of as something that is deeply seated in the human being, true, but in a way that does not imply the necessity of predestination and the absolute power of grace.

Whereas in the *Second Critique* the explanation for evil was still to be found "simply" in a free will mired in a corruptible, irrational sensibility, in the essay on *Religion Within the Limits of Reason Alone* the scope of the transcendental perspective is extended. The root of radical evil cannot reside—reads a famous passage—"in man's sensuous nature and the natural inclinations arising therefrom[. . . .] [W]e must not even be considered responsible for their existence (we cannot be, for since they are implanted in us we are not their authors). We are accountable, however, for the propensity to evil, which, as it affects the morality of the subject, is to be found in him as a free-acting being and for which it must be possible to hold him accountable as the offender."[20] In short, the introduction of a radical evil—which is inherent to the human race—must be reconcilable with the freedom of the will, so that, if it is "inextirpable by human powers," it can nevertheless be "overcome." Evil is in reality a human product, attributable to freely acting beings, who, through this freedom and not only through faith, have the capacity to distance themselves from it and elevate themselves toward the good.[21] Both good acts and bad acts derive from reason and not from the limits of our sensible nature.

This means that evil is not reason's other, it is not its negation, but rather it is that which—within reason—*corrupts* the upright faculty of the moral judgment. The judgment does in fact welcome the moral law in its maxims along with "self-love" but it performs a "reversal of incentives."[22] The incentive of self-love, and of the inclinations stemming from this sensible incentive, is assumed as "the condition of obedience to the moral law."[23] This implies that there is a subjective principle concealed under the form of the law; and that the moral law—the supreme condition, the force of upright conduct—is subordinate to that subjective principle. Reason "simply" fails to notice its mistake: that of subordinating the moral law to the sensible incentive. All the "perverse" incentives that the free will may pursue are thus grouped under the category of "self-love," "which when taken as the principle of all our maxims, is the very source of evil."[24] Evil, in essence, is nothing more than an excess of self-affirmation, an immoderate passion for one's self. Kant, according to some critics, is translating into the language of practical reason the two fundamental anthropological instances—the propensity (*Hang*) to evil, and the predisposition (*Anlage*) to good—in order to clarify the conditions of possibility of a free choice between the incentives arising from these two propensities of human nature.[25]

Without engaging in the hermeneutics of the text, we must stress once again however that for Kant's purposes it is essential to pursue the conceivability of evil as an act of freedom, as an action that expresses the "original use of [man's free] will" even at the cost of some labyrinthine, conceptual difficulties. Evil, then, is neither a substance nor a nonbeing. It is an act. It is a conduct regarding which man must be able to say that he "should have refrained from that action, whatever his temporal circumstances and entanglements; for through no cause in the world can he cease to be a freely acting being."[26]

On the one hand, then, Kant admits the innate propensity to evil of the entire human race, a propensity that "need not be formally proved in view of the multitude of crying examples which experience of the actions of men puts before our eyes."[27] On the other hand, to not undermine the fundamental assumption of his practical philosophy, it must be assumed that this propensity cannot derive merely from the weakness of a nature limited by sensible experience. It is a propensity that is rooted in the very existence of humankind, that is part of our very nature. Yet it cannot be deduced *a priori*.

This impasse stops the German philosopher from revealing the ultimate ground, the "root of evil," because by his own admission the origin remains "inscrutable" (*unherforschbar*). But it also leads him to deny the existence of human beings who can act intentionally to violate the moral law. Expressed in Kantian terms, there is no possibility for wicked actions, namely, actions that follow from the desire of individuals who incorporate the transgression of the moral law into their maxim as the prime incentive. "Man (even the most wicked) *does not*, under any maxim whatsoever, *repudiate the moral law in the manner of a rebel (renouncing obedience to it)*."[28] Kant thus seems to fall back on a distinction between evil and wickedness, between *Bösheit* and *Bösartigkeit*—which does name a possibility, the truly radical possibility of *wickedness*, but only in order to exclude it.[29] He appears to perform a supreme act of denial with his philosophy against the very thing he was able to grasp with his intuition. Human beings may have "perversity of the heart," they can pervert the order of the incentives of their will, but they cannot desire *evil as such*; they cannot will evil knowing that it is evil; they cannot rebel for the sake of rebellion: "We are not, then, to call the depravity of human nature wickedness taking the word in its strict sense as a disposition (the subjective principle of the maxims) to adopt *evil as evil* into our maxim as our incentives."[30] If that were the case, we would be dealing—he argues—with a principle that is external to freedom, in the sense of a power that "takes possession" of human beings and drags them along with a diabolical, seductive force, making them impervious to the power of the disposition to good. Indeed, for Kant, the very definition of a diabolical reason is one that posits transgression of the law as an end in itself. Human reason—he is quick to conclude—cannot fail to deduce the necessary character of the moral law, just as it cannot accept the pursuit of evil for the sake of evil. To elevate evil to the intentional aim of an action would be for him an "unthinkable contradiction." It is far more reassuring to conceive human reason as subject to deception: as a weak reason that mistakes evil for good, thus allowing evil to assume the appearance of goodness. If evil desired for its own sake contradicts the very idea of humanity, then an act that intentionally seeks evil as its end is unrepresentable.

In essence, despite having seen the demonic ground of freedom, Kant seemingly draws back rather than waver in his philosophical commitment: to wit, to not go beyond the bounds of knowledge and to maintain the difference between thinking and knowing. However, the tension that pervades his text of 1793 is unmistakable: a tissue of "scandalous" statements immediately followed by a rebuttal, as if the author were pulling up too close to a glowing hot core that he "sensed" but did not want to see. He truly seems to be struggling against himself and his intuition. Ultimately, this will turn out to be Kant's limit, vividly remarked on by those who followed in his footsteps—in uniting the problem of evil with the problem of freedom—when they attempted to solve the great aporias of radical evil by returning to the prospects he glimpsed but never accepted.

We might even wonder whether this limit—the limit of the inscrutable origin of radical evil—was precisely what later philosophers believed they could go beyond. For many, it was Schelling who successfully met the challenge to identify the true origin of radical evil. He did so in the text that marked the transition from the philosophy of identity to the so-called philosophy of freedom, which took shape between 1806 and 1820. This is his famous *Freiheitschrift* ("Freedom essay") of 1809,[31] which introduced a new definition of freedom as "the capacity for good and evil." The intensity of this "real and vital concept" swept away the previous "general," "merely formal" notion and acquired a power that would be thoroughly explored only in the twentieth century.[32] Although his treatment forms part of a metaphysical, cosmic system, Schelling is still seen as the thinker who forcefully undermined some traditional philosophical prohibitions on the question, making it possible for philosophers the likes of Nietzsche and Heidegger to think about evil and freedom together in an "abysmal" fashion. More than a few contemporary philosophers view Schelling as the thinker who successfully probed the depths of the human experience of freedom, thanks to his discovery of the interaction between *Grund* and *Abgrund*, ground and abyss.[33]

I will certainly not enter into the merits of Schelling's philosophy, its about-turns, or its debated legacy. My concern is limited to following a few nodes of the 1809 treatise that led to the conception of evil as an *ontological subversion of the principles*—the idea that lies at the heart of the Dostoevsky paradigm, and one that would continue to provide the general, fundamental schema for most twentieth-century thought on the problem, regardless of the specific content that was assigned to it from one time to the next. Although Schelling, along with the author of *Religion Within the Limits of Reason Alone*, rejects both the idea of *privatio boni* and that of *malum metaphysicum*, like Kant he cannot limit radical evil to a reversal of the incentives for an action. His criticism is directed against every philosophical and theological school—from Plato's "negation" to Spinoza's pantheism—that leads to a weakening of the ontological status of evil.[34] There is no doubt that with Schelling the solid reality of evil is reasserted without reservations. Evil cannot be confined solely to the moral dimension; it must be elevated to an active force in the real sense of the word—a force that, without falling into Gnostic dualism, nevertheless has the status of a free force capable of opposing the good. True, evil is the overturning of a proper relationship between the universal and the particular, but in the sense of an ontological reversal between two constitutive principles of reality. In short, partly thanks to the retrospective light cast on it by Heideggerian hermeneutics,[35] the *Philosophical Investigations on the Essence of Human Freedom* can be viewed as the philosophical apex of the attempt, begun by Kant, to conceive of radical evil. In its pages, the root of evil can now be thought about but also talked about, and it becomes *the very condition of freedom*.

Given that, for the idealist philosopher, the question "Where does evil come from (*unde malum*)?" calls into question an actual will to do evil for the sake of evil, and this will responds to freedom, founded in its turn on the freedom of the Absolute, its origin must inevitably be seen as residing in God. The difficulty of holding together God, evil, and freedom, so that the ground of evil independent from God can only be in God himself, is resolved by Schelling thanks to a different way of conceiving God. The deity should not be thought of as an abstract idea, but as a "living unity of forces": "God is something more real than a merely moral world order and has entirely different and more vital motive forces in himself than the desolate subtlety abstract idealists attributed to him."[36] God is a becoming, something continuously active, with internal, divergent forces at work that are in conflict with each other. If abstract visions cannot conceive of God and freedom together, for Schelling there does exist an understanding of the Unity of Being in God that does not exclude freedom, and that even makes it necessary. Schelling's "philosophy of nature" distinguishes between being as ground (*Grund*) and being as existence (*Existenz*). Expressed in other terms, God has the ground of his existence in himself.[37] Indeed, the ground is not a cause external to God; rather, it is *nature*, from which God draws himself and becomes. Hence the need to conceive of a primal ground, even if it is a non-ground (*Ungrund*), which precedes all existence and all dualities: this is what Schelling calls absolute indifference or the Undifferentiated (*Indifferenz*). Out of the Undifferentiated immediately erupts Duality, which is not yet an opposition.

What we have here is a becoming whose eternity makes it possible to think of the relationship between ground and existence as circular. The ground and existence together have an originary nature, into which the divine essence issues its "glimpse of life." The influence of the German mystic tradition—from Meister Eckhart to Jacob Böhme—is certainly discernible in Schelling's text, recognizable in the conception of creation as a perennial "inner transmutation," as "transfiguration of the initial principle of darkness into the light."[38] In other words, what we have here is the natural process of evolution, in nature, whose movement is described as an incessant activity of separation of the undifferentiated. Being emerges into beings thanks to a gradual and progressive differentiation, a continuous emergence of forms, in whose ground, however, there remains the tension of a conflict.[39] Indeed, opposing resistance to the centrifugal movement of existence, to its desire to remain within itself, is inherent in the ground as such. Schelling's focus, in short, is on the idea of a *structural duality* (between order and disorder, between light and darkness, between particular and universal) as the principle of all beings, including the supreme being.[40] It is this duality that interests me more than anything else. Each being that emerges into the light, continues Schelling, preserves a trace of the original duality: it maintains the possibility of a tension between two irreconcilably conflicting movements. On the one hand, a centrifugal force toward *singularity*, we might say, toward *ipseity*, which translates into a yearning for itself, into a persistence of the particular will; on the other hand, a centripetal force, translatable into a desire for *totality*, into a will that seeks the *universal*. Only in human beings, who, according to the famous definition, are "the deepest abyss and the loftiest sky," does being come to self-consciousness.[41] Only in human life does God come to reveal himself as existence in action. In other words, the two original tendencies of the Ground and Existence, which are inseparable in God, become differentiated and distinct when they achieve self-awareness in the human being.

Beneath the densely crafted, not always crystalline passages in Schelling's remarkable text, what becomes clearly perceptible is the philosopher's struggle to avoid both the absolute dualism of separation between the two principles of good and evil and the undifferentiated monism that encompasses and immerses the reality of evil. In God, his ground (the principle of darkness) is transformed by his very existence (the principle of light) into his actual existence. Only when God reveals himself does he rise to full actuality. God therefore needs relationship with his creatures, and it is with human beings alone that freedom becomes the power of good and evil. The separability of the principles is itself, ultimately, the possibility of good and evil. This is because the duality-unity that is in God is shattered in human beings: the principle of darkness, the non-ground (disorder) can overcome the principle of light (order): "Man is placed on that summit where he has in himself the source of self-movement toward good or evil in equal portions: the bond of principles in him is not a necessary but rather a free one. Man stands on the threshold (*Scheidepunkt*); whatever he chooses, it will be his act."[42] In the highest form of consciousness—to wit, the human—the negative side of power, the chaotic, the anarchic, can become a free act. This is evil.

What this means—the aspect that interests me—is that human freedom is such because in it is foreseen the choice for nothingness, annihilation, or chaos. It is the ontological trace of the non-ground, of darkness, that in creatures coincides with self-will—with the desire to remain closed up in themselves, to not open themselves up to the universal. It is an obstinate will on the part of beings to go against being and to elevate themselves to the totality of life, a will that can only end in death. If the divine will is the will to universalize and to totalize, the will of those who seek evil persists in particularizing. In a word, it is a refusal to open to Other than Self; it is the rejection of love, and the consequent anarchical choice for the undisputed rule of the creaturely. Hence the inevitable choice on the part of the being that "out of overweening pride (*Übermut*) to be all things, falls into non-Being."[43] Further, "The will that steps out from its being beyond nature (*das Übernatürliche*), in order as general will to make itself at once particular and creaturely, strives to reverse the relation of the principles, to elevate the ground over the cause, to use the spirit that it obtained only for the sake of the *centrum* outside the *centrum* and against creatures; from this results collapse (*Zerrüttung*) within the will itself and outside it."[44] Creatures who participate in being can choose to maintain a deep bond with it or can decide to allow themselves to be carried away by self-affirmation, to the point of abolishing it or destroying it. Hence, that which opposes and resists this bond is not a simple privation, a distancing that weakens the spirit, but a true separation, a choice made for disorder. Evil is based, therefore, "in a positive perversion or reversal of the principles (*Umkehrung der Principien*)."[45] This, for Schelling, is the root of evil in human beings, one that is far more "abysmal" than Kant's self-love. This is the heart of Schelling's conception, which the idealist philosopher arrived at by radicalizing the Kantian notion. In Heidegger's lectures on Schelling—which we will return to—he explicitly ties this vision of evil to the moment when the human being, who emerges as a self-aware being, posits itself as ground—as a subject that reduces all other beings to instruments of its own self-affirmation, to mere objects to be exploited and appropriated.[46] The truth is, evil exists precisely because human beings are spiritual, self-aware beings. Conflict can only dwell in humans: in animals conflict has yet to appear and in God it has ceased to exist.

Opposition is thus a possibility that becomes real, and it does so when the human being perverts the order of ontological principles—perverting the order of ground and existence—in a way that Kant refused to consider. The perverse will of human beings, or wickedness, goes far beyond the error and corruptibility implicated by a finite, fallible human nature. *The will to evil for the sake of evil exists*, and it is the movement that seeks to restore in the subject the union between finite and infinite, a union that can exist only in God.[47] The exaltation of human will, the revolt against the divine bond between ground and existence, creates the human illusion of divine omnipotence. This is the source of the rivalry between human beings and God. In the words of Schelling, he who commits evil is a "reversed god."[48] But human beings, as opposed to God, never have the condition of *themselves* in their power. The condition of evil is thus the pretense on the part of humans to achieve that power. Evil—to summarize in broad strokes—resides in the human will to be God.

I have drastically simplified the arguments of the *Freiheitschrift*. I certainly did not dive into the complexity of the text and I skated over the difficulties, contradictions, and ambivalences of this great work. But perhaps it is fair to say that Schelling, who sought to go beyond Kant, to refute Fichte, to avoid metaphysical dualism, and to distance himself from the Hegelian logic of an evil that justifies itself before the recollecting of Spirit, ends up stumbling into that aporia which we almost always come across when we seek to make the reality of evil coexist with the Unity and Omnipotence of God. To assert, as he does at the end, that "The initial fundamental being can never be evil in itself"[49]; to appeal to the power of love, to the force of that identity in God that is prior to evil; to admit that evil is an autonomous force, true, but it has no essence, that it is a reality, but only as opposition and not in itself, means—as Kant does in some ways—venturing into a discourse that attenuates the inflexibility of his claims. Fundamentally, in terms of the outcome, the idealist philosopher seems to weaken the radicality of his main theses. Not even Schelling, after all, really explains why some human beings commit evil seeking to do so, why they choose evil for the sake of evil, or why they choose evil instead of good.

Despite this complicated game of theoretical courage and verbal reticence, Schelling's interpretation of the link between evil and freedom remained one of the most imposing legacies for subsequent philosophy, in part thanks to the mediation of Berdyaev and Heidegger. But above all, thanks to the powerful expressiveness of Fyodor Dostoevsky and his demons, in which the forces of Schellingian disorder and nothingness—the conditions of evil—are brought to life and set in motion.

Demons: Or the Delusion of Freedom

In 1873 *Demons* was published in one volume. The work that depicts the tragedy of absolute wickedness as a tragedy of freedom is also, according to some, Dostoevsky's most perfect work: outside of Plato, its dialogs are unprecedented.[50] Dostoevsky and his demons lived during the last decades of the nineteenth century, when the term *nihilism*, a word that once raised concerns about the claimed completeness of philosophical systems,[51] now burst its way into the social and political realm. At that time nihilism became synonymous with anarchic-libertarian rebellion: a nihilist was primarily somebody who, following the "children against fathers" movement,[52] disputed the authority of tradition, calling it into question in any domain where it exerted its claims, from philosophy to political institutions, from religion to morality, from art to the family. The protest against values that, according to the nihilists, had to be brought back to what they authentically were—that is, to "nothingness"—was more dogmatic and ferocious in Russia than it was rebellious.[53]

Dostoevsky's novel, started in December 1869 under the pressure of poverty and debts, certainly reflects his concern for the social and political context. His shock at the assassination of the student Ivanov is well known.[54] It motivated his intense interest in the anarcho-nihilistic ideas of Sergey Nechayev. These were later put into systematic form in "The Catechism of the Revolutionary," a text suspected by Karl Marx to have actually been authored by Mikhail Bakunin.[55] The ideas in the pamphlet were those developed by the League of the Enlightened, whose members—according to the nihilist plan—were to occupy all state and civil positions of power in order to successfully implement the new ideal of equality. In the hands of the "nihilists," the program was radicalized and stripped down until it became nothing more than a project for general destruction. According to Nechayev's catechism, the true revolutionary could not have private interests or affections. He had to give up everything, including his own name. He had to sever ties with civilization, with its laws and its morality. The only reason he remained in the world was to better destroy it, because there was only one art known to the true revolutionary: that of killing. For this he needed to study chemistry and physics. In a sort of transvaluation of all values, fueled by hatred for contemporary society and contempt for feelings such as friendship, gratitude, and honor, the nihilist became someone who redefined good and evil in view of the new revolutionary goal:

good was anything needed for the triumph of the revolutionary cause, and evil was anything that stood in its way.

The murder certainly polarized the writer's imagination. There is no doubt that the planned destruction of Russian society, which fed the fanaticism of the younger generations, provided the backdrop against which *Demons* came into being. In a letter to the poet Apollon Majkov dated October 1870, in which he explains the meaning of the title and the epigraph taken from the Gospel of Luke,[56] Dostoevsky clearly expresses his intention to make the plot of the novel unwind in a crescendo of tensions leading up to the final explosion. Thus, some of the key figures in the novel are modeled on flesh-and-blood players from Russian history, picked out from the ranks of the nihilist-terrorists. This is particularly the case for Pyotr Verkhovensky, Nikolai Stavrogin, and Kirillov, who, we might say, represent three modes of political abuse of their own power. The dialog in part II, chapter 8, between Pyotr Verkhovensky—who impersonates Nechayev—and Nikolai Stavrogin—a fearsome tyrant over other people's minds—reads as an extreme, parodied version of the main points of the "Catechism," in which the revolutionary outlook of the nihilists is transfigured into Shigalovism. "We are going to make such an upheaval that everything will be uprooted from its foundation," Verkhovensky starts off excitedly, intent on gaining the elusive Stavrogin's allegiance to the main tenets of Shigalovism.[57] It is a doctrine that preaches universal equality, but that is achieved partly through everybody spying on everybody else. Every member of the society spies on all the others, and it is his duty to inform against them. "Every one belongs to all and all to every one. All are slaves and equal in their slavery. In extreme cases he advocates slander and murder, but the great thing about it is equality[. . . .] There has never been either freedom or equality without despotism, but in the herd there is bound to be equality, and that's Shigalovism!"[58] Despotism, Verkhovensky explains, aims to "level the mountains": it is a titanic attempt to create a society of equals. Education—an "aristocratic thirst"—has no place in this goal, which, if anything, requires science. But more than anything, it demands obedience.

The anti-egalitarian and anti-socialist polemic we read in these lines, with an acumen matched only by the writings of Nietzsche, briefly foreshadows the observations that Dostoevsky went on to develop in the legend of the Grand Inquisitor. If property and desire for individuality go together,

Pyotr Verkhovensky seems to suggest, "we will destroy that desire": "Only the necessary is necessary, that's the motto of the whole world henceforward."[59] The reign of equality and necessity can only be achieved through terror. This is the rationale for instituting a daily dose of terror in the form of denunciations, made possible by the widespread corruption that makes everyone vulnerable to being blackmailed and informed on. To suppress desire and establish obedience—this is Pyotr's special pedagogy—all talent must be stifled starting from early childhood. But none of this will be enough, he explains. For this reason he plans on resorting to massive social upheavals, which the directors will orchestrate. And so "they would all suddenly begin eating one another up, to a certain point, simply as a precaution against boredom. Boredom is an aristocratic sensation. The Shigalovians will have no desires. Desire and suffering are our lot, but Shigalovism is for the slaves."[60] In these pages Dostoevsky takes aim at another target of his fierce polemics: the Catholic Church.

For the Russian writer, the "Roman idea" on which the papacy founded its "empire" and the socialist doctrine can become allied ideals when used by the power-hungry to better construct the edifices of their political dominion—a dominion that is all the more absolute and tyrannical the more it portrays itself in words as the savior of the people's suffering and needs. "The Pope at the head, with us round him, and below us—Shigalovism," cries an increasingly agitated Pyotr Verkhovensky. At this point he is so obsessed with gaining Stavrogin's approval that he jumps from one idea to another in the hope of impressing him, finally contradicting his own nihilistic beliefs. He is even ready to admit that, unlike real nihilists without idols, he has turned Stavrogin into a true idol, the supreme idol to be placed at the head of the revolt: "You are an awful aristocrat. An aristocrat is irresistible when he goes in for democracy! [. . .] You are just the man that's needed. It's just such a man as you that I need. I know no one but you. You are the leader, you are the sun and I am your worm."[61] Even in the face of his interlocutor's dismay, Verkhovensky does not give up. He reveals his plan for Stavrogin to act as an unreal yet all-powerful ghost, by making use of his aloof, icy charisma: "We shall penetrate to the peasantry. Our party does not consist only of those who commit murder and arson[. . . .] Listen. I've reckoned them all up: a teacher who laughs with children at their God and at their cradle; is on our side. The lawyer who defends an educated murderer because he is more cultured than his victims [. . .] is one of us. The juries who acquit every criminal are ours. The prosecutor who trembles at a trial for fear he should not seem advanced enough is ours, ours."[62] Even if they do not explicitly profess the anarcho-nihilist-terrorist creed, anyone who cultivates the seed—the destruction of all principles—is "ours." On these lines, Pyotr Verkhovensky speaks with lucidity about a universal, revolutionary inebriation that now corrupts almost the entirety of the Russian people to their roots. Everywhere he looks, he sees the desire for autonomy, independence, for severing all ties with authority. One more small effort directed toward the next two generations is all that is needed to have it "in our hands," "but one or two generations of vice are essential now; monstrous, abject vice by which a man is transformed into a loathsome, cruel, egoistic reptile. That's what we need!"[63]

In a previous conversation he had already revealed to Stavrogin the secret heart of his socialism: it is a perfect costume for hiding and disguising a pure desire for power—a will to unlimited power, easily attainable by offering the many desperate people access to the signs and means of power. "This'll make you laugh," Verkhovensky assures Stavrogin, moved once again by an intense desire to gain his acceptance and admiration. "What first of all affects them terribly is a uniform. There's nothing stronger than a uniform. I purposely invent ranks and positions: I have secretaries, secret stool pigeons, treasurers, chairmen, registrars, their adjuncts—it's all very much liked and has caught on splendidly."[64]

At the most basic level of interpretation, we are completely justified in seeing a focused attack in the novel on the nihilists and terrorists of the time; but we also catch a glimpse of the signs of conservatism that will later be defined as "Dostoevskyism" (*Dostoevshchina*). This became the perspective favored by critics who pulled together the various strands of the Russian writer's thought into a coherent whole and drew from it a sort of political canon with strong overtones of antirevolutionary conservatism. This interpretative maneuver, conducted by the authors of the Konservative Revolution, for example,[65] met with a broad consensus. However, it also met with some tough opposition, beginning with that of Mikhail Bakhtin[66] and Albert Camus.[67] It was Camus who insisted, contrary to what Freud himself had argued,[68] that Dostoevsky did not make a real move away from socialism. And, in effect, the idea that Dostoevsky's criticism may very well not relate to socialism in and of itself, but only to the perverse uses of socialism that can derive from power-seekers, is confirmed once again by Pyotr Verkhovensky's admissions when Stavrogin questions him regarding his aims: "So you are really not a socialist, then, but some sort of . . . ambitious politician?" "A scoundrel, a scoundrel! [. . .] But the people must believe that we know what we are after."[69]

However, it is difficult to dispute Dostoevsky's fierce polemic against the political trends of his time and against the seed of decadence that he believed had come to the Russian people from the liberal, atheistic corruption of the West. Consider, for example, the sort of counterpoint to Turgenev's *Fathers and Children* that makes up the first part of the work, where the focus is on the ethical and social role of the generation of liberals represented by Stepan Verkhovensky, the father of the terrifying Pyotr. Behind the face of Verkhovensky senior are concealed the features of the Russian liberals: Belinsky, Mikhailovsky, Granovsky. There is no doubt that, for Dostoevsky, liberalism was the preparatory phase for nihilism; and that the generation of the fathers was responsible for the destructiveness of their children, precisely because they had abdicated their authority. In the notebooks dedicated to *Demons*,[70] Dostoevsky wrote about the close link between liberalism and the kind of antinationalism that destroys love of country; namely, the link between the generation of the fathers as bearers of abstract, lifeless ideas—liberal ones, naturally—and the generation of their children, for whom these ideas became the instrument for negating the past and destroying the present.

The son's mockery for his father is fueled by Stepan's failure to take the weight and tragedy of the real onto his shoulders. To Pyotr, his father is a pathetic intellectual, typical of the 1840s. Atheist, pro-Western, and a lukewarm believer in an "impoverished idea"—the right of free judgment as a "universal, eternal, supreme" right—everything about Stepan Trofimovich Verkhovensky appears to his son as a lie. The old man is ridiculous when swayed by pure sentimentality, and his boastful egotism makes him infantile and superficial. In short, he cries for nothing and lies about everything. He lies constantly; something that he himself confesses in the end to Varvara Petrovna, Stavrogin's mother and his own benefactor: "My friend, I've been telling lies all my life. Even when I told the truth I never spoke for the sake of the truth, but always for my own sake."[71] Almost physically incapable of distinguishing truth from falsehood, his longing for nobility of spirit hides his poverty of spirit. In reality, we realize, he uses his political banishment to lead a totally parasitic life. Not only does he not live off the fruits of his own labor, he even manages to squander the wealth produced by his landholdings. This is why he gets himself maintained by Varvara Petrovna. Worst of all, he sponges off the ideas of others. So much so that Bakhtin dubbed him "the epigone of the loftier lines of aphoristic thinking"[72]: somebody who speaks a thousand truths, only because he has none of his own, and, above all, none that are personal or deeply felt.

Dostoevsky thus establishes an ideological continuity between libertarian idealism *à la* Stepan and the murderous anarchy of the nihilists. My interest does not lie, however, in clarifying what Dostoevsky thought about the essence of Russian liberalism, in alignment with European counterrevolutionary thought; in other words, whether or not there lay hidden only mundane atheism behind his ideas of progress and humanity. What I want to stress instead is how his demons broke free of their nineteenth-century Russian context to become *the transhistorical models of an exemplary scene of evil,* one that would continue to be explicitly or implicitly evoked for a long time to come. Perhaps, then, the crucial point does not even lie in the work's "propheticism," on which Berdyaev placed so much attention. Not that he is wrong on that score: Kirillov, Stavrogin, Shatov, and all the others did not yet exist in Russia between 1860 and 1880, and they probably did prefigure the future leaders of the twentieth-century revolutionary events.[73] But more importantly than its historical premonitions, the greatness of the novel, in my opinion, lies primarily in the way the Russian writer was able to explain how the deliberate, intentional wickedness of a few actors is able, brick by brick, to construct an entire system of evil: a universe in which suffering overwhelms and annihilates everything and everyone. Because not only does he clearly show the nature of "true" radical evil in its relation to the abyss of freedom and the will to nothingness, he also foresees its collective and political use. This is where we can locate the difference between Dostoevskyism—as a canon of political conservatism—and what I am calling the Dostoevsky paradigm: a conceptual cluster that was a long-standing reference and framework for thinking about evil in its relationship to power.

If read in this perspective, then, Dostoevsky's masterpiece does not lead necessarily to the question of the relationship between liberalism and nihilism. Rather, it prompts us to wonder why the two characteristics that are so deeply rooted in Stepan Verkhovensky—lying and parasitism, or in other words, a lack of responsibility and of decisiveness—mark the spot where true demons find a possible place of engagement for their action. If parasitism and lying, perennial signs of evil, are not yet personified in the father, Stepan, in a truly wicked person they are nevertheless presented as the agents of progressive corruption, breakdown, and ruin. The old Verkhovensky is in fact the locus from which the web of entanglement between evil and power unfolds. It is not by chance, then, that Dostoevsky changed his mind at a certain point. In August 1870 he decided to replace Stepan with Stavrogin in the leading role as the anti-hero of the novel.[74] Almost as if, I like to think, he shifted from a more limited aim of political polemics to reflecting on a topic of a different nature: one that by far transcended his harsh, lucid critique of the present to become the complex, articulate answer, we might say, to the famous Kantian question: What is radical evil?

In the pages of the Russian writer, radical evil is as much a disease of the reason as it is a pathological condition of the sensibility. In both cases, it marks the breaching of a limit. Dostoevsky's phenomenology of radical evil is the skillful result of intertwining a psychology with an ontology. Above all, however, it is something that can never be reduced to the mere inclination of the subject, or to the simple result of a single, wicked action or intention. Only by interacting with everyone else do the protagonists engender the prism of radical evil. Like in Plato, where a disorder of the psyche corresponds to political and social chaos, in *Demons*, too, the energy and power of destruction are the large-scale projection, "written in large letters," of an immense hatred of being that each demon nurses in his soul. Each demon is a disconnected universe, "off its hinges." Each of them gives free rein to his own particular negative power: base instincts, cunning, pride, or envy as the case may be. But they all share the same experience of trespassing, of breaking down limits, and of violating the order of the elements. The lead role is played by absolute free will: freedom of the will taken to an extreme. Each of the protagonists, driven by his own forces, becomes delusional with omnipotence—an omnipotence that was once a divine attribute and is now turned into a human feature. It almost reads like a staging of Schelling's ontological problem: for Dostoevsky, too, the finite that seeks to elevate itself to infinity is the nesting spot for the power of evil. In the actual lives of these malicious actors one perceives a constant, common dynamic: the desire to break down the boundaries of their own finitude to make themselves not only similar to God, but equal.[75]

Indeed, it is this sort of man-God—what Stavrogin is and insists on being—who directs the scene. From the moment he arrives in the small Russian town, the public and private lives of its citizens are sucked into a destructive maelstrom, as if the main characters broke up into many parts, and these parts were no longer able to find a center of union. Pyotr Verkhovensky is the derisive representation of destructive activism; Kirillov depicts the overman who chooses nothingness as part of the whole that he believes he embodies; and Shatov takes the logic of fanaticism to an extreme, in the garb of religious nationalism. However, these vectors of evil—Titanism, extremism, fanaticism—have the same source of inspiration: Stavrogin's profound nihilism. They are contaminated by it, continuously spurred into action, in fact, by the "power of nothingness" that, as Berdyaev says, is the true heart of Nicholas Stavrogin.[76] Because if each one is a demon, each demon is a loose cannon flung into the vortex of an outburst of passions that are vile, abject, and cruel. Sadism allies itself with irony, ambition joins with superficiality, and they all set off together to begin the general destruction. The suggestion is that the power of evil becomes radical only in a relationship.

The plot of *Demons* thus spins a spider's web at whose center sits Stavrogin, who, as we read in the novel, calls to mind Hamlet, Prince Harry, and Faust: demonic figures whose characteristics are exaggerated in him, so as to present us with a kind of "anatomy" of the wicked. Stavrogin continues and completes the "chemical breakdown" of the dark side of the human soul that was begun with the underground man: the man who in the hypertrophy of his own awareness confesses to himself that he voluptuously pursues evil for the sake of evil, not out of selfishness or ignorance, selfinterest or obscurantism.[77] And Dostoevsky's analysis of this evil committed for no purpose can only be read as an unveiling of the Kantian denial.

Even though the "black soul" of *Demons* acts in many ways, his action is not for a specific purpose. He commits evil, he creates suffering and pain, because he is cynical, because he is ironic,[78] because he is violent, because he is incredibly sensual, and because he is coldly cerebral. But never for personal gain. It is almost as if he were a divine substance, endowed with infinite attributes and equally infinite behaviors, all of which lead to nothing. He is a sophisticated and elegant aristocrat, when he feels like it; a frequent visitor and instigator of the dregs of society, when it suits him. On the other hand, though, he seems generously willing to sacrifice himself, making us confused enough to wonder if some of his actions can be taken as atonement for the evil he has committed. For example, he marries a wretch, "a scrubby, feebleminded, beggarly lame girl," almost out of spite for the devastating charm that he exerts on all the women who cross his path (p. 254). In actuality, even his marriage to this "unfortunate being" (p. 191) is just an experiment to create scandal and then give him the opportunity to analyze the pity aroused in others.[79] At the same time, he is the person who leads "an ironic life," in the sense Kierkegaard gives to this notion.[80] As Pyotr Verkhovensky claims, he is a "jeering life" (p. 189), literally devoured by the demon of irony. If he commits evil, if he inflicts humiliation and shame, he often does so without any personal gain, acting with the lightheartedness typical of a child's prank. There is the unforgettable episode of his offense to Gaganov: "One of the most respectable senior members of our club . . . had acquired the innocent habit of accompanying his every word with a passionately uttered: 'No, sir, they won't lead me by the nose!'"[81] During a meeting, Stavrogin takes him literally: he grabs his nose and drags him across the room. For no reason and with no malice, accompanied only by a cheerful, mischievous smile—truly an unforgettable scene. And this is certainly not an isolated incident.[82] But Stavrogin's insolence is not restricted solely to this type of "impulsive" action. From his first appearances in the book, he behaves with the characteristic coldness that always accompanies him at crucial moments. And if "there was perhaps more anger in Nikolai Vsevolodovich" than in anyone else, "this anger was cold, calm, and, if one may put it so, reasonable, and therefore the most repulsive and terrible that can be."[83]

In a nutshell, Stavrogin, who also suffers from a hypertrophy of the consciousness of self, zealously pushes his own reason beyond good and evil, to personally prove to himself that good and evil do not exist. His freedom is a freedom without end, as Evdokimov, Berdyaev, and Pareyson all remark on. Nevertheless, paradoxically, he seems to know that once the difference between what is good and what is bad has been buried, the abyss of the "madness of freedom" opens up. He seems to have always had the premonition that the unrestricted exercise of freedom would lead him to perdition; and that this freedom beyond all boundaries would collapse, dragging him along with it and eventually crushing him. Stavrogin is not crazy. The doubling and splitting of his personality does not come from madness: they are the result of nihilism, of his abandonment of Being for

Nothing. The "demon of irony" that tells him not to believe in anything or to mock everything is what prevents the resolution of inner conflict. He sees both sides in every event,[84] and instead of deciding for one or the other of the possibilities, he chooses both.

So when the struggle (this conflict between good and evil that Dostoevsky sees battled out in the heart of every person) remains just that; when the war between the two (a source, in its turn, of the possibility of evil) does not end in the triumph of the good, the realm of the one, free will becomes perverted into freedom for evil.[85] This is why disintegration is inherent to evil. It symbolizes the madness of freedom, the same freedom that culminates in the hallucinatory doubling that leads Stavrogin to imagine himself as the devil. This visionary image is a sign that the wicked Other is perceived as real, to the point of being objectivized in the external world. Stavrogin, inhabited by evil, is a personality split in two: on the one hand, the ethical Self; and on the other, the immoral Self—leading him to say: "I am as capable now as ever before of wishing to do a good deed, and I take pleasure in that; along with it, I wish for evil and also feel pleasure."[86] He seemingly refuses to recognize the difference between an act of brutality and a gesture of supreme nobility, which he is equally capable of performing—almost as if the disgust that he feels for his own degradation exercised an enormous attraction on him; and, in addition to not being afraid of anything, as if he were dangerously attracted to death.

Every one of Stavrogin's actions produces pain and suffering, humiliation, and shame. He is the master of the spirit of negation and destruction, which in Dostoevsky's view is undoubtedly the fundamental identity of evil. But for the Russian writer, nothing about what Stavrogin has done—even the most extreme action, bordering on genuine "radical evil"—is irredeemable. Because in a certain sense, evil itself, the torture that it causes to those who commit it as well, can take the form of a path to redemption. From this perspective, torment for one's own damnation is itself an instrument of redemption. We know how important atonement through crime was for the author of *Demons*.

However, there is a limit beyond which Stavrogin's freedom crosses the threshold of any possible salvation. The circumstances and the scene where it occurs are famous: it is the story of violence against a child perpetrated by Nicholas. This is told in a crucial chapter of the novel where Stavrogin meets Bishop Tikhon and delivers him some papers "intended for distribution" in which he confesses to his act: "I, Nikolai Stavrogin, a retired officer, was living in Petersburg in the year 186–, giving myself over to debauchery in which I found no pleasure." He recounts his crime. The story reaches a climax of perversion when he dwells on how the little Matryosha was brought to suicide. Stavrogin, as he himself admits, followed the torments of the child with delight, without doing anything. He spied on her, observed her every move, and counted the seconds that separated her from the fatal act that would take her to her death as if, with the coldness of an entomologist, he were analyzing the movements of an insect. Or rather, the movements of a spider caught in a web.

The freedom that makes him capable of destruction goes past the point of no return. It does so, without any possibility for redemption, when the wickedness he is capable of has as its object the absolute innocence of the victim. It is one of the greatest literary moments in the book, but also one of its most philosophically eloquent ones. This relationship of oppression—*with an all-powerful perpetrator on the one side, faced by the total powerlessness of the victim on the other*—expresses what I believe is Dostoevsky's concept of *evil in its absolute, pure form*. In all likelihood, for the Russian writer, this extreme figuration of the relationship of power, at the most remote confine of man's humanity; this dynamic—namely, the cruelty imposed on a defenseless, innocent person epitomized by the suffering inflicted on children—is his response to the enigma of radical evil. And if in this case the radical action of evil is portrayed in the microcosm of a personal relationship between two people, a little later it will be ready to be projected on a large scale and refined, providing his twentieth century heirs with the hermeneutical key to absolute political evil.

We know that the idea of pain caused in children haunts the imagination of the writer: shortly after Stavrogin's confession, Dostoevsky once again brings it to center stage in *The Brothers Karamazov*, in the dialog between Ivan Karamazov and his brother Alyosha. In actuality, this is a superb refutation of the idea of universal harmony, an argument that claimed to dismantle the reasoning behind all theodicies, both old and new. But I am convinced that it is also, at the same time, a crystalline clarification of the link between evil and power. Now, what does the world of children represent in Dostoevsky's eyes? As Ivan remarks, the world of children is a world apart. Up until the age of seven, their nature is different from that of adults. Put simply, they represent a world without evil, the part of humanity not yet tainted by sin. But if this is true, then the violation of their innocence is the supreme crime. The violation of children appears to be the absolute crime, which even the nihilism and amorality of Ivan Karamazov is unable to accept. Assuming also that God exists and that "the small Euclidean mind of man" cannot understand it—Ivan wonders—what purpose does the suffering of children fulfill?[87] The stories that he recounts to Alyosha about the torture inflicted on them by adults, often by their own parents, also represent the "unacceptable" to his disillusioned eyes: the ultimate and irrevocable refutation of the lie of the harmony of the whole, the denial of sin as a necessary stage for salvation, the impossibility of the final reconciliation of human beings with God. "Is there in the whole world a being who would have the right to forgive and could forgive?" asks Ivan almost beside himself:

I don't want harmony. From love for humanity I don't want it. I would rather be left with the unavenged suffering. I would rather remain with my unavenged suffering and unsatisfied indignation, even if I were wrong. Besides, too high a price is asked for harmony; it's beyond our means to pay so much to enter on it. And so I hasten to give back my entrance ticket, and if I am an honest man I am bound to give it back as soon as possible. And that I'm doing. It's not God that I don't accept, Alyosha, only I most respectfully return Him the ticket.[88]

But if Ivan's rebellion, as Camus rightly points out,[89] is still an ethical revolt that reacts to the absurd "in the name of the absurd," Stavrogin's rebellion is an out-and-out attack against being itself, without any possibility of redemption: negation for the love of negation that leads not only to the nothingness of the other, but also to his own destruction. He now really is beyond the law, beyond good and beyond evil: "One can argue endlessly about everything, but what poured out of me was only negation, with no magnanimity and no force."[90] His soul seems immovable and empty, as if incapable of being touched by joy, pain, or fear. Yet even in this bleak, cold self-sufficiency, a change can be perceived: a sort of loss of aggression and the achievement of a state of perfect indifference—as if evil had reached a point beyond which it can no longer be expressed to the outside, and is thus forced to attack the source from which it issues.

The indifference that Stavrogin lapses into is indeed a disease of the emotions, but it originates from a transgression that had led his emotional and rational life into despair.[91] The reason his freedom perceived no limit to transgress ahead of him was because it had hit rock bottom. Unlike what happened in the cases narrated by Ivan, Stavrogin did not violate innocence out of amoralism, for the sadistic enjoyment of the crime, or due to the perversion of a split personality. The desecration of the little girl was a genuine experiment, an experiment to see if he could equal God's omnipotence. This is where the metaphysical origin of wickedness lies for Dostoevsky: *in pushing one's freedom to the point of competing with God.* However, when a human creature takes up this challenge—and this is crucial to understanding the problem of evil in the Russian writer—it can be played out only on the field of destruction. Wickedness, then, is not simple abuse of power driven by an excess of egotistical self-love. It is an ontological hatred: a hatred of creation and of being, simply for the fact that "it is." Wickedness follows the same direction that the human will takes when it seeks to burst the bonds of its finitude and make itself as powerful as the divine will. *Unlike God, however, human power can express itself only through destruction, never through creation.* When the human will makes the choice of refusing to open itself to being, it reveals itself as pure will to destruction: a desire for power that aims to reduce being to nothingness. Unable to create out of nothing like God, its power must at least be directed to reducing being to nothingness. It is a freedom that makes itself absolute in the only way available to human beings: *the freedom to seek nothingness in lieu of being.* As Nietzsche would later say, the will to power would rather will nothingness than not will. What seals the gratuity of this hatred toward creation is the innocence of the victim. And the power that it exercises over the innocent, in its nihilating strength, is the unequivocal sign of the radicality of evil. This is an evil whose root lies in the human being—not so much in the selfish perversion of reason, but more specifically in the delusion of a reason that believes itself to be unlimited and at the helm of a will that sees itself as absolutely free, and, as such, with pretensions to being similar to God's freedom. When humans lose their connection to God—and the sense of limit arising from that bond—the power that they exercise reveals itself solely as force, oppression, and destruction. *This is the origin of the evil of power and power as evil.*

We will come back to this on a number of occasions. As for Stavrogin—who in the final moment does not seem to fear damnation, but rather the compassion that others might feel in response to his possible repentance—we can conclude simply by recalling that when faced by the young Nicholas, Bishop Tikhon, now exhausted and disoriented, can only say:

"there is not and cannot be any greater and more terrible crime than your act with the maiden."[92]

In Stavrogin, mired in apathy, and therefore immune from any possible redemption, the gratuitous evil that he has chosen and willed as an end in itself reaches the depths of its radicality. However, as we have said, the energies of negation radiate out in different directions from this glowing hot core. The destruction of being under the guise of the "common cause" continues with the other "nihilists" in various modes. Chief among them, as we have seen, is Peter Verkhovensky, who in Bakhtin's view personifies to perfection the demon of parody. For him, "high and low are the same," just as ideas and ideals are simply screens to hide his actions behind. His aim is to ridicule everything and everyone, a universal lowering to the lowest possible level. In his hands, as Kirillov puts it, history becomes "a devil's vaudeville."[93] Every single thing he does is subordinated to the supreme pleasure he experiences in committing evil. He hates, defames, corrupts, and kills for the sake of destruction. But unlike the cynical, disinterested pride of Stavrogin, what dominates in him is pettiness and the awareness that everything can be turned into low comedy. Hence the contradiction that he carries as his banner: submissive to the point of subservience—subjugated as he is by his "idol" Stavrogin—and rebellious to the point of arrogance, he is a great manipulator and tyrant over the lives of others. Precisely because, for him, "nothing is better and nothing is worse." In fact, empty of spirit, Pyotr is a man of action, a pragmatist. He is the one in whom unscrupulous cynicism becomes the principle of organization and the political transmission belt of evil. Thrown into dynamic turmoil, he represents the unleashing of the will into action,[94] a permanent and feverish action that draws the other characters together by embroiling them in a single plot—or rather, to use the metaphor of the spider so dear to Dostoevsky, by catching them in one huge spider web. As the strategic genius of the revolutionary plan, he touches on one of the secrets for instilling obedience to power: "the good putty" that cements groups together and subjugates them is the sharing of a crime. This is a conclusion he arrives at thanks to a conversation with Stavrogin, who suggests that he "get four members of a circle to bump off a fifth on the pretense of his being an informer, and with this shed blood you'll immediately tie them together in a single knot. They'll become your slaves, they won't dare rebel or call you to accounts."[95]

It is a sham of community spirit, a collectivity held together by the "right to dishonor,"[96] so that nothing can easily gain ground, arranging itself into political and populist movements. For this reason, for most of the twentieth century, this part of *Demons* was read as a prophecy about the disastrous revolutionary failures: historical tragedies, born of nihilism, in which the link between evil and power—reaching its apex in the polarity between a subject who seeks to be all-powerful and a powerless victim—is transposed into the relationship between leader and masses, thus becoming extended to society as a whole. The same polarization, between subject-object, perpetrator-victim, was transmitted to the collective dimension, allowing it to be modeled on a similarly dualistic structure: on the one hand, a cynical leader who exploits the weaknesses of others; and, on the other, the weak masses who are devoid of any power to resist. Partly thanks to the sociology of crowds and the popularized version of Freudian theory, this relationship would later be modeled as a hypnotic bond that forms between the magical omnipotence of the leader—expressed through slogans and ideological formulas—and the totally powerless passivity of all those who allow themselves to be led, seduced, and manipulated,[97] convinced that the leader embodies the idea by which they delude themselves into submission.

If Pyotr's activist cynicism appears to be a paradigmatic example of evil in its political effects, Kirillov's "purity" seems to lie exactly on the opposite side, as if it were an antidote to his opponent's "operational nihilism." His faith in the idea of eternal, universal harmony helps Dostoevsky launch a harsh critique against the spirit of theodicies. However, in *Demons*, this attack never takes on the tone of a parody, as it does, for example, in the brilliant, famous ninth chapter of Book Eleven of *The Brothers Karamazov*, entitled "The Devil. Ivan Fyodorovich's Nightmare," which merits a brief discussion. The reason the devil's apparition upsets Ivan is not only because he recognizes him as his own hallucination, and therefore a projection of his malicious part: "You are my hallucination. You are the incarnation of myself," he announced, "but only of one side of me . . . of my thoughts and feelings, but only the nastiest and stupidest of them."[98] He is equally disturbed by the mediocre and vulnerable character of the devil, who, incredulous about his "noble" status as a fallen angel, points his finger several times at the reason for the young Karamazov's disappointment: "Yes, you expect me to do something big, something perhaps even sublime. I'm very sorry, because I only do what I can." Also: "You are really angry with me for not having appeared to you in a red glow, with thunder and lightning, with scorched wings, but have shown myself in such a modest form."[99] The devil, suffering from a cold and rheumatism, is portrayed once again as a parasite, forced to take possession of human bodies in order to take on some solidity. But this is at the expense of his power, put to a harsh test in the dialog with his double. In a world that has abandoned God in favor of nothingness, a world in which "anything goes," evil can even take the form of simple negation: it has the possibility of reducing its scope to a "mild" dialectical contradiction.

The devil who appears to Ivan in his delirium seems to parrot the Hegelian lesson, which (if I may be permitted a crudely simplified version, drawing from *Faith and Knowledge*[100]) could also be interpreted as a grandiose attempt to downplay the reality of evil and render it harmless. The reproach that Hegel directs at the previous philosophy, and in particular at Kant's, is that it was fixated on the opposition between the finite and the infinite, and on the contradistinction between being and nothingness, thus compromising our understanding of the reality of evil. In Hegel's view, this mistake prevented Kant from recognizing that evil is nothing but the stubborn refusal to see beyond this antithesis. In point of fact, the negative—in whose wide embrace the radical nature of evil seems to gather and dissolve—ensures the dynamism of the process of the spirit, forcing every moment, every "figure," to flip over into its opposite. To separate evil from good, as the simple intellect does, is thus impossible, for the reason that they are inextricably intertwined. When the Spirit is able to go beyond the false antithesis between finite and infinite, although not eliminated, evil itself is nevertheless transformed. Of course, suffering, pain, and destruction are everywhere, but reconciliation always wins out over laceration: "The wounds of the Spirit heal and leave no scars behind."[101] On these lines, evil is everywhere, inextricable from the good.

Hegel's fury against all forms of dualism could even be interpreted as a continuation of the battle against that primary—and for him, absolutely fallacious—opposition between good and evil. In his view, this antithesis was delegitimized as an "unreal" way of conceiving matter, first by Christianity, and then by philosophy, which was able to conceive of the Spirit as a synthesis between the finite and the infinite. There is no doubt that Hegel's philosophy is primarily a radical rejection of *any* kind of dualism, even one that separates humanity from God. Whether his perspective is atheistic or religious, what interests us is that his great indictment against the thought of evil as a "reality in itself" can be considered an escape into the most sophisticated of theodicies, governed by an even more effective "cunning of reason" than that of Leibniz.

In the *General Introduction* to the *Lectures on the Philosophy of History*, in fact, Hegel himself presents his thought as a theodicy, a justification of the ways of God to help us understand all the ills of the world, *including the existence of evil*. Only in this way can the thinking mind be reconciled with "the fact of the existence of evil. Indeed, nowhere is such a harmonizing view more pressingly demanded than in Universal History." For Hegel, this reconciliation "can be attained only by recognizing the positive existence, in which that negative element is a subordinate, and vanquished nullity."[102]

Before the twentieth century launched its corrosive attack against the cunning rationality of the Hegelian "negative," and before the dialectical conception of history stood accused by twentieth-century philosophers, Dostoevsky—asking himself what became of the suffering of the victims, and allying himself ideally with Kierkegaard—drew up a brilliant parody of the positivity of the negative, putting it squarely in the mouth of the devil: "Before time was, by some decree which I could never make out," confesses the devil to Ivan, "I was pre-destined 'to deny' and yet I am genuinely good-hearted and not at all inclined to negation." However, he continues, I "must go and deny, without denial there's no criticism and what would a journal be without a column of criticism? Without criticism it would be nothing but one 'hosannah'." The poor fellow, who begs for his own "annihilation," is forced to stay alive just to allow events to take place: "No, live, I am told, for there'd be nothing without you. If everything in the universe were sensible, nothing would happen. There would be no events without you, and there must be events. So against the grain I serve to produce events and do what's irrational because I am commanded to."[103] In a word, evil reduced to mere negativity, to a condition of possibility for the unfolding of the dialectical spirit—evil as a force in itself, as the destructive power and drive toward nothingness—receives in theodicy, and especially in the "Hegelian theodicy," its most powerful neutralization. As if to say that evil was simply the necessary dose of pain

and suffering required to make life interesting, to keep it from being reduced to "an endless church service; it would be holy, but tedious."[104]

Dostoevsky unleashes his sarcastic genius against the notion of evil as
a simple function of the whole, as "the x in an indeterminate equation."[105]
A few years before presenting us with the meeting between the devil and Ivan,
his irony toward Kirillov had a much more somber tone. Indeed, it is almost
tinged with the compassion that always seems to accompany his writing
when he runs into the elements of tragedy. In the case of Kirillov, the Russian
writer shows us the tragic outcome of a reasoning that pursues the core idea
of all theodicies: the idea of eternal harmony. This apperception—the idea
of harmony—can last only for a few seconds in Kirillov, "only five or six at a
time," because to be able to endure it any longer than that "one must change
physically or die."[106] Hence Kirillov's decision to kill himself, a decision explained over the course of three consecutive dialogs. He seeks death not out
of a hatred for life, but to demonstrate the absolute freedom that human beings achieve as soon as they pronounce the death of God.

This is the famous announcement—by a nihilist on the brink of
holiness—of the "new man": human beings so full of themselves and their
freedom that living or dying is a matter of indifference to them: "There will
be entire freedom when it makes no difference whether one lives or does
not live."[107] His meaning is that if life is given in exchange for pain and
fear, then whoever manages to not feel pain or fear will be able to take the
place of God, and for that person, life and death will be equivalent. Just
like Zarathustra, for the Dostoevskian *Übermensch*, too, a world without
God—and therefore without guilt and without sin—will be a transfigured
world, a world in which killing oneself, or choosing death, will not mean
denying life. As he confesses to Stavrogin, if you stop believing in the eternity of the *other* life, *this* life becomes eternal.[108] Only then will time stop
and become eternity, as it is written in the Apocalypse, in which the angel
promises that time will end as soon as everyone has achieved happiness.
When time, which is an idea, dies out in the mind, all negativity will lose
its reason for being. For Kirillov, the Christian God is actually the name
humans have given to pain and suffering; God is the bearer of all negative power. When you admit that God does not exist, even the Hegelian
demon that neutralizes evil will become unnecessary.

This seems to be the conclusion of the "overman" Kirillov, who, in
the same dialog with Stavrogin, claims as a logical consequence that he is

finally happy. *Indeed, whoever succeeds in overcoming evil is happy,* because he or she can see beyond good and evil, and discern the particular sign of the great good of the whole in everything that exists. *Because inasmuch as the good exists, it is in everything that exists*: "A leaf is good. Everything is good." If someone dies of hunger, that is good; if "someone offends and dishonors the girl," that is good. "And if someone's head gets smashed in for the child's sake, that's good, too[. . . .] Everything is good, everything. For all those who know that everything is good."

Evil, then, in an even more radical way than the many teleological neutralizations—from Leibniz to Hegel—is actually nothing but our poor, distorted, and very partial perspective. This has always been the consolation, ultimately, to which theodicy leads in the end. All we need is to shift our focus—understand that death is equal to life and that pain is a part of happiness—and evil vanishes, exposed at last as what it really is: just a name, an empty fact. All that is needed is for people to know and think that they are happy, and they would be happy: "Man is unhappy because he doesn't know he's happy; only because of that." Now, it is up to us to change the dominant way of thinking from negative to positive. And in a universe overflowing with goodness, prayer will be the "so be it and amen" that accompanies every event. "I pray to everything," says Kirillov to Stavrogin. "See, there's a spider crawling on the wall, I look and am thankful to it for crawling."[109]

Here once again is the "upside down God" typical of the atheism that Dostoevsky rejects. However, while continuing to stare into the abyss that it opens up, Kirillov's version of nihilism is not viewed with contempt.[110] The revolution that was announced by the Christian God-Man repeats, but—having had its value reversed—it now leads to the kingdom of the Man-God. This is the prophecy that Kirillov proclaims not only to Stavrogin, but also to the cynical Pyotr, whose pleasure in destruction prevents him from understanding even the perspective of universal harmony. "If there is God," Kirillov argues to Pyotr Verkhovensky, who is purely interested in taking advantage of his suicide, "then the will is all his, and I cannot get out of his will. If not, the will is all mine, and it is my duty to proclaim self-will." The fullness, the fulfillment of freedom, for Kirillov, entails the duty of putting his sovereignty to the test by killing himself. In response to these arguments, Pyotr—who wants to rouse Kirillov because he is afraid that he will change his mind, making it impossible to pin the murder of Shatov on him—answers by revealing his own petty way of dwelling in evil: "in your place, if I wanted to show self-will, I'd kill somebody else and not myself." But Kirillov, delirious with omnipotence and totally absorbed by "his idea," counters indignantly: "To kill someone else would be the lowest point of my self-will, and there's the whole of you in that. I am not you: I want the highest point, and will kill myself." "For me," he continues, "no idea is higher than that there is no God. The history of mankind is on my side. Man has done nothing but invent God, so as to live without killing himself; in that lies the whole of world history up to now."[111] As Ivan Karamazov predicts, if the idea of God has been destroyed in man, "as soon as men have all of them denied God—and I believe that period, analogous with geological periods, will come to pass— the old conception of the universe will fall of itself without cannibalism and what's more the old morality, and everything will begin anew." This will be the era of the new man, the man who "will be lifted up with a spirit of divine, titanic pride."[112]

The rational fanaticism of Kirillov, whose emotional tone is actually much closer to that of a man of faith than to someone enlightened by reason, brings us to the last figure of the relationship between evil and nihilism. This is one in which goodness is not rejected in order to choose evil; nor is a lack of difference between good and evil proclaimed in order to act indiscriminately. Rather, with a single gaze that transcends the strictly human criterion, it goes beyond the opposition between good and evil to contemplate the goodness of nature's normativity itself, because nature—and what happens in it—is the very criterion of goodness. To break the vicious circle constituted by the limits of subjective consciousness, we must accept that evil is just an illusion. It is an illusion that comes to us from suffering, which stems, in its turn, from fear of death. When we rid ourselves of this fear, we become absolute rulers over life and death. And the supreme measure of power over life is manifested through an absolute will over our own life—by deciding to end it, without pain and without regret, as a way of reuniting with the eternal in the instant. Only in this way, says Kirillov, can human beings overcome their dependency in order to achieve a subjectivity that thoroughly embodies the divine attribute of freedom. Only in this way do we prove our absolute sovereignty: to become, like God, someone who has unlimited power over life and death.

The Power of Nothingness

What can I say, in conclusion, regarding the theoretical power of Dostoevsky's novel? How do the characters depicted in *Demons* help us understand the turning point that, starting with Kant, changed our understanding of evil? To what extent were they the first "new demons"? Between theological doubts and relapses into dualism, the Russian writer still managed to demolish some of the most persistent philosophical convictions about the idea of evil. The gloomy grandeur of his characters, the "molecular" investigation of the variegated phenomenology of wickedness, managed to probe to its depths the radicality that Kant—while viewing freedom and evil as inextricably linked—refused to venture into. This means, then, not only that freedom is the constitutive element of the human condition, but also that it cannot be separated from evil—from the *a priori* of the choice between good and evil. Once knowledge of this link between freedom and evil had been acquired, it was impossible for later philosophy to disregard it.

What avenues of thought did Dostoevsky open up? Thanks largely to *Demons*, evil could no longer be understood as an autonomous principle opposed to the good. Not by chance, the devil is almost always portrayed in his role as a double: the projection of a self that expels its abject part into an external image. In a nutshell, if evil was still conceived as it was by the Gnostics, as an ontologically autonomous substance in battle with a rival one, freedom would be nothing but the instrument of a conflict that is played out apart from responsibility. And even if Dostoevsky, because of his religious convictions, constantly runs the risk of dualistically dividing humanity between the damned and the redeemed, there is no doubt that he was the one who brought this conflict inside the subject, even before Nietzsche did. In other words, he shifted the scene of the struggle between good and evil from the History of Humanity and Spirit to within the very heart of subjectivity. This is in spite of the fact that, for him, as is obvious that it must be, salvation means the two are recomposed into one. Today, in my view, quite the opposite is at stake: to prevent the one from silencing the two.

What remains unchanged, however, is that Dostoevsky cannot accept the various philosophical strategies for neutralizing evil. For him, opposing those who proclaim the absence of evil or who view it as deprivation is tantamount to defending freedom. This is why the choice of evil for the sake of evil had to be asserted. This is why he had to emphasize the power of the negative, as a force capable of action, however, and not just as the hazy area that our limited eyes are unable to see. In this way he managed to reformulate the Kantian thesis of radical evil as a "reversal of incentives." Evil is not only self-love elevated to the moral law: it is the transgression of the moral law in the spirit of revolt. It is what Kant found to be an unthinkable contradiction, the *"positive* reversal of principles" made thinkable by Schelling, which Dostoevsky's phenomenology allows us to see at first hand. Evil is not just the perversion of reason into something other than reason or the absence of reason; rather, it is the hypertrophy of the reason that moves the will toward omnipotence. When reason severs its connection with what transcends and limits it, as in Stavrogin's case, the freedom of the will gets lost in the abyss and ends up in nothingness. Like Lucifer—*God's alter ego*—evil leads to the "reversed God," to use Schelling's expression. Put in terms more appropriate to the Russian writer, inebriated with the dignity of the *imago Dei*—with being made in God's image—human beings mistake this resemblance for identity. This illusion, the illusion that we ourselves are God, *is what prompts us to climb up to the dizzying heights of our self-determination.*[113] It is as if the will that drives our love for God changed its object under the influence of pride and degenerated into a lust for the divine attributes. At this point, where the atheist dialectic becomes engaged, not only does the *idea* of the divine get substituted for the *being* of God, it is in the separation between the idea of God and the being of God that the human destiny for perdition unfolds. Wickedness, then, could be defined as a perversion of the bond that unites human beings to God, a union that is no longer nurtured by love, but by the desire on the part of human beings to embody the divine attributes, starting with omnipotence, as the will to create *ex nihilo*.

Although some of the most acute philosophical interpretations of Dostoevsky have shed light on these aspects of his thought, another trait has remained in the shadows. Not only does this work "unravel" the enigma of radical evil, it also *clarifies the conditions of possibility by relating it to the question of power*. I am convinced that this monument of Russian literature is not merely a masterful narrative on the depths of the human soul. Nor does it simply express a brilliant, learned investigation, perched between literature, philosophy, and theology, into the possible perversions that can be arrived at by a nature corrupted to the roots by original sin. In addition to the notion of wickedness that Kant had first sensed and that Schelling later conceived in metaphysical terms, in *Demons*, perhaps for the first time, the distinction between wickedness and evil took shape. What we now had was *the possibility of distinguishing between a mode of being of the subject, and the "systemic" outcome of interaction between subjects.* Precisely thanks to this difference we can state that evil is an activity, not a substance; it is the energy of a relationship, not the static translation of a principle into reality. If wickedness has to do with the structure of the individual conscience, evil is a mode of the expression of power. Or, rather, it is the occurrence in history of a wicked situation, so to speak, that is the effect of a collective interaction between trespassing freedoms.

In any case, there is no doubt that for Dostoevsky the various demons—which correspond to the different modes of being assumed by evil—all depart from a common assumption. They all posit God as a model of absolute freedom to be imitated. In a dizzying ascent of human power, they all pursue the will to determine and create being from nothingness. This is how evil enters the world, and it does so as an attribute of power. But since human omnipotence cannot be achieved through creation (no matter how much we delude ourselves, human beings will never be able to create from nothing), it must be pursued through destruction, by dominating the world in order to destroy it, and by dominating other humans in order to annihilate them. Without love of God, without faith in His infinite goodness, human power is just the visible form of evil. Thus, evil is not just death and destruction; it is the will to and desire for death and destruction. Evil is not simply nothingness that opposes itself to being; it is the will to drag being into nothingness. It is a hatred of being *qua* being; a rebellion against life as a rebellion against creation. Within this framework, truly radical evil is at work in a particular relationship in which the positions between the subjects are totally asymmetrical, as we shall see.

I am not pursuing the ridiculous goal of transforming Dostoevsky into a post-structuralist. These distinctions are not explicitly described or theorized. And more importantly, both evil and wickedness—even after being unhinged from a previous metaphysical framework—still form part of a philosophical horizon that was still essentially an onto-theology. However, in *Demons* the question of nihilism was opened up in all its ontological scope, because at play in the novel is more than just the fate of perdition that, in Dostoevsky's view, atheism held in store. There is also more involved than the political indictment of a reactionary who regarded the possible consequences of the anarchic spirit of the Russian nihilists with fear.[114] This is the text that the twentieth century used to diagnose itself as having a diabolical disease of power—a power that, exceeding all limits, had seemingly become pure energy for oppression, control, and domination, an irreducible fount of suffering and destruction.[115] Nihilism, evil, and power: these three concepts provided a triangulation within which much of the philosophy of the twentieth century believed it was possible to circumscribe the tragedies of its history and for which *Demons* set the "primary" stage.

The subsequent philosophy that inherited and relaunched the evil and nihilism equation, although no longer in the religious terms that Dostoevsky used, continued to think of power as a result of the perversion of the will into a delusion of omnipotence, as the result of a sovereign subject—whether collective or individual makes no difference—that, by raising itself up to the All, produces Nothingness. The conceptual scaffolding developed by Dostoevsky to conceive of evil was perpetuated in a sort of secularization of the theological assumptions; this is one of the main ideas of this book. This is why it makes sense to talk about a Dostoevsky paradigm, even though the idea of evil was later torn from its metaphysical and theological framework by Nietzsche. In addition to what Dostoevsky's idea helped to deconstruct with respect to the preceding tradition, we must also acknowledge the persistence of a schema that, despite perpetually new content, persisted in a structurally identical form. Unlike the characters in Dostoevsky's novels, it hardly suffices for twentieth-century individuals to open themselves to the love of Christ in order to turn their crime into punishment, their punishment into atonement, and their atonement into forgiveness and salvation. However, the implication between nihilism, evil, and power as an interaction between freedom, will, and nothingness would continue to delineate the scope of evil for a long time to come. Starting from *a certain way* of reading Nietzsche to today's revival of Lacanian ideas, passing through *some parts* of Freud and Heidegger, the long shadow of Dostoevsky remains with us and repeatedly calls into life the ghost of Stavrogin and his circle of demons. It would seem that the authentic, eternal truth of "radical evil" lay hidden inside the secret of power itself—a kind of power that ultimately makes destruction not only a means to an end, but the end in itself, and that elevates nothingness to the ultimate goal of its action.[116] Often accompanied by cruelty, the evil of power "in its pure state" is supposedly expressed in the desecration of the victim, in torment inflicted for no reason, in the pain and humiliation caused to the innocent or the defenseless, who, in addition to being powerless, are also free of guilt and sin. This is shown by the needless suffering inflicted on children that Ivan and Stavrogin talked to us about, and that for a long time provided the hermeneutical key best representing the evil-power hendiadys: the relationship evinced by an all-powerful subject who stands before an absolute victim.

Instincts, Drives, and Their Vicissitudes:
Nietzsche and Freud

Reversals and Wills: Nietzsche for the Many

In an essay that has become a classic (entitled "Dostoevsky and Nietzsche: The Philosophy of Tragedy"), when Lev Shestov recalls the philosopher's joy on discovering Dostoevsky—"the only psychologist from whom I was able to learn anything," says Nietzsche—the Russian critic draws our attention to a passing of the baton, as it were.[1] If the true critique of reason was not written by Immanuel Kant but rather is to be found within Dostoevsky's phenomenology of the underground man,[2] then Nietzsche continues the maneuver by endowing this man, and along with him Stavrogin, Kirillov, and Verkhovensky, with full philosophical dignity.

Nietzsche did likely draw on Dostoevsky's profound imagination to express his impatience with Kant's undertaking. It is not so far-fetched to imagine the characters in *Demons* providing Nietzsche with the inspiration to deconstruct the categorical imperative and thus to go beyond the limit that Kant's radical evil had placed on understanding the human animal. Indeed, from a philosophical point of view, one of the most effective objections to Kant's moral thought is found in Nietzsche's genealogy of morals. It was specifically against "pure reason" and "practical reason" that he engaged in his long, brilliant, and contradictory battle. He deployed all his resources in opposing the philosopher from Königsberg, who, in his opinion, was the most sophisticated incarnation of the metaphysical-moral lie—so much so that Kant could even dispense with a theological crutch.

Nietzsche's polemic against Kant, starting from his very first moves, was relentless and seems to have been directed against the way his adversary conceptualized evil. In Nietzsche's view, rather than starting from the presumed purity of a "free will," we must begin conceptualizing evil from the opaque tangle of instincts and passions that enmesh our reason as much as they do our will. Nihilism, Dostoevsky's "discovery," was the momentous historical opportunity that allowed Nietzsche to analyze the rise of civilization in reverse as a gradual, grandiose annihilation of life: a slow, complex process of inhibiting the vital instincts.[3]

But first things first. Nietzsche himself admitted that he was obsessed with the question of evil from an early age. At the beginning of *On the Genealogy of Morals*, he reveals that the question that set in motion his own thoughts, "my 'a priori'—[. . .] my curiosity and my suspicions," concerned the origin of good and evil: "In fact, the problem of the origin of evil pursued me even as a boy of thirteen[. . . .] I devoted to it my first childish literary trifle [. . .] and as for the 'solution' of the problem I posed at that time, well, I gave the honor to God, as was only fair, and made him the father of evil."[4] Soon Nietzsche's categorical imperative, with the same vehemence as the Kantian one, would force him to solve the question of good and evil as an "immoralist," searching for its origin in the world. Not only that, it would even oblige him to look for it in what philosophy had always considered "vile" and "low."

In choosing the problem of evil as the impetus behind his genealogical thought, Nietzsche set out to expose the values that had been established as principles in both theology and philosophy. "Where you see ideal things, I see what is—human, alas, all-too-human!"[5]: this is how he justifies, in retrospect, the title given to his 1878 work,[6] the book that put a definitive end to the "higher swindle" of morality and that, together with *The Dawn*, took shape as the beginning of a genuine "fight against the Ideal." Or, rather, a struggle to root out what lies hidden behind "the moral ideology," conducted with the genealogical, "materialistic" approach that he chose to define as "psychological."[7]

The Nietzschean genealogy, which accuses philosophers of not being able to critique values that have been elevated to principles, thus claims to be the only true psychological science. "There was no psychology at all before me," he insists.[8] Thus, what has been called psychology "has got stuck in moral prejudices and fears; it *has not dared to descend into the depths.*"[9]

This is what happened to the British scholars, who, it is true, did seek to track down the origin of good and evil, but their breakdown of the moral facts, which resorts to the principle of utility and the role of habit, remains "white" like the clouds. We must have the courage of gray, of the slow and laborious collection of documentary material. The power of moral prejudices is such that the "British psychologists" have failed to lift the veil of "goodness," to find out what lies hidden under it. Only a psychology that is conceived as "morphology and *the doctrine of the development of the will to power*" will be able to lift the veil.[10] This is because there is no fact or phenomenon—as we know—that is not in itself a sign of a force in action. The "critical" move of true philosophy for Nietzsche is thus one that calls into question values presented as principles, dismantling them in order to trace them back to the perspectives from which the valuations and judgments originated. The order of rank among values is not rooted in the world of ideas and certainly not in the law of reason; on the contrary, it is just as "immoral" "as any other thing on earth." The first objective is therefore to trace "supranatural" morality back to its nature. But not in the way that "moralistic naturalism" approaches it, as did the British philosophers or the Enlightenment thinkers like Rousseau.[11] The fact is, they have a normative idea of nature that continues to leave its imprint on the moral dichotomy of good and evil, which is hostile to life. Therefore, the first rule of "philosophizing with a hammer" consists in disposing of the underlying structure of morality, which, although it alters the meanings of good and evil, still remains caught in the same axiological polarity: "There is lacking a knowledge and consciousness of the somersaults that have already occurred in moral judgments; and of how fundamentally 'evil' has several times been renamed 'good'."[12]

The real root of the immoral nature of morality can be brought to light, then, as soon as one rids nature of any idealization. The nature spoken about by the Enlightenment sciences and philosophers is "no matter of fact": it is not a text, but "rather only a naively humanitarian emendation and perversion of meaning," with which they make concessions to the egalitarian sentiments of modern animals.[13] Now, to complete the task of unmasking morality, the first step is to deconstruct the concept of nature,[14] and to do this, as he states in several places, Nietzsche is determined to follow the thread of the body: "Nutrition, place, climate, recreation," we read, for example, in *Ecce Homo*, "[. . .]are inconceivably more important than everything one has taken to be important so far. Precisely here one must begin to *relearn*."[15]

To arrive at an understanding of how judgments about good and evil become *entrenched in the body*, or rather, of the way the energy of the body (the will to power that underlies it) is experienced, expressed, and acted on: this is the task of Nietzsche's investigation into morality. He thus learns that the ranking among values is a hierarchy that orders the perceptions of forces, into active and reactive. If the forces were not inhibited, he argues, if they had been allowed to flow freely, there would have been no need for the dichotomy of good and evil to arise. Everything that is healthy in a body gets expressed in instincts of self-defense, but *especially in those of aggression*. The natural instinct of health is thus an active force that has nothing to do with moral oppositions. The original opposition, which Nietzsche urges us repeatedly to not interpret in a symbolic sense, is the antithesis between good and bad, an opposition that expresses a physical ranking of forces. As Foucault suggests, for the German philosopher "good" is the perspective of everything that descends from above, while "bad" is the perspective of everything that seeks to rise up from below. "Good" is the perspective of those who are effectively able to place themselves in a determinate position with respect to the space and to the occupants of that space.[16] It begins from a "positioning," from being able to put oneself at a certain "distance," and proceeds from there to establishing names and orders of ranks. The narrative is a familiar one: the word "good" is imposed by those who, being upright, proud, courageous, and "pure"—relying on their pathos of distance— present themselves as the bearers of value: "The pathos of nobility and distance . . . the protracted and domineering fundamental total feeling on the part of a higher ruling order in relation to a lower order, to a 'below', that is the origin of the antithesis 'good' and 'bad'."[17] Those who say "I am good" do not measure themselves by a preexisting yardstick of valuation, but rather, they have the power to define and to affirm themselves at the exact moment that they act—as though the activity itself was what procured the energy, the affirmative energy that we immediately perceive as "good." Originally, therefore, High and Low, Noble and Vulgar were neither principles nor values; instead they were indicators of different positions, different vectors of forces, from which the process of valuation takes place.

In some passages written between November 1887 and March 1888, now collected in the *Will to Power*, Nietzsche seems to reinforce the hypothesis that for him good and evil are simply reflections of the loss of strength experienced by a healthy constitution, and that the elevation of the moral good is the body's response to the gradual corruption of its health. The more the life force diminishes, the more the body responds in terms of ideals. He therefore seems to derive the scale of values by inverting a gradation that goes from "more strength" to a degree zero, where exhaustion prevails. On the basis of this "physiological characterization of idealists," Nietzsche develops a kind of typology of human beings, both historical and cultural at the same time, whose internal divisions are established according to the fullness of the senses. The point of origin of this genealogy, the "highest type: the classical ideal,"[18] reflects the pagan idea of self-affirmation by someone who dispenses energy, because he or she perceives the fullness of the world through "the success of all the chief instincts." "Therein the highest style," confirms Nietzsche, "the grand style." The expression of the "'will to power' itself. The instinct that is most feared."[19] Nature, at the height of its wealth, gives of itself, and bestows itself unreservedly, spontaneously; it erupts and gives freely, it grasps and releases, like all things that overflow with joy and energy. It does not need to construct ideals; its own fullness is in itself divine. Nietzsche then goes on to examine those "states in which the world is seen emptier, paler, more diluted." This happens when the person who experiences it has already lost the strength of his or her senses, and has weakened the natural fullness of the instincts. This person must therefore avoid anything of "the brutal, the immediate, the animal." The move away from nature brings with it prudence: cautious and lukewarm conduct that takes the form of "removing" and "calculating." All this "choosing" and "avoiding" forges the "anemic ideal" ("the wise man," "priestly = virginal = ignorant"), the type who initiates the process of spiritualization and moralization.[20] He roughly corresponds to the man of skepticism, a type Nietzsche returns to in a number of places: "For skepticism is the most spiritual expression of a certain complex physiological condition that in ordinary language is called nervous exhaustion and sickliness."[21] When, finally, the perversion of the instincts is at its apex and the vital energy exhausted, we then find the world "more absurd, worse, poorer, more deceptive." This is how it becomes the kingdom of evil.

When the will is unable to express itself in action, when it is unable to assert itself externally, rather than stop willing, it wills that the world no longer be. At the same time it projects itself into the ideal and defines this as "good." The good, in short, is "the antinatural, antiactual, illogical." Nihilism is first and foremost an impoverished sense of the world, the consequence of a pain that can no longer, in any way, be endured. At this point "one takes, one no longer gives."[22] The culmination of the nihilistic process is arrived at when not even nihilistic ideals suffice. In this situation, all that remains is the power of negation and destruction: "one negates, one destroys," as Nietzsche says. Starting from "the pagan type," a life that is fully infused with its own force, in which nothing is deified other than this maximum fullness of life itself, we pass to a "life diluted" ("the anemic type") in which one makes "a delicate choice" arriving finally at the *negation* of life. The first step consists in idealizing a contempt for life; the last step is to champion its destruction.[23] At the beginning there is the Yes of the fullness of the senses, of a nature that blesses itself; in the end there is the No of antinature, whose power to say Yes only remains through the power to utter the No of destruction.

When the world begins to be perceived as threatening, the strategy of denial comes into play, projecting all that is weak and unnatural into the ideal. This is the moment the power of negation comes onto the scene of human life—a power that takes the name of "*ressentiment*." As suggested by Gilles Deleuze in commenting on Nietzsche's *On the Genealogy of Morals*, the deduction that sets the "ideal" into motion is the following: "You are bad *therefore* I am good."[24] But everything has changed. The negative has entered into the premise and contains the essential. He who is "antinature" postulates a non-I as a starting point, so as to be able to then posit himself as its opposite. "While every noble morality," let us recall, "develops from a triumphant affirmation of itself, slave morality from the outset says No to what is 'outside', what is 'different', what is 'not itself': and *this* No is its creative deed."[25]

In short, when life is too weak, when it lacks the strength to affirm and justify itself on its own through action, it senses the *feeling* of its own weakness and reacts not through action but by reversing the terms in a table of values—a table from which to derive judgments, the weapons used by the weak to fight and defend themselves. In order to come into being, therefore, unlike the aristocratic ethos, the slave morality requires an external, opposing world. This is how the antagonism between the positions—between the differing amounts of energy—is channeled into a dualistic struggle between opposing values. Though evil is certainly not a metaphysical substance, neither is it a given, inherent to reality. It is a problem posed by a particular human perspective, and not the perspective of the Law, which rebukes reason for making a perverse use of itself. Rather, it is the expression of *passion*, the sentiment of those who, unsuited for the harshness of the natural life, elevate desire up into an ideal, a virtue, a "should be": namely, the desire to reverse the senseless suffering that the outside force produces in them. This, then, is how evil comes into the world. This is how, according to Nietzsche, nihilism, power, and evil become intertwined.

Ultimately, the opposition between good and evil can be reduced to the reversal of an original physical polarity. Health versus illness, strength versus weakness would therefore be the "true" oppositions, inasmuch as they are rooted in the body. The brand of antinatural and mendacious is subsequently imposed on them by the moral hierarchy. As we have noted, and as we know, Friedrich Nietzsche certainly gave ample attention in his work to the distinction between healthy and sick, a distinction that unfolds in a long series of oppositions, such as strong-weak, aggressive-vengeful, and active-passive. If this were all that he had to say, his move would be simple, in that it would be a specular, reversed image of the "metaphysical lie." To grasp the meaning of good and evil, to dissolve the misunderstanding and expose the fraud, the only thing required would be to denounce the transformation and corruption of that "original" dichotomy. The will to go "beyond good and evil" in Nietzsche's philosophy could just as easily be interpreted from this perspective—making him into the accursed author who rehabilitates evil in the name of a good deemed to be such by his active, blasphemous nihilism. As a matter of fact, this is the interpretation that has been put forward, for example, by many of Nietzsche's opponents in the name of defending moral values. And it is structurally the same reading, albeit with a reversed valuation, embarked on by those who sought to reinstate a heroic morality through Nietzsche. Many interpreters of the political philosopher, especially diehard nationalists and Nazis, have declared themselves to be messengers for the realization of Nietzsche's attempt to go beyond good and evil, by trying to redeem from evil a good that had so long been stifled by history. National Socialist "readers," as we shall see, rehabilitated the will to power, making it a supreme value—a good—intending it as the rule of the strong over the weak, and thereby introducing Nietzsche into a fully dichotomous, oppositional framework. Everything depends, of course, on the significance given to the *Wille zur Macht*, contained in the essays written after *Thus Spake Zarathustra*.[26] When the "will to power" that is being reaffirmed and redeemed is a necessary will to dominate the weak on the part of the strong, then Nietzsche's ideas obviously lend themselves to being turned into an agenda of values that the political power has a duty to affirm. The Superman would thus become someone who is free from false inhibitions in reversing the valuation of good and evil from the viewpoint of the strong and powerful.

But even if one interprets the "will to power" as the instinct of freedom, mortified by guilt, to which we must return in order to restore meaning and joy to life, this fails to avert the danger of a dualistic reading.[27] As we said before, this strategy still involves a simple countermove, which merely reverses the long series of oppositions: truth-lie, health-illness, natural-unnatural. It is as if the philosophy that preaches the will to power were to put goodness on trial, to seek reparations for the damages caused to the health of the human race by this supposed virtue. According to this version, Nietzsche is combating the danger—the germ, the poison, the narcotic—in the seduction exerted by ideals that represent a serious threat to the future. Even in this case, more than a few passages justify the interpretation that all the values revolving around what is called good actually form the constellation of a true evil: the evil of negation that has exhausted life. The new morality, in short, would elevate to the supreme Good what he calls "*great health*," interpreted as the vital, powerful instinct out of which would issue the virtue of a sort of "sublime wickedness"[28]—the set of animal inclinations that have finally been rehabilitated. Nietzsche therefore seeks redemption of all the instincts that have been cursed by the all-too-human dichotomy of good and evil: "Man has all too long had an 'evil eye' for his natural inclinations, so that they have finally become inseparable from his 'bad conscience'." Would an opposite move be possible, asks Nietzsche? In other words, would it be possible to restore a good conscience to the bad man? The Good would thus become the set of all the instincts of freedom that, starting from Greek philosophy through Christianity until the exhausted modern times, have been mortified: strength, growth, taking possession of the other-than-self. And, along with these, cruelty. "To see others suffer does one good," he writes; "to make others suffer even more: this is a hard saying[. . . .] Without cruelty there is no festival: thus the longest and most ancient part of human history teaches— and in punishment there is so much that is *festive*."[29] This is partly because a great deal of sweetness, of voluptuous pleasure, comes to us from the ingredient of cruelty,[30] but also because—as Nietzsche often repeats—when humanity was unaware of the shame of cruelty it was able to lead a more serene and less gloomy life. As if to suggest that the animal innocence and joy that now create revulsion in us could be associated with a kind of lost earthly paradise to which we should return.

It is undeniable that the perspective on evil in Nietzsche's writings is complex enough to justify even this first type of interpretation. The tradition that has mortified all the instincts of freedom, vitality, and strength of the prehistoric (precivilized) animal-man is certainly to blame in his view. And the liberation of the debased instincts could therefore be the event of freedom that gives back a voice and innocence to everything that nihilism has sacrificed. In this sense the "man of the future," the "overman," would be welcomed by Nietzsche—as the person who will redeem us from both idealism and all that has germinated from it, namely, the "great nausea," the will to nothingness. If Nietzsche himself were this "antichrist," the philosopher would become the champion of a good that would be legitimized once again by its power to defeat nothingness.[31] There were more than a few twentieth-century interpreters who read Nietzsche in this way, forcing him into the vise grip of a dualistic thought.

The "beyond" as a step toward the innocence of becoming had a different meaning altogether. Being able to think in terms of a dimension where everything happens innocently and is transformed, entering into a perception of reality in which the will to power is not the will over an object, but an objectification of the vital energy, would effectively mean putting oneself into a perspective in which moral judgments no longer serve any purpose. This is because being would only be the incessant play of a differential relationship between forces that are constantly assembling and disassembling. There is no measure that transcends them, and thus, no hierarchy imposed from above; for this reason good and evil are senseless.

It might be asked whether this interpretation, best represented perhaps by Deleuze's brilliant reading, eclipses the powerful ethical instance that continues to operate in Nietzsche, although beyond a metaphysical and Christian morality of duty.[32] Does it not diminish Nietzsche's profound perception of the complexity of reality—his awareness that every process of subjectification is set into motion precisely by the perception of a difference, a negativity that imposes a judgment? That, therefore, as long as there is critical reflection, there will be, like his own *a priori*, the possibility of distinguishing between what we think is good and what we think is bad, regardless of how we name the polarity in question? It is true, as Deleuze says, that Nietzsche's great philosophical endeavor was to be able to conceive of multiplicity as the "manifestation of unity," of becoming as "the affirmation of being," and of return as "*the being of that which becomes*," so that "the Unique must be affirmed in generation and destruction." Like Heraclitus, Nietzsche sought to look deeply into the play of forces and to see "no chastisement of multiplicity." But Nietzsche also knows, like Dostoevsky's Kirillov, that one can attain that idea "only five or six [seconds] at a time," because to be able to endure it any longer "one must change physically or die."[33] Either we are transformed by it, by dying or going crazy; or inevitably the power of negative returns, and with it, the judgment.

The Interiority of Evil (Nietzsche Continued)

Perhaps, as far as the question of evil is concerned as well, we should listen more carefully to his words and to their ambivalence.[34] Do the roles of cruelty, violence, and suffering need to be contextualized in more detail? Surely Nietzsche is telling us that our way of looking at cruelty is so distorted by our "bad conscience" and moral prejudices that we are unable to see how much violence is hidden in the process that led to our condemnation of cruelty. So much cruelty and so much pleasure in that very cruelty pave the path that led to the civilizing of human beings that even "the categorical imperative smells of cruelty."[35] There is always violence, in any kind of negation of the senses: there is violence in knowledge, in transcending appearance, in reducing the new to the old, in simplifying the multiform, in ignoring contradiction.

But Nietzsche is at the same time warning us that it is not enough to get rid of the pious lie, the false promise with which Christianity and its pastoral power captured and pulled into their orbit all those who could not say Yes to life. He is not interested in a new teleological-historical construction, even under the guise of an anti-theodicy. And he has even less desire to perform an accurate historical reconstruction. He uses his "antiquarian" sources to weave the plot of a "critical kind of history" that demolishes a two-thousand-year-old "monumental history."[36] The pairs of antithetical values—"good and bad," on the one hand, and "good and evil," on the other—have been engaged in a fearful struggle on earth for thousands of years. And although we can be sure that the latter has prevailed over the former for some time now, "there are still places where the struggle is as yet undecided."[37] It is a battle that bears the *indelible marks of a conflict between two different impulses* that fuels history.[38]

Nietzschean genealogy—it must be noted at this point—is not directed toward the past. If Nietzsche seems at first glance to want to go back to an original position that is "noble and aristocratic," in actuality he is suggesting something else. He is telling us that the question of evil, and along with it the problem of suffering, is inseparable from the very birth of subjectivity. His use of the *vis polemica* must be borne in mind: while condemning the results of *ressentiment*, he is bound to acknowledge that without *ressentiment*—without its movement toward internalization—there would be no subject. Without that negation of a life that unscrupulously and cruelly affirms itself, we would not have come to the knowledge of self-awareness as we know it. There was no conscience in the so-called prehistoric period. An action was not evaluated by the intention of the actor. An action was judged purely on the basis of its consequences: "It was the retroactive force of success or failure that led men to think well or ill of an action[. . . .] Instead of the consequences, the origin: indeed a reversal of perspective!"[39] With the gaze of an immoralist, Nietzsche cannot help but observe that all this brought about at the same time a great refinement in sensibility.[40]

The striking pages that make up the second essay of the *Genealogy of Morals* recount how an asymmetrical relationship of power, in digging out a painful wedge, ends up forming our conscience.[41] His account provides us with the dynamics of an *internalization* process that will become the locus of the psyche, the soul, the spirit, reason—in a word, the subject. It is impossible not to think of Freud, but even more about the way Foucault, starting from these same pages, came to make the connections between subjection and subjectification, as we shall see. Hence, if on the one hand, *ressentiment* as Nietzsche conceives it is something dark, low, cowardly, and vulgar, it nevertheless designates the movement through which we become subjects. Nietzsche's question is well known: How did the "bad conscience" arise? How did that "serious illness" come about that man was bound to contract under the stress of "the most fundamental change he ever experienced"?[42] His answer to this question is equally famous. The situation facing "these semi-animals, well adapted to the wilderness, to war, to prowling, to adventure" was not unlike what must have happened to aquatic animals when they were forced to become land animals or die: "suddenly all their instincts were disvalued and 'suspended'." This is where the sense of inadequacy, of disorientation, originated. Deprived of their regulating drives, "they were reduced to thinking, inferring, reckoning, co-ordinating cause and effect." In short, they had to resort to their "conscience," to their most miserable organ, the one most prone to error: "I believe there has never been such a feeling of misery on earth, such a leaden discomfort—and at the same time the old instincts had not suddenly ceased to make their usual demands! Only it was hardly or rarely possible to humor them."[43] They had to seek new and, as it were, subterranean gratifications.

This is how the phenomenon of *Verinnerlichung* or internalization was set in motion, thanks to which the human being acquired its characteristic trait as the thinking animal: "All instincts that do not discharge themselves outwardly turn inward—this is what I call the *internalization* of man: thus it was that man first developed what was later called his 'soul'. The entire inner world, originally as thin as if it were stretched between two membranes, expanded and extended itself, acquired depth, breadth, and height, in the same measure as outward discharge was *inhibited*."[44] We could say that here, too, in Nietzsche as well, the negative finds a positive use for itself. But, unlike in dialectics, there is no place for synthesis. What we have instead is a precarious balance of forces, always vulnerable to the danger of tipping over into a toxic accumulation. Trapped in a vicious cycle of self-hatred, self-laceration, and torture, the forces found their way to the outside only in the immaterial mode of value judgments. This was how the antithesis between good and evil came to be, now revealed to us by Nietzsche from within and in its nascent state.

The force of an external power, such as a political organization, for example, thus seeks to restrain the human animal's ancient instincts for freedom, turning their wild, disruptive expression *against man himself*.

Hostility, cruelty, joy in persecuting, in aggression, in destruction, therefore, none of this disappeared, but it was turned against the possessors of such instincts: that is the origin of the "bad conscience."[45] Nietzsche's images are truly unforgettable of a man who, in the absence of external enemies and resistances, confined to the oppressive narrowness created by the normalization of customs, tears himself to pieces and persecutes himself. An "animal that rubbed itself raw against the bars of its cage as one tried to 'tame' it [. . .], this yearning and desperate prisoner became the inventor of the 'bad conscience'."[46] The will to attack did not recede, then; it only turned into a desire for self-aggression: "that repressed cruelty of the animal-man made inward and scared back into himself, the creature imprisoned in the 'state' so as to be tamed," invented the bad conscience in order to be able to continue causing pain. He invented the bad conscience "after the *more natural* vent for this desire to hurt had been blocked." Along this path, he mastered the religious hypothesis to push his self-martyrdom to its most horrible point of crudeness and subtlety. To wit, a debt toward God: this thought became an instrument of torture for him. As Nietzsche explains, "He apprehends in 'God' the ultimate antithesis of his own ineluctable animal instincts; he reinterprets these animal instincts themselves as a form of guilt before God, [. . .] he stretches himself upon the contradiction 'God' and 'Devil'; he ejects from himself all his denial of himself, of his nature, naturalness, and actuality, in the form of an affirmation, as something existent, corporeal, real, as God, as the holiness of God, as God the Judge, as God the Hangman, as the beyond, as eternity, as torment without end."[47]

This is how the opposition between good and evil arises and takes effect in each one of us. It has no reality outside the self. *Here lies the root of all our dualistic inclinations*: the refusal on the part of the subject to accept the drive for aggression, destruction, and negation as its own and as ineradicable. Thus, the experience of an intense, searing internal conflict is quelled only by the possibility of blaming, hating, making someone or something responsible for it—even one's own soul. The idea of evil is therefore the result of a double movement, a dynamic of externalization that follows on that first process of internalization. It consists in the projection into an outside of something that, by now, structurally inhabits the interiority of the subject: a painful perception that is prohibited from and incapable of being expressed through direct action or unmediated passion.

In the same period between November 1887 and March 1888,[48] Nietzsche expresses in the strongest terms his opinion on the destructive lie in which this dualism consists. It has led us to define a good man as someone who is cut in half: "To reduce mankind to this half-sided efficiency, to the *'good'*[. . . .] The essential demand here is that mankind should do nothing evil, that it should under no circumstances do harm or *desire* to do harm." Hence, mankind "takes good and evil for realities that contradict one another [. . .] it advises taking the side of the good, it desires that the good should renounce and oppose the evil down to its ultimate roots [. . .] it dreams, on the contrary, that it is getting back to wholeness, to unity, to strength of life: it thinks it will be a state of redemption when the inner anarchy, *the unrest between those opposing value drives, is at last put an end to*."[49] The "good" finds itself surrounded by evil, and it sees evil in every action—hence, it winds up believing that nature is evil, human beings are corrupt, and "goodness" is a form of grace. This is not the way, however, that we cease to hate, to wage war, and "to act for No."[50] In reality, this objectification of the struggle between good and evil in the external world multiplies the seeds of war and enlarges the sphere of what should be hated.

So how can we understand *Beyond Good and Evil* in the light of the dynamics that give rise to interiority? If, on the one hand, by framing his thought in terms of a physiology and psychology of morality, Nietzsche dismantles all "sublime" claims to a "transcendental Subject" or an "absolute Spirit," the purpose of this move—as has been remarked—is not to rehabilitate a natural evilness as a good whose force has received the same excommunication as the ideal. Friedrich Nietzsche is not the antichrist who blesses that which has been cursed, and curses that which has been blessed. Nor is he simply the brave demystifier who rediscovers "the accursed share." Nietzsche is primarily someone who declares war on the very structure of dualism—a structure that originates in the subject, and with the subject, as a dualistic and contradictory movement that has been turned into a hypostasis. He attacks the foundation of all metaphysical "faiths": dualism itself, the spiritual construction of a frontal opposition or of a polarity between values. "The fundamental faith of the metaphysicians is *the faith in opposite values*."[51] For Nietzsche it is a secondary, reactive development, an *a posteriori* evaluation of a situation, of the factual situation of differences between forces within the primary givenness—for him, the body.

In other words, if it is legitimate to continue speaking about "evil" as far as Nietzsche is concerned—a question we will examine in more detail—I would argue that evil has to do with the weakness of a being that is incapable of sustaining its own internal difference and that thus separates and isolates conflicting perceptions, lending them an objective reality. In the process, this being invents a soul, as a space of its own, that is separate from the body, and that believes it can expunge from itself, so as to project into the external world everything it perceives as bad. As a result, a duality, or rather, a constitutional duality of forces, *is turned into a dualistic regime of separation.* A product of powerlessness, of a repressed energy—namely, *ressentiment*—it now destroys what it itself has built: God and morality. If the vicious circle of outward projection and subsequent destruction is not stopped, the final destination is ultimate nihilism, the sort of passive nihilism that Nietzsche saw as dragging Europe toward nothingness. Dualism did indeed allow the choice, and, along with it, the exercise of the will—making it possible to say No and to negate the given—having progressively consumed the objects to be negated. The will now takes the final, fatal step of internalization. It gradually becomes the will to self-destruction of life. This is the ultimate demonstration of the fact that rather than not will, the human animal would prefer to "will nothingness."

The Freudian Scandal: The Death Drive

It has been said that Marx would be the last modern thinker in a hypothetical history of thought on evil.[52] In other words, he would be the last great thinker for whom history can provide a remedy for evil. If so, then Marx is perhaps the last great philosopher for whom evil has its own objective structure. The perspective opened up by Nietzsche and Freud certainly does look in a different direction. It is not my intention to go back over the history of philosophy *sub specie mali* for the umpteenth time. My interest lies rather in glossing a series of passages and pinning them up so that they can act as helpful signals to identify the coordinates within which, for many decades, twentieth-century continental philosophy believed it could locate the question of evil once and for all. As part of this basic mapping—regardless of which interpretative scheme one chooses—Nietzsche and Freud represent a crucial stage in the wake of the great Russian writer. In contrast to Kantian prudence, which stops short at the inscrutability of radical evil, and in the face of the Hegelian strategy, which traces it back to the dialectical power of the negative, with Nietzsche and Freud there erupts onto the scene the destructive force at work in the heart of human reality, imposing a profound redefinition of the concept of evil. No longer original sin or moral guilt, nor a state of ontological poverty or an autonomous substance, evil now appears as a set of forces that push inexorably toward nothingness. Dostoevsky's legacy is thus picked up on again, but with a strongly secularized twist.

I will touch briefly on some passages of Freud's work: on aspects that, even though making the author the target of sharp, "scientific" criticisms, played a crucial role for philosophy, making their inclusion in a hypothetical history of the idea of evil obligatory. Accordingly, I think it is important to take seriously Jacques Lacan's view of Freud's *Civilization and Its Discontents* that the purpose of the work is "to rethink the problem of evil."[53] In other words, the Freudian metapsychology—partly thanks to the results arrived at by Schopenhauer and Nietzsche—is seen as the means to a general ultimately philosophical conclusion: not only does evil exist, but it is a structural given with no remedy, inasmuch as it is the backwash from the destructive wave of an instinctual drive. This is a view that political thought was quick to translate into the hypothesis that there exists a will to power that can be understood only as the will to death of the other.

We know the impact that the First World War had on Sigmund Freud. Like many other great writers of the first half of the twentieth century, the weight of its carnage strongly marked the thought of the founder of psychoanalysis.[54] Already in his "Thoughts for the Times on War and Death,"[55] written in 1915, war—and along with it the brute fact that "people really die and no longer one by one, but in large numbers, often ten thousand in one day"—clearly plays the role of trauma, of an excess that breaks through the defenses separating us from the disorienting aspect of reality. In other words, war—and the mass death that it produces—shatters the perception of the normality of life, along with its forms and its conventions. How can we explain the brutality and destructiveness of individuals who seemed to belong to the ranks of the highest civilization? What are we to think, he wonders, about the developmental process we believed could eradicate mankind's "evil human tendencies" and replace them with "good ones" "under the influence of education and a civilized environment"?[56] Hence the bitter admission, a harbinger of significant philosophical consequences, that "in reality, there is no such thing as 'eradicating' evil tendencies." In psychological terms, his investigation shows that the most profound human essence is rooted in the deepest instinctual impulses of an elementary nature, impulses that are similar in all human beings and that likewise aim at satisfying certain primal needs. In themselves, these impulses are not good or bad. Whether they become "good" or "evil" for civilization depends—to summarize drastically—on a delicate equilibrium that internal or external factors exert on the libidinal, instinctual ambivalence of the subject.

The still detached tone of "Thoughts for the Times on War and Death," dedicated to the "passionless impartiality" of science, gave way only a few years later to a reflection on death that is much closer to the heights of philosophical speculation than to the rigor of a scientific treatise. In *Beyond the Pleasure Principle*, published in 1920, Freud reached his theoretical apex. Despite the rocky, controversial reception of the work, he never took his distance from it.[57] By analyzing the dreams of a few patients with posttraumatic neuroses, Freud entered into an unexplored area of human experience that he called "beyond the pleasure principle." In doing so, he became aware of another equilibrium of the mental apparatus. Until that time—not unlike the thinkers that Nietzsche referred to as the "British psychologists"—Freud identified the dynamics of the psyche in the human tendency to avoid unpleasure and seek pleasure. In this sense, we can say that the evil in human affairs could be seen as a side effect, an "unintended consequence" of an excessive pursuit of pleasure. But the demon of war, we might say, led him to inflict another hard blow to the humanistic pride of philosophical subjectivity. Already with the "first topography," the unconscious had usurped the sovereignty of the ego of reason. Now, what the war revealed to him about this unconscious was the absolute power that death held. It was an active force that led the inventor of psychoanalysis to appropriate and elaborate on what I have called the Dostoevsky paradigm.

Analysis of veterans and survivors, along with their "traumatic war neuroses," provided the evidence for him of how humans not only do not flee pain, they actually have a desire to seek it out. They wish to repeat the same experiences that caused their illness—proving that, in some cases, the instinct of self-preservation can entirely forgo its function. The sexual instinct no longer sufficed to explain the complex weave of instincts that rule over certain apparently incomprehensible behaviors. "The manifestations of a compulsion to repeat," Freud writes when first presenting his shocking discovery, "exhibit to a high degree an instinctual character and, when they act in opposition to the pleasure principle, give the appearance of some 'daemonic' force at work."[58] Clinical experience of trauma thus complicates the image of the unconscious, which is not reducible to an obscure zone of repressed desire. It is something that lies beyond desire itself, beyond the quest for fulfillment through a goal and an object. The Id seems to be the site of a pure instinctual impulse, with apparently no goal other than death. As if, in contradiction to every reasonable hedonistic and rational logic, in some situations human beings aspire only to sink into the abyss of evil.

Perhaps this is why Freud speaks of a "'daemonic' force" in this context, as if it were the sign of the inescapable presence of a drive toward destruction that imposes, recursively, destructive behaviors. This power of nothingness is what in the Freudian language of energetic dynamics thus takes on the name of "death drive," upsetting the distinction between sexual instincts and ego instincts, between the pleasure principle and the reality principle, that Freud had until a short time before believed to be valid. After lengthy digressions on the dynamics of elementary particles, on the drive of primitive cellular aggregates toward a return to an inorganic state, and after expressing numerous hesitations, in a concluding note, Freud finally states his discovery:

We came to know what the "sexual instincts" were[. . . .] With the hypothesis of narcissistic libido and the extension of the concept of libido to the individual cells, the sexual instinct was transformed for us into Eros, which seeks to force together and hold together the portions of living substance. What are commonly called the sexual instincts are looked upon by us as the part of Eros which is directed towards objects. Our speculations have suggested that Eros operates from the beginning of life and appears as a "life instinct" in opposition to the "death instinct" which was brought into being by the coming to life of inorganic substance. These speculations seek to solve the riddle of life by supposing that these two instincts were struggling with each other from the very first.[59]

The struggle between these two forces conjures up a sort of cosmic conflict. Freud himself admitted that the battle between life instincts and death instincts goes beyond the scope of the human psyche. The death instinct falls outside the limited sphere of subjectivity, since it represents the tendency of organic substance to return to its original inorganic state. The life instinct—which represents the tendency to aggregate the vital substance into increasingly larger and more complex units—also extends outside the dynamics of the psyche. However, the two opposing energetic directions, Freud tells us, are not usually found in isolation; they cannot be brought back to a "pure" state. As much as one can prevail over the other, for the most part we encounter them intertwined (*Vermischung*). All the more reason to conclude that it is impossible to eliminate evil.[60] On the contrary, if we identify the erotic drive, which tends to aggregate and combine, with the good, and the drive toward disintegration and the inorganic with evil— he seems to conclude—then we will have to admit that the goal of life is not Goodness but rather Evil, destruction, and death.

This is the same conclusion that Freud arrived at, in gloomier tones, in his *Civilization and Its Discontents* of 1929, in the context of a discussion on the religious feeling. Already in *Group Psychology and the Analysis of the Ego*, religion was seen as the imposition of a uniform method to protect from suffering.[61] In subsequent essays as well, including the text of 1929, religion is presented as a sort of regressive call to a collective delusion under whose shelter we can protect ourselves from the evil surrounding us on almost every turn[62]: the pain that comes from the body, which is destined to fall apart and perish; the pain that threatens us from the outside, from the destructive power of the world that can pound us down; and, finally— the hardest to accept—the pain that comes from relationships with our fellow humans. This latter kind of suffering is one that human beings delude themselves into believing can be eliminated through moral, civil, and political norms, but that, in fact, continues to blight their lives with the same power as physical and natural threats. The instincts human beings are endowed with must include an ineradicable dose of aggression. A person is not solely a possible sexual object or a potential helper for others; he is also "someone who tempts them to satisfy their aggressiveness on him, to exploit his capacity for work without compensation, to use him sexually without his consent, [. . .] to humiliate him, to cause him pain, to torture and to kill him."[63] This "cruel aggressiveness" does not act for the sake of its own benefit. Indeed, as a rule, it waits for a provocation, an excuse: it camouflages itself, putting itself to work at some goal that it would have been able to achieve anyway by far more benign means. Thus, in circumstances that are favorable, such as in the army masses during wartime, in the heat of battle when the forces that normally inhibit it are diminished, malignant aggressiveness manifests itself and "reveals man as a savage beast to whom consideration towards his own kind is something alien."[64] It is an illusion to think, as communism does, for example, that one has found "the path to deliverance from our evils" in a different socioeconomic organization. It makes no difference if everyone's essential needs are satisfied: they would still not stop regarding others as their enemy. Even if private property were abolished, aggression would exploit the differences in power and influence to its advantage. In short, we have not "altered anything in its nature."[65] In *Civilization and Its Discontents*, it is now obvious that cruelty, destructiveness, and the desire to cause pain are not transitory human characteristics contingent to specific historical and social conditions. On the contrary, some historical conditions, some brutal methods of political and social organization, are specific manifestations of the death drive (*Todestrieb*). Our most violent and destructive impulses coexist with the very development of moral codes and prohibitions. It is a dangerous illusion to think that these bulwarks of containment can offer effective, definitive protections. If the conscience—or rather the state of anxiety that will become the conscience—is essential for the emergence of morality and hence for the control of evil impulses, there are no guarantees that this shield will not be overwhelmed by the explosive force of the drives. As history shows, there are situations in which the conscience—as a point of fragile accord and energetic equilibrium of the forces—collapses.

Freud's conviction on this point is so deeply rooted that he not only emphasizes the contrast between the two drives in yet stronger terms, he even reproaches himself and his previous work for his defensive attitude toward this scandalous discovery. Yet, he argues, the phenomena of sadism and masochism had already brought him face to face with the existence of an aggressive drive alongside the erotic one. It was a denial—his own attitude—that had distracted him from the urgent need to recognize the "undeniable existence of evil." Namely, the need to acknowledge the pervasive presence of a non-erotic aggression that can explode into violent destructiveness: "I can no longer understand how we can have overlooked the ubiquity of non-erotic aggressivity and destructiveness and can have failed to give it its due place in our interpretation of life."[66] It is this same strategy of denial taken to an extreme that has led theological and religious thought to turn evil into a hypostasis. Religion and theology have not wanted or have not been able to admit to the existence of imperfection in a being made by God in his image and likeness, or to the possibility of destruction. Not being able to tolerate the coexistence of evil and divine omnipotence, the Devil thus became "the best way out as an excuse for God"—the best trick for projecting evil into the external world. This substantialization of evil in the devil, Freud adds, is the same paranoid gesture put into action by the Nazis against the Jews.[67] As an almost perfect continuation of the points made by Dostoevsky's devil when he appears to Ivan Karamazov, Sigmund Freud also appeals to Goethe and his Mephistopheles. In *Faust*, he finds a foreshadowing and a confirmation of the polarity between Eros and Thanatos of which he is now finally aware. In Goethe's masterpiece, in fact, the principle of evil is not the adversary of what is divine, holy, and moral. Rather, it is the force that opposes nature: a nature that creates, engenders, and multiplies beings. In a word, it is the churning power of death, the eternal struggle against the energy of life. The course of history takes place under the aegis of this constant tension.

The process of civilization, concludes Freud, is indeed a path down which humankind travels thanks to the drive of Eros, which progressively combines individuals into increasingly organized and sophisticated aggregations. But this program of civilization is opposed by "man's natural aggressive instinct, the hostility of each against all and of all against each." If happiness has never been achieved—on the contrary, if despite the gains of progress, the civilized world seems more than ever on the verge of collapse—it is because the impulse against life that we call the death drive is always at work in it. The latter successfully opposes the hold of the libidinal ties: "this aggressive instinct" is the offspring and main representative of "the death instinct which we have found alongside of Eros and which shares world-dominion with it. And now, I think, the meaning of the evolution of civilization is no longer obscure to us. It must present the struggle between Eros and Death, between the instinct of life and the instinct of destruction, as it works itself out in the human species. This struggle is what all life essentially consists of, and the evolution of civilization may therefore be simply described as the struggle for life of the human species."[68]

Evil is therefore no longer a mystery to psychoanalysis, which, with Freud, claims to have demolished once and for all the fictitious foundations on which philosophy and theology had placed it. It is not, in actuality, a privation of being; it is not a principle that is opposed to divine goodness; it is not a result of the original fall. But neither is it simple self-ishness or self-interest pushed to excess, or a negative dialectic that, as such, can be "repaired" and reabsorbed by the movement of the spirit of humanity. *It is a structural condition of being* that—unlike sin, or simple negation—no higher being, no final harmony, no Spirit, and ultimately no just society can ever eradicate.

As we know, the Freudian emphasis on the "cosmic" significance of his discovery led many interpreters to criticize the death drive and regard it as a hypostasis leading psychoanalysis to stray away from the sober regions of scientific rigor. For others, however, it allowed Freud's later writings to be included in the ranks of genuine philosophical thought. A prime example of this is Rüdiger Safranski, who dedicated one of the most interesting reconstructions to the idea of evil, and who views the theory of *Todestrieb* as a kind of secularized version of the Gnostic conception of "flawed creation."[69] Although admitting that Freud is not dogmatic about his views, Safranski is convinced that the theory of the death drive eliminates the possibility of human freedom—a freedom that can just as easily choose good or evil. In Safranski's view, the forces of destruction seem to be the final victors in the titanic struggle between life instincts and death instincts that takes the form of a cosmic conflict. This means the "wrong" path that led from stone to conscience is traveled back in reverse, from conscience to stone. Safranski's interpretation is debatable but certainly representative of a fairly widespread hermeneutic approach according to which the *Destruktionstrieb*, its ruinous race toward nothingness, is a natural and undeniable force against which the freedom of the subject is powerless.

Freud's metapsychological investigation, as was the case for Nietzsche's philosophy, can be and has been employed in two ways. Choosing to follow one or the other perspective leads to a divergence of paths in thought on evil. As was the case with the will to power, for the death drive as well one can maintain that thinking of it as the necessary and irredeemable component of the history of humanity means interpreting it in a simple, one-sided fashion. Be that as it may, these are the basic outlines of one of the most popular and conventional critical judgments to be issued on the later works of Freud. However, it is also a trap into which some of the critics who have used Freud's "discovery" as a tool for a new thought on the negative have fallen. There is no doubt, in fact, that the *Todestrieb* complicates even further the already problematic relationship between psychoanalysis and freedom, between a subject "no longer master in his own house" and the responsibility for his actions.

Now, Freudian analysis, which at first sight may seem like a relapse into a Manichaeism in which the life instincts correspond to the cosmic forces of good and the death instincts to those of evil, can in actuality provide arguments to land one of the most effective blows against dualism. Of course, human beings perpetrate evil. It is no longer possible to consider destructive violence toward others as the "unintended consequence" of an individual dominated by the pleasure principle. Rather, it is the expression of the drive toward death that inhabits the subject, an outward movement of evil that no law and no authority will ever be able to eradicate. No doubt, there is a tragic overtone to Freud's observations: no type of intervention, no matter how strong, can entirely extinguish this drive, because a residue will always remain in people, one that is always ready to flare up again in the form of an impulse directed toward the destructive and self-destructive repetition of evil. This is the perspective from which Freud issues his verdict on the course of civilization.

But is it a unilinear movement, inevitably projected toward ruin, or is it structurally contradictory and, as such, governable? Starting from the discovery of the death instinct, I believe that the hypothesis of an ethical instance in psychoanalysis continues to gather force in Freud's writings, to wit, the function of ambivalence. As we know, ambivalence in Freud does not simply refer to the complexity of emotions and the fluctuation of attitudes. It involves a courageous awareness that is capable of sustaining itself in an opposition, one in which *affirmation and negation are simultaneous and inseparable.*[70] In other terms, ambivalence means accepting that there is, for the ego, no possibility to choose good and eliminate evil once and for all. The ego cannot maximize, so to speak, the love that creates bonds while expecting to eliminate the aggression that destroys. Leaving behind ambivalence would mean lapsing into a dualistic attitude—which, in effect, is nothing but a figuration put into place by a powerful defense mechanism, through which we delude ourselves into believing that we can separate hatred from love, enemy from friend, or good from evil. *Because, ultimately, we delude ourselves into thinking that we can separate life from death.*

From this point of view, the work of an "ethic of honesty" or of an "ethic of maturity" arises as a humble, patient, subjective recognition of ambivalence—a position that forces us to deconstruct, again and again, every purely divisive conception of opposites.[71] We save ourselves from evil, as it were, by attempting to govern oppositions while maintaining them—in the effort to not locate the *kakon* of being in the other. The ethic of honesty thus requires us to not suppress ambivalence in the name of some delusional certainty that clarifies all shadows of doubt. To phrase it differently, in terms more consistent with our line of reasoning, it requires us to *not resolve the structural duality* of the subject into a dualistic system that absolutizes now one and then the other of the two drives. The Freudian ethic, thus conceived, would therefore imply freedom: the freedom to remain firm in ambivalence, to stay in the uncomfortable space traversed by opposing vectors, the strength to not reassemble the division of the subject into a representation of the psyche that is unitary, and thus paranoid. Evil can be contained, then, if, in the first place, we abstain from negating the negative—if we learn to face the denial that forces the magmatic reality inside the subject into an explosive, ruinous outward movement, an eruption into the fury of destruction.

Not surprisingly, there is a powerful analogy between the "story" in Nietzsche of the birth of the bad conscience and *ressentiment*, and the Freudian genealogy of hatred. If we look at *Instincts and Their Vicissitudes* of 1915—a key piece in the so-called Freudian turning point—duality becomes a structural fact, the ego's very condition of possibility.[72] As a heuristic hypothesis to explain the instinctual process, Freud refers to an original condition, to a sort of time of indifference in which human beings lived as if nothing existed outside of themselves. The Freudian argument closely resembles a mythical narrative construction, in which the initial situation, the "original reality-ego" that coincides with the indistinctness of the One, is presented as a state of absolute stillness and union, which is put to an end by birth. The other-than-self—the alterity that breaks in with the coming into the world—is perceived in the form of external stimuli, both pleasant ones, responding to what the ego needs, but also unpleasant ones, corresponding to objects that cannot be assimilated: "For the pleasure-ego the external world is divided into a part that is pleasurable, which it has incorporated into itself, and a remainder that is extraneous to it."[73] It should be noted, however, that this self-sufficient existence of the mental apparatus is a pure abstraction, as Freud himself points out. There is no One that precedes the Two. The human condition of *Hilflosigkeit*, of structural "helplessness" due to the constitution of the human subject who comes into the world always already in a state of rootlessness, of primordial dispossession—what Lacan later called failure-to-be (*manque-à-être*)—immediately places the subject at a distance from itself, in self-deferral. The "original reality-ego" immediately encounters the other; it is always already linked to alterity since it never manages to avoid the unpleasant stimuli that run counter to the mental life's tendency toward inertia. Thus, inevitably, a share of excitement structurally disturbs the tendency of the apparatus toward inertia. This is the drive (*Trieb*), which is different from the instinct. It is an innate psychological representation, whose source is on the border between the somatic and the psychic. Now, the ego's will to ignore it inevitably fails, causing pervasive hostility as a reaction, as though the ego, helpless in the face of external stimuli that it cannot master, identifies everything other than itself with the threat. This exteriority, which is irreducible and cannot be metabolized by the mental apparatus, therefore places the subject in a structural, ontological inadequacy, the harbinger of a state of excitement that will incite the ego to seek an object onto which to discharge its energetic charge.

This is how hate, the aggressive drive that can go so far as to destroy the object, accompanies the appearance of subjectivity in the world and, for Freud, structures subjectivity from the outset. As much as culture may try to limit the scope of hatred, it will prove ineradicable. Hatred is aroused against anything that intrudes into the earliest stage of narcissism, but also later, repeatedly, when faced by any perception of something that is radically extraneous. Evil, in the Freudian sense of potentially destructive aggression—and in the Nietzschean sense of resentment against the senselessness of suffering—thus ends up coinciding with the condition of possibility for subjectivity itself. It is no longer the "wound" of God, of the Spirit, or of nature; rather, it is investigated, we might say, in terms of its physiological function. The evil that theology and philosophy tried to locate outside the subject, or in an anomaly that altered its reason, becomes a disturbing but permanent guest of subjective life. On these lines, one must admit that Nietzsche and Freud really do manage to go "beyond good and evil," if we understand the two terms in the metaphysical and moral meaning that philosophy had given to them up until that point. This "beyond" was made the object of harsh condemnation, or was instead absolutized in its disruptive and innovative force. However, as has been noted, it would seem to me that the deconstruction of the traditional dichotomy does not put an end in them to the play of contrasting valuations that accompanies almost any ethical instance. Thus the judgment unfailingly returns, and the condemnation will fall on the ways by which humans try to hide and negate the negative. We will come back to the role that criticism of the negation of the negation can have in shaping a new paradigm of the conceivability of evil. For now, we will take a quick look at the legacy that the death drive has passed on—a legacy that has brought the Dostoevsky paradigm to its most extreme limit.

Beyond Morality and Beyond Pleasure: In the Footsteps of Nietzsche and Freud

Starting from the "unprecedented step" taken in *Beyond the Pleasure Principle*, philosophy has tried to probe the depths and potential of the *Todestrieb* along many paths. In a memorable interpretation of the Freudian masterpiece, Gilles Deleuze explored the meaning of "The Death Instinct" and proposed three possible answers.[74] If the central issue for Freud has to do with something that pleasure cannot account for, he argues that it must refer to the foundation of this principle. In other words, it is a matter of naming the condition of possibility of the link between a power that moves the excitation and a power that tends to negate it—between a repetition that creates unity and a repetition that dissolves, erases, and kills. For the French philosopher, this tangle explains the difficulty contained in Freud's texts, in which, he says, we find a number of indications depending on the period and context. Some of the writings by the founder of psychoanalysis presuppose a single power that repeats—a single power, at times demonic, at times beneficial, expressed in both Eros and Thanatos. Others, however, suggest that there are two qualitatively distinct natures, one that unites and the other that destroys. Still others tend to reduce the qualitative difference to a difference in rhythm and amplitude. Monism, dualism, rhythm: these are the three ways, says Deleuze, in which Freud addresses this question. And, perhaps, it could be argued that these three approaches are the three ways in which the Freudian legacy has been continued.

Now, whether the death drive is intended in one way or another is not without consequences to our inquiry. Although reflection on the topic has made an effort to maintain the complexity of Freud's thought, what has often prevailed is a dualistic interpretation. And along with it, there is the risk of identifying the conditions of evil simply with the desire for destruction, even when this desire has not been judged at all from a conventional, moral perspective. Indeed, to dramatically simplify, one theoretical approach can be distinguished from another specifically by how it rehabilitates the subversive capacity of evil. Think, for example, of Georges Bataille,[75] but also, more recently, of post-Bataille sociology, from Jean Baudrillard to Jean-Pierre Dupuy[76]—an entire cultural milieu that, under the aegis of Nietzsche and Freud's discovery, has reaffirmed the nondialectical power of absolute negation, both in its cognitive function and in its liberating capacity. To gaze without protective screens at the "accursed share" becomes the authentic gesture of any thought that is truly free, a thought capable of putting us face to face with the profundity of the real and the depth of evil that everyday life—lost as it is behind the simulacrum and in the pursuit of the useful—constantly denies. This is one of the central assumptions of Bataille's work that deeply marked the later French philosophical scene from Lacan to Deleuze, to mention only the most representative thinkers.

In the essays contained in Bataille's *Literature and Evil*, making up a sort of philosophical manifesto on evil, we read: "I believe that Evil—an acute form of Evil—[. . .] has a sovereign value for us. But this concept does not exclude morality: on the contrary, it demands a 'hypermorality'."[77] In short, although evil comes out with a positive valuation instead of a negative one, its conception remains Dostoevskian, as it were. This is so because in Bataille's case, too, evil is not synonymous with selfishness, it is not limited to causing harm, and it does not aim at acquiring some advantage. Rather, it is evil for the sake of evil, which intentionally chooses what is opposed to the good—a good that, now, is exposed as nothing different in reality from the set of goods, from interest, and from the useful. Hence, if the good is the set of conventions, norms, and laws accepted by society, then in order to be free, human beings must take the side of evil. For Bataille this means, once again, only one thing: transgression, violation, overstepping limitations and constraints. Only evil results in the act of courage that rejects a servile attitude. Only evil, or "attraction to death," therefore, makes us free.[78]

What some literary texts are able to express, unlike a philosophy that is overly committed to reason, is the truth of a death drive that is implicated in all the intense and authentic experiences of life: from Eros to the sacred, from war to sacrifice, from revolution to *dépense*. Some literature, in short, is able to talk about the persistence of this desirable form of evil as a mad "desire for freedom." Because "today" only evil manages to make us perceive the infinite—the unity of subject and object that, deep down, has always been the driving obsession behind philosophy.[79] For Bataille, this will to the absolute finds no better expression than in the works of Sade, in his askesis toward nothingness. Indeed, the work of the *"divin marquis"*—in the wake of his rediscovery by the surrealists—became the ground par excellence by which to measure the transgressive and revolutionary force of desire.[80] The greatness of the Marquis imprisoned in the Bastille (who, although having personally experienced wild abandon and ecstasy, certainly did not equal his heroes of evil in real-life action) resides primarily in the lucidity with which he analyzed these impulses toward negation, which usually remain hidden.

Preceded by the writings of Pierre Klossowski, Maurice Blanchot, and Jean Paulhan,[81] Bataille's essay on Sade's philosophy goes well beyond providing historical background and a context for Sadean ideas, consecrating "one of the most rebellious and furious men ever to have talked of rebellion and fury" as a prophet of the revolutionary impulse that lies hidden in the death drive. Pleasure does not find resolution in all that is healthful. What triggers the erotic impulse is also what destroys a being, what takes it apart *qua* definite being because the erotic drive pushes it toward the infinite state of death. We thus also—and primarily—arrive at the truth by which the being makes itself knowable through disorder and excess. This truth of disorder and excess is what Sade's imagination depicts in an extreme figuration. Bataille's text suggests that with Sade there entered onto the French stage the precursor of Stavrogin's ghost, who, like him, was possessed by the "idea of an *impossible* liberty."[82] Although Sade was an atheist, Bataille tells us, he never ceased challenging God in his writings; and, we might add, like the black hero of *Demons*, he became the spirit of infinite experimentation, to the point of reveling in sacrilege itself. In his work, the author of *Philosophy in the Bedroom* did not limit himself, then, to proposing that the republican state be founded on crime, as Klossowski would have it. Sade's work aimed to give philosophical legitimacy to "destruction as an end in itself": destruction of objects, of victims, and of the destroyer. His message is a theology in reverse, which announces the *bad* news of the *"Supremely wicked Being."* In perpetual pursuit of the absolute, at war with the "Good that condemned him," Sade substituted Evil in the place of God, which is to say, "Nature in a [furious] state of perpetual motion."[83] From this perspective it becomes understandable, Bataille seems to conclude, why the distinguishing trait of Sade's work is the act of reversal. Sade has to turn everything upside down in "an exasperated inversion" that yearns for the impossible, for the sake of new truth.[84]

The idea, then, that evil might serve as the simple antithesis of everything that is conventionally accepted as good, that it consists in violation and transgression, and that it is aimed at "pure negation as a totalizing Idea" is what Deleuze also implicitly seems to assume in his interpretation of Sade, in close continuity with that of Bataille. Thanks also to Lacan's brilliant interpretation from a few years earlier,[85] Deleuze expresses in an exemplary manner the paradigmatic relationship that evil has with the law from this perspective. Kant was the first person to reverse the classic image of the law: first the Platonic image, and later, the Christian image that the law is derived from the good. The law is a secondary principle, says Deleuze, that is contingent on a higher principle, namely, the Good. Now, the *Critique of Practical Reason* inverts this relationship by making the law something of a paradox. The law, as that which is founded on itself, which remains absolutely indeterminate in its content and which excludes a higher principle, becomes the principle on which the Good is made to depend. If with Kant, then, the Good is that which revolves around the Law, as pure form, then Sade—along with Masoch, in Deleuze's view—is the one who launched the biggest challenge to the Law,[86] a challenge by means of transgression that makes it move by opposing the law to a higher principle—one that is no longer the Good, but Evil, "the Supreme-Being-in-Evil." This is because in Sade the absolute is approachable—albeit, like the Kantian noumenon, never attainable—only through the universalization of perversion, which is to say through the desexualization of the body, by taking it apart with coldness, proceeding, then, with an intense resexualization of Thanatos.

Lacan had pointed out that Sade's morality was a genuine "antimorality," which operated by subverting point by point the value of the law and the Ten Commandments. But what Sade showed by negating them is something even more important: the relationship between evil and law. In other words, he demonstrated how and to what extent the law serves to make us perceive the absolute of evil precisely in our attempt to protect ourselves from it, from wicked enjoyment that dwells in the heart of the subject. Wickedness, which is expressed in creating suffering in the Other and in exerting violence on the Other, is, in reality, the raging sense of malaise felt toward the irreducible alterity that inhabits the subject while dispossessing it. In psychoanalysis, the question of evil is of course indistinguishable from the problem of enjoyment. Evil assumes the form, therefore, of an instinctual need that tends toward an absolute condition, beyond the pleasure principle. It is what remains lit inside the ego like something incandescent and "physically unbearable."[87]

Interpreting Sade, and rereading Freud's last writings through an almost tragic lens, Lacan arrives at a sort of complete recodification of ethics. Thanks to Freudian psychoanalysis and its "scandalous discovery," we cannot but note the definitive decline of an ontological foundation based on the Good, Truth, and the Idea. Rather, we must recognize, argues Lacan, that it is rooted in Evil, which is to say, in that "instinctual reality" which is expressed as enjoyment of destruction. In the powerful pages that fill Book VII of Lacan's seminar, devoted to the ethics of psychoanalysis, the Freudian insight about the death instinct is folded into the philosophical problem of evil, including political evil. It is this possibility of absolute, wicked enjoyment that places the subject in conflict with Civilization, with its symbolic order, and with its demand to renounce or suppress the instincts. This is the famous *jouissance*, the absolute of enjoyment, that inseparable mixture of excitement and horror that eventually overwhelms every limit and every law set up by the symbolic universe. This instinct—and not a conflict between two ethics—is what drags Antigone beyond the law of the city, beyond the symbolic barriers of the Good, and draws her relentlessly toward death.[88] Hence, the term *Das Ding*, which is used to designate the silent, disturbing reality that the unconscious is unable to translate and symbolize. The subject who does not know how to put up ramparts against the vertigo of enjoyment, a mixture of horror and fascination at its own disintegration and that of others, is dragged into the vortex of the Thing. Lacan goes back to and reassesses the idea of the unconscious as a language because it does not suffice to explain "evil." It is inadequate to understand this instinctual excess, this pleasure in violence and destruction that, as we have seen, is not amenable to any linguistic mediation.

But if in our everyday lives we take our distance from the indecency of the Thing, thanks to the Good represented by goods, by the Law and by the Beautiful, in war, in violence, and in carnage, for example, *Das Ding* once again breaks in and can become the bond of aggregation even in a public, political space. Lacan's framing of the topic has ushered in a wide range of philosophical reflections, including from political philosophers, of which Slavoj Žižek is just one of the latest examples. The excesses of political evil in the twentieth century are thus read as an ecstatic experience of a collective "solidarity-in-crime," an exaltation produced by common participation in enormous transgression. The Real of *jouissance* is thus viewed as having dragged entire strata of Nazi and Stalinist populations into a perverse state of enjoyment.[89] Put into more or less "orthodox" terms, the *Todestrieb* is still—though not always consciously—a deep-rooted *a priori* used to decipher the relationship between evil and power. This would make it seem sufficient to explain political evil as a simple, large-scale multiplication of the death instinct that dwells in individuals, once again forcing the Dostoevsky paradigm to subsume the events of the last century under its wings.

In this regard, we should not underestimate the importance—too often left unmentioned these days—of the reception given to Erich Fromm's impressive study on the *Anatomy of Human Destructiveness*.[90] In his work, Fromm distinguishes between benign and malignant aggression, tracing out a relationship between the death instinct and evil that is both linear and overly schematic. This is partly because the difficulty in Freud's attempt to hold together the life instinct and the death instinct in the same subject here gives way to a kind of dualistic elementary functioning. According to this schema, when the life instinct is able to flow in an individual, the death drive is extinguished, and vice versa. On the one hand, not just as extreme stereotypes, we have people with healthy, positive characters who like to see life aggregating in all its forms; on the other, we have psychologically impaired individuals, or "cripples," who are trapped in their destructive spirals with no way out. Evil thus takes the form of a perversion of the life instinct, a radical perversion not defined as such in terms of some sexual habit, but on the basis of a desire to inflict humiliation and mortification. Hence, sadism and necrophilia are stripped of their more usual meanings and become the characteristics of a subjectivity that demonstrates its propensity for evil. The sadist seeks to manipulate the life of others but cannot eliminate it; the necrophilic wants to destroy it. Necrophilia—the last step of "malignant aggression"—is an uncontrollable attraction to the whirlwind through which something alive is transformed into something dead. It is a passion for disintegration that seeks to tear apart every living structure. These are the human types personified by dictators of totalitarian regimes, by those who more than any others have sought to exercise limitless control over other living creatures: for when someone is able to have complete control over another human being, if he succeeds in transforming the other person into his property, he can delude himself into believing that he has soared to the heights of a God, one that holds the power of life and death.

Fromm's schema is rigid, but it does have the merit of being explicit, and above all paradigmatic. Evil, even in its collective dimension, is explained once more by the delusion of omnipotence, by the will to transcend the limits of existence that becomes a quest for dematerialized power, and an end in itself. In a beautiful essay entitled "Why Evil?"[91] André Green, who has studied the death instinct in psychoanalysis more than any other writer, continuously creating connections with philosophy in the process, offers us a kind of summary of the various ways of combining the death instinct with the problem of evil. Denial, extroversion, and paranoia are not just clinical structures but rather elements that we find at the core of social phenomena. However, they are still "relatively sensible" versions of the destructiveness that issues from the death instinct. This can indeed bind to the erotic libido and give rise to pleasure through cruelty. But extreme wickedness, the kind that represents a genuine "universal curse," emerges from the destructive impulses that have undone all libidinal ties and become "pure un-relationship." Absolute wickedness is not *jouissance*; it is not exercised in the name of enjoyment, no matter how abysmal. It performs instead in indifference and insensitivity on the part of a psyche that has ceased all imaginative activity, so that its only recourse is to unleash itself in action. To say that "evil has no explanation," states Green in a subtle polemic with Lacan—commenting on the epigraph that Claude Lanzmann chose for his film *Shoah*—means, in a sense, to answer the question "Why evil?" Evil's reason for being is in the first place to empty what exists of any meaning, by declaring that nothing has a purpose and everything depends solely on the power that can be exerted on the objects of one's appetite.

The death instinct, intertwined with the life instinct and therefore capable of being eroticized or disconnected from any investment, and therefore cold and indifferent, is the new name for the connection between evil and power. It sets up a horizon in which destruction, cruelty, and wickedness are the expression of a power that seeks to view itself as infinite and which, deprived of any purpose or meaning, pursues nothing but the annihilation of all that is. It indicates an extreme limit to thought beyond which there is no more need to investigate in order to find an explanation for evil. *Todestrieb* seems to be a secularized and "scientific" name for what the protagonists of Dostoevsky revealed to us long ago, namely, that the desire for nothingness and destruction is a part of the human being. Only then, it seems, could the assumption of Kantian radical evil, its refusal to contemplate the "active" role of a total negation, be reversed. Thus, as a concept that expresses the power of evil as absolute and unconditional, *the death instinct became the new demon of the twentieth century.*[92]

Nihilism and *Todestrieb*, conceived by Dostoevsky, Nietzsche, and Freud in different but complementary fashions, bequeathed a good part of the twentieth century with a theoretical key for interpreting its history and for allowing the wave of philosophies of death to conceptually process the traumatic experiences of their contemporary world, from world wars to genocides. The reason the destruction was unleashed so dramatically is certainly because new historical phenomena had emerged: the irruption of the masses onto the political scene, and the paroxysmal advancement of technological power. These objective conditions made power infinitely more destructive. But what gave these explanations such a strong impact, allowing them to be transformed into a genuine thought on evil, was the new demon: the death instinct. With it, evil was finally conceivable starting from the ego, from an individual whose shadowy part was no longer amputated. The scene was now occupied by the dark side of each and every person—by a structurally ineradicable evil. The twentieth century was, in actuality, the century in which Nothingness and the "accursed share" celebrated their hermeneutic victory. Because of these ideas, the anti-idealistic power of the century, at least throughout the first half, showed its true desire to go beyond good and evil.[93] Everything in the nineteenth century that had been denied and idealistically condemned now took its revenge: death, violence, cruelty, body, passions, unconscious, instincts, drives. There is definitely an aggressive side to twentieth-century culture, a culture that obsessively pursues subversion and that, for this reason, winds up absolutizing the negative, and giving it, as we have seen, a multiplicity of names. The risk involved in this revolution—of a nothing that fights against being, of an Id that declares war on the reasonableness of the ego, of an absolute of death that attacks the value of life—is that it can easily end up in a simple reversal of the previous value system, remaining trapped in its own dualistic logic.

3

Ontological Evil and the Transcendence of Evil

Malice as a Trait of Being: Heidegger

It is said that Martin Heidegger always avoided talking about evil. But is this true? Did the great thinker of the forgottenness of being—the person who restored the ontological dignity of the Nothing to thought—really not address the ethical-philosophical question that relates to it par excellence? Perhaps the truth is that this criticism, so often directed at the master of Messkirch, even by those who use his thought as a springboard for their own, in reality misinterprets his silence on Auschwitz as a failure to reflect on evil. Certainly, the number of essays on the question of evil in the ocean of Heidegger studies is minuscule.[1] But what if the question *unde malum?* was in fact the guiding star that oriented the philosopher's critical diagnosis of his contemporary world from the mid-1930s on?

It is tempting to read much of his work after the so-called *Kehre* from this perspective, as if the "turn" marked a transition from a subjectivist perspective of guilt to an ontological perspective of evil as an element of being. Starting in 1935, in fact, the philosopher began to use the term *Böse*, with the specific aim of dismantling the Leibnizian meaning of *Übel* (an evil that is physical and metaphysical at the same time) because in his eyes it signified a conception of being as presence. Later, as if to signal the extent of his critique against subjectivism, he passed from the noun *Böse*—whose Kantian assonance made it too closely tied to subjective intentionality—to the nominalized adjective *das Bösartige*. From the *Introduction to Metaphysics*,[2] through the texts on Hölderlin in the early 1940s and the famous "Letter on Humanism,"[3] until the discussion on Georg Trakl's poetry of 1953,[4] Heidegger traced out the perimeter of a full-fledged inquiry into evil. It is an inquiry that seems to accompany the fundamental step taken in *Contributions to Philosophy* toward overcoming the false separation between ontology and ethics—that of acknowledging the indissoluble link between *Ereignis* and the Nothing[5]—and with it, of an unserviceable distinction between moral evil and metaphysical evil.[6] Heidegger's thought would lead, in short, to a kind of *malum ontologicum*, neither moral nor metaphysical in character, that corresponded to the groundbreaking appearance of *Ereignis*, the specific *interaction* between Being and the being of *Da-sein*, their way of belonging to each other that marks a given horizon. It can therefore be said that Heidegger opens up the possibility of a thought on evil as event, which, as a play of revealings and concealments, "decides" the particular character of an epoch—ours in this case—as the age of the devastation of the entity in its totality.

There is a text—a crucial one, in my opinion—that can be used as evidence of my claims. I am referring to one of the three dialogs collected in *Country Path Conversations* entitled "Evening Conversation: In a Prisoner of War Camp in Russia, between a Younger and an Older Man," which is entirely devoted to the question of evil. During the spring of 1945, in the month of May, to be precise, Martin Heidegger wrote a few pages that he put in the form of a dialog, some passages of which are dazzling in their conciseness.[7] The biographical reference is certainly significant: his two sons, Jörg and Hermann, were at that moment prisoners in the hands of the Soviets. The philosopher himself left Freiburg after the bombings of November 1944 to take refuge in Messkirch, his hometown, where he found the strength to "join in thought" with the "boys" through the writing of this short text.[8] But beyond the biographical reference, to choose Russia as the backdrop for the dialog undoubtedly has a clear symbolic value. It is the land of "spirituality par excellence." Not only that, it is the land of a spirituality that more than any other would best grasp and cherish—as he declared at a certain point[9]—the profundity of his philosophy. Above all, Russia is the land of Dostoevsky. Moreover, based on Hans-Georg Gadamer's account, we know that during the years of teaching at Freiburg, Heidegger read and reread the work of the Russian writer in the famous edition by Möller van den Bruck and Merezhkovsky.[10] Heidegger was also an avid reader of Berdyaev.[11] To see the link that the author of *Demons* forged between nihilism and evil as the breeding ground for the idea of Heidegger's dialog is thus not far-fetched. The dialog can well be read, perhaps, as a preliminary coming to terms with himself—a kind of recapitulation at the end of the war in which he measures the impact of history on his thought. The two interlocutors are talking in the evening about Germany and Europe, which have been devastated by the Second World War. The paraphrases and allusions are irritating, because in this piece, as in others, they once again serve to avoid any mention of direct responsibility on the part of the Germans, a matter that Heidegger does not think merits a detailed exposition, as we shall see clearly in these pages. But much more than in other places, he does explicitly express his view of Europe's historical time during those years, referring to it, without hiding behind word games, as the very essence of evil. All around, he writes, lies "devastation" (*Verwüstung*), a devastation that is the "wound" (*Wunde*) of the times. However, he continues, only a superficial thinker can declare that the war was the sole cause of it, because the war was nothing more than the occasion on which the reality of the devastation *became event*. It is a destruction that was already at work long before the events of the war put it in plain view, before it exploded and, in the eyes of the vast majority, came to correspond with evil itself, or rather with "malice."[12] It is in this context that Heidegger gave up the use of *der Böse* to use instead *die Bösartigkeit*, especially in the neutral case of the nominalized adjective *das Bösartige*.

We might recall that in *Being and Time* he had already launched a critique against the metaphysics of the *privatio boni*.[13] Evil understood as privation, as the simple lack of a good that "should be," a *bonum debitum*, in his opinion betrayed its provenance from an ontology of being as simple presence. In a letter written in 1929 to Elisabeth Blochmann,[14] the theme was taken up again to focus on the connection between evil and nothingness. If the possibility of an authentic existence is located in the "primeval power of night" (to be distinguished from "Weltnacht," which marks the complete disappearance of the gods), then the foundation of evil is to be found in a kind of night that seeks to become day; in a situation, in other words, that negates the meaning of "Night," here synonymous with a "non-everyday" possibility of experiencing being. This is the same year that "What Is Metaphysics?" was published,[15] the work in which we see a transition from an adverbial use of "nothing"—the outcome of that initial gesture by Parmenides, who sought to nullify the nothing—to nothing as a noun. The nothing that reveals the meaning of being is differentiated from the nothing of this or that being, from "the negation of beings." It is a matter of gaining access to a more "fundamental experience" than what we get through the logical predicate, which for Heidegger—in this case in a polemic with the beginning of Hegel's *Science of Logic*—is only a pale reflection of the immense power of the nothing. "Is the nothing given only because the 'not'; i.e., negation, is given? Or is it the other way around? Are negation and the 'not' given only because the nothing is given?"[16] The nothing in question is not only the negative, that which removes and differentiates, but "the nothing itself [that] nihilates." Anticipating the discourse that will lead him to talk about "a *higher nothingness*" in the *Contributions to Philosophy*,[17] in the 1929 text a positive notion of the nothing takes shape (more aptly described as "active") that, in carrying out its dis-identifying function with respect to a rigid conception of being, takes on a revelatory function for humans with regard to the meaning of being: "Without the original revelation of the nothing, no selfhood and no freedom."[18] Selfhood (*Selbstsein*) and freedom (*Freiheit*) imply that human beings must assume responsibility for their world. But freedom and responsibility become real possibilities only when the totality of entities shows itself to be "not already otherwise decided"—in other words, when the totality of entities is not given because it is grounded on being, but as ungrounded or grounded on the nothing.

The mutual belonging of nothing, freedom, and the meaning of being, developed in 1929, still reflected the possibility of evil as *Böse* in its relationship with *Da-sein*, which he had mentioned in the letter to Blochmann. If it is the responsibility of human beings—as a consequence of our freedom—to safeguard the meaning of being by opening ourselves to the evidence of the nothing, evil would be the possibility that is opened up to us to negate such a responsibility. Hence, no matter how remote *der Böse* is from Kantian "radical evil," it is still ascribable to a subjective dimension, as it were. In other words, it still refers to an ethic, in the sense of a specific ethos assumed by a particular being-there. But even though in the *Introduction to Metaphysics* of 1935 Heidegger still seems to speak a language centered on the subject, the question of evil begins to be posed in terms of something that dominates *Da-sein*.[19] It is presented as a destructive, essential trait in opposition to the spirit, which acts as a disempowerment of the spirit (*Entmachung des Geistes*). It has the capacity, in other words, to disintegrate the spiritual forces of the members of humanity who are still able to formulate the original question.[20]

However, it was only by wrestling with Schelling's work that Heidegger began to hone his conception of evil into a genuine ontological question, for which his use of the term *das Bösartigkeit* became a necessity. His reading of Schelling's treatise of 1809 emphasizes the role that evil, not only in a moral sense, occupies in "derailing" the system of idealism: "The question of the possibility and reality of evil brings about a transformation of the question of Being."[21] Heidegger argues that idealism intended freedom as the determination of the "pure I," as self-determination for the law, as self-legislation in good will, whereas Schelling understood it as the capacity for good *and* evil, for which the possibility of evil is essential. We know what Schelling's solution was: freedom as the capacity for evil must have an origin independent from God, but if the one and only origin of the entity is and should be God, then the foundation of evil, independent of God, can lie only in God himself. In order not to fall back into the dualism that would lead to the despair of reason between two opposing powers of equal intensity, Schelling followed the path of conceiving God "more primordially"[22] so that it would be possible to consider something in God that "is" not God himself. Schelling's solution is thus a metaphysics of evil—Heidegger acknowledges—that grounds the question of Being and makes it the foundation for a system of freedom. In short, a metaphysics (of evil) acts as the foundation for a general metaphysics. "We understand the main treatise," writes Heidegger, "as a metaphysics of evil with a metaphysical intention. The supplement means the question of the nature and reality of evil lays the ground for the question of Being in general." If evil is in fact not a nothing, it must be an entity. The relationship between ground and existence is proper to an entity. And the existence of the Supreme Being, God, is conceived as a going outside of itself. This going outside of itself and revealing of self are in God himself, whose ground is, true, something distinct from God, but not "outside" of God. Therefore the ground of evil is nothing less than the ground of being-human, but it lies at the heart of God. Without following all the twists and turns Heidegger takes in his discussion of Schelling's work, what interests me at this point is to bring out a specific line of this interpretation: the one emphasizing that, because of this God who emerges from himself, becomes, reveals himself, and creates, human beings bear within themselves the craving or longing (*Sehnsucht*) to go outside themselves, to separate themselves from the ground, and at the same time to concentrate omnipotence in themselves, to see themselves as equal to God. Herein lies the "faculty of evil": in the possibility that, motivated by the desire to be the ground itself, the individual will might separate itself from the ground.[23] The possibility of this split is inherent in the essence of man, but "this separability of the two principles" is precisely the condition for the possibility of evil—that way of "being free in the sense of being a self in terms of its own essential law."[24]

Expressed differently, what is this "malice of evil" (and here we begin to encounter the terms that will appear repeatedly in the text of 1945) that turns out to be an essential possibility within the human being? It consists in a position of the will: the individual will that, although elevating itself, and thus presenting itself as a spiritual will, takes the place of the universal will by wanting to become itself the ground of the whole. What thus takes place in this will to unification of ground and existence is a reversal of the way ground and existence are joined in unity in the divine: "In this *reversal of the wills* the becoming of a *reversed god* (*Umgekehrte Gott*), of the *counter-spirit*, takes place, and thus the *upheaval* against the primal being, the *revolt* of the adversary element against the essence of Being, the *reversal* of the jointure of Being into the *disjointure* in which the ground elevates itself to existence and puts itself in the place of existence."[25] Moreover: "Thus the ground of evil lies in the primal will of the first ground which has become revealed. Evil has its ground in the ground independent of God and is nothing other than this ground, this ground as the selflike primal will which has emerged to the separate selfhood of created spirit and stepped into the place of the universal will."[26]

There is no need to pass judgment on how Heidegger sees an oscillation in the 1809 treatise between a conception of the "heretical" nothing and another nothing that is instead recaptured by the metaphysics of presence. I would rather bring attention to the conceptual and terminological framework of the concluding thesis of the work on Schelling that insists on the definition of evil as "*der Aufruhrs Verkehrung der Grundes des Willens in die Umkehrung des Gottes*" (the revolt of the reversal of the ground of the will in the reversal of God). It is the definition of perversion, of that reversal rooted in the will to the Absolute, in the will to security, which in "self-craving ground" seeks self-grounding as compensation for the indeterminacy of existence. Interestingly enough, although in Heidegger's view Schelling fails to avoid materializing the nothing, the terms used in the *Treatise*—opposition and rebellion, perversion and reversal—become the signs of a negative that is not only defective but also a nothing that acts and establishes its domination. This capacity for negation, as the possibility of reversal of the unity, is possible only in free beings. Indeed, the animal is not capable of this reversal of principles. It is never "evil," because it cannot escape its position in nature. The only being that can reverse the constituent parts of its essence is the human; the dubious privilege of being able to fall below the animal is reserved exclusively to the human. Evil is therefore the spiritual reality that transposes all the forces in such a way as to turn them against nature and against creatures, thereby arriving at the "ruin of beings."

For Heidegger, Schelling's greatness thus lies in having liberated thought from the restricted Christian concept of sin as well as from the limits of Kant's radical evil, so as to bring it to the awareness of an ontological understanding of evil. There is no doubt that many of Schelling's notions pass into Heidegger's conception. They all revolve around the theme of *Umkehrung der Seynsfüge in Ungefüge* (the *reversal* of the jointure of Being into the *disjointure*): this is the critical step, as I said earlier, that frees evil from being considered solely in the moral domain so as to connect it with the essence and truth of Being. In the crucial and most tumultuous years of his life, from 1936 to 1946, while his thought was haunted by the demon of Nietzsche, Heidegger sought allies in Schelling and in Schelling's idea of evil in his battle against Hegel and the Hegelian concept of becoming. As stated at the beginning of the *Science of Logic*, the latter is a vanishing of being and nothing into each other that, as Heidegger sees it, neutralizes a truly radical thought of the negative. We know that Nietzsche would provide him with this perspective from the point of view of an absolute finitude, but it was Schelling's idea of evil—mediated, I believe, by reading and rereading Dostoevsky and Berdyaev—that was absolutely central for bringing the phenomenon of nihilism and its philosophical importance as an event into focus.

From 1936 to 1938 Heidegger feverishly devoted himself to the composition of the *Contributions to Philosophy* (also known as the *Beiträge*). In this work, in a progressive, and we might say "grandiose" fashion, between ambiguous and contradictory passages, between strategies and argumentative counterstrategies, nihilism became the horizon in which a thought on Being could be founded as that which is destined to man (*Ereignis* as appropriation) and at the same time as that which expropriates him (*Ent-eignis*).[27] The *Contributions to Philosophy* perhaps more than any other of his writings hammers on the issue of what has been "covered over" in the tradition and how we should avoid resorting to a univocal conception of being. In the age of fully realized nihilism, the only thought remaining is one that opens to the truth of being starting from that terrible, desolate place of the "expropriation of being," from a "planetary self-destruction that has become an imminent possibility." Located in the event of appropriation-expropriation, the self will be led to the possibility of a "beyond the metaphysics of the proper and power." As noted by Reiner Schürmann, "The self, Heidegger writes, 'belongs' to the event, which in turn 'makes use of' it. Each remains unthinkable without the other."[28] What is at stake, more than ever, is a questioning of the concept of nonbeing that for two thousand years, according to Heidegger, was dependent on an idea of change as a transition from the possible to the actual, and in which the actual—according to the kinetic theory of Aristotle—is understood as what can be made. It was this Aristotelian *dynamis* that governed the proper use of the nothing in philosophy, thereby precluding any knowledge of a nothing that is "greater than any Yes."

The starting point for Heidegger's project is thus to rehabilitate the "No" as the other of being *inside* being, *while at the same time returning to the "Yes" its belonging to the "No"*—a "No" that is therefore "larger than the Yes." Whether or not Heidegger's thought on evil belongs to the Dostoevsky paradigm entirely depends on the significance we give to these statements. The constitutive correspondence of being to nothingness does not necessarily imply that Heidegger's "Nothing" must be interpreted as the principle or the primordial value on which everything is grounded.[29] Even in Heidegger's case, therefore, we sense an ambivalence, a tension in his writings, that is often overlooked or passed over in favor of a "simple" interpretation. True, there is no dearth of elements supporting an easy equation between nihilism, evil, and will to power.

In the conversation between the two prisoners, the thought of the connection between event, nothing, and self, along with the battery of terms and concepts used to examine evil in Schelling's work, reappear more clearly and explicitly. For this reason, the short text is ideal for our purposes. The critique of the concept of *malum metaphysicum*—of evil understood as a lack with respect to the perfection of the supreme entity—reemerges in force, along with the questioning of a "purely moral" vision. The Younger Man, as he calls one of the two interlocutors, does indeed confirm the Older Man's conviction that "by evil, of course, we do not mean what is morally bad, and not what is reprehensible, but rather malice (*Bösartige*)."[30] Neither simply moral nor traditionally metaphysical, evil is clearly presented here as an essential trait (*Grundzug*) of being itself. This is the reason behind Heidegger's preference for the term *das Bösartige*, which recalls the broader, "active" meaning of evil, thus shedding the static character that it would have, according to the philosopher, if it was solely the indicator of an ethical nonvalue. Malice is the event of evil, like the irruption of a disease whose symptoms have long remained latent. In effect, the philosophical tradition must be examined back to its beginnings, as if conducting a sort of clinical history. Through a deciphering of the symptoms one must be able to reconstruct the pathogenesis of the evil that has finally become visible in the wound of destruction. This is the only way a dressing can be found for it. After all, this was Heidegger's assumption starting from the *Contributions to Philosophy*, explicitly formulated here in terms of the question of evil. But if in the *Contributions* the devastation—"the defeat"—still oscillated between being just one symptom and the symptom that offers the possibility of healing, in this text, ten years later, the phenomenon unhesitatingly indicates both the diagnosis and the treatment. To be able to think of malice from a nonmoral point of view simply requires looking into what the word means: malice is insurgency or that which instigates (*das Aufrührerische*). It rests in "furiousness" (*das Grimmige*), but often while concealing its rage (*Ingrimm*), a rage that nonetheless has never ceased to threaten us. At the end of this play on words, Heidegger comes to the real definition of the essence of evil and malice: it is "the rage of insurgency," that rage which "never completely explodes and which, even when it erupts, continues to hide its true face, thus giving the impression of not existing."[31]

We may recall that under the influence of Jacob Böhme and Franz Baader, in his *Treatise* on freedom Schelling used the term *Grimm*, which referred to lack of moderation, or intemperance. In Heidegger, too—as we have already observed on several occasions with regard to his essay on Schelling—the word is intended to express the sense of the malice of evil erupting through unrestrainedness.[32] The rage of evil, which triggers insurgency and disorder, now brings us to an unstoppable devastation. And evil is that which, ontologically, directs this rage, unleashing its fury against all that is given, just as it is given. The problem clearly lies in the relationship between evil and will. This issue is introduced by the Older Man: "If [. . .] evil rests in malice [. . .] then I could almost think that malice is something pertaining to the will." Encouraged, the young man ventures: "Perhaps in general the will itself is what is evil."[33] Not the malicious will of individuals, but will in its ontological dimension: "*Das Unwesen des Seyns—das Böse—das Wille.*"[34] Devastation, then, must be thought "still more rigorously," not as resulting from malicious acts run through by "a moral badness" but as the very manifestation of the possibility of evil that has become actual. This is why "a moral indignation, even if it makes the world's general public into its mouthpiece, is not capable of doing anything against the devastation." Not only because moral superiority is not in a position to grasp or abolish or even mitigate the evil of the devastation, but because, as Nietzsche showed, the will to power, which is manifested in the devastation, works precisely through the elevation of moral values. "For it could be the case," suggests the Younger Man, "that even morality [*die Moral*], for its part, together with all the peculiar attempts to envision a world-order and make certain of a world-security for the national peoples [*Völkern*] by means of morality, are only a monstrous offspring of evil; just as the much-appealed-to 'world's general public', in its essence and product of the process that we are calling the devastation."[35]

The devastation, then—as Heidegger never tires of repeating—is not the result of the world wars, but rather the latter are a consequence of the devastation that has been destroying the earth for centuries. For this reason, condemning the individuals or "gangs" that ignite the fires of "such consequential phenomena of the devastation" is completely useless. They have a marginal role, and they are no more than "angry functionaries of their own mediocrity."[36] Desert (*Wüste*), devastation (*Verwüstung*), desolation or wasteland (*Öde*): every word that the prisoners exchange refers to a different figuration of evil, or malice, as an immense space abandoned by life—in which "life," the Younger Man tells us, must be understood as "being." The feigned innocence of the Older Man, who asks why then entities—"form[s] of 'life'"—persist, provides the pretext to explain the meaning of the paradoxical statements. The world, human beings, and the earth may indeed continue to exist, but they have nevertheless entered into the devastation, because the being of an age of devastation consists in its being abandoned by being (*Seinsverlassenheit*). And more than any others in the past, modern man is so far inside the devastation that he cannot even conceive of the idea that the true obstacle to life might arise under the imposition of "a secured and improving life": "The malice of this devastation reaches its extreme when it settles into the appearance of a secure state of the world, in order to hold out to the human a satisfactory standard of living as the highest goal of existence [*Daseins*] and to guarantee its realization."[37] But the assessment of historical ages by humans, who judge according to the criterion of what is desirable or undesirable for them, is in turn the result of the abandonment of humans by being. And even if the human, "devastated in his essence" (abandoned by being), continues to exist, in all his doing and having "he rolls into nothing."[38]

This is the reality of nihilism that Nietzsche prepared us for; however, in doing so he imprisoned his own thought in the nihilistic cage. *The "will to power" failed to find a way out of the vicious circle of nothingness.* The true agent of the devastation process was therefore the nothing. The function of malice for Heidegger is thus twofold. On the one hand, it makes visible, by bringing to the surface, what would otherwise remain imperceptible when evil is understood simplistically as the absence of good, as a nongood. In this respect, it offers humans the possibility of "healing," and "good." However, malice, as constitutive of being, is still bad because it devastates, empties of meaning, and threatens humans through their destructive action. This is also the case because malice appears in the form of the right thing to be done, as a duty to be performed, and this disguised reversal has the effect of completely disorienting people. But if evil belongs to being, and it is not a simple matter of subjective badness; if malice itself constitutes a fundamental trait of being, then all the protests and condemnations on the part of individuals are completely useless. For example, the angry functionaries who manage the epiphenomena of the devastation—beginning with those "youth" who overnight were proclaimed to be "men," an event that "ended merely with the inexperience of adolescents challenging the knowledge of elders" (referring to the SS perhaps?)—can do little in the face of a devastation to which we are ontologically destined. Constructing a moral order of the world is even more useless. Human measures, in short, can do nothing because the abandonment of beings by being is a basic trait of being itself, "outside of human guilt and atonement." As one of the two companions declares: to believe that the essential ground of being is malicious is an "awful demand" on human thinking.[39]

These ideas would have sounded scandalously provocative to many of Heidegger's students who, forced to leave Germany, had read his philosophy of *Ereignis* as a theoretical ploy to disguise the reality of evil, which they had experienced firsthand, behind the alibi of an anonymous fault of the devastation, always already inscribed in the fate of being. Of course they would have been even more outraged if they had read this dialog, and in particular its conclusions, in which the German philosopher launches into a sort of "who are we to judge." The only attitude toward what he calls the "consequential phenomena of the devastation"—war, extermination, destruction—that apparently emerges is powerlessness.[40] Heidegger's failure to perceive the traps and weakness of his "fatalistic" reading, which in the end seems to get lost in the logic of the same theodicies that he sought to oppose, is very puzzling. However, Heidegger would always remain firm in his conviction, one that was not purely theoretical, and which he explicitly states in all its premises, showing all his cards without too many sleights of hand, in these passages devoted expressly to the question of evil more than any other place in his work. If evil and being did not mutually imply one another, if the devastation, that is, had not always already been at work in being—he seems to conclude—the destruction that struck Europe with a deadly wound in the spring of 1945 would not have come to pass: "Because the devastation, insofar as it comes forth from being, is a world-event that beleaguers that earth, *humans may never presume to pass judgment on it.* For not only is the purview of everyday opining among individuals and groups always too narrow, but also because the person who passes judgment too easily falls prey here to a quarreling and an annoyance that gnaw at him; or he becomes a slave to self-righteousness who no longer sees out beyond the facade that he has hurriedly built around himself."[41] Authentic evil, the backdrop against which the omnipotence and impotence of the subject is measured, resides in the gradual *Seinsvergessenheit* that from modernity onward has become an increasingly evident ontological trait. In short, it lies in a forgottenness of being and of the mutual belonging of *Sein* and *Da-sein* that has led to the anthropocentric folly, almost as if "all Being were about Man," as if everything had been created purely for human beings. This is what lies behind the massive uprooting of humanity from its original position. Not only is the situation of things implicated in the oblivion of the truth of being—in the forgottenness of being as the occurrence of the opening, of initiality—so is the ontological status of the living. The living are viewed as isolated, unrelated, devoid of context, and therefore are perceived and treated in view of their *substitutability*.

With Heidegger, or rather thanks to the "simple" way of reading Heidegger—justified by the rest of the conversation between the two prisoners, moreover—the Dostoevsky paradigm undergoes an ontological development, so to speak. For one thing, a collective dimension now pertains to evil that is active and relational, differentiating it from individual evil. Second, it now has to do with the nihilism of a will to power that in the end proves to be a will to nothingness and the death drive, just as Nietzsche and Freud had taught us in their own ways. Despite the many ambiguities—most notably, the oscillation between a vision marked by fatalism and necessity and another by transience and contingency—the Heideggerian critique of moral, "privative" conceptions brought into focus the character of evil as "event." In other words, the malice of the devastation takes long-term dynamics to the extreme, and yet they define an "age" and provide the lineaments of a specific system of evil, illuminating its very essence. From the perspective of the truth of being and *Ereignis*, evil must be seen as *Unfug* (unfittingness, disarray), as *Unwesen* (confusion, disorder, loss of essentiality), but at the same time as *Grundzug* (basic trait). Compared to this ontological correlation, Heidegger believes, other explanations are not false, but they do prove to be inadequate. The phenomena that are the signs of malice to him—the devastation, megalomania, giganticism (*Riesenhaftigkeit*), and machinations (*Machenschaft*)—angrily threaten the earth and human beings. However, in so doing they reveal themselves as the constitutive, ontological traits of the age. There is perhaps no need to remember how deeply this interpretative structure marked twentieth-century theoretical investigations into evil.

However, from this malice, from the evil of fully realized devastation, from the desert, there also arises that which "saves." This is the beneficial, and also highly problematic, effect in the economy of Heidegger's discourse that the fellow prisoners talk about.[42] In place of the "powerless judgment" born from useless moral protest, from cowardly indignation, we must instead turn to waiting—a waiting that, devoid of purpose and without objectives, is capable of becoming pure opening to "letting come": "And, as letting come of the coming, waits in the sense of safeguarding."[43] We are familiar with the association in Heidegger between waiting, safeguarding, commemorating, and thinking: it is a connection that leads thought to the original meaning of the *logos*, understood as gathering, which can point to something beyond the metaphysical and modern reduction of thought and *ratio*. In the process, it can turn our gaze toward a human being that is "more primordial," and at the same time still "to come," with respect to subjectivity. The reason Greek pre-philosophical reflection called humans "the mortals"—defining their essence in distinction to the gods—is because it placed them in relationship with the originally all-unifying One. In reference to this One, the original conception of the divine, the mortal being, and the being who thinks belong together.

It is interesting to follow these passages of Heidegger that reflect and anticipate well-known positions repeated in his other writings, because in this context the definition of the human as the one who can die, as the only animal who knows and therefore can go toward or *have* death, is put into the plural in view of a possible overcoming of subjectivity—on this occasion a collective one—on the part of the German people. Most of the dialog between the two prisoners can be seen as counterpoint to his Rector's Address of 1934 and to the *Introduction to Metaphysics*, a counterpoint that had in actuality already started with the *Contributions to Philosophy*. In the part of this text numbered as chapter 6, entitled "The Ones to Come,"[44] Heidegger turns to the role assigned to Germany. For some critics,[45] in the *Contributions to Philosophy* the German philosopher left a legacy of his most vehement, albeit ambiguous, confrontation with National Socialism, defined in this text as a "system of the Same," along with the violent possibilities it subsumes. In short, once his thought on Being was freed from the primacy of subjectivity, Heidegger began to rethink the *Volk*. The transition that led the German philosopher to deny the prospect of a people—of a grouping, understood as self-conscious subjectivity—thus takes place in the *Contributions to Philosophy*. It is true that he still refers to a "Völkisches Prinzip"[46] or a nationalist principle that can provide a different criterion for the human being; but it had become quite different from the principle of the people that Germany had so tragically experimented with. Now, to speak authentically about a people, we must wait for the "ones to come," other "founders to come." In short, the identity of the collective principle has been suspended, as has the coming of "the Last God" and the "popular upheaval." It is true that there is still a pull toward a new kind of human being; however, the time and place that would project the force of this trajectory toward historical fulfillment are no longer included.

In the conversation between the prisoners, the ambivalent reference to "future man" in the *Contributions* is partially clarified. "Future man" cannot be abstracted from the human who, dragged along by the darkness of the devastation, constrained by the event of evil, knows how to continue waiting. If "the human is, as that being which can die, the being that waits," if, in short, thanks to its relation with its own death, the human is the being whose essence is definable as "an awaiting," then the devastation, the eruption of evil, has an eminent, active role in the opening up of this possibility.[47] Only through the devastation, which opens our eyes to the truth of evil, can we become "those who await," those who are also awaiting the definition of their essence. One certainly gets the impression that we are witnessing an important moment for Heidegger, in which he comes to terms with himself, when the previous Heidegger confronts the new Heidegger after the turn, and especially after his so-called error, attested to unequivocally by the Rector's Address. There is no more call to the self-affirmation of the German essence. The German *Volk* must abandon its plans to establish a collective self. Faced with the malice that revealed the "essence of evil," the Germans must also strive to become "those who are themselves only by abandoning themselves," those who wait toward the coming, but only by continuing to wait. If we allow ourselves while waiting to resound like "a string instrument of the most ancient provenance"—the two prisoners comfort each other— we will stop setting ourselves up over against things so as to arrange them and manipulate them, making them into objects *for* subjects.[48] Indeed, subjects can be viewed as those who are incapable of continuing to wait, those who become distressed by the uneasiness that, in destroying their tranquility, transforms beings into objects.

Here, then, is the dis-order of which man was made the bearer: the evil that comes from the "rage of insurgency" introduced to us earlier by Schelling's text. It is the condition under which the human becomes the pacesetter of the devastation, in that he chases things around in a restlessness that is foreign to them by making them into resources for his needs and items for his calculations. We will become free—we two prisoners, but also "we Germans"—when we are capable of letting be, of letting an entity be in the same manner in which it is received in its essence. The concept of freedom, therefore, is no longer based on the model of doing, dominating, and effecting. In a word, freedom can no longer be identified with the will—the will of the self-founded subject, which inevitably translates into will to power and power. Rather, freedom is to be understood as the authentic activity of thought, the same thought that, as we said, is capable of waiting. This also applies to the Germans, because only by becoming the people of poets and thinkers will they become a free people. Heidegger soothes the wounds of war and encourages Germans and himself with the belief that "the historical existence of a people and its duration" are not measured by the simple fact that "humans of its native kind" survive the annihilation and continue to live. Nor does it serve the "identity to come" to start all over at rebuilding. The pure "duration of the destiny" becomes "well-grounded" only "by means of the waiting that waits on the coming."[49] From this assumption there stems a harsh criticism against the principle of nationality and the self-affirmation of the collective self as nation, very close to the one developed in the "Letter on 'Humanism'." The idea of nation is the idea through which a people builds itself up into a Subject in whose presence everything becomes an object at its disposal. However, a people that chases after its own essence by fighting to wring recognition out of other peoples will never arrive at itself. In 1945, in a sort of historical self-correction, Heidegger states that one does not become more German by trying to discover the German character, by appealing to a supposed "German nature." As long as we remain entangled in "such intentions," we "merely chase after what is national," which is to say, taking pride in what is "naturally given."[50] On the other hand, the "international" principle is certainly not going to free us from this position of subjectivity, since it is nothing but the multiplication of the "national." However, he also feels compelled to make reference to Soviet degeneration: the principle of metaphysical subjectivity, which is stated as the ground and measure of what is actual, persists in the "uprising into work." This principle is nothing more than the active means by which the "devastation of the earth" is prepared for.[51] The conversation between the prisoners ends with a date and an observation that shed light on Heidegger's life course: "8 May 1945. On the day the world celebrated its victory, without yet recognizing that already for centuries it has been defeated by its own rebellious uprising."[52]

Nothing Is Said in Many Ways

In an essay entitled "From the Adverb 'Nothing' to the Substantive 'Nothing': Deliberations on Heidegger's Question Concerning Nothing," written in 1975,[53] Jacob Taubes takes up the ferocious attack that Rudolf Carnap had mounted against Heidegger and his concept of nothingness.[54] This attack was certainly seminal, extending its influence well beyond analytic philosophy. Although Taubes does not deny the dark side of Heidegger's philosophy, he believes that the kind of controversy championed by Carnap was culpably ignorant of the meaning of Heidegger's question on the nothing. No doubt, a generation that had found itself literally "vis-à-vis de rien" (face-to-face with nothing) could not have ignored this question. What he means by this, expressed in other terms, is that the question of the nothing was the result of an interaction between philosophical thought and historical time.

In effect, Heidegger's ontology has been the springboard for many critical inquiries that trace out a genuine hermeneutical circle between the philosophical redefinition of the idea of evil and the historical events that shocked the first half of the twentieth century. Though remaining critical of Heidegger's choices, there are many authors who benefited from his important legacy. However, there are different ways of handling this legacy in rethinking the link between evil, being, and nothingness. What is the distinguishing characteristic that differentiates between these approaches?

As we noted, not unlike Nietzsche's philosophy and Freud's work, Heidegger's thought can be interpreted in basically two ways: either as a thought that assertively and prophetically affirms the progressive destructiveness of the nothing as it continues to advance; or as the thought that, despite ambiguities, contradictions, and guilty silences, lays down the foundation for a new ontological—not metaphysical—foundation for freedom. Either a nothing that nihilates, in an anonymous, fatalistic fashion; or a principle, an ungrounded ground, that gives being its freedom, insofar as it is exposed to the possibility of being otherwise, or even to not being at all. Depending on the role attributed to the nothing, just as with Nietzschean nihilism and the Freudian *Todestrieb*, in this case, too, evil winds up being conceived in two opposing ways. Either it is identified simply with nihilism, in which there is a will to power at work that reduces being and life to nothing; or it is thought of as a negation of the constitutive, mutual belonging of being and nothingness, a "guilty" denial that produces nihilistic and "malicious" effects.

In the second part of this book we will return to the second possibility offered by the Heideggerian "nothing" and how it can be made productive even in a nonreligious context. The reason for this is because the ontology of freedom that emerged from this perspective took shape mostly in a Christian horizon, even if in a tragic version of Christianity *sui generis*.[55] The thought of Luigi Pareyson, which has continued to be developed in a number of directions by members of his school, is a prime example.[56] Another emblematic case of this tragic religious approach is the way Paul Ricoeur gives new voice to Karl Barth's "God and Nothingness": a "broken theology" that, precisely because it is willing to face the nothing, is in the position to start all over at the dreadful business of conceiving evil.[57] The fact is that nothingness must be thought of not only as deprivation and deficiency, but also as a force of corruption and destruction that is irreconcilable with the goodness of God. Barth is proof of how even theological thought is capable of conceiving of evil in other terms, differing first and foremost from theodicies, in recognizing the "positive" character of the nothing. To challenge oneself with thought about the nothing, about this "unconditioned," is the only way for this Christian philosophy "to do justice," Ricoeur explains—to do justice to the protest against human suffering, which refuses to be subsumed in the name of retribution under the category of moral evil, or to be enlisted under the banner of providence.[58]

Heidegger's thought is often traced back to the first of these alternatives. It has even been equated to a sophisticated, secularized form of Gnostic dualism.[59] In most cases, the history of metaphysics as a history of the forgottenness of being has offered an opportunity to rethink evil as a path of decline whose fate is sealed. This horizon includes theoretical approaches that can be very different from each other. For example, in spite of highly divergent theoretical objectives, the Frankfurt school's "dialectic of the Enlightenment" follows the course of *Seinsvergessenheit*—the forgottenness of Being—no less than the interpretation of history in terms of progressive "immanentism."[60] In political terms, this "simple" way of understanding the evil of nihilism leads to the interpretation of modernity as an affirmation of a globalizing technology that turns into a nihilating, total domination. We might recall the success that Ernst Jünger and his "Total Mobilization" met with in his portrayals of a society in which the individual seems to disappear, swallowed up by the technological, industrial apparatus.[61] The age of technology is a huge "machination" that reduces all human beings to mere tools. It is a universe with no openings, a world that obscures any ulterior meaning, one in which technical-scientific knowledge, which breaks through all limits, subjugates the totality of the entities in a destructive vortex in which the logical order of ends and means is reversed. In many cases, these critiques are the theoretical counterpart to the political accusation made against mass-based regimes that break down the conscience and social ties and reduce individuals to superfluous beings. No doubt, to denounce the nihilism of the age of technology is a way for thought to arrive in the most direct and simplified fashion at the root of transformations that are so alienating that they become the sign of evil per se.

There is no doubt that with Heidegger philosophy permanently leaves behind all subjective views of evil and ties its conceivability to a system of being in which politics and history play a central role. Evil can certainly no longer be dealt with as a phenomenon that is attributable exclusively to the intentionality of individual agents of evil acts. In effect, it has become impossible to identify *an active subject of guilt*—the author of the crime in its entirety. For this reason, too, the temptation to make evil correspond with "fully realized nihilism" becomes stronger and stronger. Nihilism effectively becomes synonymous with the evil that causes the West to collapse in on itself: a sort of terminal illness in which the death drive and the will to nothingness launch a furious attack against being itself. Thus, universally, "destruction" becomes the new name for political evil, preparing the way for the Dostoevsky paradigm to become the interpretative lens for the disasters of the century.

Starting specifically with the conceptual tools provided by Nietzsche, Freud, and Heidegger—from *a certain way* of understanding Nietzsche, Freud, and Heidegger—the philosophy of the midtwentieth century elevated Auschwitz to a metonymy of absolute evil. There are many thinkers of both genders who identify the series of occurrences between the two world wars as the extreme event that demolished an entire world, forcing us to rethink it from the beginning. As the apex of human destructiveness, the ground zero of Western culture, what took place in the death camps seems to have shattered a world of moral and political certainties and, along with them, the *a priori* assumptions of philosophical thought. From Günther Anders to Hannah Arendt, from Herbert Marcuse to Hans Jonas, from Karl Löwith to Leo Strauss, to mention only the most well-known names, a whole generation of scholars, mostly of Jewish origin, also had to come to terms *philosophically* with what happened.[62] Not by chance, they have come from the ranks of the "Heideggerian philosophical revolution," which they criticize, however, for having run aground in the shallows of the nihilistic drift. It has also been observed that although they read Heidegger's silence on Auschwitz as a sign of the irresponsibility of his thought, they also view it as proof that the history of the forgottenness of being told in terms of fate is no more than a sophisticated alibi for disguising yet another theodicy.

They take different positions. Above all, the answers that they feel obligated to provide in response to what appears to be the new radical evil are very different. All these thinkers are convinced, however, that a "restorative" nod, so to speak, toward a presumed lost good is not enough; the close link between ethics, ontology, and political evil must be rethought from its roots. Consider, for example, the theories put into play by Strauss and Jonas, according to which a thousand-year-old ontology has repressed the real question of the nothing, thus becoming its shadowy supporter. For this reason, they believe that the most urgent task of thought is to redefine the meaning of a moral life, of the world of values that the unprecedented evil of the twentieth century literally pulverized. To drastically simplify, Jonas argues that there is an urgent need for a new ontology in order to found a new ethics[63]; Strauss presents the disappearance of the ontological authority of the law as the driving force behind the historical disaster. However, for both, what is responsible for absolute and radical evil is the ethical nihilism lodged at the heart of the modern Western tradition. Many others share their idea that when the nihilistic view prevails unchallenged, the reasons to condemn evil—the evil of history and power—no longer exist, as Heidegger's personal bankruptcy also goes to show.

Now, within this landscape, Emmanuel Levinas and Hannah Arendt occupy a special position. What they provide us with is a perspective on evil that greatly complicates the assumptions of the nihilistic theory, and begins to throw into disarray the series of ideas that make up the Dostoevsky paradigm.

Evil as Excess: Levinas

It is evident starting from the early works of Levinas that his philosophy takes its origin from a traumatic historical experience. When we read his "Reflections on the Philosophy of Hitlerism,"[64] written in 1934, along with the slightly later essay "On Evasion," the link between his critique of metaphysics and the disastrous events in Europe in the first half of the twentieth century comes quite clearly into view. His philosophical reading of Nazism describes Hitlerism primarily as an ontology that gives precedence to the body and to its biological identity. This allows us to pinpoint the exact origin of the equivalence he makes between *conatus essendi* and evil that, in my opinion, shapes and directs his entire philosophical path. In short, Levinas thinks of Hitlerism, and the situation of "being nailed" or "bondage [*enchaînement*]" that it entails, as analogous to the actualization of the possibilities that Western metaphysics has offered, inasmuch as the latter is the product of an ontology that made the identity of the Same its basic principle.

The direct comparison with the Holocaust would lead the Jewish-Lithuanian philosopher to forge an increasingly close connection between "existential disaster" and the "ontology of the Same," an ontology erected on the principle of being as identical to itself; whence the need to revive the primacy of ethics.[65] Specifically from the evidence of these connections, Levinas's philosophy has been viewed as a progressively closer examination of the problem of evil.[66] Although the question is certainly at the center of his major works, from *On Evasion*[67] to *Existence and Existents*,[68] from *Totality and Infinity*[69] to *Otherwise Than Being or Beyond Essence*,[70] in reality only rarely does he directly address the issue. My intention is certainly not to trace the course of this progressive focus on the link between extermination, evil, and ontology. What I wish to demonstrate here through some of Levinas's texts in which the question is tackled directly is a twofold philosophical gesture that I consider to be decisive.

The appeal Levinas makes to an absolute, paradoxical ethics can be interpreted as a strategic response to all the attempts to neutralize the question of evil—above all, in answer to that obtuse will to justify the existing world known as theodicy, one of the most effective ways in which metaphysics has expressed its "idolatry of being."[71] In the essay entitled "Useless Suffering,"[72] collected in one of his last works, Levinas explicitly discusses the problem of theodicy, claiming to speak from the period when all theodicies have come to an end; in other words, from the standpoint of a century that, passing through totalitarianism, massacres, and death camps, saw all hope extinguished of being able to balance the quantity and quality of suffering with some rational justification. He recognizes that the more absurd evil is, the stronger the seductive power of theodicies becomes. According to Levinas—who was a careful reader of Dostoevsky and Nietzsche—this is because the temptation to make the suffering of the innocent bearable by giving it a meaning remains unchanged from the Book of Job to Hegel.

As a matter of fact, the real problem is "useless evil": evil that cannot be rationalized away. Appearing in its "fundamental malignancy" with the events of the twentieth century, it now stands as a genuine philosophical question and not only as a historical issue. The new phenomenon that Auschwitz impels us to think about is this: evil suffered to its utmost, regardless of the intentionality and action of the victims. In the "useless suffering" represented by the millions of deaths in the extermination of the century, Job's lament resounds in our ears once again—the cry of the just who seek to account for the senselessness of their pain.[73]

Levinas thus invites us to broaden the perspective of our investigation, so as to direct our gaze not only at the perpetrators but also at the victims. Evil, therefore, should not be investigated only from the point of view of radical freedom—of the perverse will of those who commit it. We also need to examine what is "unbearable" in the nature of evil—what is unbearable to the consciousness, because of an absurd disproportion between what someone has done and what someone has been subjected to. In this sense, before defining it any further, evil is a pure fact: the fact of suffering. Even prior to any spiritual datum, evil coincides with the condition of "extreme passivity," a paralysis that wounds and petrifies the senses: "In suffering sensibility is a vulnerability, more passive than receptivity; an encounter more passive than experience. It is precisely an evil." Evil, then, is the condition of absolute passivity, which goes beyond the oppression caused by a lack of freedom. "It is not, to tell the truth, through passivity that evil is described," he explains, "but through evil that suffering is understood[. . . .] All evil relates back to suffering. It is the *impasse* of life and of being—their absurdity—in which pain does not just somehow innocently happen to 'color' consciousness with affectivity."[74]

Levinas is describing the situation of what we might call "the absolute victim": a victim as such because he or she is released from any genuine relationship of enmity. This figure of evil did not choose to enter into a conflict or into a fight, but ends up embodying the role of the enemy by the very fact of its being how it is and not otherwise. This is the same figure that, under the name of "Muselmann," occupies the writings of Primo Levi and that, presented as "bare life," later polarized the attention of thinkers on biopower. But is there any way out of the logical vise grip of "useless suffering"? How are we to conceive it, considering that the justification for the pain of the other is certainly—in times of generalized inhumanity—the source of all immorality?

The link between evil and suffering is summarized in an exemplary manner in his article on "Transcendence and Evil," one of the few texts in which Levinas explicitly tackles the problem.[75] In this paper, written shortly before the essay on "Useless Suffering," the topic comes up in response to the publication of Philippe Nemo's book *Job and the Excess of Evil*, a powerful meditation on the Book of Job.[76] Levinas first clarifies that evil cannot be conceived as a mode, as a species, or as the culmination of a simple negation. He then addresses the issue through a comparison with the notion of "ontological difference." In his view, this concept acts for Heidegger as a "model of transcendence," which introduces nothingness into his logic—the same nothing of which *Da-sein*'s anxiety is a symptom.[77] This link between transcendence, nothingness, and anxiety is also to be found in Nemo's book, and anxiety is understood as the disclosure of nothingness. However, Levinas points out, unlike Heidegger, Nemo does not treat it as a form of affectivity, exclusively concerned with deciphering the changes internal to the self. As shown most effectively by the example of Job's suffering—suffering caused by a pain that can affect anyone at any time—the evil of anxiety speaks primarily of the horror experienced in the face of a body—one's own or someone else's—that perishes and rots. It expresses the distress arising from contact with an identity undergoing change.

What Levinas is thus suggesting here is that there exists another way to combine anxiety and evil that, in a sense, is completely overlooked by Heidegger: "Evil will indeed mean an 'end' of the world, but an end which [. . .] leads [. . .] to a beyond," elsewhere than being, and elsewhere than nothingness, "to a *beyond* that is conceived neither by negation, nor by the anxiety the philosophers of existence speak of." This dimension that has not been conceived by the philosophy of existence is excess: "In its malignancy as evil, evil is an excess." Not only because, as we have seen, its intensity goes beyond the endurable: "Evil is an excess in its very quiddity."[78]

The "essence" of evil for Levinas thus resides in the break it causes with the normal and the normative, with order and with synthesis, with the possibility of getting to the bottom of being, in a univocal fashion. The suffering it causes is the concrete and sensible manifestation of its essence, which is expressed in its being "unjustifiable": "The 'quality' of evil is this very non-integratability." If, for Kant, who is a constant reference in this paper as well, there can be no experience without synthesis and no knowledge of something that transcends experience, then the experience of evil is what really calls into question the Kantian system. This is because the evil that expresses itself in blameless suffering is a paradoxical experience whose excess can never be synthesized: "It is as though to synthesis, even the purely formal synthesis of the Kantian 'I think', capable of uniting the data however heterogeneous they may be, there would be opposed, in the form of evil, the non-synthesizable, still more heterogeneous than all heterogeneity subject to being grasped by the formal, which exposes heterogeneity in its very malignancy."[79] In short, this is not a disorder as other and opposite of order, but rather an irreducible disorder.

Is what we have here thus a sublime quality of the malignancy of evil, just like the Kantian sublime, that cannot be integrated by any idea of reason? This is certainly how Levinas's essay would been read by Jean-François Lyotard, a careful interpreter (following in the footsteps of Kant's treatment of the "Analytic of the Sublime") of philosophical interpretations that make Auschwitz synonymous with the unassimilable, of what resists any attack from dialectics.[80] For Levinas, we might recall, not only does the malignancy of evil resist being subsumed under theodicy and dialectical logic, but it also resists the possibility of being integrated into a reasonable economy—whether religious or secular makes no difference—that foresees a balance between good and evil: "In the appearing of evil, in its original phenomenality, in its quality, is announced a modality, a manner: not finding a place, the refusal of all accommodation with [. . .], a counter-nature, a monstrosity, what is disturbing and foreign of itself."[81] *This is why it is transcendence.* The excess that evil constitutes lends the preposition "ex-" its original meaning: something that cannot be traced back to a categorial form.

The emphasis Levinas places on transcendence, on the transgressive, excessive, and monstrous quality of evil, certainly holds him tightly inside the meshes of the Dostoevsky paradigm. In a certain sense, for the author of *Totality and Infinity*, too, evil preserves the sacred and mysterious aura that surrounds a theological conception of the problem. What is "Dosto-evskian" about it is the belief that true evil is incomprehensible and abyssal; and especially Dostoevskian is the idea that evil is expressed in its pure form in a power relationship so asymmetrical that it pins down into total passiv-ity an "absolute victim" who is rendered such by the useless quality of his or her suffering.

This character of excess is connected to a particular idea of the in-tentionality of evil, an idea that is completely different from the subjective intentionality of Kantian radical evil. As Levinas explains, it is as though the misfortune that "reaches me" was inevitably connected to the idea that evil was seeking me out, that it was "aiming at me."[82] It is like something directed at me not only to persecute me as the designated victim, but also, along with its horror, to offer a possibility of awakening—to push *Da-sein* out of the neutrality of being, out of the terrible power of the "il y a." Hence, it is evil as suffering and as "hatred of evil"[83] that allows us to es-cape from the idolatry of the Same and from the impersonal structure of Being: "That in the evil that pursues me the evil suffered by the other man afflicts me, that it touches me, as though from the first the other was call-ing to me, putting into question my resting on myself and my *conatus es-sendi*, as though before lamenting over my evil here below, I had to answer for the other—is not this a breakthrough of the Good in the 'intention' of which I am in my woe so exclusively aimed at?"[84] It is Levinas himself who insistently asks us to not interpret the reflection of goodness in evil as yet another dialectical reversal. The good that evil can lead us to does not bring the comfortable consequences of the final synthesis that occurs outside the scope of individual responsibility. Certainly, in the Lithuanian phi-losopher's view, the face of the other, to which the wound inflicted by evil calls our attention, is certainly the epiphany of the infinite, the power of a revelation of transcendence. But even in the case of Levinas's philosophy, another reading is possible: an interpretation that radically distances the philosopher from some of the cornerstones of Dostoevsky's conception.

In the suffering that crushes the ego and in the suffering that the ego feels for the suffering of others, a movement is set in motion that ruptures the immanence, in which we glimpse something more than a religious meaning. This is the very opening to the ethical path. What is relevant here is not the nature of the "beyond" to which existence is directed, but the fact that this excess causes an opening that does not indicate a way out of being toward nothingness, toward the destruction of creation. In a way that is different from the many others who take up the legacy of *Demons*, the good that Levinas believes can come from evil consists in breaking the circularity that characterizes the *conatus essendi*. The good resides in the possibility of suspending and weakening the imperative of being. Using a different vocabulary, we could say that thanks to the disruptive perception of useless suffering, evil is an affective experience that forces the ego to step outside its retreat into itself. It is an eruption, an emotional breach of the principle of identity of the same.

The search for meaning—this is where Levinas's discourse becomes extremely interesting—does not arise therefore from wonder in the face of being. The polemic against metaphysics primarily strives to call into question the tenacious conviction that the first, most fundamental question of philosophy regards the reason for being and for the being of beings: "The first metaphysical question is no longer Leibniz's question, 'why is there something rather than nothing?' but rather 'why is there evil rather than good?'"[85] In short, the subject—or, more accurately, the process of becoming a subject—begins not with wonder at what is, but with astonishment at the fact of something happening that should not have happened. In other words, it originates from a negative that at this point becomes the abrupt disturbance produced by the horror of evil: "The ontological difference is preceded by the difference between good and evil. *Difference itself is this latter; it is the origin of the meaningful.*"[86]

It is not the ontological question, therefore—a question that produces only tautologies, says Levinas—that gives meaning to the subject, but rather the question about the difference between good and evil. This is what founds the assumption of ethics as the first philosophy, which marks the originality of Levinas's philosophy. It does not mean that "what ought to be" comes before "what is"—I am quite certain—but rather, that a subject is led to constitute itself as such by an original opening, which consists in the perception of a break or a rupture in the order of being. The priority of the ethical over the ontological, a well-known feature of Levinas's philosophy, is rooted in its refusal to consider evil either as a simple negation or as the destiny of a nothing that nihilates. Evil is the excess that, by opposing any sort of synthesis, makes perceptible the sense of alterity.

A great deal depends on how *Da-sein* responds to horror. If the being-t/here negates it, if it closes itself before the exigency that suffering brings with it, then either the consolatory function of theodicy or the explanation of evil as an autonomous principle will triumph. In both cases, what will be assumed as given is an ontological reality toward which we are powerless. If instead we allow ourselves to be upset, if we expose ourselves to the scandal of evil, the transcendence "of what cannot be assembled into a totality" will open up a gap in subjectivity.[87] It is as if the evil that I read in the suffering of the face of the other, argues Levinas, forces me to go outside of myself, to accept or reject the demand of an infinite responsibility because it leads, as in Dostoevsky, into relation with everything and everyone—a responsibility that is even more infinite because of the fact that it haunts and pursues me with its unfulfillable demand.[88]

On the one hand, evil is *disorder*, *abyss*, and *excess*, and, as such, it is still thought of as transgression of normality; on the other hand, as has been mentioned, its transcendent character can be viewed as a cypher of the internal division of the subject. This makes it possible to distinguish between a religious transcendence, which refers to a dimension other than the subject and the world, and a transcendence internal to the subject, as it were, which in my opinion traces the movement of ethics as an immanent movement. From this perspective, the responsibility is infinite mainly because it is an endless source of disturbance for the ego. Because it can never be fulfilled, it constantly exiles the subject from the fullness of the self, thereby forcing the subject to deny any presumed self-sufficiency. The divided subject does not shun the two to reunite itself into one, as all the *Demons* would have done according to Dostoevsky. Instead, it places itself in a constant state of self-questioning, structuring itself into a truly anarchic subject. The anarchist instance does not refer to a disorder that is such because it is opposed to another, previous order, which it seeks to supplant. The sense of anarchy that can be found in Levinas's writings, and that I value greatly, is oriented toward an impossible *arché*, an unattainable return to the beginning, a two that never finds peace in the one, and that lives in a constant state of self-expropriation.

The Sacred Aura of the New Radical Evil

Not many people interpret the philosophy of Levinas as a nontheological transcendence. For the most part his thinking is considered emblematic of a position that by now has been largely called into question.

It is no coincidence that Alain Badiou, in his book *Ethics: An Essay on the Understanding of Evil*,[89] chose Levinas as the privileged target of his polemics against what he defines as the twentieth-century ethics of "radical evil." In his view, it is a religion hiding behind the appearance of an ethics. Disregarding the profound transformations that the concept of radical evil underwent during the twentieth century, the French philosopher believes that elevating Auschwitz to the symbol of evil is equivalent to reviving the Kantian idea in contemporary terms. Radical evil in this view takes on the function of cordoning off an abyss at whose edge we must stop ourselves in time, prompting us to give up on political change rather than plummet into its depths. Moreover, for Badiou the extermination of the Jews by the Nazis occupies an ambiguous position in logical terms as well.[90] On the one hand, the Holocaust plays the role of the "Totally Other," in the sense of the absolute negative; on the other, it is charged with a concrete uniqueness that is absolutely irreproducible. Auschwitz, that is, signifies something whose repetition must be prevented at all costs; or rather, something whose unrepeatability becomes the norm for any judgment regarding a concrete situation. It is therefore elevated to the status of a paradigm, although as the projection of a negative exemplarity. The Nazi extermination is radical evil because it provides our age with the unique, unequaled, inexpressible, and therefore transcendent measure of evil in and of itself. However, Badiou continues, even the act of comparison itself is effectively prevented, because it is experienced as profanation. The extermination and the Nazis are unique, unthinkable, without antecedents or descendants. Although invoked to judge every situation, in reality they remain enveloped in the impossibility of being understood. While recognizing the atrocity of the extermination of the European Jews, an atrocity that cannot be classified as transient and necessary to the movement of history, he powerfully calls the unpronounceable uniqueness of Auschwitz into question once again. For Badiou, "radical evil"—under whose name the philosophy of the twentieth century subsumes the Nazi extermination camp—exists wholly within a theological discourse. The sacredness of Auschwitz is the untouchable sacredness of the Totally Other. And Levinas is said to have become its high priest, as it were.

Now, without any doubt, for the generation that was personally marked by the signs of exile, or even of deportation and internment, the moment of discovery of the death camps was charged with an aura of the absolute and the demonic, in philosophical terms as well. We might recall, however, the words of Maurice Blanchot that Levinas explicitly quotes in "Useless Suffering": "I think that all the dead of the Gulag and all the other places of torture in our political century are present when one speaks of Auschwitz."[91] And he continues, unequivocally: "This is the century that in thirty years has known two world wars, the totalitarianisms of right and left, Hitlerism and Stalinism, Hiroshima, the Gulag, and the genocides of Auschwitz and Cambodia. This is the century that is drawing to a close in the obsessive fear of the return of everything these barbaric names stood for: suffering and evil inflicted deliberately, but in a manner no reason sets limits to, in the exasperation of a reason become political and detached from all ethics."[92] Perhaps what Badiou does not want to entirely grasp about the paradigm—concerned as he is that something "unpronounce-able" might hinder access to the possibility of political praxis—is its dynamics of exemplarity. He repeats the same criticism that Slavoj Žižek directs against the idea of totalitarianism, and against Hannah Arendt's notion of "radical evil."

As I have just argued with regard to Levinas, and as I will argue with regard to Arendt, the task these thinkers undertake is much more complicated than the neo-Marxist simplification that Žižek and Badiou propose to us. I am therefore convinced that to classify twentieth-century attempts to name the "excessiveness of Auschwitz" as false ideological consciousness is reductive.[93] Badiou does, however, help us grasp an element of truth that is absolutely vital.

It was not the sacredness of Auschwitz that placed an impassable limit on thought, as the French philosopher maintains. It is rather the subsuming of evil under the hegemony of the Dostoevsky paradigm that entangled the conceivability of Auschwitz in the meshes of transcendence, the absolute, excess, the nihilistic drift, the death instinct, the destiny of nothingness, and history. As I have insisted, there is no doubt that this interpretive scheme, rooted in a theoretical context that long preceded the extermination of the Jews, has enriched and extended its hermeneutic power to the point of including the key experiences of the twentieth century within its nihilistic hypothesis: war that becomes total, global exploitation that ravages the planet, and above all, the death camp. These especially are the new phenomenal modes by which evil manifests itself in history, and for which there seems to be no better explanation than "a pure unleashing of the will to death," now transformed into a crushing power. In short, the name of Auschwitz became conceptually pronounceable partly thanks to the "discoveries" of Nietzsche, Freud, and Heidegger, which, having been unilaterally accepted, came to epitomize the insights of Schelling and Dostoevsky: thanks, then, to the idea of a will to power that "would rather will nothingness than not will"; thanks to the disruptive force that the death instinct made conceivable; and thanks to a history of being that deciphered the will/necessity to annihilation in the devastation wrought by technology.

I believe the time has come to leave behind the Dostoevsky paradigm. We need to abandon it more than anything in order to understand the radical evil of the twentieth century. This cluster of concepts makes it impossible to probe some folds of the concreteness of the event, and it is likely to catch us up in traps that philosophy fell into for two thousand years, whenever it tried to address the problem of evil. There is no doubt that having kept our eyes fixed on the abysmality of the subject and of history has taught us a lot about the new figures from the last century. But this point of view, fundamentally, slips steadily toward an identification of evil either with subjective wickedness or with suprahistorical malignancy. Evil is not only the sum of the maliciousness and wickedness of the subjects; it cannot be understood by looking only at the vertigo of nothingness that upsets the ego. Nor is it conceivable only in the terms of disaster to which the history of being and nihilism deliver us.

Of course, there is an event, or rather a series of events, that we can and must define as "ultimate evil." These are events, however, that have to do with conjunctures of circumstances and ideas, with political choices and historical occurrences, with specific intentions and passive internalizations, all of which, in the end, are contingently knotted together in a fatal weave of atrocities and destruction, one in which evil—the elemental evil that comes from the *fact of suffering*, a suffering that every individual causes and is subjected to—has been turned into a system, so to speak, and has become an event, saturating an entire area of time and space. The exterminations and mass killings that continue to occur have performed the function of examples to the best of their ability. And the *Shoah* has certainly occupied a privileged place. This does not mean—especially not today—that we should comply with the prohibition on the pronounceability of a name. Not only must we keep thinking about politics after Auschwitz,[94] we may just as well begin our thought with Auschwitz, by comparing its basic traits with those of other places that, like the death camp, set the scene for extreme evil.

I think it behooves us, then, to ask a question: Between the malice of devastation, and freedom as the delusion of omnipotence, which eventually cancels itself out; between the planetary organization of technology, and the revolt of the ego against being, what has the twentieth century bequeathed us for understanding evil, for breaking its substance down into the elements of a relationship? What tools do we have at our disposal to understand that the scene of evil is a complex scene, where the power of nothingness and the death drive do not reign absolute at all? Political philosophy has remained so stuck in the paradigm we are examining that it has never completely freed itself from a conception of power that is heavily influenced by this "grandiose" idea of evil. It has continued, that is, to think of the relationship of power, and *a fortiori* the power relationship that is turned into an event of evil, along the binary lines of a dualistic, rigidly polarized conception. That is to say, the hermeneutic key incessantly put forward by twentieth-century philosophy is the clear distinction between the omnipotent action of the evil actor and the totally passive inaction of a subject who is deprived of any capacity to react; as if the eternal Dostoevskian scene of the violation of children—the quintessential innocent victim—were to be endlessly repeated. After all, if we take a close look, the darkest, most terrible power relations in our history have been modeled according to this schema: *evil demons* on one side and *absolute victims* on the other. Even today, as much as we acknowledge the extreme complexity of the scenarios, we never manage to completely free ourselves from this *a priori*. It is a metaphysical and theological *a priori* that continues to affect us, often unconsciously, in our deciphering of power relations. It is as though we refuse to look deeply and do not want to become aware of what happens before arriving at that final scene of domination, where, it is true, the most absolute asymmetry does indeed reign.

However, abandoning the Dostoevsky paradigm does not mean believing that atrocities are no longer atrocious, that cruelty is no longer cruel, that violence is no longer savage; and above all it does not mean that the victim is no longer the victim and the perpetrator is no longer the perpetrator. To break evil down into the characteristics that have made it such, and thus to leave behind a metaphysical investigation in order to take the route of a microphysical analysis, it is not enough to think about it using the schema of transcendence and the absolutization of death. We have to investigate it in its historical and contingent immanence: to realign it, that is, on the plane of human relations that are *always also power relations*.

Although transcendence does not reveal an otherworldly dimension to us—which is why Levinas's work is so valuable—it does show us the movement that ties a subject to the question of evil, a movement that, in my opinion, is essential to the formation of ethical subjectivity. There is no doubt that evil and its detectability, as such, have to do with the structure of subjectivity; this was the greatest acquisition of philosophy from Kantian radical evil onward. However, this is so not in the sense of an abyssal freedom that comes to it from that "elsewhere," in which the subject's choice for nothing or for being takes root, but in the primary significance of the realization that the question of evil, in its difference from the good, is absurd when considered outside the scope of becoming subjects. As Nietzsche had made perfectly clear to philosophical thought (and Hegel before him, although with a different lexicon), within the confines of the formation of subjectivity there is neither good nor bad. This is because evil is intelligible only insofar as it can be distinguished from the banal, "innocent" violence that organic life occasionally runs into while seeking to preserve its being. Without this process of subjectification, of becoming subjects, all that exists is the more or less cruel innocence of life's becoming. We can speak of evil only in relation to a human animal that has been able to put to use its capacity to place itself within a meaning-building process at the service of its mortal life. This is because meaning itself is structured around the perception of a difference: the difference between what strikes us and makes us suffer and what leaves us peacefully in the confines of our self. There is no such thing as a subject, we might say, then, before this distinction—a distinction not only between the perception of what is good for us and what is bad for us, but one that extends into reflection on good and evil. But there is no question of good and evil without the locus where an original division can be recorded. In this sense, probably, the claim that ethics comes before ontology can be confusing, as if we were to think of them as separate domains, even within a single subject. But if a question about the meaning of being is posed, it is because a process of subjectivation has occurred and is occurring—and along with it, the question of good and evil that a life asks itself in order to enter into a process of individuation from being. The question of evil—clearly, not the answer—is thus a rupture: the immanent rupture of the indifference and immediacy of becoming. This is what Badiou designates as event. And perhaps it is true that to not perceive the difference, to not ask oneself the question about good and evil, may be the first step one takes to enter into a scene of evil.

INTERLUDE: HYPERMORAL BIOPOLITICS

4

Thanatopolitics and Absolute Victims

Before focusing on an alternative perspective from which to regard the event of evil, we need to look into the relevance of a few questions that have converged in current discussions on biopower. In the economy of my discourse, these represent an intermediate space connecting and intersecting the two genealogies of the relationship between evil and power: the one we have just reconstructed of the Dostoevsky paradigm, and that of the "paradigm of mediocre demons" that takes shape in the second part of this book. In order to unsubstantialize the supposed essence of evil and de-absolutize the omnipotence of a destruction-seeking, evil subjectivity, our first task is to dismantle a demonological idea of power and turn instead to an analytics that forgoes evaluating domination based solely on its capacity for death and will to death. As I see it, this is the direction taken by thought on biopolitics. Even as it attempts to understand the elevation of life to an undisputed value of modernity, biopolitics implicitly shifts the point of view toward evil. This allows us to observe evil as if it were no longer simply the realm of nothingness. For this reason, it is worth looking at some of the main topics that have entered into the discussion on biopower.[1] This is especially the case where totalitarian biopower is concerned, particularly the Nazi model, which in the extreme excesses of its practice brought into the open one of the paradoxes of biopower. Any attempt to rethink the relationship between evil and power can certainly not avoid returning to this historical scene, to how it has been interpreted, and to some of the texts that created its narrative.

One of the main merits of this broad hermeneutic horizon, encompassing both philosophical and historical studies, is that it has definitively shifted attention away from the omnipotent will of the actors to the suffering of those who bore the brunt of those actions. However, it is also important to point out its limits—the limits of certain philosophical approaches that, in the interest of emphasizing the novelty of biopower, end up neglecting the strong continuity of Nazi biopower with the metaphysical and, so to speak, "hypermoral" tradition; and, more generally, the limit of a critical inquiry that, in my opinion, maintains a dualistic schema in its understanding of power. The following sections clarify the main implications of these interpretations.

In the Name of Life: Arendt and Foucault

"If I could enclose all the evil of our time in one image, I would choose this image which is familiar to me: an emaciated man, with head dropped and shoulders curved, on whose face and in whose eyes not a trace of a thought is to be seen."[2] The type of prisoner portrayed in this description is by now headed for final destruction: the concentration camp inmate who has been transformed by deprivation into a sort of lifeless, biological remnant. He reacts mechanically to hunger, cold, and fatigue. In other words, he has been transformed into a being for whom any room for choice has been eliminated. This figure is a composite made from the anonymous mass of the "drowned" who populated the camps, who marched and labored without speaking, because by then they were too empty to truly suffer: "One hesitates to call them living: one hesitates to call their death death, in the face of which they have no fear, as they are too tired to understand."[3] The preparation of the "men in decay" was methodical, marked by gradual, well-defined stages: from repeated offenses against their sense of modesty to violence aimed specifically at humiliating them, from bursts of terror to practices of savage derision, from the absurd rhythms of forced labor to a totally inadequate diet.

This is Primo Levi's unforgettable, paradigmatic figure of the "Muselmann" in his book *If This Is a Man*, which also provided the opportunity to introduce the equation between evil and absolute victim that, as we have seen in the case of Levinas, occupied center-stage in a number of political philosophy works that appeared in the final decades of the last century. The literature on the extermination camps, especially works written by survivors, bears witness to a limit experience: that of a life de-subjectified, as it were, and stripped down to the last of its relational and symbolic identities, reduced to mere biological processuality. The historical sciences and the social sciences, philosophy, and literature have all focused their attention on it.

This means—as we will have occasion to repeat—that the gaze directed toward the actors in the scene of evil definitely changed its object and perspective. The experience and the testimony of the victims took on capital importance. From the point of view of history and historiography, this shift has been noted many times. There was talk of an "era of the witness,"[4] of a transition from the condemnation of the perpetrators to compassion for the victims, the ending of "the myth of the soldier-hero"—of the resistant—and the triumph of the victim.[5] What has perhaps not been sufficiently emphasized are the implications that this shift has had in rethinking the idea of evil. To sum up briefly, when viewed from the perspective of those who design and implement the killing, evil can be understood as the ultimate cypher of the enigma of freedom, the dark side of the subject's power. A gaze focused on the victim's experience, on the other hand, sees evil as a total lack of freedom, one that calls out to be deciphered and probed. What has been described, then, is a shift in focus from an analysis of the connection and links between evil and the all-powerful freedom of the perpetrators, to an examination of the destructive process through which a human life, with its inextricable intertwining of freedom and predetermination, is reduced to a thing—or rather to an "absolute victim."

In recovering the expressive force of a silence that in the Muselmann becomes a paradoxical witnessing, Giorgio Agamben has led contemporary philosophical discussion in reexamining Foucault's notion of biopower from the perspective of thanatopolitics.[6] It is safe to say that with *Homo sacer* and *Remnants of Auschwitz* he indirectly but unequivocally involved biopolitics in a rethinking of the evil and power hendiadys. This is because evil is now representable in a form of life that has become "bare life": the ultimate expression, the final outcome of a relationship of power that leads to the production of what he calls *homo sacer*, which, like Primo Levi's Muselmann, can be killed without committing homicide. Certainly, the question of "bare life," which was developed out of the distinction between *zoe* and *bios*, is controversial. Agamben argues that the distinction was elaborated by Arendt and not by Foucault, who failed to think it through. Jacques Derrida, perhaps rightly, denies the opposition between *zoe* and *bios*, saying that the difference between "bare life" and "qualified life" cannot be traced.[7]

Nevertheless, what I said earlier still holds: from Derrida[8] to Roberto Esposito,[9] to mention only the most frequently cited names, there have been many authors who have accepted the challenge that Agamben re-launched in the mid-1990s. This is a challenge that in my eyes takes on a specific meaning: the attempt to conceive the opposition between evil and freedom no longer only in terms of a choice between political regimes, as it was conceived by post–World War II political philosophy, but in the onto-logical terms of a different degree of destructiveness that the inevitable in-tertwining of life and power manifests under certain circumstances. These are precisely the circumstances that—explicitly or implicitly—characterize the phenomenology of evil for thinkers who follow in Agamben's footsteps as well: it is an extreme phenomenology that is at the same time exemplary.

As *Homo sacer* explains, what we might call the "biopolitical para-digm" arose at the intersection of the notions that Arendt and Foucault mobilized to rethink modern power. Thanatopolitics is not just one spe-cific case of this paradigm's application, but rather, as we will show, the question that opens the path to its very conceptualization. This is not to understate the differences—even radical ones—that separate the two au-thors, but rather to question the effectiveness of a theoretical perspective that has opened up from the intersection of both their works. The very different terminology and styles of Arendt and Foucault converge in lo-cating a single turning point: that is, they are concentrated on identify-ing and characterizing the discontinuity represented in modern politics by the inclusion of life—understood in its biological aspect and as species—in the mechanisms and calculations of political power. For both thinkers, the *zoe* that had been excluded from the field of vision of politics in an-cient times, and that was politically insignificant in the Ancien Régime, because as creaturely life it belonged to God, came to the fore as part of the strategic aims of the state and became the very foundation of its legit-imacy and its sovereignty.[10] Although Arendt never used the terms "bio-power" or "biopolitics," there are many comparisons that can be made between her work and Foucault's. In *The Will to Knowledge*, for example, one of the crucial passages sounds thoroughly Arendtian: "For millennia, man remained what he was for Aristotle: a living animal with the additional capacity for a political existence; modern man is an animal whose politics places his existence as a living being in question."[11] This statement seems to confirm the fact that the play of opposites set up by Arendt in *The Human Condition* and in her preceding works is also valid for Foucault: namely, a sharp contrast between the politics of the ancient world and modern politics based mostly on the different role that life—understood as "mere biological living"—plays in the functioning and legitimacy of political power. For Arendt, the Greek polis, which continued to exist through Aristotle's *Politics*, was sustained, although with some contradictions, on the basis of a strict separation between the realm of necessity (the body and its needs, family and economic life) and the realm of freedom (the interaction, mostly linguistic and agonistic, between citizens).

The emergence of life as a "public matter"—biopower in Foucault's terms—would mark the final escape from a classical model of separation between humankind seen as a living being, as pure animal life, and humankind understood as a political actor, as citizen. For Arendt, this break coincided with the rise of political economy and the transformation of labor[12]: when life, understood as a natural process, burst onto the public scene, when the traits of the *animal laborans*, that is, became elevated to the main characteristics of the social and political space.[13] What was extinguished during this transition, in her opinion, was the chance for a politics based on freedom instead of a politics based on security. The notion of society in Arendt has precisely this function: to connect the dimension of "life itself," originally a private and "invisible" dimension, to the collective, supra-individual dimension. When the goal of politics becomes to safeguard and increase the life of society, as a totality; when the political signifies to guarantee and strengthen the safety and productivity of society, as a whole, then the original link between politics and freedom, between political action and the granting of meaning to the "who" becomes unhinged—because for Arendt what freedom means in the first place is a transcendence of concern for one's own survival. Already in "Introduction *into* Politics" we read[14]:

Although, to be sure, the proponents of these two views—that the state and politics are institutions indispensable to freedom, and that they are institutions indispensable to life—are scarcely aware of it, the two theories stand in unbridgeable opposition to each other. It makes a huge difference whether freedom or life is posited as the highest of all goods—as the standard by which all political action is guided and judged. If we think of politics by its very nature, and despite all its permutations, as having arisen out of the polis and being still under its charge, then the linkage of politics and life results in an inner contradiction that cancels and destroys what is specifically political about politics.[15]

Without entering into the merits of Arendt's gap between life and politics, which responds precisely to the necessity-freedom dichotomy, we need only recall that her criticism of liberalism must be viewed in this perspective. Despite the emphasis on the notion of freedom, liberal thought and practice, which are focused on material well-being, are fully included in the process of "de-politicization" that for Arendt dramatically traces out the "parabola" of modernity.

When it comes to Foucault, however, we can begin to speak of biopolitics in reference to the transition that took place between the late seventeenth century and the middle of the eighteenth century, when along with sovereign power and disciplinary authority over individual bodies there entered onto the scene a series of practices and disciplines of knowledge (medicine, demography, public health, statistics, urban planning) whose object was the population and the *general life* of the population as a good to be increased and protected. We can say, then, that for both authors we enter into a context that is modern and biopolitical when power is no longer only concerned with the life and death of the individual, but also with the vital process of society and the population as a whole—that is, when life becomes a sort of collective entity, on whose basis regular phenomena can be deduced and predictions can be made. The conceptual function of society, conceived by Arendt as a general idea, is very similar to the notion of population as it is conceived by Foucault.[16] Indeed, both of them call our attention to the paradox presented by liberalism. Despite its emphasis on freedom, it was liberal thought that opened the door to a conception of society as a network of economic relations requiring the security and improvement of the life of the population in order to operate in a "virtuous" way. As a first approximation, therefore, one may say that, according to the meaning that can be inferred from the works of these two authors, biopolitics is neither a historical category nor a true paradigm yet. If anything, it is a heuristic tool for bringing into view a crucial discontinuity in the continuum of Western power, an epistemic discontinuity, Foucault would say, or a historical-metaphysical one, as Arendt might say. In particular, it is a tool for recording the changes in configurations of power in different social-historical eras, beginning first of all with the radical discontinuity between Greek politics and modern sovereignty.

Unlike what Agamben argues,[17] in Arendt we detect a very tight bond between the observations contained in *The Origins of Totalitarianism* about the extermination camps and "nonpersons," and those in *The Human Condition* on the birth of the social and the triumph of the *animal laborans*. It is not entirely accurate to state—as Agamben still does—that Foucault failed to investigate the locus of modern biopolitics par excellence: the extermination camp. Both Arendt and Foucault, in their own ways, did in fact attempt to think through the complicated relationship of continuity and discontinuity that connects the modern form of biopower—the power that has taken charge of life even in its biological aspect—to the extreme, revelatory event represented by the genocides of the twentieth century. Both view Auschwitz, and in many ways the Soviet camps as well, as the extreme pathology of power, but at the same time as the fulfillment of a politics, however paroxysmal it may be, that has elevated life into a universal category with an undisputed value. The risk implicit in biopolitics is racism: not just the historic kind with an ethnic or biological basis, but, more generally, racism as a mental attitude that predisposes one to distinguish between lives that are worthy of being protected and improved and lives marked for disposal. It is the danger of a politics like that of the modern era, which has oriented itself from the outset starting from the absolute *a priori* of "life in itself."

This risk is a long-term trend, but it became explosively visible in the "genocidal passion" of the twentieth century. In this regard, the fact that the two authors share the need to conceive of power from a perspective that goes beyond what seems to be the obsession of political philosophy—the face-off between state sovereignty and individuals as bearers of rights—is no coincidence and certainly bears noting. To give priority to the legal doctrine of sovereignty, for Arendt and Foucault, would mean compromising a deep understanding of the experience of power, because power can no longer serve as a hegemonic image of a law that prescribes the limit of what is permitted and what is prohibited. Power is better thought of as *dynamis* and *energeia*, as a play of actions and resistances, as a set of plural relations, which define the role and the temporary identity of the actors only at the time when they are actualized. Hence, a static geometry of power, which stifles its movement in a predictable temporality and a blocked subjectivity, is rejected. This means, at the same time, breaking with a vision of power as a simple tool of an already-given reality in favor of a "performative" concept of power, one that itself produces new realities. Again, I am not denying the differences between the two perspectives, nor is it my intention to suggest that Foucault is any less careful in many respects than Arendt in order to avoid falling back into the meshes of a philosophical theory of power. His analysis seeks precisely to avoid the "simple" conflict between power and domination to which Arendt resorts. But it also seeks, above all, to highlight how the categories that revolve around the concept of state and the juridical theory of sovereignty mask the dense and complicated weave of dynamics between individuals, which involve their bodies and their daily relationships. But all this is well known.

I would, however, reiterate that the modern state paradigm of power is called into question by both authors not solely and primarily because of its theoretical weakness, but stemming from the impact of a concrete experience and how both, each in their own way, develop the force of history as philosophical-political exemplarity. Although this genealogy is well known and recognized with regard to Arendt, it often remains overlooked in relation to Foucault.[18] This is because for both authors, totalitarian domination, which Arendt called "totalitarianism" and Foucault, distrusting the instrumental use made of the term during the Cold War,[19] preferred to call "state racism," is not only a category of politology. It is not an ideal type created by political science, used to record the degree of restriction of freedom in regimes that have abolished pluralism. Rather, it is the historical example of the crystallization of specific relations, of certain circumstances that are structured so as to transform the lives of millions of human beings into an object devoid of meaning. In other words, it is the historical example in which, in the name of life, the new figure of the "absolute victim" made its appearance.[20] This means, then, that the extermination camps, a product of thanatopolitics to which various mechanisms of power gave rise, are the historical experience in which are rooted both Arendt's and Foucault's thought on power.

Given these presuppositions, it is legitimate to ask, however, whether Arendt's idea of radical evil can be ascribed to a so-called biopolitical perspective. In 1951, in concluding *The Origins of Totalitarianism*, she wrote:

When the impossible was made possible it became . . . absolute evil[. . . .] It is inherent in our entire philosophical tradition that we cannot conceive of a "radical evil," and this is true both for Christian theology, which conceded even to the

Devil himself a celestial origin, as well as for Kant, the only philosopher who, in the word he coined for it, at least must have suspected the existence of this evil even though he immediately rationalized it in the concept of a "perverted ill will." Therefore, we actually have nothing to fall back on in order to understand a phenomenon that nevertheless confronts us with its overpowering reality[. . . .] There is only one thing that seems to be discernible: we may say that radical evil has emerged in connection with a system in which all men have become equally superfluous.[21]

"Radical evil" would seem to indicate the surplus—the lack of proportion—that occurred during the extermination. This appears to be confirmed by the answer she gave to Karl Jaspers, who already in December 1946 had reproached her for giving an aura of "satanic greatness" to the Nazi phenomenon just by using the expression radical evil. "But still," she retorted to the teacher who later became a close friend, "there is a difference between a man who sets out to murder his old aunt and people who without considering the economic usefulness of their actions at all [. . .] build factories to produce corpses. Perhaps what is behind it all is only that individual human beings did not kill other individual human beings for human reasons, *but that an organized attempt was made to eradicate the concept of the human being*."[22] When put to the test by Auschwitz, in short, Arendt's conception of radical evil expresses the urgency of giving voice to something much more "limitless" than what the expression signified in Kant.

Just as for Schelling, Nietzsche, Freud, and Heidegger, evil in her opinion cannot be reduced to a will that puts some particular interest before the moral law. The horror of the camps now stands for a genuine ontological crime,[23] one that, in going beyond the threshold of "anything goes," is pushed forward, so to speak, into another place "where anything has become possible." From her correspondence with Jaspers to the exchange of letters with Eric Voegelin,[24] passing through all the essays and articles related to totalitarianism, of course,[25] evil is therefore thought of as something "beyond measure." It is the modern hubris that is revealed in the will to destroy the human being as we have hitherto known it in order to construct a new kind of human nature. The political evil that crossed over the line of comprehensible and punishable crimes went beyond the vices still thought of as "human," such as selfishness, envy, greed, resentment, lust for power, or cowardice. Many of the elements in the diagnosis of absolute and radical evil during these years recall both Heidegger's idea of evil as the devastation and the destructiveness implicit in the desire for omnipotence. This is to say that at this point Arendt is clearly still working within the Dostoevsky paradigm, one that understands evil as the will to infinite power, as an abyssal freedom that turns into hatred for being and for creation, and that therefore devastates, nihilates, and destroys. Her approach to the problem is still strongly marked by the "power of nothingness" to which Heidegger's philosophy had given so much importance.

However, if carefully examined, also from the retrospective light of *The Human Condition* and the manuscripts on Marx,[26] Arendt's explanation for the extermination—and along with it, for evil—becomes considerably more complex, venturing far beyond the schema that the proponents of the "nihilistic theorem" rely on to analyze the deep-rooted interplay between life and power. Read philosophically, the destructive force of total power can be explained only partly through the lens of the abyssal freedom of evil subjects. It finds a powerful *a priori* in the necessity that we have seen to be characteristic of life, understood in the sense of mere biological repetition. The modern metaphysical framework within which are located both theories of race and faith in the dialectical movement of history is in fact provided by the elevation of life itself— of "mere life"—to a supreme value. As clearly expressed in *The Human Condition*, the new absolute of life—which replaces the transcendental sacredness of the Christian eternal life (which had, in its turn, revolutionized the human-world relationship in the classical world[27])—redirects the search for meaning toward the prospect of a new immortality. Individual lives, now subjugated to the new, natural, and undetermined force of *zoe*, are not only dragged into the current of necessity; their individual importance is also sacrificed to the universal. This is the passion— Arendt seems to suggest—that moved the last century, prompting it to devise that series of abstract collective subjects behind which pulses the one and only power: the anonymous power of life. Spirit, Humanity, Race, Class are the many names by which Western culture has expressed its faith in the new, modern idol: the life of the great, organic—but immortal—body of the human species. For Arendt too, then, here the paradox of radical evil is already prefigured: not only an uncontrollable drive toward nothingness but also an insatiable need for life are what produced the horror of the twentieth century. Certainly Arendt viewed the extermination camp as the locus that revealed the conditions of possibility for a political power that can strike at life from all sides, in the sense of directly attacking it in its presumed "bareness," starting from the absolute priority of the value of life. She grasped the link, that is, between a power acting in the name of the necessity of life, "radical evil," and the production of the "absolute victim."

In "Mankind and Terror," written in 1953, Arendt briefly described the process by which individuals are reified, the transformation of "who" into "what": in other words, the construction of the "absolute victim." The *via crucis* toward the Muselmann proceeds through graduated stages of depersonalization. First, the moment of arbitrary arrest, when faith in a so-called legal personality is crushed. This is not so much because the arrest is unfair, but because it bears no relation to the actions or opinions of the person. The next phase is the disintegration of the moral structure. By separating the camps from the rest of the world, the sense of reality is made to waver, while any attempt to sacrifice one's own life by refusing to wait for the final blow is made to seem vain, senseless, and ridiculous. In the final phase we reach the destruction of individuality as such, through prolonged internment in the camp and the institutionalization of torture. The end result is the reduction of human beings to the lowest possible common denominator, namely to a bundle of biological, "identical reactions." "For a totalitarian government to achieve its goal of total control over the governed," she writes, "people have to be deprived not only of their freedom but also of their instincts and drives, which are not programmed to produce identical reactions in all of us but always move different individuals to different acts."[28] No individual life is put to death anymore, no one with a name, with an unmistakable identity, but only a completely indistinguishable and indefinable specimen of a degenerate living species. This, for Arendt, is what remains of Auschwitz. Whenever this individual life is stripped of all its masks, one after the other—from citizenship to affective relationships and emotional spontaneity, to the possibility of choice—it is exposed to the danger of being totally altered, to the point of becoming indistinguishable even as a body, the extreme limit characterizing the mass of camp corpses. From this, we reach the final result: that of a collective, "absolute victim." What remains, then, is the opening to a historical, but limitless, possibility of evil, which continues to threaten us whenever the stages are followed to progressively remove individual human lives, step by step, from their world in order to deliver them up to the necessary, indistinct current of the One Single General Life.[29]

More than twenty years after Arendt's earliest thoughts on the topic, Foucault returned via the notion of biopolitics to investigate the destructive potential of a power that was capable of reducing many individual lives into one single life and that, as perhaps never before in history, succeeded in joining together the many members of a *demos* into the great, united body of the *ethnos*: a population that is identical to itself. Using a more analytical approach, choosing to investigate the disciplines of the new sciences, at first glance it might seem to us that nothing is more distant from the emotional and somewhat metaphysical tone of Arendt's philosophy. However, as early as *The Order of Things*, the theoretical problem that Foucault labored over was not simply that of scientific statements, but that of the implications of an "ontology of life."[30] Or rather, the epistemological but also ontological significance of the rupture that led "life" and the life sciences to take the place of natural history. Along with "work" and "language," "life" is the epistemic *a priori* that upset the classical order of relation between words and things; a kind of meta-concept that not only guided the life sciences but also affected the way that political power works. Whence Foucault's growing interest in the interaction between different forms of scientific knowledge and power, until arriving in the mid-1970s at the theme of biopolitics.

As Deleuze notes,[31] with Foucault's work we now find ourselves in an analysis of concrete *dispositifs* that, at first glance, appear very distant from Arendt's philosophical genealogies of the 1950s. Retraced in Foucault's analysis of "state racism" are the peculiar ways in which the three main vectors of modern politics—sovereignty, disciplinary power, and biopower—are interwoven and mutually determined. Although sovereignty gives rise to an unambiguous vertical relationship, polarized into a subject (ruler), on the one hand, and on the other, an object (the subjugated subject), other types of power will need to be flanked alongside sovereignty in order to give it more dynamism and extensive coverage.

In *The Will to Knowledge*, but even more clearly in the lectures in the collection entitled *"Society Must Be Defended,"* Foucault presents us with the emergence of two other technologies of power alongside sovereignty that "from the eighteenth century onward [. . .] were established at different times and which were superimposed." On the one hand, we have a technical discipline: it produces the individualizing effects centered on the body, manipulating it as the source of forces that requires it to be shaped and molded.

These are the so-called disciplines: multiple practices that operate on the individual through upbringing, schooling, and training. In short, they produce the individual as a docile and disciplined body so as to make it useful to the community and to the relationship of obedience imposed by laws and norms. On the other hand, we have a technology that is centered not on the body but on biological life, "which brings together the mass effects characteristic of a population and which tries to control the series of random events that can occur in a living mass, a technology which tries to predict the probability of those events."[32] Biopower is distinguished from classical state sovereignty because of its encompassing character, which caters to the "productivity" of life, pushing concern about death to its perimeter. In a political system guided by the *a priori* of life, a turning point takes place in Foucault's view when biopower inscribes racism inside the mechanisms of the state: "[Racism] had already been in existence for a very long time," but it was biopower that allowed it to be inscribed within the state mechanisms. "As a result," he explains, "the modern state can scarcely function without becoming involved with racism at some point, within certain limits and subject to certain conditions."[33] It is quite clear that in this context the ideological claims of racism are not under analysis. Far from being a simple expression of mutual hatred between races, and irreducible to a political maneuver that seeks to channel hostilities running through the social body into a mythical adversary, the specificity of modern racism is linked rather to a technique of power: "So racism is bound up with the workings of a State that is obliged to use race, the elimination of races and the purification of the race, to exercise its sovereign power."[34] In the sphere of a power that has taken charge of life, racism is the dispositif that makes it possible to separate what must live from what must die. Through the criterion of the greater or lesser vitality of humans as a whole, power can be exercised by treating a population as a mixture of races; it can divide the species into subgroups. In a word, it can fragment, hierarchize, and establish breaks in the biological continuum that has become its new object: the population. It can also put to work the relationship of war—"if you want to live, the other must die"—in a completely new and "biological" way. Racism makes it possible to say that "'The more inferior species die out, the more abnormal individuals are eliminated, the fewer degenerates there will be in the species as a whole, and the more I—as species rather than individual—can live, the stronger I will be, the more vigorous I will be. I will be able to proliferate'."[35]

This is how death, or rather the act of putting to death, becomes admissible in biopolitics. Killing is not accepted in the name of triumphing over adversaries, of putting an end to a conflict or a war. Death is justified if it aims to eliminate some biological danger, hence, if it is directed at strengthening the species or race: "In a normalizing society, race or racism is the precondition that makes killing acceptable[. . . .] Once the State functions in the biopower mode, racism alone can justify the murderous function of the State."[36]

In Foucault's perspective, Nazism and "the socialist State" delineate the paroxysmal outcome of the mechanisms of biopower that were instituted at the beginning of the eighteenth century. Disciplinary power and biopower: all this permeated and sustained Nazi society to the extreme. "No society," he wrote, "could be more disciplinary or more concerned with providing insurance than that established, or at least planned, by the Nazis[. . . .] But this society in which insurance and reassurance were universal, this universally disciplinary and regulatory society, was also a society which unleashed murderous power, or in other words, the old sovereign right to take life."[37] But now, not only do the top echelons of the state participate in this sovereign power; in a sense, in a limit sense, so does the entire society. The practice of informing granted the power of life and death potentially to anyone. The originality of Nazism lies in having made the two powers completely coincide. Never before had they so completely overlapped: the sovereign power to kill, to the extreme that anyone can kill anyone; and biopower, which cultivates, protects, and organizes life.

There was, in Nazism, a coincidence between a generalized biopower and a dictatorship that was at once absolute and retransmitted throughout the entire social body by this fantastic extension of the right to kill and of exposure to death. We have an absolutely racist State, an absolutely murderous State, and an absolutely suicidal State[. . . .] The three were necessarily superimposed, and the result was of course both "the final solution" [. . .] of the years 1942–1943, and then Telegram 71, in which, in April 1945, Hitler gave the order to destroy the German people's own living conditions. The final solution for the other races, and the absolute suicide of the [German] race. *That is where this mechanism inscribed in the workings of the State leads.*[38]

Nazism is not alone in exemplifying the extreme destructiveness to which the logic of biopolitics can arrive. As remote as the socialist state and socialism in general may appear from the biologistic frenzy of National Socialism, they, too, are "racists." This is the tenor of Foucault's provocation. Racism is not just about doctrinal statements. Rather, it is the discourse that the political power circuit pronounces in order to get itself going; it is what ignites a dispositif of forces that must continue to separate and distinguish, to select and discard in order to keep moving. The logic of purification allows people to be put to death with the rigor and moral neutrality of a scientific experiment. Above all, it allows death to be justified by not calling it by its name, and instead by appealing to the supreme good of life and its maximization. "One thing at least is certain," writes Foucault; "Socialism has made no critique of the theme of biopower, which developed at the end of the eighteenth century and throughout the nineteenth; it has in fact taken it up, developed, reimplanted, and modified it in certain respects."[39] Whether socialism seeks to eliminate the state, or to strengthen it in order to better bring it down, it has never questioned the assumptions of biopower. Above all, in "the socialist State," there is no ethnic racism at work, but an evolutionist racism that distinguishes between the normal and the mentally ill, between revolutionaries and saboteurs, and that in any case, working at full speed to discriminate between those who should die and those who should live, has *organized the total management of life.*[40]

What, then, does this dispositif called "State racism" represent? What theoretical significance does this specific historical configuration hold? As Deleuze recalled, a dispositif is a set, a "tangle" of lines and vectors that, although oriented in different directions, intersect each other according to accidental but not random modalities. The elements or variables in play—knowledge, power, and subjectivity—are mutually intertwined, but also in tension with each other. Which means, leaving behind Deleuze's figuration, that subjects are indeed determined by the power structures peculiar to the particular dispositif, but they do not reproduce them exactly. What we have are relationships between lines of force that, as such, constantly change direction because of the pressures that one exerts on the other and vice versa. It can be said that for Foucault it is in these deviations, in these movements, that the condition of possibility for freedom is located. In his later works, in fact, he arrived at a clear distinction between power and violence, separating them from each other by virtue of the space of freedom that remains, or does not remain, open. What defines a relationship of power is a mode of action that does not act directly and immediately on others by treating them as objects. Instead, it acts on their actions: one action on another action, on existing actions, or on those that may arise, in the present or the future. A relationship of violence acts on the body or on things; it forces, subdues, tortures, destroys, or bars all possibilities. Its opposite pole can only be passivity; and if it comes up against any resistance, it has no other option but to try to minimize it. On the other hand, for it to really be a power relationship, it can only be articulated on the basis of two elements that are indispensable to it: "that [. . .] (the one over whom power is exercised) be thoroughly recognized and maintained to the very end as a person who acts; and that, faced with a relationship of power, a whole field of responses, reactions, results, and possible inventions may open up."[41]

If freedom is the resistance that consists in the deviation of a subject in the reproduction of lines of power, then the particular tangle of the totalitarian dispositif is the configuration that has best succeeded in destroying the possibility of resistance on the part of the subject. State racism is thus a particular constellation in which a specific form of subjugation is produced that extinguishes the very possibility of subjectification, so to speak. It is the scene where interaction is suspended, where power, in short, is transformed from a relationship between actions into domination of direct violence on bodies; and the bodies, the bodies of the victims, are so passive that the perception is that they can be killed without committing a crime. In other words, it is the situation that produces the absolute victim, Levi's Muselmann, Agamben's "bare life," and what "encloses all the evil of our time in one image," which in the context of a biopolitical analysis, can no longer be explained starting from the power of death, but only from the absolute of life.

Beginning with Levinas, continuing with Arendt and Foucault, the path that continental philosophy took after World War II progressively disrupted the assumptions of the Dostoevsky paradigm. Evil, unlike wickedness, is not solely a relationship. It is not only a systemic effect that crystallizes subjects and events, digging a wedge in the continuity of history. It exacerbates its intensity, qualitatively and quantitatively, along with what we might call an ontological rupture, to wit, when the axiological framework changes and life, its energy, its duration, and its productivity become the supreme good. The relationship between evil and power continues to be conceptually modeled on an "anatomy of human destructiveness." However, the context of the nihilistic explanation gets more complicated and is forced to deal with the enigma of human freedom that out of the desire to be infinite seeks death, as well as with the paradox of life that to universalize and erect itself to the height of a supreme value must celebrate the insignificance of an individual's death. What Arendt and Foucault identified, then, could be described as a shift in perspective that leads to different questions on the meaning of evil being posed as soon as the gaze is broken from the hegemonic presence of the perpetrator and his or her freedom to focus instead on the victim and his or her nullification. Evil is no longer viewed as the strategy of a nothing that arrives at the destruction of the entity in its totality, but rather—and this is certainly much clearer in Foucault—the paradoxical outcome of maximizing the power of life. It is a power that reaches its destructive apex when it manages to organize itself into a principle that, elevated into a norm, makes the body of the totality homogeneous. This is in part because the principle is introjected as a moral duty both by the population and by the individual.[42]

Although the more well-trodden of the philosophical genealogies is called into question by thought on biopower, two paths still remain to be closely explored. The first leads us to question the process of subjectification, and in particular of those subjects that are not "evil demons" or "absolute victims," so to speak. I mean those subjects who occupy the so-called gray zone, the intermediate space that unites and separates the two extreme poles of the interaction. This is the most densely populated land, the one most burdened by the roots of evil, but at the same time the one that philosophy has most left unexplored. This territory will be covered in the last part of this book. The second, and more urgent genealogy at this point, requires us to look beyond the deconstruction of the tradition performed by Arendt and search deeper into the microphysics of biopower analyzed by Foucault. The thought on biopolitics that originated with these two writers, even the most recent, leaves us without any answer as to how and why these victims become such as they are. We still have no answer as to which symbolic order, introjected, shared, and transmitted, forms the basis for some bodies to be turned into waste bodies of which we must rid ourselves and make ourselves clean. As anthropologists have always taught us, culture works primarily in the interaction between a biological or anatomical given and an order of norms.

We must therefore investigate the *a prioris* of these constructions that the symbolic force sets up, a force that does not simply structure the individual unconscious but also imposes itself on all those who take part in its system of assumptions.

The Absolute Victim: Biologization or Moralization?

Muselmann, homo sacer, zoe, the chain of synonyms leads us to the image that Levi saw as symbolizing all the evil of the century. The passive pole in the power relationship is what draws our attention now. From George Orwell[43] to Wolfgang Sofsky,[44] from Emmanuel Levinas to Giorgio Agamben, literature, philosophy, and the historical disciplines have focused their eye more and more explicitly on the figure of the defenseless victim. As a result, the field of investigation has shifted from the "pleasure of cruelty" to the pain of the victim, someone reduced to total passivity. Or, to put it better, the focus has shifted toward the final outcome of the act of violence, which can no longer be considered a relationship of power, precisely because one of the two subjects is being extinguished *qua* subject. It would seem that the truth about evil lies much more in the suffering from it than in the perpetrating of it.

What we have here is undoubtedly a different schema of intelligibility regarding political evil, a cluster of concepts that run the gambit from a purely subjective idea of evil—hence, aimed at grasping the actor's evil attitude and intention—to a notion that we might call the "bureaucratization of evil."[45] Indeed, the task is to explain a twofold process of routinization: that of the killing, performed on a victim who has been made anonymous and one in a series; and that of the perpetrator, no longer a demon thirsting for blood and motivated by a desire for nothingness, but simply a cog in a machine. Every genocidal system is said to follow the same script: a process that starts from a situation of "de-individualization" and "moral disengagement," culminating in all-out "dehumanization." It begins with restricting freedom, proceeds to the uprooting of individuals from the flow of their meaningful relationships, and then freezes them into a reifying identity. Perceiving one part of the population as subhuman, inhuman, impure, and contagious thus facilitates the progressive slide of individuals toward massacre. This perception is thought to perform an adaptive function of sorts: on the one hand, it serves to suspend the emotional reaction of the perpetrators; and on the other, it legitimates the massacre of bodies *en masse* as a regretful but necessary practice.

In other words, for the bodies of the victims to be destroyed *en masse*—this is the starting assumption—not only must they be perceived as foreign and harmful, in the eyes of the perpetrators they must above all be devoid of any human meaning: they must be deprived of their subjectivity. As the experts on genocide agree, this is how one goes about creating "bare life"[46]: this is a life that can be killed without the killers perceiving that they are committing a murder and, thanks to the new axiological and epistemological framework—that of Life—they can be allowed to die in order to "make live." Also, even though the many historians who have studied the extermination and the philosophers who have occupied themselves with the advent of the biopolitical may employ different terminologies and methodologies, they all agree in viewing the emergence of the new biological and medical sciences during the course of the nineteenth century as having facilitated this operation. Evolutionist theories, in particular, are viewed as having allowed racial theories to inscribe conflicts into the context of a naturalization of history and politics, making it possible to conceive and implement the annihilation of entire categories of people in the guise of medical prophylaxis or disinfestation. Violent action would no longer be perceived as a transgression because it would be reinscribed in a friend-enemy relationship of this sort: there is a subject who preserves his or her human identity and there is a victim who, having been stripped of his or her subjecthood, is perceived *solely* as the bearer of biological life, devoid of human significance. This enables *the shutting down* of the genocidal agent's *sense of morality*.

Without doubt, the new life sciences provided innumerable opportunities for the spurious "science of race" to be used as a tool for desubjectivizing the victim: the storehouse of new images and neologisms that they made available is one example. As we know well, not only were the Jews figured as parasites, the entire history of the twentieth century teemed with microorganisms that had to be disposed of.[47] The microbiological lexicon spared no one: fantasies were nurtured about cleansing counterrevolutionary parasites who threatened the salvation of the Russian Revolution just as they were about the menacing Kosovar bacilli who undermined the physical integrity of the heroic people of Serbia. The reduction of the other to the status of animal, which accompanied the characterization of the enemy, was bolstered by an entire science with its new domains and new vocabulary, especially when the enemy needed to be placed outside an ordinary context of judgment.

The political imagination has always employed an assorted bestiary to represent anyone who lies outside the law of the polis or is antagonistic. Consider the image that Plato made classic: the tyrant who nurtures an irrepressible, "lawless wild-beast nature." The tyrant fosters and cultivates the "wild beast" that dwells in every man, turning it into a "multitudinous, many-headed monster."[48] The freedom of the tyrant is absolute, making it comparable to godly freedom, but its lack of restraint—its leonine ferocity and elementary, animal compulsiveness—drags him down to the level of the beast. This is the same as what Aristotle observed about those who make themselves similar to beasts or gods by living outside the polis, the political community.

The idea we glimpse here is that of an almost "demonic" overstepping of human limits, in which the confines of the divine and the bestial begin to mingle. It expresses the same tension toward a "beyond" suspended between superhumanity and savagery that we also recognize, albeit in radically different contexts, in the Hobbesian appeal to the majestic grandeur of the Leviathan, and in what made Machiavelli so adept at recasting the foxes and the lions that populate the works of the ancients, from Cicero to Plutarch.

These allusions are simply meant to stress that these figures of wild beasts and cunning beings tended for the most part to shift the human image into a region "beyond the human," *in a dizzying overstepping of limits that went as far as the savage and the horrible, but never so far as the repellent and the abject.* These images almost always portrayed those who stood at the top of the political relationship, at the active pole of those who hold power: sovereigns, tyrants, and commanders. However, at the same time, there was another current of animalization running through the texts in this tradition that was very often used to represent those at the bottom, those who rebel: the animal image emphasizes their primitive instinct, their "low," deficient being; it is a current that projects human beings "below" the human. In short, face-to-face or side-by-side with the image of a mighty, fearsome wildness, there coexisted what we might describe as the simply zoological figure of animal obtuseness. What appears to be conveyed in these two animalistic representations is *a bi-directional movement of the human being's animal possibilities*: on the one hand, a thrust that propels us beyond the human; on the other, a trajectory that leads us beneath the law of man. To represent the warping of full humanity we have, on the one side, the image of the animal that we might dub "hyper-human," like a powerful, wild beast that is almost heroic and virtuous. On the other, we have an image that highlights the deficient status of the animal and its abysmal inferiority compared to the human. This latter assumption, that of the ontological inferiority of the animal, is what has legitimated the unanimous, constant dominion of humans over beasts since the time of the Old Testament. And it is based on this assumption that the sacrifice and the killing of animals have never been considered immoral in Western culture and others.

Now, this second bias, resumed in the figure of the animal as a lowly being, is what continued to occupy increasingly more space in the political imaginary of late modernity. Reinterpreted and reinforced by the new scientific discourses of medicine, biology, criminology, and psychopathology, the representation of the enemy as a fierce, savage, barbarian faded away, gradually replaced by the baseness of animalization. According to Foucault's reconstruction, these are the sciences that accompanied the birth of what is now referred to as biopolitics. The figures of vile animals continued to abound in a growing distance from the human until arriving at the last rungs, occupied by parasites and pathogens. This became the preferred storehouse for racist discourse to draw from, not only or primarily for its metaphors but especially for its "literal" references. Racial theory, especially in its evolutionist versions, functioned as an effective vehicle for the "naturalization" and "biologization" of the object of power, thus carrying out a direct political and discriminatory functionalization of the biological given. It took form as the theoretical justification for a practice that created hierarchies and differentiated beings, including and excluding them from the range of the human, while at the same time lending coherence and solidity to society as a whole.

The representation of conflict expressed in racial terms called into play fewer and fewer lions, tigers, and wolves while depicting more and more rats, fleas, and lice, the killing of which was perceived as a simple practice of hygiene and healing. In other terms, whereas the former meaning of animalization implied passions, involvement, and possibly a sense of transgression, the latter encouraged detachment, coldness, and *especially moral indifference*. Persecution could thus be organized as a planned, systematic undertaking for healing the body politic. The biologistic formulation in which the dehumanization of the future victims was phrased numbed perception of the crimes and led to the separation between healthy blood and infected blood being represented as routine work, to be carried out in the name of life—for its enhancement and perpetuation. In this change of context, the word "extermination," and the function of the extermination as a practice in general, thus changed meaning, by deriving it from a definition of the enemy that had been shifted from one lexical and epistemic domain to another.[49] Anti-Jewish racism certainly lends itself more than any other type to providing examples of this shift. From this perspective, racial theory melded perfectly with the age-old theme of the Jewish parasite, thus in the first instance becoming an antisemitic doctrine. In the tangle of positivism and racism wound tightly together by the force of the new disciplines—from medicine to experimental microbiology, and from anthropology to eugenics—the racist approach received a sort of noble, scientific investiture. It was thus able to present its own strategies of power as medical planning. In this medical-scientific context, the imaginary was populated by security needs and fantasies of purification. However, outside of it, according to most post-Foucauldian historical interpreters and philosophers, genocide remained unrepresentable and unfeasible.

This is the perspective adopted by studies on the role that doctors and biomedical research played in the Third Reich.[50] At the heart of the National Socialist ideology, there apparently lay the conviction that the German nation, as a *real* political body, was suffering from a disease caused by a potentially deadly infection—triggered by infectious agents that, to start with, were identifiable with the Jewish microorganism. Fascinated by the power of these corporeal fantasies, Hitler and his followers conceived their mission as a sequence of therapeutic phases. After an accurate, but ruthless, diagnosis of the disease, they had to act according to the most rigorous, scientific logic of cause and effect, without shirking the weight of their responsibility for the treatment.

At various points in his speeches and writings, the Führer used the idea of Germany as a real organic body. Dazzled by the power of the metaphor, he continually returned to the relationship between cell and body: it was an inextricable bond that charged every cell with the responsibility for the health of the whole. We know how powerful this appeal was: rather than treating individual patients, doctors now felt called on to care for the entire German people; their mission was to become "biological soldiers" serving "the great idea of the National Socialist biological state structure."[51] The growing success of medical and biological sciences, whose discoveries in the last decades of the nineteenth century led to the isolation of many disease-carrying microorganisms, prompted the Nazi imaginary to literalize the metaphor of Germany as a political body. Hitler thus became celebrated as the "Great Physician" of the German nation, the "Robert Koch" of politics.[52] This makes sense of what Rudolf Hess proclaimed about National Socialism in a mass gathering in 1934, when he described it as nothing more than "applied biology."[53]

In a word, Germany expressed its power of death, its absolute thanatopolitics, by fully assuming the identity of a biocracy: the power of life. The result of this contamination of politics and social science by the medical and scientific discourse was a specific political-military therapy.[54] The connection between the therapeutic proclamations in the name of enhancing life and the drift into thanatopolitics was therefore not a contradiction, but rather a deep bond.

The two-thousand-year-old biological metaphors, which the political lexicon had always co-opted, were freed from any conceptual mediation and literalized to the point of tearing down any divisions between biology and politics; more specifically, according to some interpreters, this total biopower was marked by a specific specialization of medicine and biology, that of immunology. According to Richard Koenigsberg,[55] Hitler and his men expected Germany to conform to the law of the immune system, and it did so. In the same way any other organism singled out and recognized cells foreign to it and automatically destroyed them, so did the German body politic.

The view that the unprecedented destructiveness of the Nazi genocide is linked to this sort of immunological strategy is also the guiding force behind Roberto Esposito's interpretation. In his previously mentioned *Bios*, the analogy between the Nazi regime and the immune system occupies center-stage in his philosophical reading of the historical phenomenon. Following a hermeneutic paradigm expertly put to the test in previous works,[56] he believes that the category of "immunization" clarifies the link left unresolved in Foucault's work between biopower and its drift into thanatopolitics in the nineteenth century. The logic inherent in the functioning of the immune system would explain the perverse, but deep, association between the protection of life—a genuine *"a priori* of Nazi politics"—and the simultaneous negation and destruction of life. The impressive epidemiological repertoire used by the ideologues and functionaries of the Third Reich to depict their enemies and victims displaced their aggression into the sphere of defensive action needed for survival. In this shifted context, death was therefore understood not as the negation of life but as the immunological strategy required to expunge the infected part. In this frantic process of literalizing the medical metaphor, autoimmune disease is the figure that would explain the double tie between obsession for life and health on the one hand, and continuous extermination on the other. No longer content with attacking and annihilating the supposed "bacilli," "bacteria," "viruses," and "microbes," the immune system of the great body of Germany began to perceive a large part of its own organs as a threat as well. For Esposito, sterilization, "the anticipatory suppression of birth," and the elimination of those who threatened the life of Germany are to be understood as dispositifs of radical immunization.

But what is the premise founding this biopolitical reading of the relationship between life and death in Nazi politics? The texts that Esposito analyzes convince him that Nazism is not, and can never be, a fully developed philosophy, *because it is already a fully developed biology.*[57] In other words, the Nazi regime's "vitalistic" vision of the world alongside its biopolitical practices of putting to death mark a sharp break with both modernity and the philosophical tradition. Unlike the aberrations of "real socialism," into which the Nazi crimes are usually assimilated, the thanatopolitics of the Third Reich break with our civilization. If it is still possible to say that communism "realizes"—however perversely—some of the currents of our tradition, the same cannot be said for Nazism. In this view, Nazi politics not only used the biomedical studies of the time for rhetorical and legitimizing purposes, it entirely identified with them, turning itself into a full-fledged biocracy. It was a novel form of power that blew away the old political and ethical criteria.

However, is this way of viewing extreme biologization not a way of leading us back, although via a different route, to the idea of political evil as a suspension or destruction of all moral criteria? Even if this is not Esposito's intention, do we not run the risk of yielding to simplifying theorems that insist on discontinuity, and thus on evil as breaks in the continuous duration of goodness? Is what we have here really a slippage of discursive regimes and epistemic thresholds that sweep aside or even crush and negate the centuries-old conceptions of evil in one and the same movement? If this were the case, Nazi thanatopolitics would be the supreme emblem of political evil—partly accountable to a metamorphosis of the very idea of evil—and its active agents would be the bearers of this new conception. According to this view, a vitalist barbarism thus prevailed, burying the traditional oppositions in a sort of grotesque Nietzschean overcoming of metaphysics and morality. Based on the new *a priori* provided by the life sciences, this view portrays evil as being reduced entirely to disease, to the pathological dimension that threatens and endangers the health of the body. But in this way, by viewing the extermination as something lying beyond all moralities, does the biopolitical theory not run the risk of lending a hand to the "nihilistic" stance?

This equivalence between horror and abandonment of morality was certainly not established solely by common sense. A large number of highly rigorous studies have understood Nazism as a disinhibited, brazen pursuit of immorality—giving perhaps too much credit to some of Hitler's quotes, according to which we should free ourselves forever of that absurd "Jewish invention" of the "conscience." The Shoah has been thought of as the supreme crime, not only because of the results and methods of operation, but also because of its desire to revolutionize the moral conscience of Europe. From this argument it follows that if evil resulted from a betrayal of values, then to walk away from evil and prevent its return, all we need to do is restore these values.

I am not saying that biopolitical, post-Foucauldian readings are direct mouthpieces for this position. However, I would like to emphasize that, unlike Foucault's last works, as we shall see, they overlook strong continuities visible in the background of the turning point marked by Nazi ideology. I truly think that the Third Reich's vision of the world, at least for some of its most influential exponents, should be examined as a morality, indeed, as a hypermorality—primarily because I believe that the "virtuous" intentions of the many perpetrators need to be taken seriously, not just viewed as rhetorical, cynical strategies. Many actors or protagonists of the scene of evil perceived themselves as the executors of a supreme moral law, which prompted them to act in conformity with that imperative. The famous speech Heinrich Himmler gave to the heads of the SS on October 4, 1943, in Posen (Poznan), exhorting them to be loyal to the universal, is emblematic.[58] He invited them to stop placing a particular violation before their ethical duty: "The extermination of the Jewish people" is a duty. In the face of this duty, "along they all come, all the 80 million upright Germans, and each one has his decent Jew." It is not as if Himmler does not understand the unconscious urge of his listeners to be exempted from this tough task. He knows what it means to look on "when a hundred bodies lie together, when there are five hundred, or when there are a thousand." But this is where "our virtue" lies: to have observed all this and remained decent ("anständig geblieben zu sein"). "We have the moral duty" ("wir haben die Pflicht") to the German people, "to kill this people who would kill us," but "we don't want [. . .] to get sick and die from the same bacillus that we have exterminated." Himmler is proud to say that "our conscience," our soul, our interiority, have remained intact: "And we have suffered no defect within us, in our soul, or in our character" ("Und wir haben keinen Schaden in unserem Innern, in unserer Seele, in unserem Charakter daran genommen").

As much as National Socialism was applied biology, as much as it ultimately developed into a biocracy, it nevertheless remained powerfully marked by moral choices. What led to mass murder was not the neutrality of value relativism typical of the scientistic worldview; rather, it was a hypermoral vision of the world, strongly characterized, like all hypermoralities, by the fundamental distinction between good and evil. Certainly, *dehumanization*—which operates through medicalization and animalization—is an effective hermeneutic lens for understanding mass exterminations. But the emphasis placed on the legitimizing and anesthetizing role played *by the new life sciences* in regard to racism leads to genocide—especially the Nazi genocide—being located in a place "beyond good and evil" that suspended the basic assumptions of our cultural tradition. What I believe instead, as I shall argue, is that as much as the racial theories were marked by the "novelty" of the biological and medical sciences, they continued to powerfully convey a sense of the ancient moral distinctions tied to the traditional ontological categories. In fact, far from asserting, as we often read, that in racist discourse the body of the future extermination victim is emptied of human and moral meaning, I believe that on the contrary we should say that the future victim's body is "saturated" with meaning—both human and moral—although the meaning of these terms needs to be clearly specified.

How then are we to interpret the obsession for enhancing life? Could it be that the insistence on purity that is so easily formulated in the health versus disease opposition has always had to do with a dualistic perception whose sway, in reality, was never broken?[59] It is a dualism that ultimately responds to the need to separate life from death, identifying life with goodness and death with evil—a dualism that has probably never been defeated, even when the theologians and philosophers believed they had overcome it through the idea of *privatio boni*, the ontological deficiency, or with the justification provided by theodicies. Saying that death—in other words, evil—does not exist, or that it is mere appearance, has never sufficed to allow life—the good—to eternally *be*. This, I believe, is why dualism is always quick to make a comeback.

In the racist biocracy, too, more than ever perhaps, the traditional concepts of evil—the dualistic conception and the idea of evil as appearance—continued to reign, savagely pitting against each other the absolute power of life and the disintegrating power of death. This opposition between life and death, whose content and contexts have changed over the course of history, has nevertheless always continued to function according to the structural schema of the struggle between good and evil. Evil must be fought in order for the good to triumph; death must be defeated so that life can be perpetuated. Thus the antithesis between health and disease, as the fundamental opposition between human and nonhuman, must be conceived along the fundamental lines that have traced the difference between good and evil. Far from achieving the "beyond good and evil" to which certain unilateral readers of Nietzsche aspired, the return to life, to nature, and to biological laws was promptly reworked into an axiological alternative, in which good and evil returned to their rigid normative positions.

From this perspective, certain tropes of racist discourse prove to be choice places for deciphering the interweaving between the new scientific lexicon, imprinted by the rationality of the medical and biological sciences, and the eternal structure of the moral dichotomy. This supports the fact that antisemitism and Nazi racism in general are not simply a perversion of Darwinian biologism. Rather, they are nurtured by much older cultural legacies that are profoundly rooted in our tradition of thought. Even during that dark night when there supposedly reigned a nihilistic absence of values, the eternal *a priori* of all antitheses continued to function in the cultural storehouse: the omnipresent separation between life and death, to-gether with the fixed premise behind the great denial asserting that death is nothing but an illusory appearance. The oppositional machine present in every thought on evil has thus remained lodged in the very heart of mod-ern and late-modern biopower.

Perhaps we need to take another look, then, at the division between two distinct types of antisemitism proposed by an attentive, intelligent, and remarkably prescient reader like Eric Voegelin. In his *Race and State*, published in the spring of 1933 and withdrawn from circulation a few months later,[60] the Austrian philosopher stated that starting from Ernest Renan there descend two opposing "ideas of Judaism."[61] The first, says Voegelin, has an exclusively spiritual meaning, the example being Renan's antithesis between Aryan and Jew—a sort of psychological type that does not have the devastating consequence of physical, racial determinism. The second type is designed to classify and disqualify the "Jewish race" by as-similating the body of Jews to an animal breed, based on zoological crite-ria. Voegelin understands the simultaneity of the two directions but sees them as two parallel paths that never meet up. What remains unseen is the deadly mixture that can explode when the two registers intersect. In many respects, Voegelin "spares" "psychological and spiritual Judaism," not so much because he was too early to see the pernicious effects of the inter-weaving between the "spiritual" and the "animal," but because the sepa-ration is in a certain sense essential to his own convictions. If evil occurs when the opening toward transcendence is blocked, as he believes, then biology and the natural sciences—along with the methods that they intro-duce—must be considered responsible for the disaster. In other words, he too is unwilling to recognize that the antisemitism arising out of Nazism was not simply a degeneration or depravation of biologism. He does not want to admit that there are much older, inherited cultural forces at work; and that, therefore, in a much more problematic fashion for Westerners, *depravation lies at the core of our tradition.*

Parasites, Souls, and Demons

"Watch out! This is the world enemy, the destroyer of civilizations, the parasite that insinuates itself into nations, the offspring of chaos, the incarnation of evil, the demon of decadence who has appeared."[62] This speech given by Joseph Goebbels in 1937, at a party rally in Nuremberg, provides a perfect example of the overlapping of these two registers. The Jew is made to play the role of the hidden manipulator, concerned only for personal gain, while the Aryan is portrayed as someone intent solely on the common good. The Jew is materialistic and exploitative, while the Nordic type is spiritual and generous, and so on, following a script according to which each and every positive aspect of German identity corresponds to a negative Jewish characteristic that needs to be counteracted and combated.

Those represented as Jews are ghosts who change from period to period, but in medieval Christianity they were branded with a dualistic mark that continued to act as an ordering principle for differentiating between the good Christian and the dangerous Jew. It was Christianity that inextricably linked the Jew to the figure of the devil, passing on to subsequent history the dichotomous structure that shaped the antithesis between Jew and non-Jew. The Jew is the Antichrist, the plague, the scourge, the locust, the vampire—in short, one of the incarnations of the principle of evil.[63] As such, the *res publica christiana* must be prepared to respond appropriately so as to preserve the good that it safeguards.

The theme of the parasite is one of the most interesting threads to follow in the interweaving between a theological and metaphysical concept of evil and its reshaping into a naturalistic, zoological, and biological concept. Without the slightest pretense of reconstructing an exhaustive, complete picture of the topic, in the next section this thread is pursued through a few texts that make up what could be called the antisemitic tradition. The semantics of the term "parasite," more than any other word, show us that racism is a field crisscrossed by vectors with various meanings, coming from several directions. Antisemitic racism, in particular, because of the considerable literature available on the topic, offers the clearest, biggest wealth of materials in support. As shown in the brief quote from Goebbels' speech, the figure of the parasite welds together linguistic elements drawn from different, distant spheres of the real world.

It seems that in Athens, *parasitos*—from the union of *para* and *sito*, someone who eats nearby—was the name given to people employed to provide religious and civil services who benefited from dividing up the remains of the sacrificial victims or from levying taxes on meat and fish. That is why with the creation of Epicharmus, in the fifth century BCE, the parasite became a comic character representing a person with no particular talents who perfects his abilities to procure free food for himself. In the sixteenth century, thanks to the recovery of the classical sources, the word entered along with its derogatory character into the lexicon of European languages and became synonymous with a contemptible human type who lives at other people's expense. The German term *Schmarotzer* indicates the dual meaning that it would later bear: it is the equivalent of the English "sponger" and the Italian *scroccone*, with a morally negative connotation, but it also denotes a parasite understood in the biological sense, making its entrance into the natural sciences, starting in the eighteenth century, first in botany and then in animal biology. The parasite is an example of the phenomenon in biology that takes the name of symbiosis, allowing a constant relationship to be established between two organisms from different species. A parasitical relationship is one in which the relation is advantageous for one of the two symbionts—the parasite, of course—and harmful to the other, who in technical terms is known as the host. The term *parasite* therefore designates an organism that lives at the expense of an organism from another species, establishing itself on the outside of its host (ectoparasite), or inside (endoparasite). In any case, the parasite is an organism that lives by feeding off its host, thereby causing harm; but unlike what happens in the relationship between a predator and its prey, which brings about immediate death, the damage is invisible and delayed. This brings us to the last phase of animalization through "deficiency" that we spoke about earlier, with references to clearly demarcated natural realms populated by viruses, bacteria, mosquitoes, lice, and ticks as well as weeds and fungi. Their description, however, is never neutral and detached, and carries connotations of a dirty, ugly, dejected world. In short, in this realm of organisms killing is no more than an act of defense necessary for the health and survival of the "host." This is why parasite, more than any other term, lent itself to this dual scientific and moral meaning that was eventually put into play for describing the enemy.

The term gives voice better than any other to the fear of *Verjudung*, the specter of Judaization that haunted the German imagination, both as a specter of omnipotent political and economic dominion and a fear of mental and cultural "contagion."[64] When the emphasis that Romanticism put on the "organic" was united with metaphors taken from the natural sciences, starting as early as the late eighteenth century, the figure of the *Volkskörper*—often understood by the conservative parties as "racial body"—found a perfect correlate in the image of poisonous penetration. In the mixture of *völkisch* (folkish) ideology, social Darwinism, eugenicism, and "Nordic racism" that typified Germany at the beginning of the twentieth century, allusions to the parasite were something everybody could agree on. Biologists, medical doctors, eugenicists, anthropologists, an excited and frightened middle class, rabble rousers—a large, variegated array of Germans—were finally able to give a name, function, and face to the secret, corrosive power held, in their eyes, by the Jews. It was a parasite that was intent on destroying the body of the race by means of Bolshevism, capitalism, or intellectualism, as circumstances dictated; in any case, the Jew was eating away at the integrity of the German *Volkskörper*.

The hatred toward those who suck blood, going back to the medieval blood libel fantasies, was redoubled by contempt and resentment for those who were believed to exploit the host nation. The Jew became responsible for the disasters caused by industrialization, modernization, and capitalism[65]; he was the negative pole in the opposition between *Kultur* and *Zivilisation*, between *Gemeinschaft* and *Gesellschaft*, that sparked European antimodernism.[66] From Heinrich von Treitschke's heroic nationalism[67] to the provocative brilliance of Otto Weininger,[68] from the sociology of Ferdinand Tönnies to the economics of Werner Sombart, passing through the social philosophy of the brilliant Georg Simmel,[69] even the respectable face of the German intelligentsia launched the culture of the twentieth century with the well-known opposition between the community spirit of the Germans versus the "disintegrative" power of the uprooted Jews, the *bodenlos*. It was an opposition that would perpetuate itself in a long series of dichotomies, at whose head the adversaries now loomed starkly in battle, face to face: the *Judentum* versus the *Deutschtum*. This is the dichotomous vision that tied the Jew to economic, political, and intellectual abstraction and decadence, presenting the Jewish people as a corrosive force eating away at the authentic and the concrete, with the capacity to drag everything toward nothingness.

Toward the end of the nineteenth century, the French repertoire provided by the likes of Alphonse Toussenel and Édouard Drumont passed into German hands.[70] Out of the reprehensible name "Jew"—already developed as a concept—they were able to shape a veritable category of the spirit, embodied by the figure of the parasite, which became the vehicle for an exterminatory racism. There was Wilhelm Marr, the inventor of the successful neologism "antisemitism"[71]; and Eugen Carl Dühring's *The Jewish Question: A Racial Moral and Cultural Question with a World-historical Answer*, published in 1881, the founding text of the antisemitic gospel.[72] In this book, Dühring is quite confident in stating that because Jews are parasites, they act as a marker in signaling a society's state of corruption. The Jew makes his appearance whenever the fabric of a community begins to unravel: this is the situation that allows his nature to be best expressed, bringing the work of disintegration to completion. These are the same outlooks we find in the highly influential manual of antisemitism published for the first time a few years later by Theodor Fritsch.[73] Statistics in hand, Fritsch reluctantly unveils the slow, inexorable penetration of Jews into the German body, through a detailed account of Jews employed in all the most important positions, from politics to entertainment, from the economy to the media, and from publishing to academia. An apparently less resentful form of antisemitism, like that of the orientalist Paul de Lagarde,[74] also testifies to the fruition of a long series of assimilations. In this work, the Jew is described as a trichina, a worm that works its way into the gut and from there incysts itself, propagating to the muscles and throughout the entire body. As parasites, the Jewish foreigners who invade every European state are the carriers of decadence. There can be no compromise with "worms and parasites"; their nature can never be transformed through education.[75] They must be exterminated and annihilated as soon as possible.

Even though its author never embraced National Socialism, and indeed was opposed by the regime, one of the most influential books in twentieth-century Germany in contributing to the image of the Jew as the "corrosive creature" par excellence was Otto Spengler's *The Decline of the West* of 1923, especially the chapter on "Problems of the Arabian Culture."[76] Under the rubric of "Historical Pseudomorphoses," the Jewish civilization is presented as an exemplary case of "foreign and ancient" civilizations that encumber other, more vital civilizations—to the point of suffocating them and stopping them from reaching self-awareness.[77] All the elements of parasitism are included: the parasitic organism that carries the host organism toward a slow death, impeding it from expressing its essence and manifesting its fully developed form. Judaism, a part of the Arabian culture, is a nation without nation. And even though Jerusalem is recognized as a sacred place, it is neither the fatherland nor the spiritual center of Jewishness. The dispersion of the Jewish people does not originate, therefore, from the destruction of the Temple, but from its being a collective form of life without roots and without a land. Its ideal form of nation has always been restricted to the synagogue: a "pure abstract assembly," emptied of concrete experiences, which has led to the progressive disintegration of all feeling of lineage. In short, it is an abstract, empty spirituality that reveals the "corrosive nature" of the Jews, who are carriers of toxic cynicism and a nomadic way of life. Because of these characteristics, and in spite of any good intentions they are shown, they are destined to be a foreign body in the life of other nations.

These are the commonplaces that we find in some of the works by elite German intellectuals at the beginning of the century. They combine the image of the parasite with the idea of a Jewish race without any of its own creativity, which can only exist by exploiting other races and other host nations (*Die Wirtsvölker*). A sponger, bloodsucker, exploiter of other people's values, an enemy of work, a lover of financial returns, and a moneylender: anticapitalistic obsessions are melded with counterrevolutionary fantasies, solidifying the new figure of social and political evil in the unproductive and harmful figure of the Jew.[78]

This is the weave of evil characteristics that typify Hitler's idea of the Jew, listed by Eberhard Jäckel in a famous book from the late 1960s. The Jew "is a maggot in a rotting corpse; he is a plague worse than the Black Death of former times; a germ carrier of the worst sort; mankind's eternal germ of disunion; the drone which insinuates its way into the rest of mankind; the spider that slowly sucks the people's blood out of its pores; the pack of rats fighting bloodily among themselves; the parasite in the body of other peoples; the typical parasite; a sponger who, like a harmful bacillus, continues to spread; the eternal bloodsucker; the peoples' parasite; the peoples' vampire."[79]

In effect, not one of the commonplaces from the long history of antisemitism is omitted from *Mein Kampf*. If in the eyes of the world the Jew appears as a bearer of culture, this is a good that he plundered from other peoples.[80] He absorbs foreign cultures and reproduces them, which is how he corrupts them. He is an artist of metamorphoses; indeed, he has succeeded at the greatest of hoaxes, passing himself off as German. And with the German language he continues "to think his Jewish thoughts." "The dangerous mistake" left in circulation by "anti-Jewish science"—which Hitler wants to correct and refine—is the identification of the Jew as a nomad. The fact that Jews do not have their own land and their own culture should not suggest that they are nomadic. In fact, nomads live from the yield of their own labor, and if they change their location it is only because the territory where they have settled is infertile. The idea that people should live off their own work and from toiling on the land is a mentality entirely unknown to the Jews. Therefore, concludes Hitler, the Jew is not a nomad but simply "a parasite in the body of other nations." As such, he is perpetually in search of a feeding ground to nourish his race: "a sponger, who like a noxious bacillus keeps spreading as soon as a favorable medium invites him." But wherever he manages to penetrate, he brings on the death of his host.[81] Through pandering and money, the Jew has insinuated himself into places that he had been expelled from: "No persecution can deter him from his type of human exploitation."[82] His most powerful weapon is deceit, and the lie he has most fruitfully exploited is that he is part of a religious community. In reality, Jewish doctrine is devoid of faith, serving only to reinforce his blood—his racial community.

Here the Jew is once again depicted as the standard bearer of nothingness: he believes in nothing, and sets his sights on nothing positive. All he wants, as he worms his way into the nerve ganglia of the German people, is to drag them down to destruction. And if the masses seek to defeat this "scourge of God" after having historically experienced this calamity of nature, then they act purely in self-defense. In short, we must reverse the decline that the German princes also had a hand in creating: forever in need of more money, "they made a pact with the devil and landed in hell."[83] If this does not happen, if a stop is not put to the racial desecration of the Jews, who intentionally infect the blood of their host, it will be the end of the German people. The only consolation is that, in line with the logic of a parasitic existence, the parasite will die along with its host: "After the death of his victim, the vampire sooner or later dies too."[84]

Although it is true that the term *parasite* undergoes an even more "naturalistic" transformation in Hitler's writing compared to how it was used in previous antisemitism, we must not forget the conceptual toolkit that accompanies and overlaps this "biologization." The eye of the naturalist always sees through the lens of the moralist. Take, for example, the infamous chapter 11, "Nation and Race": the classification of an assorted bestiary, including foxes, geese, rats, horses, and so on, actually conceals a deadly campaign of contempt for the lower species, who are "guilty" of trying to undermine the purity of the superior races. On the one hand, Hitler uses the argument of autoregulation in nature, playing at a sort of Nietzschean innocence of becoming that only celebrates the strength of the strong; on the other hand, here we find him moralizing what nature has produced in history. The lowering of the Aryan race, its "physical and intellectual regression" beginning with a slow but steady contagion, is the supreme misdeed, tantamount to a "sin against the will of the eternal creator," a "struggle with the principles to which he himself owes his existence as a man."[85] In other words, in the midst of a massive hodgepodge of plans, making genetics overlap with history, naturalness is replaced by sin: the opposing value system—*the dualism between good and evil*—*comes to life once again, in one of its most powerful forms.* Although Hitler claims that he despises the current morality, composed of stupid do-gooderisms, in reality good and evil polarize both a bestiary that is presented as a simple naturalistic observation and a historic process that is presented as obeying natural necessity. His moral amoralism—in a simplified, moronic Nietzscheanism—reaches a Manichean apotheosis in the final struggle between the Jew and the Aryan. The former "destroys the fundamental basis of all civilization," not unlike Dostoevsky's demons who experience their absolute freedom by dragging the world down with them into nothingness. Everything in *Mein Kampf* points to the demonic nature of the Jew. The Jew not only destroys the German race, economy, and political life "with satanic joy in his face," he also torpedoes moral values. "Culturally he contaminates art, literature, the theater, makes a mockery of natural feeling"; he overturns ideals of beauty, dignity, and nobility. From a religious point of view, he mocks all religions. And like all genuine nihilists, he represents ethics and morality as "outmoded."[86]

What to say then, from an ethical and philosophical point of view, about the book that has been held up as emblematic of political evil in the West? Perhaps it helps us to understand that the *evil* embodied by racism *was not committed because good and evil had been surpassed.* It did not occur because nihilism—which presupposes tearing down the barriers between good and evil—had succeeded in its demonic plan. Nor did it take place because (as a still deep-seated theory would have it, from André Glucksmann to Pope Benedict XVI) nihilism bore fruit and reached its destructive apex thanks to the lack of moral judgment in a positive science that only posed questions about health and disease, or about what is useful and what is harmful. If it is true—as the promoters of genocide as a hygienic act of disinfestation argue—that zoological and biological metaphors were made literal, their naturalistic innocence was immediately tainted by guilt. In other words, these naturalistic metaphors were projected onto a moral universe so powerful that the fight of good against evil stopped at nothing.

In my opinion, this is the aspect overshadowed today by the interpretation of political evil in terms of biopower. If biopolitics transformed into thanatopolitics, if political evil was truly absolute, it is also because the historical scene was first and foremost a battlefield on which the fight of good against evil was waged with unparalleled tenacity—with the intent of saving life from the looming threat of death's nihilistic drift. It was fought according to the dualism of the topology that we all ultimately resort to when it becomes necessary to issue a definitive judgment on evil.

And thus the image of evil personified by the Jew was portrayed with the despicable, demonic features of the perfect nihilistic agent: from the Faustian "spirit who denies everything" to the parasite that sucks the lifeblood of its host, dragging it stealthily toward death; and at the same time, as the devil in battle with God against the curse of organic degeneration. The Jew was depicted with all the traits that lead to the usual final scene of the *fullness of being doing battle against nonbeing*.

We find a much more "cultivated" support for this view in the other major book of evil, considered to be incomparably more "theoretical" than the popular *Mein Kampf*: the massive, visionary *Myth of the Twentieth Century* by Alfred Rosenberg.[87] Published for the first time in 1930, it was reprinted many times, with more than a million copies of the new edition coming off the press in 1942. In this text, too, there is a firmly rooted identification between *Schmarotzertum* and *Judentum*, though not before warning us that the phenomenon to be investigated is not to be examined with a moral judgment, but rather as a biological fact, "in exactly the same way as we speak of parasitical phenomena in the plant and animal world." As the sack crab bores through the posterior of the pocket crab, sucking out all its vital energies, in the same way the Jew has penetrated into the open wounds in the body of the people, absorbing and exhausting its creative forces and ultimately dragging it toward a final collapse.[88] However, in this case too the neutrality of the naturalist only manages to keep its distance and balanced view with some difficulty. A few lines below, the parasite returns, likened to the devastating power of the eternal principle that opposes the good. What is presented as biological knowledge, the detached investigation of parasitic diseases, gives way to allusions of ancient demons, which are far more powerful at provoking an emotional response. The Good is achieved when a noble lineage—the Germanic lineage of today, the Hellenic one of yesterday—successfully achieves its supreme spiritual value, which is intimately allied with the perfect form of its bodily appearance. This form expresses the realization of the idea, the type, and the soul of the people. The concept of idea, type, and soul all relate to a notion of myth that, in its turn, differs greatly from a narrative reconstruction of origins as well as from a simple, objective representation. The strength of myth lies in carrying out the Good: a "coming into form," an individualization that contrasts the "disembodied," abstract, and generalized identity of what Rosenberg calls "absolutes without limits."[89] By this he means the divinities of the monotheistic religions and the universal concepts of philosophy. However, in his view, the Germany of "today" is finally drawing on the true German myth. "Until now" the *Volk* had never managed to achieve a mythical identity, its own true form. The power of myth lies in the projection of a "dream image" with which we can identify: the absolute is not outside us, but rather it is the dream in which we can see ourselves. Myth must therefore embody itself in a figure or a type.[90]

Myth, dream, soul, and type are, in Rosenberg's vision, inextricably intertwined in the pursuit of the supreme Good. Type is the realization of the "embodied" identity, which takes form and is set in motion by the dream: the type is simultaneously the model and the realization, the "idea" and the "formation" of identity. In contrast to Christian dualism, the soul finds its freedom in the "Gestalt," in the figure or form—in an embodied configuration. The soul is free, in other words, if it is able to capture, organize, and materialize a form; it must be able to circumscribe or trace a perimeter around the indeterminate within a figure and make it visible. To take liberties with a more familiar philosophical vocabulary, in this theoretical framework we might say that the type or the soul has the transcendental function of making a body visible, of marking its placement in time and space. But in this context, then, race is nothing but the outer form of a particular soul. Language alone, despite its specificity, is insufficient to generate an identity: it belongs to the realm of the universal. If it is not to remain something abstract, myth must also be nourished with blood and soil, with matter and nature. However, it must be noted that in this case matter and nature are not those we would expect to see in a discourse aspiring to a scientific status, treated as unadorned facts, objectively observed. Nature is understood as mythical power, as Idea, as a sort of impersonal force that dreams itself up through its types. The Aryans of antiquity are the Greeks, the people who gave shape to their soul, who created the *Darstellung* (representation) or *Gestaltung* (configuration) of their race in the absolute delineation of artistic form. For Rosenberg's Greek-Aryans, however, art is "an organic art which produces life." In the same way, the soul of the German people realizes itself by embodying itself in its Type, Blood, and Race.[91]

This creative, "figurative" power counters an opposing force that springs from the "Jewish parasitical dream of world domination."[92] In book 3, dedicated to *Das kommende Reich*, the kingdom to come, Rosenberg dwells on the corrosive power of the eternal Jew, base and materialistic, who tries to take advantage of the Nordic spirit in some pernicious way the moment it shows any signs of weakening. The Jewish people are moved by their own dream and myth, those of world domination—the dream and myth that for approximately three thousand years have driven the "black magic of politics and trade." Mephistopheles, made immortal by Goethe, reveals the same inner structure that is found, says Rosenberg, in the current bosses of the economic markets, in the lords of the world press, or in the senior officials of the League of Nations. Their diabolical plan is to conquer world power, not heroically by victory in battle, but in secret and in the shadows, by enslaving peoples through finance. The Jewish demon, therefore, does not pursue world domination as a conqueror, but through a web of subterfuges and squalor; not by fighting, but by creeping; not by putting himself at the service of authentic values, but by exploiting the decadence of values. "This," it is argued, "is the direction of this parasite, strong of strong—these things constitute his law according to which he has moved and from which he will never escape as long as he exists."[93]

The new commonplace of the Jew-parasite that must be eradicated thus melds with the particular *Weltanschauung* (image, intuition, idea) which will provide the great mythology to be materialized and that is finally within Germany's reach. In the chaotic tangle of traditions, discursive registers, and philosophical premises, the distinction between good and evil acts as a load-bearing structure, without ever deciding between a vision that is idealistic, Platonic, neo-Kantian, confused and convulsive—although not unfounded—and a convoluted, although not invented, mythological and literary Manicheanism.[94]

Voegelin is therefore not entirely wrong in judging *The Myth of the Twentieth Century* as the most emblematic work of racial thought that, in his opinion, is expressed as "a political religion marked by Manichean dualism."[95] The Austrian philosopher describes an uninterrupted philosophical path departing from Fichte's idea of a Kingdom of God opposed to the Kingdom of the devil. This idea merged with German nationalism, which, to construct an identity of its own, had to give form to a counter-identity that took on the characteristics of a "counter-kingdom" or an "anti-kingdom." In modern German history, this counterreality almost always corresponded with the Jewish people, understood not only as a religious community but as a "state within a state." In racial theories, this dualistic vision led to the idea of the Nordic race—Aryan, German, or Germanic, as it was variously called—nurturing itself on the idea of a counterrace. That is, it demanded an opposing, mirror-image construction in order to reveal the positive characteristics of the Aryan race by contrast.[96] Rosenberg's Manichean tone is undeniable. Today we find ourselves poised, warns the future head of the Eastern European territories, before the final struggle between two great spirits who lie worlds apart. The battle fought by "German genius with the Jewish demon" will probably be a fight to the death.[97] Relying on an antisemitic authority of his time,[98] Rosenberg opines: "The evil demon of Jewry is [. . .] Phariseeism. It is certainly the bearer of the hope of the Messiah, but simultaneously is the guardian which prevents any Messiah from arriving."[99] What does Rosenberg mean by Phariseeism? The answer to this question reveals the truth behind the binary schema: the Jew is nihilism personified. In other words, the Jew embodies the destructive force opposed to action and the active world; the Jew embodies the will to destruction ensuring that nothing good, concrete, or effective can be created. "A demonic emotion" dwells in the hearts of the Jews, making them the lords of destruction.[100] Unlike the Buddhist—continues Rosenberg—who would be innocently pleased if the world around him fell asleep, the pharisaical Jew can do nothing but deny, because this is the only way he can exercise his immense will to power. The malevolent Jewish will finds its raison d'être in repeatedly destroying Life, which "take[s] on shape again and again."[101] The Jews "are the spirit which always denies, and with an ecstatic affirmation of a

Utopian existence which can never be, conceal[s] the arrival of the Messiah. They would have to hang themselves like Judas, if the latter really came, since they are completely incapable of yea saying."[102] The Pharisee is the same thing as the parasite, the obstacle preventing life from taking shape, because it is blocked from pursuing its own individual growth. The Pharisee, also known as the parasite, thus has no *Seelengestalt*, and consequently no *Rassengestalt* either: no race and no soul, no soul of the race, and consequently no ability to take shape as type. The Jew's true condition is defined by his lack of an organic race and the desire to destroy other races. The Jews thus represent "the anti-race," *Die Gegenrasse*,[103] demonstrated by the variety of their outward appearances. The idea of their being the "chosen" people is ridiculous and grotesque. How could a god have ever chosen a people without a soul and without a race? How could a god have chosen the demon of eternal denial? It is a cunning lie that they use to mask their inability to ever say yes to the great European creations.

Rosenberg's readings of Goethe, Nietzsche, and Schopenhauer join here in the "meditation" on Dostoevsky's *Demons*—nothing in the European heritage is passed over in his effort to describe the Jewish demon, the Pharisee, the parasite. The destructive impulse, the relentless war against all forms of European culture, throws in its forces with international anarchism, which tirelessly corrodes all manifestations of the Nordic soul.[104] Judaism is actually a chimeric form of Phariseeism—an unreality—because it is firmly rooted in nothingness, because it is in fact "nothing," a simulacrum, the masking of a corpse. It is death all dolled up that seeks to deceive us, passing itself off as life. Devoid of anything substantial, the Jew is a nothing and it is as such that he acts, by destroying and annihilating. He drags being toward nothingness. The final battle, inevitably, will be the fight of Life against Death.

Beings Devoid of Their Own Nature

The Aryan type, then, has no adversary in a Jewish type, who stands before him with his defined, immutable core of essential characteristics. The enemy of the Nordic type is in the first place an anti-type, whose essence is to be devoid of its own nature. The enemy of the Aryan type is thus the absence of type, the *Gegenrasse*—devoid of soul and essence— that somehow alters Rosenberg's Manichean dualism. In his writings, the dualism between the principle of Good, which wages war against the principle of Evil, coexists unwittingly with the idea of the *privatio boni*; or, more precisely, in this case with the pre-Christian idea of evil as ontological defectiveness, an evil that gets worse and worse until arriving at the last step—the simulacrum, or forms that lack a type, the adaptive, metamorphic methods of a foreign, defective substance that disintegrates through contagion. Pharisee, parasite, demon, or other: although the names change, one thing remains the same—the nothingness that dwells inside the Jew and that marks his participation in evil.

Plato was the philosopher that Rosenberg and some other major Nazi intellectuals drew on in addition to Nietzsche in delineating their political, moral, and racial world. Their interpretation originates from the idealization of Greek culture that ran through German Romanticism and that developed its nationalistic vein through the "Platonism" of Stefan George-Kreis.[105] An author like Hans K. F. Günther, less esoteric than Rosenberg and more "scientific" than Hitler, managed to successfully combine "raceology," ethics, politics, and philosophy for a wide, diverse audience. Defined by Julius Evola as one of the most widely read writers during Nazism,[106] in all his works Günther advances his thesis of the close correspondence between physical, mental, and spiritual traits. The Nordic person is naturally distinguished by strong individuality, group loyalty, effectiveness and productivity, a carefully deliberated judgment, *Führergeist* (the spirit of a leader), and warrior strengths. Here we find the idea that the ancient Hellenic peoples represented the highest example of "Nordic character," which was then corrupted by widespread interbreeding between peoples. The Nordic character acquires all its vividness when compared and contrasted with the features of the Eastern European race: these peoples, starting with the Jews, of course, lack a deep and consistent creativity, since they are irresponsive to work and effort, affected only by an excitability that spurs them to transgression and falsehood.

Plato serves as a warning to Germany, so that it will not repeat the mistakes that led to the decline of the great Greek civilization. The German people must revive and even relive in a "still more authentic" form the Greek beginning, the origin of true European culture; it must finally give shape to Platonic anthropology, politics, and philosophy.[107] Plato provides a valuable criterion by which to differentiate humanity according to degrees of value, starting from the Good and gradually moving downward toward Evil. In *Platon als Hüter des Lebens* (Plato as the Guardian of Life) and *Humanitas*—the two books by Günther that almost any good National Socialist would have owned[108]—*The Republic* (especially Book V), *The Statesman*, and *The Laws* offer the design for the perfect human specimen, the idea to be fulfilled that Germany will be able to bring into reality through spiritual purification. This process is essentially one of biological selection, the choice of a "transparently Nordic" elite in which "the blond image of divinity" may finally shine forth again. As in Rosenberg's *Myth*, Beauty and Goodness partake of Truth when they become real and living. This is the *kalokagathia* (the Greek ideal of the inextricable connection between being good and being beautiful) that the Third Reich must advance from idea into reality, transmitting the ideal of individual perfection into a humanity made pure and perfect by the process of selection.[109] Plato knows that virtue is a matter of race, and he was not concerned with the life of the individual, but rather with the superior value of racial identity achieved through a process of purification that, in Günther's terminology, is indistinguishable from a process of cleansing. Günther supports his claims with a long sequence of quotations playing on the two meanings of the German term *Auslese* (election and purification), both of which are synonyms of the Greek *ekloghe*. The ethical and political goal of the *politeia* consists in the optimal management of the people's life, making the best prosper and eliminating the worst.

By emphasizing the "monistic" passage that Plato supposedly made in *The Republic*, thereby attenuating the duality between body and soul, Günther refines the idea of the Good as the soul of the race's fulfillment of its essence. The Nazi interpretation of Plato's text is only partly prejudicial. Since the soul is determined by the idea of life, it must be immortal. According to Nazi anthropological monism, the body—at least the Aryan body—is no longer meant to be transcended; rather, it becomes the external, phenomenal expression of an interiority or noumenon of the soul. Further, since Plato believes that the polis is "man written in capital letters," the body to be preserved and no longer transcended is not the individual body, but the body of the *genos*: the body of the race, or more precisely, the expression of the eternal soul of the race. Thus, justice and health are no longer related metaphorically; their relation becomes one of literal identity. The Good, which corresponds to the justice of the city, *is* the health of the *genos*. And the health of the *genos* is the fulfillment of justice and the Good. *Kallipolis* thus implies health, but health presupposes its identity with the Good—a moral choice that expresses the right way to make a people just through selection.

Gunther's monism is built on a system of dual separations and oppositions that reestablish and found the selective mechanism and that transform selection into a true dialectical process of *askesis*, required to attain the One. Life is realized only if the life of the *genos*—the race—prospers and grows. Far from being a natural, biological, material given, the race as type must be pursued through selection, which enables the process of adaptation to the idea, to "True Life," to the eternal life of the eternal soul, which, as a normative ideal, extends the movement of approximation and purification into an infinite period of time: "Plato advocates for his people all kinds of selective tests, because they allow the separation of the healthy from the unworthy. The gaze is always turned toward totality, toward the descendants of the future, toward the masses of young people who have yet to come into the world: thus Plato, unconcerned with individual cases, acquires the sort of imperturbability that we easily attribute to nature. *Similar to nature: so accommodating to the ideal Type and so uncaring of the individual life.*"[110] Measured against the "total psycho-physical ideal," whatever appears to be bad must be eliminated, something that becomes a moral duty. Putting people to death is thus inherent in the purification of the race and the health of the polis; it is a conception that adheres to Greek thought as it does to Roman and Germanic thought.

It is the duty of the Nordic spirit, embodied "today" by the German people, to eliminate as far as possible the contradictions between body and soul, race and people, people and nation, so as to finally bring into reality the Idea, the Type, the One and Eternal Soul—in a word, the Good.[111] As Günther seems to conclude, this is how a people is created. Based on Plato, the only state that can call itself "good" is one that is not content with being the guardian of laws and borders, education and prosperity, but that also becomes the guardian and creator of life, in the fullest sense of the term. The only country that can recapture Plato's heritage is Germany, because of a proximity of blood that is also a proximity of spirit. Only Germany knows that the distinction between noble and ignoble is not a social, educational, or class issue, but rather an ontological distinction—an opposition between pure and impure.[112] There is no escape from the soul of the race, because nobody can escape from his or her own body, which is, precisely, an expression of the type: "For the Hellenes there was nothing spiritual which did not affect the body, nothing corporeal which did not also affect the soul. This is the spirit of the Nordic race. The medieval Church has dangerously inculcated in Western man the idea that the body belongs to the domain of sin. This is the spirit of the Levantine race."[113]

But the reality of the Good—which consists in the perfect correspondence between body and soul in the Nordic type—is not matched by an equally unique reality of evil, corresponding to the Jewish-Levantine type. As for Rosenberg, the polarity between good and evil, between type and anti-type, becomes more complicated. The perfect correspondence between body, soul, and type, as regards the Jew, presents a difficulty: it is that of the tall, blond, and *falsely* distinguished Jew. Günther refers to this issue, in this book and elsewhere,[114] but it is dealt with more extensively in a work by a dear friend and colleague of his, *Race and Soul: An Introduction to the Meaning of Corporeal Morphology*.[115] Written by the anthropologist Ludwig Ferdinand Clauss, it was published for the first time in 1929, also met with great success, and went through numerous reprints. Clauss stated that he followed a neutral method of field investigation: this involves observing the type in an environment whose original characteristics are still intact. Thus, his study focuses on profiles of these archetypal representatives—some verified in person and many analyzed from photographic images. This is why the book surveys a German worker from Friesland, a Swedish farmer, and also a Norwegian house servant as examples of an uncontaminated "Nordic Type." Whatever their social position, if they are really Nordic, they will show "the same rhythm in their features [. . .], that is to say, lines that follow a single morphology, one and the same style." This Nordic style expresses extroversion and a will to reach out to the world (*Ausgriff*). They have slender, agile bodies testifying to their predisposition to attack and predation.[116] Nordic men are their own masters even when they serve others; they are men of action, vigorous and responsible. Their heads are oblong and "projected forward"; their bodies stand upright; everything in their physique reflects their way of living, their psyche, and their soul. Actually, their propensity is not physical in itself: the origin of their attitude makes use of the physical to express itself, to make itself visible and realize itself in the world. All of the terms that Clauss uses refer to a hypothetical dynamic nature of the soul, which is expressed in the movement of the body. Every soul has its own form that materializes in a given body: "The form is the tracing of the lines of the soul." The body is not "a thing in itself"; it is a physical manifestation of the life of the soul. Take, for example, a tall stature: it is the best visible demonstration of a spiritual dimension. As in Rosenberg, body and soul are two faces of the same reality.

After a lengthy analysis of contrasting character and form as expressed by different races—the character pertains to the individual, and to a certain extent can change, while the form is a pure, eternal element and pertains to the type—in the fifth chapter of the book we finally arrive at his examination of the "man of redemption,"[117] meaning, the Near-Eastern race. The image we are asked to focus our attention on, photograph number 85, is that of a Kurdish Jew: a humble desert laborer who represents "his race at an elemental, primitive level." In other words, he offers an archetype that is impossible to find in the Germany of the day, says Clauss, because German Jews have strayed from this primeval model by intellectualizing themselves. But the truth of the Jewish nature can be read precisely from the Semitic-Bedouin features offered by photograph number 85. That is why, when observed using the *Seelengestalt* or "soul form" method, the features of the Jew reveal an "essential coarseness." The nose—a large mass of flesh—the pendulous lips, the gaze—under heavy eyelids that almost cover the eyes—everything faces downward, showing a figure who will always be a stranger to elegance; not because he is a laborer, but because "natural elegance only pertains to those who are actively turned toward the world."

Now, this is where Clauss recalls with pride his own epistemological assumptions, that every race is in itself a value: "In itself, when there is conformity to the soul of the race, there is neither good nor evil." In the world of this morphological racism, evil comes with the degeneration that signifies departure from the purity of the type. And no race has moved farther from its own identity than the Jewish one. This is partly because the dualistic, schizophrenic, ascetic, and emotional nature of the Jews plunges them toward excessive, wanton behaviors. Proof of this—deducible once again from crucial image number 85—is the way in which this Jewish laborer grabs hold of the object given to him by the photographer. With a suspicious, inward-turning look, he proceeds, almost by groping, so to speak, stealthily and warily examining his surroundings. He is not sure who the gift comes from and he would like to "look inside" the person who brought it to him: "An expression like this does not reflect the will to give form, to shape, to produce a new reality from the observed object. It expresses rather the desire to know—the will that gets expressed in the long sessions of the rabbinic schools. Although this man has not attended the schools—and therefore is not, according to the ancient tradition, 'a good Jew'—this trait emerges nonetheless."[118]

Although the nature of this race appears to be its lack of a stable, fixed nature, one permanent trait can be established. This is *Vergeistlichung*, or spiritualization, which is inimical to all instincts of vitality and safety and which tends to internalize everything and transform all physical drives into spiritual phenomena (*umdeuten Geistiges*). The spirit also lives in the Nordic type, but it does not absorb all other phenomena. For the genuine Nordic, "the soul and body form a unity that must expand freely and with force in order to achieve a fully lived, fully affirmative life."[119] The human type in the photo—our Jewish laborer—will never have the opportunity to achieve this positive experience. His essence consists of suspicion, resentment, trickery for circumventing obstacles, and deception for getting hold of things.

In other words, in this supposedly value-free classification, which claims to go, Nietzsche-like, "beyond good and evil," the Jew becomes in reality what throws into disorder the uniqueness of the Good: the perfect correspondence between soul and type. In Clauss as well, then, the Jew returns as the bearer of all negativity, becoming the paradigm of negation without synthesis, the disintegration of the One. This is especially true of the bodily semblance, which cannot redeem its deficient status by working toward the idea through *askesis*.

This is precisely what is revealed by the man of humble origin portrayed in the photo: an inability to rise toward the true idea, a propensity toward the bottom—a movement that is indicative of life's slow fading away. The lines of his form express a soul's tortuous work on itself and against itself: "There is nothing simple and straightforward about this type." Nothing about it is ever spontaneous or original. More than anything, Clauss seems to conclude, the Jew is never unambiguous—contrary to the Greek and, later, the Nordic man. He is double: internally divided between spirit and flesh, and divided from others because of his uncertain identity, which garners mistrust and resentment. What, then, is hidden behind his spiritual and sacral aura? A brute material that, no matter how much he tries, will "never become fully realized spirituality." The Jew is deficient by definition because, owing to the law to which he is subject, his knowledge will never lead to an answer. For this reason, the Jew disguises his desire for being and power under the mask of intellectuality—an intellectuality that he cultivates and exhibits (to pick up on the parasite theme again) at the expense of the peoples who host him. When he fails to attain the sort of spiritualization that would in theory (but only in theory) be in keeping with his type, he thus turns to the worship of abstract systems—those of economy and finance—appropriating all the material values of the world in which he lives.

Clauss's learned and falsely impartial style crumbles when it comes to the theory of "double depravation." Not only does the Jew inherently lack an identity, because the Middle Easterner can never achieve perfection by attaining the spiritual truth of his type, this imperfect being is often led to redouble his inauthenticity. Eager for a spirituality that he cannot achieve because he lacks a genuine, intimate, direct relationship with God, rancorous about an unattainable world domination, his resentment turns into a lack of moderation, an absence of limits, and dissolute greed: in a word, hatred toward the world. Clauss goes so far as to say that "they [the Jews] live for the sole purpose of hating and transforming their lives into a single-minded revenge against everything that lives." All the values of their race, "which they go on about in the name of their law, transmute into their opposites." This explains how this being, because of its inability to conform to its type, becomes the standard-bearer of nihilism: "Instead of sacralizing them [spiritual values], he desacralizes them; instead of going beyond the cult of the flesh, he makes it into an idol; instead of attaining spiritualization, he disseminates materialism."[120] Even when the Jew takes on the appearance of a German—in stature, bearing, a fierce look, light-colored eyes, high forehead, and so on—what lies hidden and ready to pounce is the great nihilist, the true enemy of humanity.

The morphological theory of racism is therefore forced to introduce an inconsistency into its metaphysics of form: for Rosenberg as well as for the more "sober" authors, Günther and Clauss, the Jewish race ranges in an often unconscious alternation between the being with the bodily expression of a low, vile, and often evil soul and the being who is pure simulacrum, pure appearance that does not correspond to any idea and does not possess its own essence. We thus understand what prevented Germany, the sole heir of the Hellenic idea, from bringing the high values of the Greeks into reality, by embodying them. If the good needs to be restored, and if it consists in a sameness between essence and appearance, between soul and body, then the nihilistic semblance—which undermines that sameness by making itself the bearer of eternal differing, as the herald of nothingness—must be eliminated and expunged.

This is how one goes about restoring the value of life, the value of the good, the only good life that can properly be called "human": when participation in the idea of a human life lived in accordance with justice will finally be possible, in which body and soul are united, and reason, passions, and instincts are in close harmony. Hence, humanism must not be opposed, as some proponents of "provincial National Socialism believe," but rather its original meaning must be achieved in its true opposition to nihilism.

Indeed, *Humanitas* is the title of a booklet published by Günther in 1937 that would become a sort of bible or founding text for a theoretical circle in the SS who promoted a racially based United Europe. The text obsessively returns to the theme of German-Hellenic brotherhood, based on a common origin from Nordic stock located in Central Europe during the Neolithic age. The human greatness that developed "thanks to an uninterrupted process of selection," starting from a few families in Greece and Rome is, and will always remain, the ideal representative for the Nordic soul. The value of *humanitas* rests in this greatness, brought into reality and strengthened by racial selection. As the apex of history, the ancient Greco-Roman world was where life was one and the same as the good. It was Stoicism that began the process of eroding this correspondence, by taking humanism in a direction that was hostile to the laws of life, by pursuing supposedly moral goals that are suited only to the isolated individual, indifferent to the health and safety of the *genos*. Hellenism in general is a culture of "reaction," of decadence and interbreeding; it is the symbol of a world that is degenerating.[121] Authentic *humanitas*, in its noble meaning as a hymn to life, was gradually eroded, starting with Hellenism, by the process of de-Nordification (*Entnordung*) and degeneration. The Hellenic-Germanic concept is aristocratic: it demands the victory of man over everything in him that is lowly, over every physical and hedonistic weakness. It requires firmness, contempt for the utilitarian, moderation, decorum, and discretion. To this inner dignity and nobility there corresponds the lofty, proud body of the Nordic type.[122] *Humanitas* is thus the ideal of a Nordic purity that can always be improved; it is the Platonic idea that at times is transformed in Günther's philosophy into Kant's noumenon. What is important for the supporters of the Nordic good is that Nazism—unlike the philosophies of the past—offers a historic opportunity of "embodying" these absolutes, the idea or the noumenon, and phenomenalizing them.

Despite the brute simplifications, the logic of the discourse is stringent: "The idea of *humanitas* has an equivalent in the same Indo-Germanic ideal of the noble man who in the Hellas, in a more strictly selective context, produced the two notions of *eugeneia* and *kalokagathia*."[123] This value was lost when it was transformed into an ideal of individual perfection. The Platonic correspondence between man, soul, and polis became perverse and debased into a fake humanistic ideal, which exalts the individual—who is nothing on his own—in his nullity, in his isolation and abstractness, in his unreality.[124] It has fallen to the German people to bring the idea of *humanitas* into the German context, whose values when examined closely—like the original Indo-Germanic ones—are those of life itself, which seeks to assert itself and be strengthened. True *humanitas* "is a task to be performed, a model to be attained [. . .], an ideal of racial and marital selection, because only a concept that distinguishes between the best and the worst can preserve true ethics and ideals."[125] The lesson (*Lektion*) of humanism is selection (*Selektion*).[126]

"Learned" Nazi literature pursued an intensive undertaking to redefine the human being that borrowed its idea of the good from the philosophical tradition, based partly on Plato's works. The new concept of *humanitas* as it coincided with the *bonum* thus decreed that one part of humanity was incapable of raising itself up to partake of the idea, to reach reality. In a nutshell, not everyone is born human. True humanity—the idea, the soul, the type, the good—is something one partakes of. It is *not* the purview of *anybody*. One rejoins humanity through a course of purification, improvement, and selection: the Platonic process of ascension toward the Idea. However, it is not a path that each individual soul can achieve in relation to the particular "earthly body" that it has ended up in. It is not the "still Socratic" Plato who appeals to the Nazis of *Gestalt* metaphysics; rather, it is the Plato who seems to diminish the soul-body dualism to almost nothing and who is secretly united with an odd "loyalty to the land," viewed by some as Nietzschean. Solidly connected, enclosed in a rigid and ineluctable system of correspondences, man is in other words the expression of the soul of the race, understood Platonically, as "Man written in capital letters." This is the Macroanthropos who will start the ascending path of the *synagoghe*, the process of approximation and of conforming to the idea, which is at the same time always and already the return to the One. This will take place through the selection of the material that the people are made from; through the purging of bodies that are the expression of an evil soul, or of bodies that only *simulate the type*: parasites that insinuate themselves into the limbs of the great body of the race, that do not belong to it and who try stealthily to annihilate it. And this is the point: Jews are by and large simulacra, that is to say impure bodies because they are deprived of a soul, or more precisely unable to partake of a soul of their own, that of the *genos*. The Jews are not only a different type and a different soul of an inferior race: they are the anti-type par excellence.

What drives these theories of race, therefore, is not simply a push toward differentiation, building up the construction of the positive image of a particular community through opposition to its contrary, mirror image. Is not simply a matter of countering rootedness, in the soil and in the blood, to uprootedness; historical and concrete being to abstract, ahistorical being; moral autonomy to the external observance of the laws; the personality of the type, solid in its correspondence with body, soul, and spirit, to mere appearance concealing nothingness. What we have here, as we said at the beginning, is the original matrix that governs all dualistic oppositions: the original act that opposes good to evil, life to death, and being to nonbeing.

In line with the metaphysics of form that we have analyzed (which may have found a home beyond the theoretical circle of the SS), if bodies are the mirror of the soul, and if true souls participate in a single, great soul, in the process of approximation-purification, the bodies must become a single body.[127] It does not suffice, then, to transform the body of the impure enemy or harmful parasite into a corpse, or to prove that this body (*soma*) has always already been a tomb (*sema*), the container of a soul without life, always already absent. For the body to finally, thoroughly partake of the soul of the race—the Nordic idea that continues to exert its mythical force—it must reach the eternal Aryan body, the expression of an eternal soul. On the one hand, then, we have a corpse that finally shows itself to be precisely that, doing justice to its lack of essence, and its *Seenlos* (soulless) and *Gestaltlos* (Gestalt-less) being. On the other hand, we have a great, uncorrupted body, the expression of a pure soul, whose health and justice imply victory over all pathogenic and corruptive agents.

What are the Nazi thanatopolitics that employed racial theories, as Foucault argued, to decide who should live—and how—and who should die—and when? The biopolitical analysis introduced by the French philosopher could perhaps be understood as a conscious rejection of the Dostoevsky paradigm. In other words, this is an interpretation of the relationship between evil and power that does not limit itself to the will to death, the *Todestrieb*, or to nihilism as its key for understanding political evil. As we have said before, if we read Foucault's reconstructions as a "critical ontology" of the present, it is the absolutization of life, with its strategies of universalization, that is called into question and becomes the object of investigation. Moreover, from the analysis that we conducted on the Nazi texts, it is clear that thanatopolitics are run through with and drawn to the will to affirm life, to the will for individual lives to converge in the unceasing, universal Life: a life that to become One can only expunge from itself the irrepressible ghost of what constantly threatens and corrodes it—the ghost that "denies everything" and is the spirit of nothingness.

The ancient gesture of metaphysics that discerns good from evil and makes life the equivalent of good and death the equivalent of evil is thus repeated once again. Both in its evolutionist version and in its "morphological" version, "German vitalism"—if we can call it that—reveals the other side that always accompanies the act of separating life from death: that is, their mutual absolutization. It is an absolutization of life that necessarily involves death, because when compared to life, understood as a synthetic unit, individual beings are just passing instants. And in some cases, they are spurious and illusory concretions to be amended so that the power of life can flourish.

Vile animal, Pharisee, antirace, demon, simulacrum, parasite, semblance of soul: all of these figures, which in the Nazi world mostly represented Jews but which could potentially denote anyone, wherever they invoke the purity and power of life, are not simple carriers of the negative that pass through the positive. Whether the Jew is represented as a base, harmful form of animal life, whether he appears as a demon or a vampire, or whether he is portrayed as the element that is never identical to itself that erodes and disintegrates the identity of others, he is never perceived solely as a pathogenic excrescence that a healthy body must rid itself of, with the scientific coolness of a doctor with regard to a disease. The Jew embodies ontological defectiveness, or, better still, the root of all defectiveness: the structural lack of the negative. He has therefore been endowed with great force: the force of evil as the power of nothingness, which is active and not only passive, which drags everything that is life-giving into its nonbeing, through corruption, degeneration, and contagion.

Jewishness, along with all the lives that are not worthy of being lived, was therefore viewed by the Nazis as the symbol of nihilism, understood as a nothingness that advances and progressively nihilates; in the same way Nazism, in its turn, was to become the historical expression in which we view in action the fully realized expression of our culture's nihilistic turn. Nihilism is called the great ghost of the last century, against which everyone has fought in turn and which everyone identifies as absolute evil: this holds for the perpetrators of yesterday as it does for contemporary critics of those perpetrators. This is because nihilism is the great polemical idol that sustains the ideological war of late modernity. Nazism and Communism, Catholicism and liberalism, each tacks the blame for nihilism on the other. They all believed that they could stop the disastrous flow of events by appealing to the supreme value of life.

Those who engaged in battle to eliminate parasites, unmask the Pharisees, and annihilate the demons—a battle that was meant to destroy those who in their eyes were the bearers of nothingness and destruction—did the same thing, in the name of life. But a fight in the name of the same value was also engaged in by many critics of political evil par excellence. They belong to the ranks of interpreters who read Nietzsche, Freud, and Heidegger in a simple, univocal manner; who used Nietzsche, Freud, and Heidegger, interwoven with the Dostoevsky paradigm, to think about the last century as the time of the death drive, of inexorable "machination," of civilization as a systematic undertaking for the domination of man over man—in a word, those who have conceived of political evil as the absolutization of death.

Thus, in the biopolitics introduced by Foucault we really can pick up on a specific challenge to the nihilism theory, directed at examining the course of the twentieth century that maximizes the value of life—its preservation, the increase of its intensity, its duration, the optimization of its production capacity—and that makes life the focus of the objectives of power and knowledge. For this reason, the concept of biopower stands as an alternative to the Dostoevsky paradigm, which, often even unconsciously, has served to frame the catastrophes of modernity. This is where the innovative strength of Foucault's explanation lies, in highlighting the destructive potential of biopower, not by presenting it as a perversion of reason but through a careful reconstruction of governmental strategies and specific dispositifs, and of the manner in which they work hand in hand with sovereignty.

However, biopolitics as treated in *"Society Must Be Defended"* and in *The Will to Knowledge* is also a philosophical inquiry. It is an inquiry that, rather than following the theories of the philosophy of history, asks how the racist discourse made it possible to distribute sovereignty so widely throughout the social body. Post-Foucauldian interpretations have given differing answers to these questions. Not all of them have placed an emphasis on the fact that, if read in philosophical terms, thanatopolitics, precisely in its absolutizing of life, leads to the configuration of the final scene: the fight of life against death, of being against nonbeing. Even thinkers such as Roberto Esposito who have grasped the significance of this ultimate fight of life against death in Nazi thanatopolitics have not always seen its "hypermoral" character: the extreme, ultimative moralization of a final battle between what is supposed to be good against what is alleged to be evil.

Now, for contemporary philosophy that has grasped and reflected on the significance of this final struggle, that has detected the paradoxical, "useless suffering" of the absolute victim, and that has felt called on to respond with its own thought, what theoretical strategies has it adopted? How has it responded to this version of life that has been made the bearer of death? It has taken sides with those who have been identified with evil. It has put itself in the place of those accused of corrupting life, who were deprived of their lives. It has put itself in the place of animals, parasites, and all beings considered to be devoid of their own nature. *It has put itself in the place of the absolute victim.* We have seen Giorgio Agamben do this, placing "anyone" in the same "zone of indistinguishability" as the Muselmann. This is no different from Esposito's move, who in the figure of the "Third person" and the "Impersonal" has found the locus of a life that casts down the weapons of discrimination that has always led to human beings defining themselves as persons. Adriana Cavarero did the same thing when, as an instant of resistance to horror, she assumed the point of view of the innocent, "defenseless victim" struck by the "horrorist event."[128]

These are "protective" gestures, so to speak, that reactivate the critical potential of the undetermined, the a-subjective, the becoming plural, life as impersonal flow, and the absolute potency of the powerless. *All these thinkers basically want to leave evil behind by siding with what a malicious politics had to define as evil in order to be able to exert itself.* The implication is that this is the only viable avenue for jettisoning the subject, which, as long as it remains such, will inevitably unleash power and along with it reduce the non-I to object. It suggests that this is the only way to disable the metaphysical dispositif, by leaping, in a single bound, outside the circle of subjectivity. But maybe they turn on evil too quickly by so promptly taking a stand on the side of the polarity opposed to the one that they view as directing, disposing, and leading people toward a conduct of power that transforms into domination.

Does putting yourself on the side of bare life, the impersonal, the defenseless, and the animal not ultimately mean continuing to think about the power of a dualistic conception?[129] In other words, does it not mean taking for granted that political evil is a scene occupied by only two players: on one side the perpetrator, the guilty, cruel subject, and on the other the subject completely transformed into an object, turned into a Muselmann or bare life? Perhaps, a better question is whether this is a way of skipping the intermediate steps necessary to fully understand what is happening in the scenes of evil.

The scene of evil is not simply a *folie à deux*, as Orwell would have it. It is not wickedness that adds up and multiplies on a collective scale to make up a sort of Rousseau-like "general will" to nothingness, as it is played out in *Demons*. Before getting to the point at which power relations congeal into total domination, before omnipotent violence is unleashed and pours down onto the defenseless, before suffering becomes the senseless pain of those who passively endure it, there always exist games of actions and reactions. There exist gray areas, ones that are still open, in which a plurality of subjects share the space and divide the weight and privilege of their small or large slice of freedom.

Of course, the savage, perverse imaginary that has forged and filled up the content of "hypermoralization" has worked for others in addition to those who devised it. The hypermoral context of a strong opposition between good and evil has also served, perhaps first and foremost, to reassure those who followed the path of disinterest—those who had no particular urgency to express their hatred, but who acquiesced on the basis of a normative justification to not intervene; those who legitimized their nonjudgment.

This normativity of nonjudgment, then, this morality that has so often taught that to judge is the shadow of that first sin committed by our forefathers—the sin of disobedience—is probably what needs to be examined as a carrier of political evil, as its effective transmission belt. How do we become obedient subjects, and how is another way of subjectivation possible? How are we to conceive the conditions of possibility for evil, or resistance to evil—an evil that is not reduced to more or less outrageous, unyielding episodes of cruelty and wickedness? Evil, I will never tire of repeating, is an event that makes itself into a system. However, it is not the anonymous system of a fatalistic history. Rather, it is a system in the sense of a tangle of subjectivities, a network of relations, whose threads pull together into a pernicious event thanks to the perfect complementarity between (a few) wicked actors and originators, (a few) zealous, committed agents, and (many) acquiescent, not simply indifferent spectators. Only this combination can produce the absolute victim as the ongoing condition of a power system that makes itself into domination.

PART II

MEDIOCRE DEMONS: TOWARD A NEW PARADIGM

The Legend of the Grand Inquisitor
Reinterpreted from Below

The Pastoral Power of the Grand Inquisitor

"The Grand Inquisitor," the legendary "story within a story" that makes up the fifth book of part two of *The Brothers Karamazov*, in some ways complicates, but in other ways simplifies, the perspective of *Demons*. In Ivan's "literary fantasy," told to his brother Alyosha, not without a certain willingness to hurt his feelings, the relationship between evil and power established in the previous work is partially revised. It no longer offers us the spectacle of an interaction between the many and various ways of encroaching on human freedom. No longer does disorder burst forth from the pages, nor do we view any terrorist practices put in motion by the anarchic and destructive tendencies of the protagonists. The link between evil, nihilism, and power is firmly established, but it is portrayed from another angle, which will lead us to look in a different direction. What comes under examination is a specific configuration of the political relationship according to which evil, to succeed in its aim of domination and oppression, plays the part of the good. This allows another important piece to be added to the Dostoevsky paradigm.

The scene is familiar to us. During a sweltering night in Seville, when by the decision of a cardinal of the Inquisition a hundred "evil heretics were burnt" to the glory of God, Jesus Christ returns on earth.[1] He is motivated by the desire to dwell only for a moment among men, among the humble who have never stopped waiting for him and who recognize him immediately. Even the Grand Inquisitor has no doubts about the identity of the Son of God and precisely for this reason loses no time in arresting him. During the night, protected from the eyes of the crowd, the old man decides to visit him in prison; more than anything, he decides to tell him the truth about power and tell it directly to Him in whose name he governs. Certainly, as in *Demons*, Dostoevsky expresses his own anti-Catholic sentiment by giving voice to his condemnation of a power that is by now completely worldly and that exploits and betrays the Gospel message. The story also gives a glimpse of his harsh assessment of "Genevan and socialist ideas" from Western Europe, borrowed by the Russian youth. When Catholicism and socialism are transformed into instruments for gaining and maintaining political power, they inevitably sacrifice their truth on the altar of inquisitorial reasoning. They become the masks behind which the "demonic face of power" hides, whose future history Dostoevsky is thought to have predicted.[2] Poised between tragedy and lucidity, the soliloquy of the Grand Inquisitor is without a doubt a thought experiment offered to us by the Russian on what, at first sight, appears to be the inescapable and cunning wickedness of people who hold positions of power. We are presented with what could be described as a table of "political cynicism" across the ages, from which we can deduce the constants in the one-to-one correspondence between the false altruism of the One—or at most, of the few—and the passive obedience of the many.

According to this view, similar to Faust, the Grand Inquisitor has made a pact with the devil—with the "Anti-Christic" forces of worldly domination—whose wickedness he is now willing to recognize in the intimacy of his face-to-face meeting with Jesus Christ. As if it were a long-awaited opportunity, the liberating tones of the old man's confession are also tinged with anger and resentment: "Perhaps you precisely want to hear it from my lips. Listen, then: we are not with you, but with him, that is our secret! For a long time now—eight centuries already—we have not been with you, but with him."[3] For at least eight hundred years, the Church has been siding with the power of evil, since "we took from him what you so indignantly rejected": Rome and the sword of Caesar. And for even a longer time, he continues, addressing the Son of God, we have made it our task to correct your deed, in your name, but against you, by basing our empire on *miracle, mystery, and authority*.[4] These are the three forces through which faith in Christ was transformed into the official religion of the Roman Empire, creating the model for all political domination over human beings.

What comes into view here, then, is the classic Dostoevskian picture on the phenomenology of the powerful—of those who know the truth and hide it to forge the tools to more effectively achieve obedience through falsehood. Once again we have the demonic freedom that consciously chooses evil, that seeks evil precisely because it is evil, thereby elevating itself in imitation of the divine power. People "will marvel at us," at those of us who hold power, confides the Grand Inquisitor, and they will "look upon us as gods," not only because "we will say that we are obedient to you and rule in your name," but also because we will take your place, he seems to conclude. In other words, power is a lie: he speaks in the name of God while working on behalf of "'The dread and intelligent spirit, the spirit of self-destruction and non-being'."[5] But above all, power is still identical with evil because it claims to take the place of God.

Dostoevsky's last work thus offers us one of the most magnificent examples of polarization of the political field: on the one hand, we have a sovereign subject, whether made up of one person or a chosen few, who is all-powerful and guilty; and on the other, as "one man," the many who are totally passive and obedient, partly because they are tricked into it by the highest authority of the powerful. The scene simplifies the plural topology of *Demons*: in the Grand Inquisitor there are only two poles that structure the relationship. However, the framework of the Dostoevsky paradigm gets more complicated, bringing into full light the ambivalent reality of the pastoral form of power: the generous, "positive" tendency that seems to herald the modern structure of biopower in terms of a freedom-happiness dialectic. This is why the innocent dualism that Alyosha proposes to his brother and that for a long time has provided the hermeneutic key to Ivan's "poem" is unconvincing[6]: if the Inquisitor, the Church, and the Antichrist are evil, then Jesus, true Christianity, and love are good.

If Stavrogin and his friends pursued evil in order to prove their abyssal freedom in choosing to reject the good, the Grand Inquisitor has at least the ability to confuse us about the objectives of his work. He seems to remind us that if power truly consisted solely in negating, exploiting, and oppressing, it would never achieve the obedience that it almost always does. There must be another dimension at work in the balance of power, then, that makes the majority accept and perhaps even seek to give up self-rule and freedom. Hence, this means that the powerful, in addition to exploiting weaknesses, first know how to understand and seize on them. In some way the powerful lend their ear to weaknesses and are able to take charge of them. The visionary greatness of the Grand Inquisitor, in effect, lies in having understood that the strength of tyrants consists not only in consenting wholeheartedly to the three great temptations faced by Christ in the desert, but also in managing them in a positive manner—because miracle, mystery, and authority, the foundations of power over human beings, *respond to real needs that must be cultivated and in many cases made to grow.* This is what Dostoevsky's discourse on human nature hinges on, making it one of the immortal chapters in "European conservatism," as Peter Sloterdijk observes, but also, I believe, one of the few answers to the question of what motivates "voluntary servitude." It is a response more radical still than the one given by Tocqueville's "tyranny of the majority" and by the many later diagnoses of mass society, matched in depth and foresight only by those of Nietzsche.

Humanity is undoubtedly marked by freedom, by that poisoned gift that Christ brought with him onto the earth and that places human beings before the painful choice between good and evil. "You desired the free love of man, that he should follow you freely[. . . .] Instead of the firm ancient law, man had henceforth to decide for himself, with a free heart, what is good and what is evil,"[7] the anguished cardinal presses on while the Son of God remains in silence. But if man is free, he is also feeble, cowardly, lying, depraved, fickle, and more than anything "made a rebel,"[8] a slave, with the character of a rebel, or a rebel who seeks slavery. This is the thought that returns obsessively in Dostoevsky's writings and that here becomes the pivot around which the dramatic lucidity of the Grand Inquisitor rotates. Only a very few, continues the old man, have had and will have the courage for this terrible freedom and unhappiness; "a hundred thousand sufferers" in all, who have taken and will take upon themselves the curse of the knowledge of good and evil, and the choice between the two. And what will all the others make of their being free, considering that "nothing has ever been more insufferable for man and for human society than freedom!"?[9]

So begins the indictment against the Savior who, in reality, is the one who destined human beings to unhappiness. This is where the Inquisitor character is revealed in all its ambivalence, making the task of judging it a difficult one. We certainly cannot be satisfied with the evaluation made by the angelic Alyosha: the Grand Inquisitor, as a mimetic principle of the good, but with the opposite sign, is the only agent responsible for evil. True, he does wish to dominate human beings, and to this end he seizes on and interprets their weaknesses and their fears. However, in a sense, he himself has been caught in his own trap. There is something convincing in his pathetic reference to self-sacrifice and in the accusation he expresses to Jesus Christ that not only did Jesus go into the world "empty-handed," he also did not have true compassion for human beings. The cardinal truly believes that humanity should be saved from its own freedom—a freedom that is a crushing, tormenting burden. The Inquisitor himself has passed through the experience of Christ: "Know that I, too, was in the wilderness, and I, too, ate locusts and roots; that I, too, blessed freedom, with which you have blessed mankind, and I, too, was preparing to enter the number of your chosen ones."[10] However, he "opened his eyes," turned his back on the folly of Jesus and, above all, decided not to take sides with the proud so as to stay on the side of the humble and the weak. Yes, indeed, he did so in order to join those who genuinely love humanity—to join the shepherds of Roman Catholicism. The flock has in fact been saved by the work of the Church, argues the Inquisitor, which, in apparent continuity with the legacy of Christ, has amended the Gospel, as we have said, to the point of sacrificing the gift of freedom for happiness; or rather, for an innocent, infantile form of contentment, particularly unburdened by the weight of choice. Because—this is how his confession to Jesus can be interpreted, I think—it is the sheep who want to barter their free will—their conscience—for a small, but guaranteed, earthly happiness.

Thus, there is a great force at the disposal of powerful people: the ability to respond to an infinite flow of requests and desires that come from below, by manipulating it. In the eyes of the cardinal, this flow can be summed up in the human need to placate the anguish of the soul with bread, in the need to serve and to obey, to liberate oneself from the painful freedom of choice. All of them, "thousands of millions of happy babes," will believe themselves to be living in freedom: "These people are more certain than ever before that they are completely free, and at the same time they themselves have brought us their freedom and obediently laid it at our feet."[11]

Dostoevsky therefore knows, and more importantly reveals to us, that it is this tendency, the most fundamental and deeply rooted one, as it were, that is what power sinks its hooks into: the tendency that can be endlessly abused and manipulated for dispensation, for unburdening, which leads human beings to give up the fatigue of having to endlessly make judgments in favor of safety and bread—in a word, the guarantee of life. If Jesus had heard the spirit of nothingness in the desert, if he had accepted the Devil's suggestion to change stones into bread, humanity would have run after him "like sheep, grateful and obedient." As the Inquisitor logically decrees, "give man bread and he will bow down to you, for there is nothing more indisputable than bread." If the Son of God had been so humble as to ensure the loaves of bread, he would have provided a response to the universal, perpetual anxiety of man, to the worry that torments him: to gorge oneself on material goods, but at the same time to find someone to kneel down before. It is the desire for authority, the desire for the One that Étienne de La Boétie speaks about, the desire that authority appear *to each and every one of us* as indisputable, permitting a *universal* genuflection: "For the care of these pitiful creatures is not just to find something before which I or some other man can bow down to but to find something that everyone else will also believe in and bow down to, for it must needs be *all together*."[12] Then they will appreciate once and for all the goodness of the standing submission, because we, continues the Inquisitor, "shall give them quiet, humble happiness, the happiness of feeble creatures"; we shall prove to them that they are pitiful children "but that a child's happiness is sweeter than any other."[13] Small sins will also be permitted; indeed, they will become effective instruments of control and conformism.

Spinoza reminded us that those who hold power are constantly in need of telling themselves and others that people suffer from sad passions and that stoking these passions makes people increasingly passive and subduable.[14] Now, to the old Inquisitor, human nature is clear: we are ready to bow down and obey, especially if everybody does it together, *en masse*, as soon as they are offered the chance to fill the vacuum and chase away the sense of uncertainty. The set of human needs—bread, miracles, mystery, and authority—nourishes the evil of power, in a circularity that seems, to Dostoevsky speaking as the Inquisitor, impossible to break. Is this the great secret that explains obedience to power, then? Is it perhaps the cunning altruism of the powerful in promising earthly happiness, which intersects with the desire of the many to absolutize the value and duration of life? Is it the dovetailing between the need of the sheep to be saved and the opportunistic sacrifice of the shepherds who promise salvation that relentlessly legitimizes the recurrence of political evil in history?

Certainly the reality is a little more complicated, especially for us today, we who are not so easily persuaded by the evidence of a human nature and who are unable to identify with the same sharp clarity as Dostoevsky exactly where power really resides and what forms it takes. However, if there is an element of truth in the words of the Grand Inquisitor, it appears more clearly than ever before in our democratic societies. This is the point from which we will have to start over in the attempt to investigate the workings of a political relationship: beginning not only from the evil structure of subjects who hold the monopoly of violence, but also and especially from the support that comes to them "from below." From a below that, unlike what the old man believed, although not composed of a universally shared human nature, represents an area that has remained unexamined by supporters of the Dostoevsky paradigm. Paradoxically, ahead of all others, it is the Russian writer who points the way for us to explore a different genealogy of the evil-power hendiadys, thus offering an escape route from the conceptual constellation whose structure was originally provided by his works.

The Crime of Obedience and the Normality of Evil

To understand how power can be transformed into a system of evil, then, we must change perspective. Explaining it with nihilism, the death drive, and the desire for power is not enough. We cannot arrive at an adequate understanding by examining the destructiveness of the many bearers of nothingness. The point is not, as I have repeated several times, to arrive at the conclusion that the perpetrators do not exist or that they are innocent, and that the victims are guilty. Our aim is to break down these logical dichotomies and transform them into a field of forces and tensions in which the antinomies lose their essential identities. As Dostoevsky himself saw, this allows us to examine the desire for norms and subordination, which, apart from a few exceptions, philosophers have either not wanted to take on or have not known how to, preferring instead to continue thinking about political evil in terms of the grandiose schema based on the omnipotence of transgression.

The historical disciplines and some currents of social psychology were the first to understand the need to escape from an interpretation of evil locked into this dualistic vision—as a relationship, we might say, between absolute subjects and objects. More directly pressured by historical facts than philosophy was, perhaps, they provided the first theoretical framework for understanding the novelty of something that at first glance strikes us as an oxymoron: crimes of obedience. In the same way sociology and social psychology went beyond theories of a "criminal personality" or a "collective psychopathology," for some time now historians have questioned the role that the perpetrators' wicked disposition played in historical tragedies.

Starting from the great, groundbreaking work by Raul Hilberg, *The Destruction of the European Jews*,[15] to the most recent historiography on the Shoah and, more generally, on genocides,[16] attention has increasingly turned to a collective subject composed of different types who played more or less active roles: from the actual perpetrators of the slaughters to passive witnesses who limited themselves to turning their head the other way. It is a set composed of so-called common people who certainly avoided situations that would turn them into victims; however, they did not take the initiative and the role performed by those who originated the evil. The main role in carrying out the extermination is viewed as no longer being performed by the demonic will of a criminal elite, but rather by the function of the bureaucracy and the administration on the one hand, and of acquiescent or indifferent observers on the other.

In a similar move, social psychologists began to ask themselves about the "ordinariness" of the minds of people who went so far as to massacre defenseless men, women, and children on an industrial scale. In the 1970s, two famous researchers devised experiments to challenge the hegemonic, and in some respects reassuring, theory on the "authoritarian personality."[17] According to this theory there exist radically different human types: personalities with a propensity to evil, and personalities with a propensity to normal behavior. The work of Philip Zimbardo and Stanley Milgram became "classics"—people talked about the "Milgram Paradigm"[18]—not only in social psychology but in the entire cluster of disciplines engaged with thought on the "banality of evil."

In short, both historians and social scientists have brought into focus that "gray zone" which throws into disorder the reassuring geometry, so to speak, of the agents who create scenes of evil—and which introduces the difficult issue of the involuntarily guilty. From the most detailed and documented studies to the most provocative and polemical essays, the data that researchers now focus on regard the supporting function that obedience, conformism, alignment, silence, and denial played, aside from the extreme positions of the victims or perpetrators, in crystallizing our contemporary image of evil around the scenes of a genocide. The strong point of these studies is their recognition of how pervasive the dynamic is that leads individuals to submerge themselves in their roles. Because of this dynamic, violence, abuse of power, and mistreatment are not viewed as the outcome of an uncontrollable aggressive impulse, but as the product of practices and techniques designed to produce submission. Because the iron grip of the role is legitimated by authority or expresses a powerful group identity, it leaves no freedom of movement.

However, assuming that the people involved in the scenes of evil are normal participants does not suffice to delineate the scope of the normality of evil. In my opinion, it is not enough to argue simply that there is no need for a pathological personality in order to participate in evil, just a servile humanity that is prone to conform, as these studies implicitly establish. Above all, it does not suffice to conclude that, in the end, because of the inherent pliability and fragility of human nature, we can act cruelly because what we are and what we become depends on the influence of the environment and the interaction between the various systems—biological, geographical, economic, and ideological—that govern our lives.

I think that "the normality of evil" implies something more than these simple observations. Does philosophy not have something to add to this structural, systemic framework that reminds us how fragile our capacity to resist is, and how detrimental it is to think of ourselves as being beyond all temptation? If we continue to talk about evil and we want to think about it as a network of relations, however, we must introduce a theoretical space for freedom and responsibility, even if it is only a counterfactual one, into this structural game of roles and situations. We must also understand that before these chilling scenarios that pin victims and perpetrators into fixed roles, there exists an interval of spaces and movements that must be examined in depth, despite the degree of coercion involved in the particular circumstances. With this premise, we can look through the works of contemporary philosophy for a different genealogy of the criteria of evil, one unlike what prevalent philosophical narratives have always provided, and unlike the scenario exemplified by the Dostoevsky paradigm.

The text that gave rise to the possibility of thinking about evil along this new genealogical and conceptual path is the renowned *Eichmann in Jerusalem: A Report on the Banality of Evil,*[19] the series of articles on the Eichmann trial that Hannah Arendt wrote for the *New Yorker*, later published as a book. There are some books that can transform particular occurrences into events that are emblematic of their times, to the point of redefining the theoretical discourses of the age. Arendt's is one of these books: without a doubt, more than any other, it helped to transform the trial of the Nazi criminal Adolf Eichmann, held in Jerusalem in 1961 and 1962, into a genuine theoretical *a priori*. It has been discussed a great deal at various times, so there is little reason to revisit the ideas that rang out as completely discreditable at the time of publication: from her descriptions of Eichmann as a diligent bureaucrat to his absolutely ordinary personality, to the accusation of "collaborationism" that she made against the heads of the Jewish councils.

From a distance of almost fifty years, it is more interesting to try to understand the legacy of *Eichmann in Jerusalem*. As a columnist and chronicler, there is no doubt that Arendt erred by being hasty and incautious. The role of the Jewish councils and Eichmann has been reexamined and reassessed by numerous works since then, contradicting Arendt's rash assertions on several points. But if she stepped over the line as far as the factual reconstruction is concerned, as a political thinker she won the match. First of all, there is agreement today in viewing in this trial what Arendt intuitively perceived in her time: a turning point in Israel's self-perception, the start of Israel's construction of its identity through the remembrance of the Shoah. There is no doubt that Arendt glimpsed the dangers and contradictions that this could lead to right from the outset.

But in terms of political philosophy, how are we to understand her criticism of the trial as opportunism, its rhetoric of collective guilt, its celebration of the exclusivity of Jewish victims? How are we to interpret the provocation launched by her use of the term "banality" and the intention she brandished to question the responsibilities of the Jewish councils? What was fermenting in Arendt's mind? Perhaps a rethinking of the categories with which she had redefined Kant's radicality of evil *sub specie Auschwitz*? Perhaps she was forming the opinion that this cluster of concepts had not shown itself to fit reality closely enough to be able to grasp the most elementary or molecular aspects of evil—aspects that are so disturbing to us because they are so widespread in our contemporary world. Moreover, was it pure sarcasm on her part to take Eichmann seriously in his role as a Zionist, so devoted to the cause that he spoke impeccable Hebrew? And what are we to say about her juxtaposition of Eichmann's behavior to Kantian philosophy? At the very least, we are forced to recognize that if Arendt started out to write a journalistic report, what she came back with was a philosophical reflection on evil; or rather, with a series of questions that, although left unanswered by their author, today enable us to conceive of evil in a different way.[20]

Because she passed away before completing *The Life of the Mind*, Arendt did not have time to develop her set of ideas connecting evil with an absence of judgment. Instead of elaborating a structured, systematic examination of the topic, she associated these ideas with the proper name of Adolf Eichmann. Unlike Stavrogin, Eichmann is not a literary character, so the historical reality of what he was severely limits the uses to be made of him by theoretical thought. Nonetheless, it makes no sense to blame Arendt's text on the trial for historically distorting the Nazi criminal's profile. Arendt availed herself of a paradigmatic function that, in this case, she played out through a flesh-and-bones individual. We can thus speak about a singular phenomenon that provides a new theoretical construct with a face and makes it intelligible the instant it exhibits its exemplarity.

Eichmann, we might say, is the anti-Stavrogin. Even from a philosophical point of view, he is the mirror-image opposite of Dostoevsky's anti-heroes, in the sense that he performs evil not by transgressing the law for the sake of evil but by fully observing the law, regardless of its content. Consequently, like Sade (Lacan and Deleuze's Sade[21]), he too draws attention to the "scandal" of Kantian law intended as pure form and incarnation of the Good in and of itself. Let us recall what Lacan and Deleuze argued. Kant was the first person to turn the classical image of the law upside down, so that the law is no longer founded on the good; now, instead, the law as such sets itself up as the good. If we follow this reasoning to the point of paradox, we can thus say that Eichmann has good reason to be defined as Kantian. Eichmann is someone who commits evil, but as a side effect of action aimed at conforming to the good, which is to say, conforming to the law as such. Arendt's hasty equation between Kantianism and Nazism was made possible by these premises. It is an equation that was certainly worked out starting from an overly simplified reading of Kant—also true in the case of Michel Onfray[22]—but that nevertheless points to a crucial ethical-philosophical question. It is the problem of a political philosophy, and more generally of a philosophical and theological thought that has always looked to obedience as the obligatory *dispositif* needed to make a power relationship work—because, in reality, obedience has always been thought of as the antidote for human defectiveness, which, according to various schemas, predisposes human beings to figures of evil.

Apart from the historical reality of the Nazi criminal's actions, then, his exemplarity initially guided Arendt's investigation in the direction of an ethical perspective, and certainly not in the direction of rehabilitating Kantian morality. It is true that in writing about the accused in the Jerusalem trial she resumes the harsh polemic that she had begun previously in *The Origins of Totalitarianism* on the dangerous self-referentiality of logical reasoning—something in which Eichmann appears to take refuge. The idea also resurfaces that the success of totalitarian ideologies is related to the fact that they offer security to a human mind thirsty for consistency and certainty. Eichmann, endowed purely with a deductive capacity, as it would seem, adheres rigidly to the application of absolutely predictable rules, so much so that in court, his continuous appeal to duty, to obedience to the law, and to the execution of orders appears as more than a defensive strategy. During the early days of the regime, he behaved like a lot of people who were not opposed to Nazism because they were impressed by its success and unable to issue a judgment against what they considered to be a verdict of history. Like the minds of all those who went along with the regime, the mind of Eichmann refused to let in anything that in one way or another might contradict his system of reference. This is why it turned out to be so easy to adhere to the new dictates of the prevailing moral law in Germany. He fully complied with the imperative of the new order, whose commandment was changed from "Thou shalt not kill" to "Thou shalt kill": "Thou shalt kill" all beings guilty of evading the parameters of humanity established by the regime. Eichmann thus served Arendt as an extreme and sometimes—it must be admitted—convoluted example to illustrate her long-held theoretical convictions.

As a cypher of the ethical collapse of an entire society, he also provided the opportunity to redefine the meaning of the terms on which "our moral tradition" was built. It is a tradition that has ultimately proved to be not much more than what the etymological meaning of "moral" suggests:

a code of norms, habits, and customs that can be replaced with the same ease with which festive traditions are changed. Eichmann is not distinguished by any pathology. In some ways he truly did conduct himself morally. Under normal conditions, argues Arendt, many of those who were to become functionaries of the regime would never have even imagined committing crimes of this sort. As long as they lived in a society where the rules did not require the elimination of beings regarded as entirely superfluous, they behaved as honest citizens. But the moment the killing of Jews became a moral duty, they applied a new categorical imperative without the slightest hesitation. Eichmann did not need to "'close his ears to the voice of conscience', not because he had none, but because his conscience spoke with a 'respectable voice', with the voice of respectable society around him." Eichmann, therefore, was not deaf to the voice of conscience because he fell prey to the slavery of the passions or because he succumbed to the delusion of reason; he listened to his conscience, which spoke in the language of the collectivity, which was connected in its turn to the terms and validity of the new law.[23]

In the wake of Arendt's observations on Eichmann's normality, I believe we can identify the traces of a profound theoretical nucleus that brings Socrates, Kant, and Nietzsche into dialog, bequeathing to us a possible cluster of concepts for rethinking evil.

The Antinomy Between Ethics and Life, and Between Ethics and Law

An important text by Arendt named "Some Questions of Moral Philosophy" has only recently appeared in print.[24] The essay incorporates the lectures that she gave between 1965 and 1966 at the New School for Social Research in New York and at the University of Chicago. They may very well be considered the long-sought missing link between her account of the trial and her ideas on judgment from the 1970s. From her lectures it becomes clear that in addition to being a journalistic slogan, the expression "banality of evil" was also the beginning of a full-fledged moral philosophy, one that, although not developed further in subsequent works, stands as one of the most important legacies of twentieth-century thought. As far as I am concerned, even though the "banality of evil" encapsulates the challenge represented by this legacy, I prefer to talk about the "normality of evil." In fact, I believe that the adjective "banal" was an unfortunate choice, not so much because it is offensive to the memory of the victims, but because it fails to capture the novel aspects of a vision that sought to break with previous moral philosophy. What landmarks did Arendt turn to when setting out on her exploration of ethics? She proceeded with Nietzsche to dismantle the "idols" of morality, and alongside Kant she asserted the value of autonomy, while at the same time seeking to break out of Kantian universalism by returning to Socrates. In her view, these philosophical schemas, or rather, some of the ideas included in them, are able to express an ethical instance that, under certain circumstances, can entail a strong political value.

The rigor with which the separations between ethics and politics, and between the public and private spheres, were traced out in *The Human Condition* is replaced in this text by the awareness of an inextricable interweaving between the spheres of the "human condition." Most likely, it is in this regard that Eichmann proved to be exemplary. If, on the one hand, his case presented the opportunity to deconstruct the idea of intentional evil, on the other hand he offered the chance to return to the question of evil—evil as interaction and as system—from the perspective of the consent given by individuals. Arendt's investigation shifts its focus onto the subjective modalities that support political evil by implicitly asking the question of how a normal mind is structured so as to reach the point of performing particular actions and following specific orders. This is how the prohibition on the untouchable sanctity of Auschwitz came to be violated, and more generally how the metaphysical taboo on an ultimately inexplicable evil was breached. I am convinced that it was only from the perspective gained from the 1960s onward—when she began to delve into the life of the mind—that Arendt truly began to leave behind the unilateralism of the Dostoevsky paradigm. At the very least, it was the ideas occasioned by her work on the trial that set off the inquiry into a constellation of concepts that serve to think about evil in its normality and not only in its abysmality.

In the transition from the "radicality" to the "banality" of evil, as evidenced by her lectures from 1965 and 1966, it became clear to Arendt that she could no longer invoke the usual moral traditions—from the philosophical ones of Aristotelianism and Kantianism to religious ones. It was no longer conceivable for her to qualify as moral the adaptation of the particular to the universal: the "Thou shalt [*du sollst*]" is empty per se and it can even go so far as to justify the impossibility of resisting evil. And it certainly no longer suffices to conceive of virtue as the *subjective habitus*— acquirable and teachable—that contributes to constructing and maintaining a shared ethos. Whether one follows Kant's universalism or Aristotelian communitarianism, morality remains dangerously at risk of political manipulation. At this point, however, the important point to focus on would seem to be the true ethical value of a behavior. This becomes clear precisely in situations where morality comes into conflict with politics and with the law, under circumstances in which the reasons for following one or the other can constitute a real dilemma.

Before going on, it might be useful to recall that in "Some Questions of Moral Philosophy" Arendt does not make a distinction between "morality" and "ethics." And it is interesting to note that although Nazism and Stalinism are viewed as structurally related in the horizon of the "radicalism of evil," from the new perspective only Nazi Germany brought about a genuine ethical revolution in her eyes. From a moral point of view, the Stalinist crimes did not overturn the traditional parameters. These crimes were kept hidden, or justified as temporary, albeit painful, means that were necessary for the success of the "good cause." Arendt is convinced that even the most energetic revolutionaries believed that once social circumstances were changed, humankind would continue to follow the moral precepts whose obviousness was known to everyone. Hitler and his officers had instead "announced a new set of values," designed in accordance with the imperative of the new law. Overnight, the confidence of entire generations in the self-evidence of the moral conscience, in the "natural" capacity to discern good from evil, was shattered.[25] Only the Nazis, therefore, forced the contemporary world to take note of the fact that ethical distinctions are not something obvious; that the conscience is not some kind of organ with which we are naturally endowed.

From within Nazism, the true ethical question was posed not so much by the creators of the criminal political system, by those who committed evil "for the sake of evil." The most disturbing problem was in reality represented by the large number of those who were neither demons nor fanatics, but who simply lacked any motivation for refusing to act in accordance with the law. In a piece written during the same period as the lectures, Arendt stated, "The moral problem arose only with the phenomenon of 'coordination' [. . .] with this, as it were, honest overnight change of opinion that befell a great majority of public figures in all walks of life and all ramifications of culture."[26] What are we to think of the conscience, then? That everyone suddenly became deaf to its voice, perhaps?

It was Nietzsche (whose prophecy, she believes, was only partially understood) who warned us that there is something illusionary in the self-evidence of the conscience and moral values: it is a trick that veils reality and that for Arendt as well must be unmasked before we can approach the question of good and evil anew. But if Nietzsche was right in attributing to the Christian virtues and precepts a desire to negate the world, Arendt distanced herself from the faith in whose name he fought against the ascetic ideal. This is because the norm that Nietzsche chose as his point of reference for orienting himself was unacceptable in her eyes. Thus begins Arendt's confrontation with Nietzsche, which runs throughout the entire series of lectures. In her opinion, Nietzsche not only interpreted the collapse of the moral idols as a result of pressure exerted on them by the onslaught of life, he also elevated life itself—what Arendt calls "the simple fact of living"—to the supreme value. Arendt's reading is too simple, of course. But it is an interpretation that serves her to set up her own attack on the ethics of the "Main Tradition," starting from the idea that if ethics made sense and continue to do so, the reason is because the underlying assumption has always been that life—"staying alive"—has no legitimation in itself. This is a strong premise that the author embraces here, as in many other places, without offering any supporting arguments. That is to say, she fails to clearly explain to us why life needs to be redeemed from its elementary materiality. For that matter, as is well known, this assumption underlies her entire political conception and criticism of the modern era, which has been accused of sacrificing the greatness of action to labor, to the preservation of biological life.

Now, it is precisely from this statement about Nietzsche, considered so obvious by Arendt, that I would like to start my analysis of these pages that, on the one hand, attack the positions of Christian morality and modern morality, but on the other hand emphasize that any ethical discourse must assume life is *not* the highest good for mortals. The reference to ancient Greece plays a central role on this occasion as well. We know that for the Greeks *philopsychia* (love of life, attachment to life, such that one's aim is the preservation of life) somehow expresses cowardice, a lack of courage, often punished by being condemned to a miserable life, with the *philopsychos* being expelled from the battle—that is, from the scene that offers the opportunity to "win immortality for oneself." According to the Greek conception, a life that is never put at risk for something higher is practically unworthy of being lived. This is quite different from the assumption of the Christian ethos, which recognizes that life can be "sacrificed" for something higher, it is true, but assumes that for humankind, living is the supreme good. For this reason, the revolution that fully manifests in modernity and that leads to a reversal of the hierarchy between life and the world actually dates back to Christianity and to the value assumed by life, as a gift from God, in the new axiological universe. In any case, as we have already suggested, there remains no doubt that the ethical discourse always implied— and for Arendt should always continue to imply—that there is something different at stake beyond the simple procreation and subsistence of the biological organism. If the ultimate good ever really became the survival of the human species, in her view we would be well beyond an ethical inquiry.

In these pages Arendt quickly disposes of the question of the value of life in itself, just as she issues a hasty judgment on Nietzsche's philosophy, almost in line with the "simple" interpretations we have discussed earlier in this book. It is as if Nietzsche restricted himself to saying that on the basis of his transvaluation everything that impedes life is to be understood as evil, and everything that accepts, confirms, and strengthens life is to be associated with good. As much as Arendt agrees with the perspectivism of the German philosopher, the strong influence of Kant's philosophy is undeniable. By this I mean that Arendt never fully disputes the separation between the realm of necessity and the realm of freedom.[27]

Arendt's horizon of inquiry is thus strongly marked by a dichotomy between necessity and freedom that it is too sharply defined. This horizon does not block her access, however, to the possibility of taking unexpected paths that radically distance her from Kantianism. Playing Nietzsche against Kant, as a first move, but then playing Kant against Nietzsche, Arendt is finally able to formulate the question: What is this "something else" that concerns the individual and its singularity and that exceeds its living, understood as surviving? What is this thing that exceeds mere life, that makes a human being a singularity and endows it with an ethical status? What is it that in its absence hypothetically introduces the possibility of evil? By binding the categorical imperative to the "fact of reason," in her eyes Kant had the great merit of freeing morality from the heavy burden of religious discourse. We know what Kant said in this regard: "We will not hold actions to be obligatory because they are God's commands but will rather regard them as divine commands because we are internally obligated by them."[28] The explicit admission that "nobody, not even the deity, is an originator of moral laws"[29] was undoubtedly a blow to traditional ethics, one whose force was equaled only by that of Nietzsche's hammer. It was a blow that allowed a genuine moral philosophy to arise, since it was finally released from the question of a superior, religious authority, and connected instead to the relationship that human beings have with themselves—with their reason. As one entity among others, human beings are overwhelmed by a sense of powerlessness about the nothingness that they will return to; however, they do have access to freedom by virtue of the singular responsibility to which they are destined by Practical Reason. Although this is the Kantian heritage that must be preserved, it needs to be reworked.

With regard to the issue of the difference between good and evil, and the nature of the subject who perceives this difference, the distance that separates Arendt from Kant becomes profound. As much as the German philosopher tried to separate the ethical discourse from the religious one, in which, as we were saying, the relationship of obedience to an external law dominates, in Arendt's opinion he remains trapped in the vertical structure of the command relationship. The categorical imperative is not objectionable so much because of the contradictions—more than a few, as she sees it—that it introduces into the corpus of Kantian philosophy, but because its form brings back through the window what practical philosophy had chased out the door.[30] The "Thou shalt" not only can prove to be "*Hirngespintse* [phantasms]," "empty concepts," but with the separation between Reason and Will it returns to that subjective dynamic whose morality Kant had put into question. The Good—or Good Will—is the result of a struggle that takes place within the self along a vertical, authoritarian trajectory: the "Thou shalt" of the commanding will must be answered blindly by the Reason with "Yes. I will."[31] The command-obedience relationship of religious morality thus takes up residence in the very heart of the subject, who once again identifies the good with fulfilling an order, and evil with transgressing it.

Arendt's true polemical objective is more general, and concerns the imprint left in ethics by the religious conception from which not even

Kant, in her opinion, managed to free himself. This is obviously where Nietzsche plays an essential role. I believe that these pages can be read as an attack against the way Christianity has contributed to making the conscience a mechanism for neutralizing conflict, and thus a device for relieving people of responsibility. Halfway between a cognitive status and a moral one, in Christian thought the conscience is transformed into the tool for hearing and fulfilling the divine watchword, mainly thanks to the role of the will: the faculty, discovered with Paul and Augustine, to be able to say yes or no to the precepts of reason. Let us not forget the context of this indictment. It is not a historical-philosophical reconstruction, but the acknowledgment of the bankruptcy of ethics that took place in the twentieth century: the reflection on the events—which Eichmann emblematizes—that, in Arendt's opinion, forever deprived us of the possibility of believing that "morality goes without saying." The causes behind the collapse in ethics may in fact include exactly what strong believers in "totalitarian evil as a product of secularization" have pointed to as the only salvation for civilization: the sanctity of the obligation of moral precepts. What is now under accusation, therefore, is the long-standing tradition that based its foundation on the command-obedience relationship—not only for the political sphere, but also for the ethical life of the individual. This type of relationship—the vertical one that demands obedience—has proved to be a completely effective strategy for anesthetizing the critical judgment. For this reason Arendt writes, "Much would be gained if we could eliminate this pernicious word 'obedience' from our vocabulary."[32]

The same verticality is to be found in the dynamics of the will, "which among all other faculties got so power hungry." In fact, it wants to command both the body and the reason, and thus splits the I into two opposing instances, a civil war that can only be resolved by the defeat of one of the two contenders: "Hence the most important manifestation of the will is to give orders. But it now turns out that to be obeyed, the will must at the same time consent or will obedience."[33] And to consent it must *silence* any form of opposition, by putting the opposite party completely out of the game—*by forgetting, by denying* the resistance that fuels the opposing movement. Only in this way can the Two—created by the conflict generated by the will between one part that wants and the other that does not—unify into the One that acts to carry out the order.[34] A will that remains divided has a paralyzing effect, but the unity achieved by the will is aimed at a necessary behavior. In short, the will is the faculty that, having been discovered in the religious sphere, has monopolized the entire ethical life of the mind, reducing it to a matter of conforming to commands.

This means conceiving of the good as something given, as something external, Arendt continues, to which the subject must adapt and the consequent potential loss of responsibility in acting. In the revealed religions the good is pursued without questioning why the good is good: one simply obeys the command that the good imposes. Since it is willed by God, the good can only be precisely that. Even Thomas Aquinas, argues Arendt, "the greatest rationalizer of Christianity,"[35] came to admit that the ultimate reason a certain precept is just and should be followed lies in the fact that it was established by God. In short, the moment Christianity became a defined set of ideas and practices, it transformed the opposition between the "I want" and the "Thou shalt" from an inner conflict into a relationship between, on the one hand the voice of God or of the ecclesiastical authorities that imparts the commandments, and on the other hand the human being who can obey and live morally or disobey and live in sin. This is how individuals are deprived of the ability to question themselves, to learn instead that the moral activity is a conforming behavior. So much so that, in this context, the criteria of just and unjust, rather than corresponding to the criteria of morality or immorality, become indicators of conformity and nonconformity.[36] In no other text does Arendt push her critique of Christianity so far, almost to the point of identifying it as the real origin of conformism—the matrix of a subjectivity structured on the basis of the normativity of the absence of judgment, and therefore prone to yield to evil. Perhaps I am projecting too much into my reading of these passages, but I truly believe that the complex that keeps banality of evil, responsibility, and judgment united takes its start precisely from this schematic but pointed critique that Arendt directs against the current of Christian morality that flowed practically unimpeded into the secularized West. In a word, starting from Christianity a moral thinking predominated that ultimately identified the conscience as the locus where the inner dialectic was brought to its end.[37]

Starting out from these kinds of considerations, the issue of the reflective judgment took up an increasing amount of space in Arendt's thought. The always possible intertwining between politics and evil now found a restraint in the very ability to judge, thanks to a judgment that can distinguish between what is right and what is wrong, even in the absence of laws and shared criteria.[38] The moral judgment is therefore akin to the Kantian judgment of taste, which states that "I like it or I don't." Because it is not a determinate judgment, which subsumes the particular under the universal, but a reflective judgment, it cannot depend on rules established *a priori*.[39] In "Some Questions of Moral Philosophy," "those few" who refused to consent to the regime provide the author with a prime example of the ethical effectiveness of the ability to judge. Although any avenues to "political responsibility" were closed to them, she argues, the possibility of nonparticipation was still open, a road taken not by diehard champions of the permanence of moral values but rather by those who were not accustomed to complying with the prejudged. In refusing to participate, the criterion of these few was not the application of a universal law to the particular case, but the simple impossibility of living with themselves if they had done certain acts. And it is at this point that the emphasis on autonomy, originating from Kant, must be able to be joined up with the critical, negative power of the Socratic *daimon*.

Those few who did not fall into line, says Arendt, behaved as if they had put into practice the teachings of Socrates: it is better to suffer wrong than to do wrong, and it is better for me, being one, to stand against the whole world than against myself. It is as if they had followed the premise of these Socratic propositions: not only do I live with others, I also live with myself, and this living with myself in some cases takes precedence over everything else. In some exceptional moments, like the Socratic *daimon* who understands when it is time "*not* to do" something, the capacity of thought—the wind of thought that "destroys [. . .] values, doctrines, theories, even convictions"—can be transformed *immediately* into action.[40] No particular culture is necessary, therefore, for the judgment that arises as a condition of possibility for abstaining from evil; what is required instead is the ability to create friction with the present, to distance oneself from the context. And whenever this capacity is lacking, there is always the potential for the banality of evil.

What is the significance of these allusions to Socrates, so powerfully expressed in the lectures of the mid-1960s? Arendt feels the need to reflect on what has been lost over the long process of constituting the ethical conscience that began with Christianity, or rather, with Plato's distancing of himself from Socratic ignorance. Certainly, to define which aspect of ethics has been obscured is a difficult task, and one that is always prone to contradictions; all she can do is turn to fragments of the philosophical tradition, so that they can speak on her behalf. In the background of the Socratic moral propositions—it is better to suffer an evil than to commit one; "being One," it would be better for me to be at odds with the whole world than with myself—there lies, for Arendt, a "plural," or more precisely a "dual and horizontal," conception of the I, which is the only thing that makes judgment possible. It is this duality that would later be transformed and betrayed in the inner struggle of the moral conscience: the struggle of the will against desire, on the one hand, but also against reason, on the other. In Socrates, if there is something that resembles the conscience, the reason that sustains it is "neither sheer intellect to be applied to whatever might be at hand, nor contemplation,"[41] but a capacity of thought to split itself into two and return constantly to itself. It almost resembles a continuous double movement: escaping outside the closed circle of self-referentiality, and then returning to itself in order to remember and review what it saw and experienced. In these passages, as well as in those written during the same period in her *Denktagebuch*, there are some interesting ideas on the relationship between thinking and remembering. The safest way to avoid getting into conflict with ourselves, says Arendt, is to forget. However, we cannot process something in the memory unless it has previously become an object of thought—unless it has been given a key place in the silent dialog with ourselves. In this sense, thought is the activity thanks to which the I returns to what it has done and to what it has seen. And evil, Arendt states here, undoubtedly has something to do with the deterioration of this capacity.[42] On this point she has no doubt: the worst crimes that we have witnessed today are committed by "those who don't remember because they have never given thought to the matter, and, without remembrance, nothing can hold them back."[43]

Thus, for Hannah Arendt, human beings are not "rational animals." Rather, they are "thinking animals." We now understand what this "something more" and "different" is for Socrates-Arendt that exceeds the factuality of the vital process, what constitutes that element of immanent transcendence, we might say, that in her opinion justifies human life and that makes it worthy of being lived. In this sense, thought is not only an ethical activity—the authentic ethical activity, in fact—because it makes judgment possible, but because it is in itself the activity that qualifies a living being as a human being. It is not "the fact of reason" and its imperative law but the division between the self and itself that forms the condition for the possibility of thought and at the same time the transcendentals of freedom, responsibility, and the imputability of evil.[44]

What we usually call a person or a personality, as distinguished from a mere human being or a nobody, actually grows out of this root-striking process of thinking. [. . .] If he is a thinking being, rooted in his thoughts and remembrances, and hence knowing that he has to live with himself, there will be limits to what he can permit himself to do, and these limits will not be imposed on him from the outside, but will be self-set. These limits can change considerably and uncomfortably from person to person, from country to country, from century to century; *but limitless, extreme evil is possible only where these self-grown roots, which automatically limit possibilities, are entirely absent.* They were absent where men skid only over the surface of events, where they permit themselves to be carried away without ever penetrating into whatever depth they may be capable of.[45]

The image of an ingenuous Arendt with still overly "humanistic" traits might be reinforced from these references to thought as the quality that is proper to the human being.[46] The status of Arendt's subject and its humanity remains an unresolved hermeneutic puzzle. On the one hand, the *who* is constituted by the relational weave in which it has always been caught up, a subject who becomes such because from the outset it takes part in a game of recognition and reciprocal visibility with others. Thus, in non-Arendtian terms, one can say that the very activity of thinking starts out from the impact that the outside has on the inside—it is nurtured by the perpetual outward and inward movement. On the other hand, the ability to think and remember often appears to be a mysterious gift, potentially bestowed on everyone, whose actualization and workings are not further investigated.

However, if we read these lectures together with some notes written during the same period in her *Denktagebuch*, in the retrospective light of *The Life of the Mind*, we see a path that is far from naïve. The splitting inside the subject is not the product of that mysterious, critical capacity signaled by the Socratic *daimon*. Rather, it seems to correspond to a conflict between the temporal perceptions of the I: between the part of the Self that experiences itself as subject to time, change, and death; and the part, called "the I of Apperception," that, although inseparable from the events of the corporeal, mortal I, cannot help but perceive itself as immortal.

The dualism in Arendt's thought between biological life and the life of the mind seems to become blurred: already during these years the experience of thought as experience of the eternal is connected to a particular bodily experience, during which, under certain conditions of solitude, concentration, and quiet—the conditions that make thought possible—the body represents itself as immortal. *The Life of the Mind* later returns to examine this perceptual illusion of eternity on whose foundation are built both the metaphysical reason and the belief in the immortality of the soul. But for now it is interesting to note that, in the context of the notes made in 1966,[47] conflict within the I is closely related to the problem of evil. Among the conditions that facilitate evil—which is now clearly understood as the absence of judgment—we can include the exclusive victory of one of the two perceptions over the other. It is as if Arendt were telling us—and this is important—that evil, or rather, the type of subjectivity linked to the possible occurrence of evil, *is actualized more easily when*, among the perspectives from which the I perceives itself, only a single instance *affirms itself as hegemonic*, an instance that when absolutized negates the other. Whether the viewpoint of death triumphs (that of a finitude who only cares about its obsession with the disappearance of itself and others) or whether the sense of omnipotence of the "I of Apperception" (who feels eternal and universal) wins out, the separation of this entanglement must surely be one of the conditions of evil. This is because it blocks the movement of thought that is the exclusive source of the judgment—the same judgment that is capable of being critical of the present and of opening itself to imagining the suffering of others.

Does this not perhaps provide a different perspective from which to look to the dialectic between life and death that is at work from the outset in Arendt's thought? In *The Origins of Totalitarianism* she gave voice to the historic paradox of such an intense attachment to biological life and of a fear so obsessed with death that it delivered life—or more precisely, individual lives—over to the omnipresent power of death.[48] Now, however, this dynamic has to be located at its point of engagement within the subject itself. This is what affords the possibility of breaking down the formation of the events of evil into their microphysical structure. The question that we must ask ourselves, then, is no longer the metaphysical one: "What is evil?" We will never arrive at a definition. Instead, we must try to understand how and why we arrive at an experience of power that gets crystallized into a system of domination because of the effect, so to speak, of a quantity-quality dialectic. We want to know *how* the network of relations that produces it is organized; but even more importantly, *how* the mind of a person who supports and therefore reinforces the event of evil works, in "physiological" terms. To observe the event of evil from the perspective of political decisions or historical trends no longer suffices; rather, it must be scrutinized "from below."

We have dwelt a number of times on the possible philosophical interpretations of conflicts within the self. In the case of Hannah Arendt as well—or perhaps especially in her case—on the basis of a particular way of reading her work, the ethical implications are clear and, as in the case of Nietzsche, from a particular way of reading his work, they go against one of the most deeply rooted convictions about the topology of evil. From Augustine to Schelling, to speak only of the thinkers we have examined, the subject that commits evil manifests a recurring phenomenology: one of inner duality that becomes a full-blown splitting in Dostoevsky's dark heroes, for example. Inner strife is thus viewed as the source of both subjective malevolence as well as evil in history. This is why, for a large part of Christian and modern moral philosophy, it must cease: the Two must be brought back to the One. Only in this way can its subversive force be extinguished. This is also how the wicked nature of the absolute demons is placated.

However, as it has been repeatedly proven in reality, the Two is not the condition of wicked action, and furthermore, evil does not simply coincide with wickedness. Wickedness alone can no longer explain all the occurrences of evil. The Dostoevsky paradigm must therefore go along with a genealogy—for the most part still waiting to be traced out—that locates the "blame" in the normativity of nonjudgment and passivity, in the docility and obstinacy of defending and enhancing life.[49] These phenomenologies of evil are more widespread than the pathologies of the dispensers of death, and not only because of the generic, ubiquitous pressure that the system, the context, and the institution exert on those involved, as the "psychologists of evil" simply assert. These are the very people, with their lack of thought and judgment, on whom Arendt sought to shift our gaze.

A Different Genealogy: The Evil of Docility

Subjection as a Remedy for Pride

The problem with obedience and docility—their role in diminishing a sense of responsibility—was a question Hannah Arendt had already looked into before she wrote the book on Eichmann's trial. It is no coincidence that she *always* played Kant's ethics and aesthetics against each other.[1] His ethics extol obedience and compliance to the law, but his aesthetics are potentially "subversive" since they disrupt the system of subsumability under universality. While she was working on "Introduction *into* Politics" in July 1955, she recorded some brilliant ideas that might have developed into an organized inquiry into the relationship between obedience and evil.[2] However, these notes in the *Denktagebuch*, which she got back to only a few years before her death, were never systematically arranged. In these pages, Arendt asked herself how it ever came to pass that an attitude of obedience got elevated to a supreme virtue. How did a behavior that was so contemptible to the Greeks end up as the highest ethical value? What prompted her to pose these questions was the section in Thomas Aquinas's *Summa Theologiae* (specifically IIa–IIae, *quaestio* 162, *articulus* 5), where Thomas directly opposed *superbia* to *humilitas*, defining the latter as *subiectio hominis ad Deum* (subjection of man to God). The curious fact, notes Arendt, is that pride is not defined simply as *rebellio* against God. As Thomas recites from Ecclesiasticus 10:14, instead, "The beginning of the pride of man is to apostatize [Douay: 'fall off'] from God," which in her view opens up many possible interpretations. The one that would prevail, she tells us, accompanied by useful political effects, is that when human beings disobey other human beings, this behavior is also a sign of man's original betrayal of God. Given that the first human action—transgression—was the product of pride, Christianity had no difficulty in "psychologizing" such behavior by transforming it into a given inherent in the human being. Over time, modeling human beings on their innate predisposition to rebellion and disobedience offered advantageous political results.

As an assiduous reader of the Patristics and a scholar of Augustine, the fundamental role that the dialectic between *superbia* and *humilitas* played in shaping the peculiar character of original sin could hardly have escaped her. However, in that context she did not undertake what could have developed into a radical genealogical inquiry into the link between docility and evil. She did go back to the Pauline and Augustinian texts in the last work of her life, to probe the cornerstones that they laid in the "foundation" of the faculty of the will. But in the notes from 1955, the juxtaposition between evil, power, and obedience was still only hinted at. Thus, although Arendt left us clear traces of the problematic interweaving between these three factors, she never fully formulated the implications ensuing from it.

We know from Genesis 3 how evil got into human beings, and through them into the world. Immediately after the story of the divine creation, we come to the narrative of the first human act. Adam's action shattered the state of perfection and innocence, without time and without history, in which the relationship between God and his creatures was immediate and harmonious. The instant man acted for the first time, he committed a transgression: not a free action—an autonomous, creative initiative—but a reactive act of opposition. The first thing a human being did was break the only order that God had issued: do not feed yourself on "the tree of the knowledge of good and evil." As the serpent insinuates, knowledge of good and evil signifies making oneself similar to God. Compared to other cosmogonies and theogonies, from *Gilgamesh* to the many Nordic sagas, the original sin in Genesis 3 takes the form of guilt attributable to freedom—a freedom that is inseparable from disobedience. However, this guilt cannot be redeemed by human forces alone. As a consequence of this first act, human beings can be saved only by divine action, because the evil introduced by the disobedience of the first parent remains as an indelible wound of man's separation from God. And, as Paul Ricoeur remarks, although the narrative includes figures like the serpent that seem to shift the question of evil to an outside that is "always already there,"[3] there is no question that disobedience is identified with the original, radical evil—the source of all evil on earth. The propensity to evil is inscribed in the first creature and this propensity is transmitted to every other human being, because from that *action*, the rebellion against God—the first, original sin—there arises a *condition*.[4]

Disobedience, then, is not a consequence of the corruption of human nature but is, we might say, the *original event* that introduces corruption into human nature. God, "the Author of all natures but not of their defects, created man good; but man, corrupt by choice and condemned by justice, has produced a progeny that is both corrupt and condemned."[5] God created the human race from a single, unique man in order to bind his descendants in divine harmony, peace, and love. But the act of disobedience disrupted the ontological order.[6] The disobedience of the first human being, which transmits the original blemish to all the others, leads to the spiritual death from which, as St. Paul tells us, we can be saved only by the sacrifice of Christ. However, the evil of sin, even if redeemed by the Son of God, remains as a stain on humanity, which thus remains marked by evil even though the sin was committed by only one of its members. Baptism therefore has the function of renewing the salvific sacrifice of Christ for each and every person, one at a time. Even if Augustine tries to complicate and blur the scope of this original breach, attempting to provide an essentially moral reading of the evil of the original sin, the assumption of an ontologically corrupt human nature as a result of the moral transgression of the will still remains: "[N]o member of this race would ever have died had not the first two—one created from nothing and the second from the first—*merited this death by disobedience. The sin which they committed was so great that it impaired all human nature*—in this sense, that the nature has been transmitted to posterity with a propensity to sin and a necessity to die."[7] Thomas Aquinas considerably attenuated the ontological scope of sin, in his turn, by making canonical the difference between *peccatum personae* (imputable to the individual) and *peccatum naturae* (original sin), which is potentially transmitted to everyone through biological reproduction but is made actual only by the choices of the individual soul who sins.[8] However, the inherent ambiguity that structures the idea of original sin was never resolved.

Modernity took the direction of gradually weakening the literal interpretation of Adam and Eve's action, but the equation between evil and transgression—between disobedience and corruption—has remained forever fixed as an undisputed *a priori* in the question of evil.

Now, if the fall is not originary—and this is what Arendt seizes on in her 1955 notes—if the *status naturae lapsae* is a consequence of the rebellion that shattered the uncontaminated unity and tranquility of the original state, then disobedience, which is integral to pride, is the constitutive feature that delineates the anthropological defectiveness of humankind as a whole. It is what cast human beings into *this* world marked by suffering and death. It is what caused the rupture with the eternal and the entry into time and history, decadence and disorder.[9] Human innocence—as God created us—consisted in a state of perfect obedience, corresponding to the body's "happy" subjection to the soul. But the moment the rebellious will entered onto the scene, all was lost. Disobedience itself lost its character as a free event to become a permanent disposition that can be restrained only by the imposition of a *humilitas*, the attitude intended to become the *habitus* and *ethos* of the *subiectio hominis ad Deum*. As a consequence of this act of disobedience, human beings therefore lost their innocence and pleasure and acquired guilt and toil as their essential state of hardship. Their inner world is torn by the conflict between the desire to return to God and the desire for the world. Punished in its likeness to God, the human creature now shares partly in the fate of the irrational creatures. This is why their need for final salvation is equaled by their need for a master and a sovereign during their earthly sojourn, which leads to a life of relations structured inevitably by man's abuse of power over other men, by property, by concupiscence, and by the need for law.

This, then, is the inextricable relationship between transgression, evil, death, and power structure—the new earthly condition of human beings, who remain perpetually poised between their finite horizon and the desire for the infinite. Despite even radical differences in the content of each of these terms, the association between transgression, evil, death, and power, as we have seen, remains substantially the same all the way to Heidegger and Levinas.[10] What sealed the unbreakable bond between human beings—evil, and death, on the one hand, and power, on the other, which was made necessary by the interaction of the three terms—was therefore an original act of transgression.

We know what became one of the most effective ways for Christianity to remedy the evils arising from disobedience and pride. Sin brings with it the need for power, but through power the possibility of salvation as well. Although sin brought with it death, it also made possible the need, and along with it the opportunity, for redemption in the other life. The power of human beings over other human beings is certainly "*libido dominandi*," lust for power and a manifestation of sin—in a word, evil. But when properly directed and used to guide people toward obedience, it is also the sign of God's love: He who can no longer be simply a Creator but must also become a ruler to govern over the differences between human beings, because although human beings were made equal to each other by God and in God, by sinning they have become different and rebellious in the world and therefore in need of a guide. To lead people toward salvation from eternal death, it is necessary to use a power that is not only a desire to dominate but also a desire to take care: "For those who care for the rest, rule,—the husband the wife, the parents the children, the masters the servants; and they who are cared for obey,—the women their husbands, the children their parents, the servants their masters. But in the family of the just man who lives by faith and is as yet a pilgrim journeying on to the celestial city, even those who rule serve those whom they seem to command."[11] The exercise of power as care—in the analogy with shepherding and domestic power—means not only to command but also "*imperare potentia rationis*," to rule by the power of reason.[12] If those who exercise the power of command put themselves at the service of God, they do not impart orders out of a passion for power, but rather in order to direct those who must obey toward the good. If there was no power of care, which is expressed through the command-obedience relationship, nature would move relentlessly forward into corruption.

Earthly obedience thus appears to perform a dual function. On the one hand, it is undoubtedly the scar of a wound, the cypher of guilt. If the initial disobedience from pride had not taken place, there would be no power requiring obedience to the orders that it imparts. The state of innocence stood in immediate divine communication, with no breaks or rifts. On the other hand, obedience can now lead back to *humilitas*; it is the path along which we can establish a worldly relationship that in some way disables the root of pride. The order of nature willed by God did not intend human beings to have power over other human beings. God did not intend "that his rational creature, who was made in His image, should have dominion over anything but the irrational creation,—not man over man, but man over the beasts."[13] However, since guilt has reduced human beings to irrational creatures, the power of some humans over others must become similar to that of shepherds. This is what divine justice now desires. The model of power is thus drawn from the relationship between shepherds and their herds, which also sets an example for the relationship between a man and his companion, and for the relationship between a father and his children. In short, political power as care, as pastoral power, implies obedience as an indispensable antidote against evil—the evil that entered into the human condition as a result of the sin of pride caused by Adam's disobedience.

What are we to say, then, to close the circle of our constant references to Dostoevsky? If *Demons* recounts the evil of power as a result of the abyssal freedom and desire for destruction on the part of those who seek to make themselves equal to God, the legend of the Grand Inquisitor shows the pastoral, altruistic face of a power that demands obedience in exchange for the possibility of salvation. *Demons* warns of the dangers that we risk by making ourselves equal to God at the dizzying point of our self-determination; the legend of the Grand Inquisitor shows the ambivalence of a command that can become corrupted into idolatry of power, but that can also serve as a remedy for sin. Certainly, what is never put into question in either case is the salvific, beneficial role of obedience and humility—because freedom is always posited (and Dostoevsky stands purely as an exemplary case) as the *imago* of divine omnipotence, of the absolute will of God who is able to create *ex nihilo*.[14] Evil comes into the world the moment the creature tries to imitate God by disobeying the limitation to which it is bound. What else can the object of human desire for omnipotence be except lust for power and dominion over other human beings? Herein lies the sway of evil for those who rule over others—unless some of them accept the burden of governing on behalf of God, by imposing the sort of order and obedience that hark back, even if only obliquely, to the perfect obedience and perfect harmony of the original state. Society, even the best society, must therefore guide individual human beings in the awareness that they are completely unable to control themselves on their own. In some way, as we have seen, this theological belief is perpetuated in the secular argument that transforms the first sin of disobedience into the root of the inherent desire for human freedom, which can become corrupted in seeking to go beyond its own limits.

But what if the power of God was conceived on the basis of another model? What if it had not followed the path that leads from nothingness to being? Would we perhaps think about our freedom in a different way? Would freedom have been liberated from the anxiety of nonbeing as damnation from which we must be saved? Would freedom have been liberated from the condemnation of the judgment—from the fact that judging or discriminating between what is good and what is evil, between what is right and what is wrong, means seeking to resemble God—and thus from arrogance?

These unanswered questions seem to suggest that questioning the necessary correlation between disobedience, evil, death, and power could be the real issue at stake in a different philosophical genealogy—one that does not simply claim to go beyond good and evil, but continues to investigate the problem of evil and searches for it exactly where the condition of possibility for redemption was always thought to lie. This hypothetical branch of philosophy is what we attempt to reconstruct in the following sections.

A Relationship Between Forces: The Nietzsche of a Few

The thinker who brought into question the assumptions of the "political equation" that was established on the basis of Genesis 3 and then actually overturned them is undoubtedly the Nietzsche that we encounter in his last major writings. At the time of *The Birth of Tragedy*, the anti-Rousseau and anti-Kant polemic somehow induced him to accept the "counterrevolutionary" presuppositions, and thus to not discuss the assumptions relating to sin. Starting from *Zarathustra*, however, he appears to want to explicitly break with the basic assumptions of the Christian tradition. The parallel the reader is led to accept—between Jesus Christ and Zarathustra—is not simply intended as a parody. Nor is it limited to preaching the "alternative Good News."[15] His intention is to arrive at a gaze liberated from all the mystifications imposed by *ressentiment* and codified by metaphysics and religion. This perspective opens up the possibility for an interpretation of the link between evil and power that is very different from the reactionary, conservative tradition, but also from that of political thought in general. This is so much the case that it can be said that the strategy deployed in the 1885 masterpiece—to go "Beyond Good and

Evil"—does respond to the need to describe the prospects for assessing traditional morality from another set of eyes. But it also fulfills the desire to bring into the open the stratagems used by Christian pastoral power to weld the formula of political domination to the idea of sin and to unmask the cunning with which it made obedience the remedy for the evil that was first expressed as disobedience.

Nietzsche points his finger at the "invention" of original sin, and to carry out his polemic he must rewrite (I think it can be interpreted this way) the first step taken by humankind along the path toward a propensity for evil. On this point Deleuze is right: Nietzsche brought to completion what Kant had only just begun. However, it also needs to be added, he did this not only as far as *The Critique of Pure Reason* is concerned, but also with regard to *Religion Within the Limits of Reason Alone*, in which the concept of radical evil is intended to oppose the question of the predestination of the human race to original sin. Nietzsche appears to accuse Kant of failing to dismantle the scaffolding of the secular construction that pastoral power had erected on the idea of man's natural wickedness—a construction that, although now collapsing under the impetus of its own nihilistic thrust, still retains its foundations intact. Nietzsche's entire corpus, at least from the writings after *Thus Spake Zarathustra*, especially *Beyond Good and Evil* and *On the Genealogy of Morals*, can thus be thought of as a long, circuitous, indirect commentary on Genesis 3. What gets investigated between the lines is not the predisposition to evil expressed by disobedience, but the evil that emerges from the reactive passivity of *ressentiment*. Instead of interpreting evil as a cypher of the pain human beings feel as a consequence of their finite nature, he critiques the evil that the vital energy has to be subjected to in order to become docile, so as to be saved by the same power that wounded it. In a manner that is sometimes subtle and sometimes heavy-handed, Nietzsche points his finger at the brilliant invention that turned a bad conscience and sense of guilt into the indelible scars of sin. He counters them with the innocence of a life that is able to express what is in its power.

The doctrine of sin must not therefore be fought on the ground of Kant's radical evil or even on that of Rousseau, which simply reverses the times and places of the "fall." What should be challenged, rather, are its theological premises, revealing their practical functionality. Through an elaborate inhibitory psychology, in the first instance Christianity denied the innocence of pain and chance that inevitably causes pain. "Pain has been robbed of innocence," Nietzsche never tires of repeating.[16] Christianity then postulated that conditions of peace were natural and original, that "God created man happy, idle, innocent, and immortal," so that real life would seem like a false, fallen, sinful existence, in which suffering, struggle, and effort appear as something corrupt, as signs of inauthenticity and the fall, which must be remedied. Here is the trick: *think about life*, from Adam's disobedience on, as a curse, *as the state into which sin has injected death* and from which we must be saved. If humankind can become free, in the sense of free from sin, it will do so not thanks to its own actions but because it is redeemed by the sacrifice of others, namely, the sacrifice of Christ. The promise made in exchange for obedience and humility consists in a life that is immortal, happy, and devoid of pain. But why, the philosopher asks provocatively, would we ever want a life that is idle, immortal, and happy? "Why are guilt, work, death, suffering [. . .] contrary to the supreme desiderata?" And what if fully abundant strength is characterized precisely by the fact that it wants to "create, suffer, go under"?[17]

If this is the essence of Nietzsche's conviction, it is obvious that in his eyes the link between evil and power takes on a very different meaning from the one conferred on it by the entire spectrum of counterrevolutionary and reactionary thought. For those who see 1789 as the date that sealed the disaster of modern politics, the "democratic and socialist" age is the result of the crisis in the principle of authority. There is no doubt that this genealogical linearity does not apply to Nietzsche's thought. As far as he is concerned, there is a path that can be followed dictated by an altogether different logic, that is, to see decadence not as the outcome of a gradual delegitimization of the obligation to obey but as the paradoxical universalization of obedience itself, understood as having a more profound meaning than simple consent to a command. As has been said, it is clear that wanting to read Nietzsche in this way involves a philosophical choice that is anything but obvious. It means taking the will to power as a first ontological given that cannot be simply turned into a political project. In sharp contrast with the "fascist" simplifications, and generally with the advocates of a Nietzsche who is "cut in half," the *Wille zur Macht* would essentially be extended back to the very foundation of life, to its incessant principle of organization and disorganization. Therefore, as Deleuze suggests, it means asserting that every phenomenon is in itself the manifestation of a set of forces, since every force is in an essential relationship with another. The Nietzschean world would be a plural universe whose atoms, in reality, are not indivisible but rather sets of forces. If the being of force is plural, and if only force can be related to another force, then the differential element of this relation is called will to power. The will to power, therefore—and this is a crucial point—is not expressed as the will to exert itself on an object and dominate it. It is a will that seeks to manifest itself by relating to another will. In this interpretative horizon, the body itself—a product of the forces that make it up—would be organized according to a hierarchy between the quantity of forces with a different direction. Whence the origin of the contrast between active and passive, which does not consist, therefore, in a different quality originating in the will to power that is good in some people and evil in others.[18]

Obedience Has Never Been a Virtue

How, then, are we to interpret the relationship between forces and Nietzsche's eulogy of differences, in political terms as well, and how are we to assess it? As we know, broad nationalist simplifications in Nietzsche's thought—from *völkisch* to full-blown Nazi—view the principle of difference as a principle of the ranking of values between political and anthropological affiliations, based on one's social position by birth or race. If we really believed that Nietzsche's thought preached this caste-based or racist mapping of the human being, he would be championing a political dualism in which there would be an aristocratic people on the one hand and a population of slaves on the other, with the consequent distinction between a good power and a bad power, manifested in the distance between an active command and a passive obedience. However, refuting this easy opposition, which merely flips the commonsense idea of what is good and what is evil, does not mean that we can evade the crudeness of some of his hyperboles. Rather, we must acknowledge that the principle of the strong's will to dominate over the weak is easily transposable into politics. Nor can we dispose of the embarrassment provoked by many of the aphorisms by making his sister responsible for them, by blaming them on the "cut-and-paste" editing she performed in order to be able to translate a "scabrous" selection of them into the National-Populist language of the Thousand Year Reich. Nevertheless, the question of evil in relation to power continues to be asked. With Nietzsche and starting from Nietzsche, it arises along with the question of the subject, along two lines of thought: in the first place, because along with the movement of an I that returns to itself there arose the linguistic invention that corresponds to the concept of evil (a thread we already pulled through in the chapter on Nietzsche in the first part of this book). It is involved in the formation of interiority, explained by the German philosopher as the folding inside of an energy, and of its power, which is unable to flow to the outside. The second way the question of the subject is implicated in the question of evil is because, using this specific mode of subjectification, the apparatuses of a relation of domination can best be operated by the "entrepreneurs of *ressentiment*." This is what makes Nietzsche's denunciation of the dismal picture of the last man so interesting. It serves to show him how the ground for nihilism was prepared by a general domestication, thanks to which the government of men managed the demands of *ressentiment*, the reactive forces. In a word, another reading of Nietzsche is possible without the need to make his work completely "impolitical"—without turning it into metaphors and hiding the traces of his political preoccupation. It requires following the path of his critique of pastoral power and, without pushing it too far, deriving from this critique a challenge to the political principle of obedience—or better, of a certain way of obeying—that can transform a physiological balance of power into an event of evil.

As always, Nietzsche is ambivalent, of course. In some passages he seems to justify or even appreciate obedience, conformism, and servility for everyone who lacks the strength to act. However, in his criticism of apathy and passivity, his antidemocratic polemic allows us to locate one of the rare places in which political philosophy seems to offer the possibility of another genealogy of the connection between evil and power. The genealogy inferable from Nietzsche seems to have reaped the precious insights contained in the legend of the Grand Inquisitor, and then extended them into an area that remained unexplored by the great Russian writer.

The evil of power, therefore, has nothing to do with a will to power that original sin, as disobedience, would seem to presume. On the contrary, in 1884 he writes, "*The root of all evil*: that the slavish morality of meekness, selflessness, absolute obedience, has triumphed." Radical evil is thus that which reveals itself, with no ambiguity whatsoever, in the fact that "the higher men" are either racked by guilt or, ultimately, having "measured themselves according to the standard of the virtue of slaves—found they were 'proud'."[19] The human type corresponding to the triumphant morality of *ressentiment* is none other than the "last man," whose phenomenology indicates the apex of the nihilistic trajectory, politically marked by full affirmation of the herd morality.[20] Certainly, Nietzsche's philosophical radicalism does not make him a master of terminological and conceptual distinctions. In his writings liberalism, democracy, and socialism are often confused and overlap. Briefly, the age of democracy is the time of the "last men": narrow and petty, useful and utilitarian, measurable and measuring, equal and mediocre, weak and meek, and yet strongly convinced that this is how they finally invented happiness. Democratic morality, which at this point has triumphed "almost everywhere," at first sight appears to be a good glue for the political community with its idea of equality. But for Nietzsche, under the lofty values (justice, brotherhood, solidarity) there lies concealed a general decadence that defends universal pettiness and weakness, by cultivating them.

I do not think that Nietzsche is simply seeking antidemocracy followers; rather, he wants to disorient his readers, to prompt them to question their habitual, deeply rooted convictions, specifically the ones relating to "modern democratic ideas." He wants to show them the other face of democracy, the dark side of the democratic human type, who believes he has invented happiness only because he has "left the regions where it was hard to live," who believes himself capable of love for humanity only because he is now incapable of withstanding conflict. If democratic, "modern men" are now at the forefront, this is only because they are horrified by the strain of extremes. They want to live in comfort and their supposed goodness is nothing but their desire not to be hurt by anyone. The democratic type is the supporter of the cowardly virtues, of which the most unbearable for Nietzsche is the hypocrisy of those who hold a position of real power. In fact, "even those who command hypocritically feign the virtues of those who serve. 'I serve, you serve, we serve'—thus prays even the hypocrisy of the rulers—and woe if the first lord is *merely* the first servant!"[21] Nietzsche fails to rein in his contempt for these followers of the democratic taste, for the new "levelers" and "brotherhood enthusiasts who call themselves socialists" for whom nothing is valuable except a life of well-being, free from danger, and pain, unburdened of everything that creates worry.[22] Thus, they are lovers of equality because they are always the most suspicious of any differences, and while they are incapable of admiring others, they want to be validated and affirmed. The democratic types lend themselves better to offering gentleness and meekness in exchange for a guide than people of any other age. The important thing, suggests Nietzsche, is that they never be told that someone is commanding and, consequently, that they are obeying. Remember: "I serve, you serve, we serve" is the required slogan of the new political legitimacy, because all that matters is that the new master-servants be able to convince the democratic type that they are the guarantors of their secure, good life. Thus, far from being the expression of a progressive affirmation of subjective freedom, of the triumph of humankind who has finally achieved adulthood, democracy is rather the fulfillment and final phase of a long process of subjugation and containment of the vital energy. From this process, what we have learned to call virtue is fear rather than courage, *ressentiment* rather than action, and obedience rather than self-determination. The last man, therefore, is he who is aware of his new numerical strength, endowing himself with political potency as well.

At first glance these pages seem to resume the invaluable insights of Tocqueville in *Democracy in America*: his lucid, ambivalent look on the "passion for equality of conditions" and on the mimetic desire produced by conformism and uniformity.[23] Equally Tocquevillian is Nietzsche's condemnation of a homogenizing process that although constantly gaining more ground paradoxically increases the risk of overturning into tyranny. But even though for the French writer the issue is primarily the "tyranny of the majority," for Nietzsche the possibility for anyone who wants to affirm his or her superiority over the masses to become a tyrant grows at the same time. These are the well-known statements pointed to by those who support a view of Nietzsche as a racist and advocate of slavery. In many places the German philosopher does indeed state that the new political and social conditions brought on by the leveling, the "mediocritization of man," is "likely in the highest degree to give birth to exceptional human beings of the most dangerous and attractive quality."[24] The democratization advances, generating a "type that is prepared for slavery in the subtlest sense," but it may happen in "single, exceptional cases" that a strong man will appear. Democracy can prove to be "an involuntary arrangement for the cultivation of tyrants—taking that word in every sense, including the most spiritual."[25] Also because, as Nietzsche reminds us with regularity, it is much easier to control a Christian people than a non-Christian people. This is the "extra step" Nietzsche's criticism of democracy takes. What makes it more radical than both Tocqueville's polemic and Dostoevsky's harsh analysis is that he identifies the continuity between Christianity and the modern world as lying in a subjectification process that rendered the human animal docile, manipulable, and obedient. He explains the political implications of this change to us as well, confronting us with one of the first, most powerful explorations of the interweaving between subjectivity and power. The exemplarity of the classical world also serves this purpose: to show us, by contrast, how an entire experience of the world and the self was lost.

The world of Christian morality, he explains, resulted from a long process that is marked by an "anti-political" bias. In its religious or secularized form, Christianity conquered all spheres of life, thereby eliminating *real* politics, or more precisely, a "political" conception of life. It neutralized the "truth" of the Greek *agon* (contest, struggle). Nietzsche's reassessment of this concept shaped his theoretical vision, inspired his formulation of the "will to power," and especially provided the driving force behind his critique of the present. We know that Nietzsche's writing took its start from his encounter with the Homeric poems and their concept of struggle, especially in the *Iliad*.[26] The Homeric *arete* (excellence) issued from the various forms of contests—from war to tournaments—that in turn expressed a world of struggle that served as Nietzsche's tool for shattering the reigning image in his time of a Hellenism that was measured and Olympian. Moreover, it almost seems in his work as if the battlefield where Hector and Achilles faced each other, united by an identical passion for *agon*, becomes the standard by which to measure the transformations of the subject and power. To the end, this agonistic schema—originating both in Heraclitus and Homer—remained one of his criteria by which to judge the meaning of existence. If contest and struggle are the essence of Hellenism—the sign of greatness that embraces every sphere of the real—then the political also draws its value from the well of agonism. What agonism implies in war, but also in daily behavior, is the will to distinguish oneself, to express oneself, and to win immortality for oneself; it is an unrelenting stimulus to memorable action, which is an integral part of how individual perfection is accomplished. For Nietzsche, just as for Heraclitus, *dike* is *polemos*: the political relation "according to justice" is struggle *inter pares*, between men of equal value. Even when the struggle takes place between unequal forces, so that someone wins and someone loses, the clash between the two competitors presupposes respect for the value of others, and admiration for the greatness of one's adversary. As a matter of fact, only in a horizontal *agon* "between equals" can politics put into action the desire that human beings have to transcend themselves and give meaning to their lives. In truth, life is nothing but this will: not the will to self-preservation, but the will to expand, to compete, and to outdo oneself.

In the first section of *On the Genealogy of Morals*, Nietzsche returns to the idea of politics as a relation *inter pares*, one of "mutual suspicion and jealousy," as the product of a noble morality—in other words, a self-affirming one that "develops from a triumphant affirmation of itself."[27] It is in this context, and not in the Gospel, that true "love of one's enemies" finds its place: "How much reverence has a noble man for his enemies!—and such reverence is a bridge to love[. . . .] For he desires his enemy for himself, as his mark of distinction; he can endure no other enemy than one in whom there is nothing to despise and *very much* to honor!"[28] The Roman, Arabian, Germanic, Japanese nobility, the Homeric heroes, the Scandinavian Vikings,[29] these are the "men of action" who express in the arena their contempt for security, for the preservation of the body and life. It is an aristocracy of *agathoi*, "complete men," overflowing with force and energy who have not yet learned to separate action from happiness. These are the people who self-defined themselves as "good men," not on the basis of some *a posteriori* evaluation, beyond action, but because they are "good at,"[30] in other words, capable of manifesting their power *immediately*, thanks to the opportunity provided by contest and by the greatness of their enemies. In short, a passion for contest, *agon*, and being form a single whole, just as subject and predicate are indistinguishable in a vision that sees no subject prior to or outside action. But what is even more important for our inquiry is to note how degrading, lowering, and humiliating the enemy are extraneous to this political relationship *inter pares*; and to observe how instead *ressentiment* functions to compellingly introduce this need. Indeed, it is the "man of *ressentiment*" who ushers in a vertical perspective of the political relation: a relationship whose vector begins from above and heads toward the bottom, basing itself on devaluing the other and contempt as a substitute for action. The admiration and fear we had previously now become lowering and moralization: "He [the man of *ressentiment*] has conceived 'the evil enemy', '*the Evil One*', and this in fact is his basic concept, from which he then evolves, as an afterthought and pendant, a 'good one'—himself!"[31] He does not present himself in terms of his value, as we have said; instead, he needs to model himself in opposition to something outside himself, something other than himself.

Starting from the *Gay Science*, Nietzsche is persuaded that *ressentiment*, and the moralization of the world along with it, have transformed the "horizontal" clash between forces into a vertical type of relation—a high-low relationship in which the fighting continues, but by other means, with value judgments, that is. The *ressentiment* of Christian morality therefore neutralizes the spirit of political contest—true politics—and inaugurates a lengthy era that is antipolitical and destructive toward political action. The last stage in this process is democracy, when all those who would never have been able to brave the greatness of the contest now enter into the public sphere.[32]

To undertake a genealogy of morals that is able to reconstruct the dynamics of the new pastoral mode of the relationship between subject and power thus also means to reveal the point of origin, the "scandalous trigger" of the virtues belonging to the modern subject that change the perspective of the political relationship. Meekness, self-control, moderation, fairness, kindness, tolerance do not arise as expressions of a subject that has finally risen out of its minority status, of a subject that autonomously gives laws to itself. These virtues are rather signs of old scars, adaptation strategies that respond to an "original" pain. In the lengthy second essay in *On the Genealogy of Morals*,[33] Nietzsche describes in the most effective manner possible the anthropological leap ("the most fundamental change he ever experienced") that brought the human animal to the formation of conscience and bad conscience, from whose subtle, cruel, dialectical play it produced a tamed and meek human being, malleable and willing to meet the needs of society, a creature who was predictable and calculable; in brief, the responsible and obedient individual who was necessary more than ever for democratic society. It is certainly not my intention to run through the passages describing the role played by fear and punishment, as well as that played by the relationship between creditor and debtor, in producing "man as we have known him." I would just like to point out that it is primarily based on these pages that the philosophical anthropology of the twentieth century—from Helmuth Plessner to Arnold Gehlen and Max Scheler all the way to Peter Sloterdijk—formulated their own hypotheses about humankind as an incomplete animal, unfit for life, characterized, however, in the first place by its absolute will to live and because of this by the need to "stabilize" its world through institutions and moral beliefs, legal norms, and behavioral customs. From these pages, too, Michel Foucault drew his inspiration for his thought on what he called "pastoral power."

We have already talked about how Nietzsche describes the phenomenon of internalization taking place.[34] Because of this process, a will that is unable to directly express itself in action resorts to the cunning trick of transforming its own passivity into a moral virtue. A "material" impossibility, an objective impossibility, is thus elevated into choice: the choice for good and the rejection of evil. Along with this moral lie, Nietzsche wants to unmask the related political lie of free consent to obedience. The origin of political domination (for which in this context he uses the term "state") is not a gradual, intentional passage to which individuals consent because they are aware of the complexity of their needs; nor does it take form by means of the instrument posited by the illusory theory called contractualism. The origin of "vertical politics" is a sudden violence; it is an unexpected event—a rupture, an inevitable fatality.

I employed the word "state": it is obvious what is meant—some pack of blond beasts of prey, a conqueror and master race which, organized for war and with the ability to organize, unhesitatingly lays its terrible claws upon a populace perhaps tremendously superior in numbers but still formless and nomad. *That is after all how the "state" began on earth*: I think that sentimentalism which would have it begin with a "contract" has been disposed of[. . . .] One does not reckon with such natures; they come like fate, without reason, consideration, pretext; they appear as lightning appears, too terrible, too sudden, too convincing, too "different" even to be hated. Their work is an instinctive creation and imposition of forms—they are the most involuntary, unconscious artists there are [. . .] a ruling structure that lives, in which parts and functions are delimited and coordinated, in which nothing whatever finds a place that has not first been assigned a "meaning" in relation to the whole.[35]

Nietzsche has no interest in demonstrating the historical authenticity of his reconstruction of the origin of the state. It is meant to serve as the hypothesis for an "original break" to explain the grip that the salvific mechanisms "of the priestly power" have on the state of subjugation out of which obedient conformism gets its start. Pastoral power, the power of what Nietzsche calls the "priestly caste," manages and organizes the *ressentiment* of the weak toward the strongest members of society. It channels the power of their malaise toward the outside, onto others and against others. And when this fails, when the mere presence of the other-than-self no longer suffices to explain evil, then they manage to transform suffering into a condition of punishment.[36] "Quite so, my sheep! someone must be to blame for it: but you yourself are this someone, *you alone are to blame for it—you alone are to blame for yourself.*"[37] These are the famous words that Nietzsche puts in the mouth of the shepherd when the latter introduces the idea of sin onto the scene, the magnificent idea that "has been the greatest event so far in the history of the sick soul."[38] Here we have "the entire antisensualistic metaphysic of the priests, that makes men indolent and overrefined," to which the ascetic ideals of our Judeo-Christian tradition owe their origin.

The process of internalization is what makes human beings potentially insecure, potentially in need of a shepherd to guide them. And the state is not pervasive enough, not familiar or reassuring or aggregating enough; indeed, "directing the conscience" escapes it.[39] Pastoral power was able to find a place for itself in this vacuum by managing, directing, and manipulating *ressentiment* and the need for guidance. In this way, responding to a request that originated from the bottom, it managed to weld the political relationship into a perfect mechanism for control and obedience. Now, the democratic age, an offspring of that same pastoral power, is currently destroying everything that it had built: God and morality. In fact, if *ressentiment* is allowed to flow in its own vicious circle, that movement of projection onto the outside and destruction of what is externalized as object can only lead to the nihilism that is dragging Europe toward its collapse—and all this without the I being able to regain its self-government.

In the journey started by pastoral power, Nietzsche seems to conclude, the democratic outcome marks the successful internalization of the herd instinct. What we will see from what Nietzsche writes, then, is a progressive, relentless slide from reverent obedience to an external authority, from a form of obedience that in some way is a sign of recognition of a distance and a difference, to an obedience that is automatic, so to speak. In other words, we will shift from a form of obedience, understood as an explicit means to satisfy the goal of securing oneself, to a passive and compliant obedience to the already internalized command—which expresses itself in a spontaneous anticipation of the demand for submission. In short, *pastoral power establishes the value of passivity as a general rule of conduct, a value that becomes a universal virtue in a democracy.*[40]

In his ironic praise of the astute workings of the ascetic priest, Nietzsche nevertheless acknowledges the greatness and strength of a culture—that of Christianity and more generally of philosophy—that was able to develop a symbolic order out of suffering and pain. These pages of his posthumous fragments from 1887 to 1888, in which Nietzsche describes the human animal's need for meaning, are beautiful and intense, and certainly not wanting in clarity compared to later psychoanalysis. It is as if he were telling us that the problem of evil arises from the impossibility of acting—and from the resulting frustration—on the part of a human being that in order to "save itself" reinvented itself as soul, as interiority, as a consciousness endowed with its own mysterious, innermost freedom. But, more profoundly, he also seems to be telling us that the *very idea of evil is inseparable from the human animal's search for meaning*—the same animal that, even though capable of withstanding pain, is unable to tolerate the randomness and senselessness of pain. This is why Nietzsche never tires of repeating that "pain has been robbed of innocence." He knows that to give meaning to pain, to explain it as "evil" makes the pain bearable, regardless of whether it is caused by the wickedness of others or by original sin. A culprit and a *telos*, sin and redemption: these are the skillful stratagems that attenuate the absurdity of suffering.

Nietzsche is aware that if, on the one hand, ascetic ideals are untruthful revaluations, on the other hand, thanks to them—and to the process of internationalization that they are rooted in—the human animal has become "an interesting animal." As he explains in *On the Genealogy of Morals*: "For with the priests *everything* becomes more dangerous, not only cures and remedies, but also arrogance, revenge, acuteness, profligacy, love, lust to rule, virtue, disease—but it is only fair to add that it was on the soil of this *essentially dangerous* form of human existence, the priestly form, that man first became *an interesting animal*, that only here did the human soul in a higher sense acquire depth and become evil [*böse*]—and these are the two basic respects in which man has hitherto been superior to other beasts!"[41]

"Human history would be altogether too stupid a thing without the spirit that the impotent have introduced into it."[42] Nietzsche thus acknowl-

edges that if "the ascetic priest" is in reality a transhistorical figure, its function must respond to a need that is constant and deep. In §11 of the third essay in *On the Genealogy of Morals*, we read: "For consider how regularly and universally the ascetic priest appears in almost every age; he belongs to no one race; he prospers everywhere; he emerges from every class of society[. . . .] It must be a necessity of the first order that again and again promotes the growth and prosperity of the *life-inimical species*—it must indeed be in the *interest of life itself that such a self-contradictory type does not die out.*"[43]

In the face of a "positive," creative morality guided by the pathos of distance—that of the strong and of the conquerors—what takes form by reaction is the morality of the herd, which conveys a force that is different but no less powerful in any case: *the force capable of transforming weakness and impotence into goodness, and obedience into virtue.*[44] In summary, expressed in terms that are not properly Nietzschean, we can say that "pastoral power" is the first model of a relationship, repeated and internalized, in which giving up the power of the self over itself and over action is consecrated as the virtue of obedience, thanks to a sort of positive revaluation of fear and insecurity. The shepherd will from now on be responsible for the salvation of every sheep and of the whole flock, but for this purpose he or she must have access to the truth and freedom of their consciences. This is precisely when obedience is elevated to a virtue, passing from a means to obtain something definite, to an end in itself: the achievement of a permanent state of the soul, in which the sheep simultaneously pursue the good of one and all by constantly submitting themselves to their shepherd-pastor.

Nietzsche seeks to bring to light the suffering, fear, and violence that constitute the origin of politics, social morality, the ethics of sacrifice, collective responsibility, and the compact between the individual and the community. He is warning us that democratic self-determination is nothing but a form of obedience so successful it no longer requires coercion and sensational punishments. But he is also saying that in the "perverse" and "sick" act that lowers strength and nobility to vices at the same time it elevates weakness and servility to virtues, what is at work in the original "reversal" of values, which are the basis for reinforcing *every* political and social order, is the will to life that would rather change from positive to negative than cease to exist. Nietzsche is ultimately suggesting we question the meekness and the passivity of the virtues that were "invented" and exalted by the Christian ethic, and that, in his opinion, were transported directly, although in a secularized version, into political virtues during the age of democracy. Egalitarianism and universal justice, obedience and conformism—masked by the veil of trust and confidence in democratic self-determination—are in reality vectors of a precise will to life that acts as a force for the progressive destruction of differences, as a continuous process of homologation, which shuns and devours every "pathos of distance," both upwardly and downwardly. As Nietzsche incessantly repeats, "difference engenders hatred."[45] But a life removed from the physiological conflict generated by differences is, for Nietzsche, a life that is forced to deny itself. The "tragic" observation of such an irreducible dynamic, first of all within life itself and only secondarily transposable into political conflicts, marks, I believe, the profound distance of the German philosopher from the large and undefined counterrevolutionary "galaxy," with its "simple" desire to reinstate a supposedly shattered order.

This, in my opinion, is the great deconstructive contribution—controversial and disputable, political and "impolitical" at the same time—that Nietzsche has to offer political thought and the question of the evil of power. The fact that in the democratic desert there may arise the "overman," the strong spirit, who is free and capable of contesting this life that seeks to preserve itself by annihilating itself, is certainly a good sign, and perhaps a proactive one, in Nietzsche's thought. But whether or not this can be expressed in terms of the good of a political project for a particular nation, a particular people, or a single dominating race is something I am really unable to pin down in his texts—not even in the posthumous fragments on the will to power.[46] True, Nietzsche does not say a single thing about obedience and inertia; sometimes they are presented only as the nihilistic effects caused by the weakening of life. But mostly he presents them as the cunning strategies of a life that seeks to preserve itself. It is not possible then to divide between an "anti-nature" morality and politics, and a "second-nature" morality and politics. Heuristically, he presents to us a will that is positive power, which creates values by itself, manifests itself, and seeks to increase. This stands in opposition to a will to life that has no other objective than to preserve itself, does not express itself, and instead reacts, retroacts, thus returning, resentful and cowering, to its source. But if the will to power is not the will to dominate and instead a relationship between different energies; if it is not the "thing in itself" of absolute energy, able to turn the weak into a function of the strong and instead is composed of opposing vectors, then everything gets more complicated. No wonder that Nietzsche criticizes Darwinism and its assessment of the instinct for self-preservation as the original nucleus of life from which all further understanding of the existing world is to be derived.

In reality, the desire for life whose sole purpose is to preserve itself is viewed by Nietzsche as the heart and engine of nihilism, the source of all types of passivity: a will that is no less reactive than *ressentiment*, seeking mimicry, tending toward fast adaptation, and searching for union in associations and collectivities. For him, these are all symptoms of a great weakness[47]: "Physiologists should think again before positing the 'instinct of preservation' as the cardinal drive in an organic creature. *A living thing wants above all to discharge its force*; 'preservation' is only a consequence of this."[48] And again: "The weaker presses to the stronger from a need for nourishment; it wants to get under it, if possible to become one with it. The stronger, on the contrary, drives others away; it does not want to perish in this manner; it grows and in growing it splits itself into two or more parts. The greater the impulse toward unity, the more firmly may one conclude that weakness is present; the greater the impulse towards variety, differentiation, inner decay, the more force is present."[49]

Now, all the Christian and democratic virtues—derived, I repeat once more, from that first postulate of the equality of all souls before God—all the virtues of modern man, are for Nietzsche strategies put into action from the inability to express one's power. Hence his critique of obedience as hypocrisy, as the prudent transfiguration of *ressentiment* into the virtue of "subordination." Behind "pride in duty" hides in reality the fatalism and resignation that lead to the "idealization, deification of him who commands."[50] Better to submit, therefore, than respond with one's own action and power. Here is Kant's petty "You must": "'Do right and fear no man': i.e., to do one's duty according to a definite rude scheme within which a community exists."[51] But in all these virtues related to moral obedience, the will to power of a life that fights for its continuity, that fights to continue to exist, that fights against death, comes to the surface in any case. Nietzsche will say that "the ascetic ideal is an artifice for the preservation of life" that struggles against death.[52]

Goodness as Inner Anarchy

So who is the person who manages to go beyond good and evil? Surely it is the person who manages to transcend the *ressentiment* that for Nietzsche is inseparable from the evil of nihilism. But what type of politics and morality would be able to carry this person beyond pastoral or democratic management of *ressentiment*? Is it really the order of the strong man, the Superman of the aristocracy, understood in the common sense of the term? In short, the order of those who, never holding back from bad conscience or remorse, put their will to power directly into action?

In §260 of *Beyond Good and Evil*, entitled "What is noble," Nietzsche writes:

Wandering through the many subtler and coarser moralities which have so far been prevalent on earth, or still are prevalent, I found that certain features recurred regularly together and were closely associated—until I finally discovered two basic types and one basic difference. There are *master morality* and *slave morality*—I add immediately that in all higher and more mixed cultures there also appear attempts at mediation between these two moralities, and yet more often the interpenetration and mutual misunderstanding of both, and at times they occur directly alongside each other—even within the same human being, within a *single* soul.[53]

It is true that in his genealogical exploration, the German philosopher traced out the physiognomy of two human types, or rather, two modes of conduct. But perhaps it would be more correct to say that he set up an antithesis of types as a hypothesis to denote two alternative possibilities for subjectification. As Deleuze would say, "a typology of forces, an ethic of the corresponding ways of being"[54]: the perspective of the self-affirming ethos that human beings forge through action and will versus the dynamics of *ressentiment*—a passive reaction—that operates through introversion as a strategy in response to the perception of its own weakness. However, the fact that Nietzsche views these modes of being as intermingling is not emphasized frequently enough. It is our need to simplify that presents them to us as a real alternative: on the one hand, the desire for power, and on the other, a creeping decadence that struggles to avoid totally succumbing. However, the philosopher tells us, everyone who does not die too young is a decadent for almost half his or her life.[55] What significance are we to give to this statement?

I think that the conditions of evil, even for Nietzsche, are not "simple." That is to say, they are not simply embodied in the "last man" and his system of power. I think they should be identified rather in the progressive hegemony of a single type, or more precisely, of a single attitude: denying oneself as a field of opposing forces, and because of this denial, allowing oneself to be dragged into the "hemiplegia of virtue," into that "peace of soul" that Nietzsche defines as a "chronic disease." "Whence comes the hemiplegia of virtue, the invention of the good man?" Nietzsche asks in the spring of 1888.

The demand is that man should castrate himself, of those instincts with which [. . .] he can cause harm, can be angry, can demand revenge[. . . .] This unnaturalness corresponds, then, to that dualistic conception of a merely good and a merely evil creature [. . .]; in the former are summarized all the positive, in the latter all the negative forces, intentions, states.—Such a manner of valuing believes itself to be "idealistic"; it does not doubt that, in the conception of "the good," it has posited a supreme desideratum[. . . .] It does not even consider it settled that this antithesis of good and evil is conditional on the existence of both; on the contrary, the latter should vanish and the former remain.

This way of thinking, useful for convincing human animals to be meek and obedient, starts off from the absurd assumption that "takes good and evil for realities that contradict one another" and not as complementary value concepts: "*It therewith actually denies life, which has in all its instincts both Yes and No.*" And this way of thinking imagines, indeed dreams about, a single, unitary state, in which one can put an end to "the inner anarchy, the unrest between those opposing value drives."[56] "What is mediocre in the typical man?" asks Nietzsche. "That he does not understand the necessity for the *reverse side of things*; that he combats evils as if one could dispense with them; that he will not take the one with the other."[57] These, then, are the people who allow evil to grow inside themselves; those who want to *approve of* one part by abolishing the others; those who pursue the *ideal* as something that can be isolated, those who are never more in contact with anything harmful, bad, dangerous, enigmatic, or destructive.

Anyone who is able to counter all this, Nietzsche will call "aristocratic." As he asserts, "Our insight is that with every growth of man, his other side must grow too; that the *highest* man [. . .] would be the man who represented the antithetical character of existence most strongly."[58] Anyone who can sustain his or her own inner duality, without hypostatizing it into two separate entities—an inside and an outside, into a self of goodness who must fight against an "other-than-self of evil," whose presence is a constant threat—is noble. By not taking sides on the front line of the battle between opposing substances, the aristocrat never falls into the clutches of the power that promises to liberate us.

This was the secret that the Grand Inquisitor had used his powerful intelligence to figure out, stopping however within the confines of the dualistic relationship. Nietzsche looks more deeply into this very relationship and grasps the power that lies at its heart. He understands that each submission, each vertical relationship, appeals to the desire of subjects to be freed from evil so as to reconstitute themselves as a homogeneous whole, to pacify their inner world. He realizes that the desire to be free once and for all of conflict in order to continue to live in tranquility actually makes us slaves of a utilitarian logic, which leads us to accept the identity that someone else imposes on us. It leads us to "choose" to become what those who save want us to become. This is how we consent to making ourselves into a stable, fixed identity: making ourselves into something objectivizable, employable, usable, and replaceable.

This is how, for Nietzsche, we give up on making ourselves aristocratic, which is to say, bearers of true responsibility. We are constantly waiting for something from outside to justify, save, legitimize, authorize. This is how we become obedient subjects. It is not only a relationship of command and obedience, of an authority who decides and a subservient subject who performs. At play is a complex process of subjectification that requires adaptation and identification to the game of rules thanks to which we feel "saved" or kept alive. This is how a dynamic of the subject is modeled that remains in force even when—as the letter of the democratic spirit would have it—people want to call themselves—or they proclaim themselves to be—a sovereign.[59] Going beyond good and evil, then, means conceding "a tragic yes to life," without getting trapped and blackmailed by the promise of a revaluation of suffering, and without deluding oneself by the hope of giving a meaning to the senselessness of pain. *It means knowing how to remain a field of opposing forces.* This does not mean we remain a perpetual flow of impersonal energies because, for Nietzsche, human beings are defined by their need to give themselves a form. The human animal must fashion itself, it must curb its instincts—without eradicating them, though.

In *Ecce Homo* he reveals to us the meaning of that incessant war taking place inside one person. Nietzsche presents himself as a field of forces, within which sickness has the liberating force of an inescapable death sentence, making him a master of dis-identifications: "I have the know-how to reverse perspectives." With the perspective of the sick he has learned to look at the *healthiest* values, and from the perspective of superabundant life he has practiced perceiving the symptoms of decadence: "Looking from the perspective of the sick toward healthier concepts and values and, conversely, looking again from the fullness and self-assurance of a rich life down into the secret work of the instinct of decadence—in this I have had the longest training, my truest experience; if in anything, I became master in this. Now I know how, have the know-how, to reverse perspectives."[60] He feels this vicious alternation within himself because his own life, his illness, has become his philosophy of experience. Human life has a dual structure. For this reason, real power does not lie in forcing oneself or something outside of oneself, but in being able to give oneself a form that reorders the warring forces within the self: forces that always and only reach equilibriums that promptly shatter and reassemble once again. Moral dualism has instead turned the human animal into a "herd animal," by bringing it up to deny and amputate its inherent duality. This herd animal is contemptible not because it is weaker, belonging as it does to a human category with an inferior status, but because it has been brought up in the faith of non-freedom. It has been taught that "only as a bigot is one on the right path to god."[61] It has been taught to unburden itself of any tension with itself and thus to delegate to others the management and cessation of conflict. In short, it has been taught to be dependent.

Life, in being active, is tension—the will to overcome obstacles, the need to go beyond ourselves. Life is the will to power, but not in the sense of desiring the objects of power as tools required to dominate others— "men who want power for the sake of the *happiness* power provides: political parties."[62] Some want power even at the cost of damaging their well-being and happiness: these are the ambitious ones, the glory seekers. But some want power simply to make sure it does not fall into the hands of others, whom they do not want to depend on. Aristocratic thus describes someone who does not want to be dependent. Nobility is not conferred by birth or by virtue of belonging to a particular social class; it is not a question of status, but of the ability to recognize the structural duality of life, without ever denying it.

The question that concludes *Beyond Good and Evil*—"What is noble?"—is not intended to serve as a way of demarcating the aristocracy from the plebeian class. The ultimate root of the noble attitude—before the social game of parts reconnected it to a dynasty and a rank—is distance, understood as the freedom and capacity to dis-identify oneself: to be divided, "to detach oneself," to put oneself in perspective with regard to all one's surroundings. It means to always be *also* somewhere else. Certainly, the split between self and self does cause suffering, and no one knew this better than Nietzsche. But he also knew that the game of continuously putting together and casting off identifications is the movement of freedom. The only genuine virtue, for him, is to accept that, as Zarathustra said, life is yes (affirmation), but it is also no (negation). Not surprisingly, the Nietzschean hero, the noble par excellence, is a slave. Epictetus is emblematic of someone who is not a master and does not want to be one. Life based on "justice," in the style of Heraclitus, is a life that does not seek to curb its own going beyond itself. Therefore, it is a life that seeks to get to the bottom of itself, to its end, without bartering its own demise for subordination.

Giorgio Colli stated that the only readers made uncomfortable by reading Nietzsche are those who have realized that the philosopher is not putting forward a doctrine. When there is a doctrine at stake, the answer is simple: you accept it or reject it. The discomfort strikes us, he argues, when we feel judged, or explored in all our "psychological nakedness," stripped of the protective masks afforded us by memberships and ideologies. "What if Nietzsche told us about himself," he asks, "and, in describing himself, laid bare all the ambivalences and contradictions of all human animals who are able to be brutally honest with themselves?"[63] If this is the case, then perhaps evil does exist for Nietzsche and, as it did for a minority strand of the twentieth century, its potentiality can be actualized in the cessation of *polemos*, of the tension that exists between the forces inside the self; evil can arise out of the state in which there is no longer any difference perceived whatsoever.

Thus, between the many ambiguities and contradictions, between the many affirmations that we have no desire to listen to in Nietzsche's writings, the possibility emerges of conceiving evil differently. Not so much by going beyond good and evil to proclaim the innocence of what has traditionally been thought of as evil; and certainly not in the sense of reversing good and evil, as Nietzsche's "hemiplegic interpreters" have done. Rather, starting with Nietzsche, the possibility presents itself of conceiving the conditions for stopping the circularity between evil and power, thanks to a sort of "ethical revolution" of the subject. Foucault's ethics as care of the self take up this legacy and respond to this challenge.

Strategies of Obedience and the Ethos of Freedom

Power in Itself Is Not Evil (Foucault)

In his last interview, published three days after his death,[1] Michel Foucault turned once again to his connection with the philosophy of Friedrich Nietzsche. "My entire philosophical development," he says, "was determined by my reading of Heidegger. I nevertheless recognize that Nietzsche outweighed him[. . . .] My knowledge of Nietzsche certainly is better than my knowledge of Heidegger. Nevertheless, these are the two fundamental experiences I have had." He then explains that the real philosophical turning point for him coincided with his rereading of Nietzsche after his "encounter" with Heidegger. And, significantly, this is how he concludes: "Do you mean to say that my fundamental Nietzscheanism might be at the origin of different misunderstandings? [. . .] I can only respond by saying that I am simply Nietzschean."[2]

The fact that Foucault's thought follows in the long wake of the "Nietzsche-Renaissance" is widely known. Foucault himself mentioned it to anyone who asked him for an account of his intellectual influences. Every one of his interpreters has underlined the strong impact that Nietzsche's philosophy had on Foucault's thought, in terms of both method and content. However, this connection has been claimed more often than it has been probed in any detail. The two names are so closely associated that anyone with a desire to criticize Foucault need only dust off the traditional accusation of irrationalism directed at Nietzsche. As an example, we need only recall Jürgen Habermas, who likened the German philosopher's role to that of a "turntable," from which there spun out the various routes taken by romantic irrationalism in attacking the modern subject and modern reason, from Adorno to Derrida, passing through Foucault.[3] I would not presume to dig into the folds of this theoretical relationship. What I would like to do, in a much more limited fashion, is explain the meaning of the statement, "I am simply Nietzschean." In what way is Foucault Nietzschean? In what way is he *simply* Nietzschean? Does the question of evil—its genealogy, its redefinition, its connection with power and the will to power, its relationship with life and death—play a central role for Michel Foucault as it does for Friedrich Nietzsche?

In addition to the texts devoted specifically to Nietzsche, Foucault's references to the German philosopher run throughout his entire oeuvre.[4] By restoring speech to madness, Nietzsche was the demon who prompted the French thinker to redeem "unreason" from the blame that reason had placed on it; it was Nietzsche who flanked Foucault in his critique of the idea of truth. It was primarily under Nietzsche's guidance that Foucault performed his dual task: on the one hand, demolishing the pretense of the self-sufficiency of subjectivity, and on the other, redefining the concept of power. Thanks to the Nietzschean will to power—or rather, thanks to a certain way of construing it that was passed on via Heidegger and Deleuze—it is therefore possible, as we have said, to interpret power relations between subjects as relations between forces. Although the *Wille zur Macht* is not a substance and not even something that some people are endowed with and others lack, Foucault adopted it as a complex, strategic situation: an intersection and clash between the multiple forces that pass through individuals. The will to power therefore serves as a privileged conceptual lens through which to observe what happens and which vectors pass between the subjects when they are in a power relationship.

In a word, it was Nietzsche who first taught Foucault that one should be suspicious of the exclusively coercive and repressive representation of the idea of power: the representation that stages power on one side and the subject on the other as if they were two separate, simply opposing entities, as do modern contractualism and the theory of state sovereignty. In classic legal theory, in fact, power is considered to be similar to a good: a right that you possess and, as such, something that can be transferred or alienated, partially or totally, through a particular legal act.[5] Law is neither the alibi nor the truth of power, just as the state is not its essential locus. Power is coextensive with the entire social body. Subjects and power give rise to a network of relationships inside of which there runs an energy that continuously reshapes the consolidated structures. These relations never appear in forms that are pure and autonomous; rather, they insinuate themselves into other types of relations, with which they play a role that is simultaneously determined and determining. Certainly their intertwining and their connections give rise to what Foucault calls "general facts of domination," but it is not possible to establish a first fact that founds a political domination.

He continued to discuss the meaning to be given to his idea of power on many occasions, until finally, near the end of his life, he arrived at a crystal-clear statement that put the various meanings and semantic differences into order. In what was perhaps one of his most important interviews, given in January 1984, published with the title "The Ethic of Care of the Self as a Practice of Freedom,"[6] the problem of the relationship between the subject and practices of power was given its most rigorous treatment. The paradox of the double bind between practices of subjugation and processes of subjectification—in other words, the dynamics by which the subject is constituted by relations of power such that along with subjugation there simultaneously occurs subjectification—is clearly stated. We will return later to the workings of these practices of self upon self that give rise to subjective conscience. For now we will limit ourselves to clarifying the dual function of power, the dynamic defined by Judith Butler as the scandal that Foucault brought to light, namely, the fact that we are dominated by an external power and simultaneously constituted by that same power; the fact that power forms the subject and at the same time lays down the conditions of its existence and the trajectory of its desire.[7]

If, then, on the one hand power negates the sphere of freedom and the desire of the subject by means of the law and prohibitions, on the other hand power affirms and produces; it causes actions to be performed and behaviors to come into existence. This is what prompted the criticism against Foucault that he allowed no room for resistance and freedom inside the network running between power, truth, and subject. Above all, say his critics, he did not provide any criteria for assessing political practices, since the difference between one type of exercise of power and another dissolves in the resigned observation that "everything is power." The possibility of appealing to some form of judgment is thus precluded, since the subject is deprived of the weapon of criticism along with the criterion of truth, because every truth results from a "play of perspectives" between knowledge and power.

This is why, at the urging of his interviewers, Michel Foucault seized on the opportunity to clarify his position once and for all. As we noted earlier,[8] by doing so he gave us a possible clue for interpreting his contribution to the problem of the relationship between evil and power. Of course, he can only reject the naïve idea expressed by all those, like Sartre for example, who declare that "power is evil"—because power means "strategic games" and the phenomenologies of these games can differ widely from one another.[9] In and of themselves, because there is no such thing as a society without power relations—that is, without strategies by which people seek to determine the conduct of others—these relations are neither good nor bad. Nevertheless, Foucault introduces a further and more nuanced distinction, bringing into focus the differences among "strategic games between liberties," "governmental technologies," and "states of domination." Strategic relationships are, so to speak, the condition of possibility for every relationship of power, from love relationships to more rigidly formal ones. This *a priori* consists in an attempt by some to determine the conduct of others, an attempt that meets with or collides with the aspiration on the part of the latter to not allow their conduct to be determined by the former, or to determine the conduct of the former in their turn. In short, the configuration of each relationship between subjects is what, in a Nietzschean fashion, implies a force, the manifestation of an energy or a will with respect to the action of others. In this regard, it is important to keep in mind Foucault's definition of power as "a mode of action upon the actions of others."[10]

Governmental technologies, instead, correspond to a more specific level of the manifestation of these relations: that of instruments and dispositifs (games of truth) through which certain modes of conduct are imparted and adopted. In short, the governmental technologies involve the constitution of a political hub that sets out, through these strategies, to govern others. It is often through these techniques, Foucault remarks, that states of domination are established and maintained. Often defined confusingly as "power," these states of domination are in reality situations in which the relations are so fixed, so frozen, that the structures they shape are totally asymmetrical and immobilized, with one pole of the relation having extremely limited margins of freedom. States of domination, such as Nazi thanatopolitics, are places and times in which the interactions are locked into place instead of being mobile. Within the infinite range of ways in which relations of power come into being, therefore, there can arise constellations that paralyze the freedom of the subjects involved. Although he does not say so explicitly, in my opinion these are the specific situations that Foucault sees as corresponding to the ancient question of the connection uniting evil and power. Though it no longer makes sense to simply distinguish between good power and bad power, and although we can no longer conceive of a situation in which relations of power do not exist, this does not imply that all ethical instances—and with them, the inevitable reference to the idea of evil—are dropped from Foucault's discourse. The criterion for evaluating a system of power, for deciding on its acceptability or rejection, resides in the distance that separates this whole from a "state of domination." This is so much the case that a new antimony can almost be forced out of Foucault: an opposition between evil (the apex of subjective dependence in a state of domination) and freedom (the least dependence possible that subjects can have on other people's determinations of their conduct). What was a synonymy—the traditional equivalence between evil, power, and freedom—has now become an antinomy; this is what would prompt Foucault to say that *where there is evil there is no longer power*.

Relations of power exist, in fact, only to the extent that subjects are free, which is to say, when they can change the circumstances: "In order to exercise a relation of power, there must be on both sides at least a certain form of liberty."[11] When one of the two subjects is completely under the other's command, when one becomes a thing in the other's hands—an object on which endless, limitless violence can be exerted—then relations of power cease to exist. But until that time, up to the threshold of the limit case of total domination, wherever there is power there is necessarily the possibility of resistance. Indeed, if the possibility to resist did not exist—through violence, escape, or deception, with the use of strategies that can reverse or at least change the circumstances—power would not exist, since it would lack even an object on which to discharge itself and the space within which to express itself. This way of thinking about power in terms of "microphysics," as we know, was the great innovation that Foucault introduced into political philosophy: it is a way whose Nietzschean assumptions were never put into question, despite several changes in direction that Foucault took along his path.[12]

It is as if Foucault felt the need, toward the late 1970s, to once again rethink the play between continuities and discontinuities that had served him in reconstructing the historical events of power. In the 1978 course entitled "Security, Territory, Population," focused on the concept of "governmentality," we see him at a crucial crossroads, I believe.[13] Presented in the beginning lectures as a historical study into the "art of governing"—an art that flourished from the beginning of the seventeenth century—Foucault's investigation ends by raising a question that is more philosophical than historical in nature. On the one hand, he defines "governmentality" as "the ensemble formed by institutions, procedures, analyses and reflection, calculations, and tactics that allow the exercise of the very specific, albeit very complex power that has the population as its target."[14] On the other hand, the term comes to designate a "line of force" that cuts across epochs, a centuries-old tendency that was the *a priori* of how political relations between people in the West were conceived and organized. In a word, Foucault is suggesting that we regard the series of political events that culminated in the neoliberal practices of World War II as an extremely long course, one from which in reality we have never really strayed. Thus, even before the concept of government sets up a finite, circumscribed ensemble of apparatuses, it establishes a fundamental historical continuity.

The Instance of "Pure Obedience": The Government of Men

In the fifth lecture, given on February 8, 1978, with the pretext of retracing the semantic history of the notion of government, Foucault in reality begins a long interlude on "pastoral power."[15] The idea implicit in his argument is as powerful as it is questionable on historical grounds: there is a deep bond that must be examined between the "government of souls," or the "economy of souls," of the first Christian centuries and the "government of men" that marked the horizon within which Western politics is inscribed. The connection consists in the structure of a specific relationship between subjects that Foucault proposes to call "pastoral relationships." This interaction does not refer to some natural human propensity and it is not eternal; rather, it had a beginning in time and it was constructed layer on layer. As such, it can be observed and the nuts and bolts of its workings can be taken apart.

The rise of the Christian pastorate—irreducible to the Jewish pastorate and to the pre-Christian pastorate of the East from which in any case it took its start—marks a rupture with a different political world. This is the world of the ancient Greeks, for whom the idea that human beings are the object or the material on which to exercise a kind of control and guidance similar to what is exercised in the extrapolitical realm—for example, on things and animals of the *oikos*—is completely foreign. Foucault is not particularly "scientific" in his analysis of the Eastern origin of this type of power. However, the traits that he sets out as characterizing it are crucial: he underlines its nomadic character, and that it is not bound to a territory or to the vicissitudes of a city, but rather to a population, both as a whole and in its individual members: "Anyway, one thing clearly emerges through all these meanings, which is that one never governs a state, a territory, or a political structure. Those whom one governs are people, individuals, or groups[. . . .] Those whom one governs are people."[16] In terms of its historical phenomenology, the bond between the wandering Hebrew people and their God that leads them from one land to another represents one of the first relationships that can be represented, thanks to the image of the relationship between the shepherd and his flock. The shepherd is a guide, who has no designs on the power of the collective organization, however; all he cares about is the salvation of his sheep, as a whole and individually. And salvation is obtained first by ensuring nourishment, by leading the flock to the best pastures, by making sure that all the animals eat and are properly fed. What we have, then, is a power that aims to do good. No longer the good of the city, however, in its primarily political meaning, but good understood as the well-being of those who wish to be led and who, for this reason, accept subordination. In other words, pastoral power is a power that cares, that is concerned, that seeks to prevent suffering, that goes in search of lost sheep and treats the sheep that are injured and in pain. As a result, the power of the shepherd never appears as a manifestation of power and superiority. Nor does it express a repressive instance; rather, it manifests itself as a duty, as the task of safeguarding and keeping watch, to be performed with zeal and devotion. "Pastoral power is fundamentally a beneficent power" because its purpose is to keep evil away from every sheep and from the whole flock.

The shepherd is the intermediary between the flock and salvation and as such does not act for his own glory or for his own wealth, but labors altruistically for others, to the point of sacrificing himself: ". . . sacrifice of the shepherd for his flock, the sacrifice of himself for the whole of the flock, and the sacrifice of the whole of his flock for each of the sheep."[17] One and all belong to each other in a mutual sacrificial relationship whose purpose is final salvation. Unlike the Hebrew pastorate, in which God acts directly as the shepherd who leads the people toward the promised land, the Christian pastorate introduces a strong element of mediation. The architect of salvation is not the pastor. He can only administer and plan the paths, thus arriving at managing "a subtle economy of merit and fault" that presupposes a careful analysis of the mechanisms of transfer, the procedures of reversal, and the games by means of which opposing elements balance each other. The Christian pastorate breaks the direct link between salvation, law, and truth, by establishing a mediated, "transversal" relationship between them that gives rise to a complex mechanics of subordination, a sort of accounting of the soul, of its vices and virtues.[18]

Thanks to the mediation of Christianity, especially after its institutionalization into a state religion, the structure of pastoral power, so alien to Greco-Roman thought, penetrated throughout the Western world. The Church made a specific form of power out of it that insinuated itself, with all of its dispositifs, into the heart of the Roman Empire. I am not going to enter into what these hypotheses owe to theories of secularization, from Max Weber to Hans Blumenberg, by way of Walter Benjamin and Carl Schmitt. Foucault states that he keeps his distance from them, although I am not sure to what extent his studies are able to remain faithful to this intention.[19] He directs the reader's attention toward a series of constants in how people enter into agreements with someone who promises them the good and salvation, by which they obey rules of behavior, and by which they embody a truth. The emphasis is placed on the constants of a pastoral power from which no "antipastoral revolution" has yet freed us. What seems to have been conveyed into modern politics, and what marks a permanent feature of our political universe, is the framework of a relationship based on the exchange between dependence and salvation, regardless of whether salvation is to be understood as the immortality of the soul or as the material well-being of the population. "This pastoral power [. . .]," writes Foucault, "no doubt underwent considerable transformations during these fifteen centuries of its history. It was no doubt shifted, broken up, transformed and integrated in various forms, but basically it has never been truly abolished. And I am very likely still mistaken when I situate the end of the pastoral age in the eighteenth century, for in fact *pastoral power in its typology, organization and mode of functioning, pastoral power exercised as power, is doubtless something from which we have still not freed ourselves.*"[20]

More than as a precise reconstruction of events and caesuras, the history of the pastorate appears to serve as a parameter for measuring the different procedures for the government of men. But how did this specific constellation make its way into history? How does a relationship of subordination get cemented—especially as far as the subservient party is concerned?[21] What are the gears that, by fitting together so perfectly, have made this relationship of care and protection not only the political relation par excellence, but also the norm for all proper behavior? To arrive at a better understanding (this is Foucault's usual move), we must distance ourselves from the supposed obviousness of this relationship, highlight its historicity, and investigate, *from inside*, how the rationale of the vertical link between an injunction and obedience to it is structured. Foucault emphasizes the novelty of the Christian pastorate for political thought. In the first place, he wants us to grasp what an unprecedented turning point it was that elevated "pure obedience" to an ideal. "The Christian pastorate," he tells us, "has organized something completely different that seems to me to be foreign to Greek practice, and this is what we could call the insistence on 'pure obedience' that is to say, on obedience as a unitary, highly valued type of conduct in which the essence of its *raison d'être* is in itself. What I mean is this. Everyone knows [. . .] that Christianity is not a religion of the law; it is a religion of what God wills for each in particular."[22]

Foucault's strategy, used here as elsewhere, is to proceed by stark oppositions, in order to make the force of the statements more effective. In this case, the contrast is played out between the individual of the pastoral power and the Greek citizen. The latter agrees to be directed only by the law or by persuasion, by the orders of the city or by the rhetoric of men: two different spheres, but in no case attributable to the instance of pure obedience. A sphere of respect does exist for the laws, for the decisions of the assembly and the magistrates whose orders are addressed to all in equal measure. And along with this, there is the insidious sphere of people who try to persuade other people, like the orator who convinces his public to act in a certain way, the physician who convinces the sick person to follow a certain treatment, and the philosopher who wants to teach how to arrive at the truth. These are attempts to persuade, even deceive, but they are never attempts to obtain obedience as a good in itself, as an ethical and political value.[23]

How does obedience ensconce itself inside the subject's heart, as its permanent state and ultimate end? What is the point at which external pressures are introjected into the hetero-directed? How does it happen that dependency—the object of the highest contempt in the Greek world—becomes the value of moral behavior par excellence? To this, almost like a programmatic outline of the courses of the 1980s, Foucault responds by turning his gaze to the first Christian monastic communities. It would seem that in these forms of collective life, the practice of obedience underwent a decisive passage from instrumental action to supreme moral principle, from a transitional means for reaching an end to a permanent state toward which to aim. Through the texts of the Christian Fathers, the lectures of February 15 and 22 on the pastorate of the early centuries of the Christian era describe the birth of the "government of souls" presented as the "art of arts." The shepherd is not analogous to a judge and even less to a sovereign state. The most fitting similarity makes him akin to a physician. Of course, he will make known the law and the will of God, which is equally valid for everyone, but as the physician he must be able to intervene through an individualizing treatment.

In the course of 1978, the term *apatheia* is the marker of this passage between these two modes of conceiving the relationship of subordination, the ancient and the Christian.[24] To define the "permanent state" of submission, during the early centuries Christianity used *apatheia*, the same term that Greek philosophy, and Stoicism in particular, had designated as the control the individual can exert over his or her passions through the exercise of reason. When a Greek disciple accepted subordination, by agreeing to be put under the direction and guidance of a philosophy master, he or she did so in order to arrive at a state of liberation from the passions. To keep the *pathe* at bay meant to fight against the passive forces that escape our control, thereby enslaving us, making us slaves to our own bodily instincts and also to the reality of the external world. Through *apatheia*, therefore, one attains self-mastery. If one obeys and renounces, as in Stoic philosophy and in late Epicureanism, the purpose is to liberate oneself from a state of subjection and passivity in order to achieve an active state.

When *apatheia* was transmitted from the Greeks and the Romans to the Christian Fathers, who translated it with *impassibilitas*,[25] it went on to acquire a meaning for them that was quite different from the original. For early Christianity, the absence of passions, *apatheia*, means renouncing the disturbances that come from the body, renouncing one's own judgment and one's own will. In a word, it is a renunciation of everything that involves the self in a demented craving for self-affirmation. In Foucault's "*Omnes et singulatim*" lecture, more emphasis is placed on the political significance that the Christian *apatheia* acquired. To induce mortification of the self involves detachment from the world, disinterest and indifference to what is happening in history and in the city.[26]

For Foucault there is no doubt that this is a crucial step: Christian *apatheia* as abstention from the self's obstinate practice of judgment and of willfulness exerted over the self, as the deliverance of oneself over to the protection of a pastoral guide, does seem to be the point where a condition of "complete subordination" becomes elevated to a virtue, whose value would be transmitted over the centuries. "Complete subordination means three things. First, it is a relationship of submission, but not submission to a law or a principle of order, and not even to a reasonable injunction, or to some reasoned principles or conclusions. It is a relationship of the submission of one individual to another. The relationship of submission of one individual to another, correlating an individual who directs and an individual who is directed, is not only a condition of Christian obedience, it is its very principle. And the person who is directed must accept submission and obey within this individual relationship."[27] As the price to be paid on the long road leading to salvation, therefore, the pastoral relationship implies being humble: assuming the sort of humility that consists in "knowing that any will of one's own is an evil will." Starting from this assumption one must "act so that one's will, as one's own will, is dead, that is to say so that there is no other will but not to have any will." The pastoral relationship, in short, requires "the definitive and complete renunciation of one's own will."[28] This, then, is the Christian masterpiece: the invention of pure obedience as the supreme principle. It is not obedience to the law, to a city, or to reason, but rather the obedience of someone to someone else who guides them. This is a principle that has managed not only to direct the conduct of the faithful in religious communities, but also to establish itself, first, in the institutional structure of the Church, and then, to assert itself *as a structural model, as a canon for arranging and organizing power relations between people.* If it has proved to be so pervasive and so persistent, this is because it has successfully worked on the deep tissue of subjectivity. In fact, it was a hugely powerful agent of subjective individualization, a subjectification that is built on the model of submission. The government of men was thus prepared to become the network of continuous deferrals to the responsibilities of others: in the power game of the sheep and shepherds, in reality no one acts according to their own will and their own judgment. The shepherd does not direct "the sheep" for the pleasure he feels in leading them; he does not command out of a liking for resolving and overcoming resistance; he does not require to know the truth of other people's thoughts in order to keep them in check. No, the shepherd is a servant and minister of the truth and salvation of others, making himself obedient in his turn, so that he too can receive his salvation and his truth from someone else. In the network of reciprocal links between obediences, in that "field of generalized obedience," as Foucault defines it, commanding is just another way for someone to comply in their turn with the duty of obedience. Ultimately, therefore, there is no locus of responsibility and of final decision with regard to the control of behaviors or the direction of consciences, but only *an endless web of subordination.* It is endless, as we have seen, because one subordinate always refers to another source of command, and because, as we will see, even within one's own core, the extinguishing of the will and the expropriation of the judgment is an interminable task.

Clearly, the hidden text that orients this interpretation is *On the Genealogy of Morals*, in which Nietzsche "completely" rewrites Western history, presenting it as a long and painful process of moralization that is inseparable from a gradual universalization of subjection and obedience.[29] We have already discussed how Nietzsche interprets the birth of the conscience, how it arises from a movement that internalizes the instincts and how it continues to work, fueled by the antinomy between good and evil, by projecting the conflict that structurally inhabits the individual onto the outside, onto an "other-than-self." We have repeatedly pointed out that for Nietzsche all dualistic thinking takes root precisely in this conflict, which feels unbearable to the subject. Thanks to the intervention of pastoral power, for Nietzsche even before Foucault, it was in this context that the practice of obedience—self-mortification as redemption from evil—grew into such a "scandalous" offshoot compared to that of the Greek world.

I believe that it is really true, then, as Foucault said in the interview with which we started, that Nietzsche outweighed Heidegger for him. Starting with the focus on the "government of men," Foucault seems to have convinced himself that a new *On the Genealogy of Morals* had to be written. Until then, the double movement of subjugation and subjectification had been examined and explained, on the basis of the power-knowledge equation, in reference to the production of disciplined bodies or to the construction of "biological masses."[30] Now his investigation extended its reach to the very structuring of the conscience, or rather, to the way the interiority that would be called consciousness, soul, or ego was carved out from inside the life of an individual. Speaking in Foucauldian terms, we might say that what was being investigated was why a body takes on the subjugation, why the subject accepts the subordination, almost as if Foucault now felt that what he needed to examine was an affective aspect of power relations. It is as if he realized that dealing with modern politics solely in terms of the dispositifs of power, stopping short at the totalizing and individualizing dynamics of the state and disciplines of knowledge, was no longer enough. It no longer sufficed to reconstruct an epochal genealogy—more Heideggerian than Nietzschean—of power systems. This type of analysis had to be accompanied by a radical questioning of how the subject becomes such: first, by turning in on itself, and second, by surrendering itself to the power of others, by virtue of a principle of authority and truth "outside."[31] I think it is safe to say that by the time the course of 1978 began, Foucault had started down a path that led him, in Nietzsche's footsteps, to analyze the play of forces *within* the subject. He moved in this direction in order to probe *from inside what triggers the "scandalous" virtues of obedience and compliant behavior—which prove to be the most solid glue for cementing relations of power in relations of domination.* The Nietzschean explanation of subordination, the sudden domination of strong individuals who impose a political organization on the weakest ones, perhaps was still too steeped in naturalism for Foucault. The quality of the meek, humble, and obedient subject required instead a tropological explanation, so to speak, the material of which was provided by the techniques of penitence and the examination of the conscience found in early monasticism.

If what we are dealing with is a "pastoral" revolution from whose long-term consequences we have not yet managed to escape, it is obvious that, for Foucault, narrating the history of moral subjectification is one and the same as making a critical diagnosis of the present. As far as the supposed obviousness of this figure of the subject is concerned—its presumed naturalness—the historical/genealogical analysis works primarily as a "counterfactual" gauge. For Foucault, much more so than for Nietzsche, the birth of the conscience is not a precise moment, but—as he reminds us in the *Hermeneutics of the Subject*—a complex process with its steps, its conflicts, its slow developments, and its headlong rushes.[32] The obligation of telling the truth about oneself, which becomes identified with the necessary condition for salvation, plays a major role in the dynamics of this process. *The Will to Knowledge* (*The History of Sexuality Volume 1*) had already focused on the function of confession and penitence in relation to the turning point marked by Tridentine Catholicism. In the course he gave in 1978 and even more so in the one in 1980, the focus was instead shifted onto the techniques of spiritual direction, examined from three perspectives: the relationship with the master, the examination of conscience, and the verbalization of thoughts. What he describes is the emergence of a new technique involving the production of a true discourse about oneself when absolute obedience to a "director of conscience" is demanded. Hence, Foucault is no longer interested in the "moral psychology of the flesh," but in the subject's relation to the truth about itself.[33]

To show the rise of the conscience through the double movement of turning in on oneself and objectification, the writings of the monk John Cassian proved to be extremely useful. Already studied during the course of 1978, Cassian's texts are more closely analyzed in the course of 1980 entitled "On the Government of the Living." Although only recently available in French,[34] we can read summaries and various excerpts of these lectures in English in some of Foucault's writings from the same period: in the seminar "Technologies of the Self,"[35] and in "The Battle for Chastity."[36] The attention of the French philosopher was shifting increasingly from the general structure of pastoral power to its dispositif inherited from Greco-Roman antiquity that led the subject to produce "reflexive acts of truth" with a view to salvation. Christianity thus appears to be marked by a double system of complementary truths: one truth as a "system of faith," requiring the faithful to adhere to the truth of the doctrine, and another truth as "a regime of confession," which requires the exposure of one's own individual truth through regulated actions.

Foucault first focused on the works of Tertullian in the lectures of February 13 and 20, 1980.[37] In these he glimpsed a redefinition of the concept of original sin that is crucial for our inquiry. Not only is sin darkness and error, it is now said to designate a genuine perversion of human nature, owing to the introduction of Satan into the human soul at the time of birth. Because of this change in the ontological status of sin, one must now undergo intense purification before being baptized. To chase the stranger—the enemy—out of the soul, a fierce battle must be waged; but on a closer look, the battle is against Satan himself, against the evil that lurks in the meanders of the soul and that intensifies its attacks during the time preceding baptism. The soul must be constantly wary of itself. To arrive at the truth, the inner flow of one's thoughts must be continuously and meticulously exposed. The only way to check one's progress in the fight against the devil is through this reporting. This is the only way to demonstrate the transformation of one's nature. Believers must first declare themselves sinners and publicly display their guilt through the practice of *publicatio sui* or *exomologesis*.[38]

Foucault analyzes the writings of Cassian in the light of the innovations introduced by Tertullian so as to grasp the innovations that were introduced with respect to the "spiritual exercises" of ancient Greek and Roman practices. Basing his reading mainly on Cassian's *Institutes* and *Conferences*,[39] the French philosopher resumes his discussion on "pastoral techniques." As he sees it, what the pre-Christian world referred to as "philosophical techniques" were maintained in their structure, but they evolved in response to the new content.[40]

His intention is clearly not to offer a detailed analysis of the works by the founder of monastic institutions, but rather, as I have pointed out, to use the passages on the examination of the conscience in order to decipher the process by which the Christian subject was constituted, whose structure then passed into modern subjectivity. What is particularly relevant for the purposes of our inquiry is that in the eyes of Foucault, the works of Cassian are the best entryway for grasping the significance of monastic life as a practice of obedience and as a struggle against evil. In his 1982 essay "The Battle for Chastity," Foucault says that precisely because of the new concept of original sin, there occurred a shift from an economy based on codes of behavior, which codified permitted or forbidden actions, to the practice of continuous verbalization of one's thoughts.

It was a transition during which the idea of the presence of evil presided over subjectification: the subject had to be structured so as to be able to wage the battle against the enemy within, who had to be hunted down and chased out of the soul. As we said, to ensure that the battle was won, every single representation of the imagination and every hidden movement of thought had to be exposed to the authority of a superior. One of the *Conferences* of Cassian is dedicated to *discretio*, the faculty of judging and examining one's thoughts.[41] The presence of evil in the soul is what prevents even the most expert and irreprehensible monk from being able to trust his own judgment, writes Cassian, because the devil acts through illusion and deception, transmitting thoughts—*cogitationes*—that seem harmless but are such as to lead the monk astray and lure him into error. This is why the examination of the conscience is necessary. It serves to check what kind of thoughts are passing through one's mind and to flush out Satan, who mixes evil thoughts with good ones. Whence the metaphors that Cassian uses: thoughts are like grains and the conscience is like the mill store of the capable miller who separates the good grains from the bad ones; the conscience must act on our thoughts the way an officer separates troops, the good ones marching to the right and the bad ones to the left; and finally, the conscience is the money changer of the self, who examines coins, checking what metal they are made from and where they came from.[42] Only by following these practices, by constantly trying to flush out one's own sins and weaknesses, can we dispel evil, the Evil One. To expel all that is impure, we must be relentlessly vigilant and permanently suspicious with regard to the self: "This subjectivization is linked with a process of self-knowledge which makes the obligation to seek and state the truth about oneself an indispensable and permanent condition of this asceticism; and if there is subjectivization, it also involves an indeterminate objectivization of the self by the self-indeterminate in the sense that one must be forever extending as far as possible the range of one's thoughts, however insignificant and innocent they may appear to be."[43] But if our judgment is weak, corruptible, and unreliable, how are we to separate the good from the bad? "[A] wrong thought," writes Cassian, "is enfeebled at the moment that it is discovered: and even before the sentence of discretion has been given, the foul serpent is by the power of confession dragged out, so to speak, from his dark under-ground cavern, and in some sense shown up and sent away in disgrace."[44] Evil has power over us only insofar as it succeeds in hiding. The simple fact of external-izing and objectivizing the thought under which it might have hidden results in immediate purification for the believer. Unlike good thoughts, bad thoughts are very difficult to express, "for evil is hidden and unstated. Because evil thoughts cannot be expressed without difficulty and shame, the cosmological difference between light and dark, between verbaliza-tion and sin, secrecy and silence, between God and the devil, may not emerge."[45] What we have here is an *aliturgical* act, a ritual of manifest-ing the truth that has purifying and salvific effects in itself for those who perform it.

However, we cannot be the judges of ourselves, Foucault reminds us. The evil inside us forces us to submit ourselves to an external evaluation. The degree to which the superior—the director of conscience—is virtuous makes no difference. The examination of the self is secondary to the contin-uous verbalization of one's thoughts and absolute obedience to authority. The important thing for the monk is to confess, to prostrate himself, and to make himself infinitely humble toward the other; only then—thanks to the prostration and the confession of the truth—does the devil leave.[46]

As Foucault had already remarked in *Security, Territory, Population*, the state of *apatheia* induces humility and prostration, for which the monk, feeling the lowest of the low, does not judge the goodness of his superior but puts himself in the position—as a condition and goal for salvation—to receive orders from anyone, thereby constantly renewing the relationship of obedience. The reason the monk does this, let us recall once again, is be-cause being humble and obedient not only means recognizing that we are sinners, it also means acknowledging that our judgment and will—without a guide—are powerless and evil. Foucault also mentions the fifth chapter of the *Rule*, in which Saint Benedict describes what defines a good monk: "They no longer live by their free will, *ambulates alieno judicio et imperio*, in marching under the judgment and the *imperium* of another, they always desire that someone command them."[47]

I am convinced that these lectures provide one of the most sophisti-cated philosophical signposts for the "normativity of nonjudgment," the pivot around which the alternative genealogy of the link between evil and power rotates. First of all, the texts Foucault discusses shed light on how, in many ways, heteronomy dominates the dynamics of subjectification, and how this arises primarily thanks to a substantive idea of evil. Evil is the Other inside who corrupts and seeks to destroy and who will only be vanquished with the help of a different Other, the superior—only because the latter, in his turn, is subjected to the Almighty Other. The idea of the existence of evil, which takes possession of the individual's soul through original sin, thus serves as a powerful device to eliminate the autonomous constitution of the self. Christian subjectification implies an objectification of the conflict between the forces inside us so that they can be dualistically ordered on the outside into a good part and a bad part. This is the only way that the other, the director of conscience, can eradicate the evil part from the person being directed. In exchange for salvation, the disciple should not only speak the truth about himself to the person who directs him, he must also ensure that his conduct conforms to the rules of the person to whom he is subordinated. Starting at this time, and continuing for a long period in the West, the subject remained fixed to this identity.

What happens in the formation of Christian subjectivity is a strange game of splittings and reassemblings, a game whose dynamics are critically determined by the idea of evil. For Foucault as well, in a way that is very similar to Nietzsche's, the human animal seems to give itself over to obedience, meekness, and conformism whenever it is unable to bear the burden of its inner differences. Whenever the conflict raging inside feels unbearable, it expels the battle to the outside, structuring this conflict into a dualistic schema. This is the source of the ego's need to see salvation as the return to the One: to the One of the Self and to the One with God, assured by the mediation of the pastoral authority. The human animal must fight an incessant battle to obtain its salvation, then, which is attainable in exchange for unwavering submission to the divine power and to the power of its ministers. Humans can certainly not trust themselves; they can become subjects of truth only under conditions of subjection to the other. From this time on, the structural character of the subject and the relationship between subjects revolved around two poles: a profound, hidden truth—threatened by evil—that required the aid of objectivizing introspection; and a final salvation that could only come from outside, from a transcendent plane. This is how the individual was shaped into subordination and obedience. It is quite clear that the form of subjectification Foucault is talking about was not limited solely to the early centuries of Christianity; on the contrary, in spite of being secularized and emancipated from theology, it continued to persist.

This, then, is how the circularity between subject and power is structured in the West: if power requires submission and obedience to determine the conduct of others, the same is required by individuals to fulfill their need for someone or something that transcends them, be it God or the norm. Submission and obedience serve them in order to receive confirmation from others, and from the other, of their redemption, that is, *the promise of salvation from the danger of death*. This need is what we must now identify as one of the possible carriers of political evil—because focusing our attention on the desire for destruction does not suffice.

I may be stretching my interpretation of Foucault's work, but I believe that his shift from biopower to an interest in the "practices of the self" can be viewed from this perspective. On the one hand, pastoral power explains the very long duration of altruistic dynamics, during which the practices of power managed at various times to organize their objectives and their strategies and transform themselves, in some cases, into total domination by promising to protect life and improve it. On the other hand, the investigation into the governing of behaviors serves to formulate a possible answer to a new question, relating to the "affective" dynamic of the relationship of subordination, so to speak. This regards what Judith Butler called the question about the "psychic life of power": What brings an individual to desire and accept his or her own subjection? Why do we do nothing to prevent certain historical and political contexts from turning into scenes of evil?

The Ethos of Freedom

Nietzsche's work must thus be pursued to ascertain what other ways have existed in history for constituting the self, primarily to compare these with the *habitus* that became hegemonic starting from the pastoral revolution. Out of the structure of the obedient subject that we have just brought to light, we now begin to glimpse the features of a different possibility of subjectification. There is no doubt that this investigation into the practices of the self, which also began as a historical study, was part of Foucault's plan for an ontology of the present: a critical thought that problematizes things as they are, especially in how they present themselves as necessary.[48] Although up to 1980 the "care of the self" and the spiritual exercises of ancient Greece and Rome served Foucault above all as a background against which to view the rupture represented by the technique of Christian subjectification, later on the pre-Christian ethos took on a different meaning. It served as an example, I believe, to demonstrate the feasibility of an idea of autonomy that is exempt, however, from the "blackmail of the Enlightenment."[49] By this he means that if you accept the tradition of the Enlightenment, then you must remain faithful to the assumptions of its rationalism. But if you are trying instead to escape its principles of rationality, then the idea of autonomy has to be given up. I believe that the challenge of Foucault's later work can be expressed as a search for a possible "self-determination" that, in avoiding any reference to a universal and necessary law, is as much in contrast with the hetero-determination of the obedient, Christian subject as it is with the absoluteness of Kantian autonomy. Indeed, autonomy should not be pursued in terms of self-affirmation, but rather in terms of the continuous possibility of revoking the authority that the Other—master, director, God, sovereign, or simply the political and social context—claims to exert over us. In this sense, the ethic of the care of self is in the first instance the demand for freedom, a freedom understood as the possibility of being different from everything that claims to be necessary, without really being so.

I am not alone in believing that what Foucault sought in ancient ethics—from the classical Greeks to the Stoics, from the Skeptics to the Cynics—was an immanent ethics, that is to say, a way to give oneself an ethical subjectivity that does not refer to a "beyond" outside the times and places of individual lives. For Foucault, in a word, it was a matter of conducting "untimely" research: of searching between the folds of ancient ethics for a method in which the relationship between subject, truth, and salvation forms *a constellation that is different from the one structuring the geometry of the obedient subject*, the subject that maintains and nurtures a power that is liable to transform itself into a state of domination. What he sought was a practice of the self with itself, in relation to its own life and to its own death, that leads neither to an inner dualistic split nor to a tutelage dependent on the outside. This means seeking in the ancient world the traces and the signposts of an extremely fragile balance: how to allow the divergent forces within the subject to coexist, ungoverned, without tearing the subject apart; but while averting the possibility that what brings them back into unity is some external, salvific power. This may be forcing my interpretation, but I truly believe that in studying the ancient ethics, Foucault was reposing the Nietzschean question par excellence: the possibility of an ethics beyond the substantive, moral dichotomy of good and evil, a dichotomy that in its dualistic and moralizing attitude was certainly the monopoly of the Christian way of forming the subject. Nevertheless—this is the difficulty posed by this challenge—both Nietzsche and Foucault knew that *to become ethical subjects* means having to *perceive*, and to be able to continue to perceive, *a difference* that inevitably distinguishes between *good and evil.* This is all the truer because, as we have seen, although for Foucault power is not in itself evil, there undoubtedly occur conditions under which power does become evil: when an excess of domination precludes any room for freedom. These are the circumstances under which power stops circulating, in which the pervasive, microphysical movement between actions and reactions gets crystallized into a static, macrophysical state of domination: as in Nazi thanatopolitics, for example, in which pastoral power, the sovereignty of putting to death, and governmental technologies became intertwined. But how do we avoid this hardening process? How do we prevent the unbalanced growth of power into an immobile, totally asymmetrical relationship?

Foucault's response cannot rely on universal, abstract ideas that designate and dictate the norms of liberation. This refusal is what drives him to the search for an ethic that is not universal, not normative, not transcendent, and yet that is able to answer the question of political evil that continues to endure. Unlike how he views liberal theory, and in a certain sense also Marxism, he can no longer be satisfied with halting the frontiers of evil through the project of harnessing and balancing sovereignty or through planning the disappearance of the state. Rather, the possibility for the propagation of evil must be pulled out by its roots. It is as if the French philosopher were telling us that we must change our perspective and invest in the resistance that issues from the very source of power relations, which is to say, the subject; or rather, the locus where the subject is structured and acquires its force of action. This is the Foucauldian ethic of the self: to look within individuals for possible points of withdrawal, of disidentification from the normativity of power. The issue at stake, therefore, is to understand how the subject is able to organize itself internally as a field of opposing forces and in what way this arrangement can ensure autonomy and independence to the greatest possible extent.[50]

If the Christian question leads to defining and establishing "who we are and what we are," the question that Foucault wants to relaunch for an ontology of the present has the classical Greek tone of "What should we do with ourselves?" and "How are we to think of ourselves?" If the ultimate resistance to political power can be situated only in the subject itself, or rather in the method that this subject adopts in shaping the relationship with the self, then—as in Hannah Arendt—the dimension of thought and of the critical capacity take on a political value. This does not mean that the course entitled "The Hermeneutics of the Subject," which was held in 1982, leads off with a self-referential vision of the self. On the contrary, in Foucault's mind the practical and ethical techniques of antiquity—those of the first and second centuries C.E. especially—show that the subject can be structured only through a connection with some alterity or otherness, a particular political regime, the director of conscience, the master, and so on, depending on the context. The government of the self is always in relation to the government of others, but it is a relationship that nevertheless takes place in a dimension that is immanent, one that aims to achieve self-determination.

Both the self and the other are rooted in a strict plane of immanence. The authority that we grant the other is not something that legitimates us or penalizes us; rather, it is the instrument by which we tend to make our lives as little hetero-directed as possible. It was noted that if the modern subject—exemplified by the Cartesian *ego* for Foucault—is capable of truth *a priori*, the ancient subject has access to the truth thanks only to a "spiritual" transformation of the self.[51] Arriving at the truth is not so much a gnoseological matter as it is an ethical value. For this reason, the Delphic injunction to "know yourself" is inseparable from the exhortation urging "care of the self." The figure of Socrates in Plato's *Apology* exemplifies someone who now devotes his life to persuading himself and others to take care of their own transformation. Foucault locates one of the possible precedents of the later theories of ancient Greek philosophy in the connection between care of the self and the government of others put forward in some of Plato's texts, particularly in the *First Alcibiades*.[52] And although care of the self in the Hellenistic world became more markedly the fortifying practice of a subject that began to see itself as a weak self, it nevertheless remained an ethic of self-mastery and self-government.

As on many other occasions, Foucault's historical research aligned itself with his philosophical intentions. As I see it, there are two leads to follow in these pages of his: the relationship of the subject with salvation, and the relationship of the subject with death. These are the themes that returned to dominate the courses on *parrhesia*. Now, what does it mean to be "saved" for the Hellenistic ethical philosophies of the first two centuries? It meant, first of all, equipping oneself to become a locus that is safe and inaccessible to the outside—a refuge from events and from other people, but also from one's own passions. Never, Foucault points out, does salvation refer to the drama of an event that makes us jump from negative to positive[53]: "the term salvation refers to nothing else but life itself."[54] A notion of salvation aimed at overcoming death, at pursuing eternity, or another world, is never at stake in this thought. Salvation is an activity that is put together piece by piece over an entire lifetime and whose only agent is the subject itself, as it acts in its field of relations. The finality of this undertaking, its end point, is simply to make us inaccessible to the evils brought on by misfortunes, accidents, and diseases. The moment the subject attains self-mastery—the certainty that nothing can disturb it—the very moment it has fortified himself to the point of self-sufficiency (as Foucault interprets the ideals of ataraxy and autarchy), it has reached its own salvation. Of course, this must be renewed through unremittingly vigilant attention and myriad activities relating to its conduct: "*One saves oneself for the self, one is saved by the self, one saves oneself in order to arrive at nothing other than oneself.*"[55] The type of salvation sought in Hellenistic and Roman thought is by now far removed from that represented by the city in classical philosophy, but it is just as remote from a religious purpose that, being inseparable from a dualistic conception of existence, must posit a dramatic transition from false to true, from nothing to being.

Unlike in Christianity, in which the truth can be reached if you come to know the depth of one's soul, in Hellenism it is obtained through a sort of relational knowledge, which allows individuals to arm themselves to resist attacks from the outside world. This resistance is tempered and forged through a continuous, deconstructive management of one's identifications. What emerges from reading Epictetus, Seneca, and Marcus Aurelius is how different these various strategies are, and yet how similar they are in their result. Whether it is a matter of Seneca's "looking down from on high" (letter 84, "On Gathering Ideas") or of Marcus Aurelius's "immersion on the spot," the aim is to break down contingent identities to the point of perceiving one's singularity in the totality of the world. Foucault analyzes many texts and passages in his effort to reconstruct the paradoxical ambivalence of Stoic ethics for us. While viewing the subject as nothing but the infinitely small part of a nature that encompasses everything, precisely because the subject is aware of its own fragility and weakness, Stoic ethics teach the subject to accept the real for what it is, but to combat it and do everything one can to oppose it. Philosophical *askesis* also serves for this purpose. Above all, this is the purpose of *meditatio malorum*, which can be learned by putting oneself under the guidance of a master. In this culture, to meditate on death is to practice an extremely powerful dislocation of the identity. This is not equivalent to the knowledge that sooner or later one must die; it does not mean that the subject thinks about death as an object. It means putting oneself, through the exercise of thought, into the state of someone who is close to death and therefore living as if it were one's last days. This thought shakes the subject up, disturbing and dislocating it, but at the same time preparing and fortifying it. As opposed to fear, this practice strengthens subjects and motivates them to focus on the "completion" of their lives. "The exercise, thinking about death," explains Foucault, "is only a means for taking this cross-section view of life which enables one to grasp the value of the present, or again to carry out the great loop of memorization, by which one totalizes one's life and reveals it as it is."[56] Far from being an escape route projected into the future or an excuse for giving up one's critical capacity, unlike in Christianity, the thought of death enhances both one's judgment regarding the present and the ability to recollect in order to make sense of the past.

The Hellenistic and Roman ethic is a fragment, then, that Foucault tears from history in order to provide us with an example of how a *bios* manages to make itself into an *ethos*, and how an *ethos* can become a *praxis*; in other words, how to assume a stance for taking the present "against the grain." For Foucault, the ethics of late antiquity are therefore an example of the "virtualization" of subjective identity—or, better still, they are the opportunity to show that there is more than one way of becoming subjects. If we are not born subjects but become them, then the practices constituting the self are not limited solely to the ones that have proven to be successful in the history of the "rational animal." The Foucauldian appeal to "déprendre de soi-même [to get free of oneself, to lose one's fondness for oneself]"[57] is an exhortation to detach oneself from parts of the self—from ways of being and acting—that keep us bound to powers that seem intolerable to us or that we simply no longer acknowledge. This is the substance of what it means to chose an ethos and to give oneself a form: it is not an aesthetic choice, in the sense of "making one's life a work of art," but rather a recognition of the self as a singular event that reveals the incommensurability of a space within which we can accept or resist the pressures of power.

Socratic Demons

In the difficult task of giving shape to one's life, of impressing an ethos on one's *bios* outside of universal norms, *parrhesia* as an expression of the self and as a style continued to capture more of Foucault's attention. In a paper delivered a year before his death, in a eulogy of "ethical resistance" admirably hidden under a lexical clarification that could have come from a historian of ancient Greek thought, there is an explicit call to a responsibility that is totally different from the one inaugurated by pastoral power. Let us carefully consider every single word of the definition that he gives of *parrhesia* as this was conceived in democratic Athens: "a kind of verbal activity where the speaker has a specific relation to truth through frankness, a certain relationship to his own life through danger, a certain type of relation to himself or other people through criticism (self-criticism or criticism of other people), and a specific relation to moral law through freedom and duty[. . . .] In *parrhesia*, the speaker uses his freedom and chooses frankness instead of persuasion, truth instead of falsehood or silence, the risk of death instead of life and security, criticism instead of flattery, and moral duty instead of self-interest and moral apathy."[58]

Already during the 1982 course "The Hermeneutics of the Subject," the ethics of *parrhesia* made its appearance as political praxis that is opposed to the adulation of the powerful, and as a discursive technique that is the opposite of rhetoric. In this context, the truth that the speaker puts into action has primarily an ethical effect. Truth is *ethopoietica*; it starts from the bottom and rises up to strike those who are above. It is irrelevant whether the content of the statement is true, if the *parrhesiastes* gains legitimacy on ethical grounds. The *parrhesiastes* states a truth that is in the form of a personal opinion, but that is not valued solely as a simple point of view. He expresses himself and acts inasmuch as he testifies firsthand to the force of the enunciation. The confidence in the truthfulness of his words derives from the fact that, along with the facts, he asserts his belief in the truth of what he says. Because he believes in them, he applies this truth to his existence; he literally makes his life true. He shows the correspondence between facts and words in a perfect indivisibility between *logos* and *bios*.

With the course begun in 1983, published as *The Government of Self and Others*,[59] but above all with the last lectures he gave before his death, only recently published under the title *The Courage of Truth*,[60] Foucault shifted his gaze to a direct link between life and truth that was even more radical than the one put forward by the Stoic ethic, tempted as it was to appeal to the normativity of the law of nature. From the *parrhesia* of Creusa in Euripides' *Ion*, up to the *parrhesia* of the Cynics, by way of *parrhesia* as the philosophy of Socrates, the criterion for establishing the truth of a parrhesiastic enunciation is the close correspondence between *logoi* and *erga*. As we saw in the passage just quoted, whether we are talking about the assembly of the polis or of philosophical discourse, the ethical traits that denote authentic *parrhesia* remain constant: courage, risk—even of death—frankness, and personal involvement distinguish the *parrhesiastes* from other types of people who live in the city. Socrates follows his daemon, who showed him the way of philosophical "truth telling," one that is just as useful to the city as the way of speech in the public square. Indeed, in practice there is absolutely nothing solipsistic about it: *parrhesia* is aimed at inciting others to engage in the "care of the self." This is because Socrates' unique mission is to ensure that others will take care of themselves, their reason, their soul, and their truth.

An entire chapter remains to be written on how the figure of Socrates was used in twentieth-century philosophy: on how he was called on to give voice to the way a singular ethos, resistant to any predetermined and functional political planning, succeeds in itself becoming praxis, perhaps the only praxis capable of short-circuiting power from below. We saw Socrates in Arendt, we are seeing him in Foucault, and we will see him in the philosophy of dissent. It is no coincidence that we will find Socrates in many thinkers who, in facing the nexus between evil and power, feel that they cannot resort to the restoration of a shattered normativity, but instead seek the possible emergence of freedom in the space that removes normativity from power. Thus, even as a "Nietzschean," Foucault cannot entirely share Nietzsche's assessment of Socrates. What he does in fact, as did Arendt and much of nineteenth-century philosophy, is set up a partition that is more complicated than one between the Socratic Socrates and the Platonic Socrates—a distinction that has to do with a certain way of giving oneself an ethics in relation to truth.

Foucault's passion for clear-cut conceptual oppositions thus comes to the fore once again. Whereas during the 1982 course the opposition that developed was between "knowledge of self" and "care of the self," now it is rooted in the bifurcation of the Platonic philosophy. This is a crucial place in Foucault, because in my opinion the dual mode of becoming subjects becomes clearly evident, through the words of Socrates, as an antagonism between two paths. Starting with the Platonic dialogs, two possible philosophical journeys were opened up that bind ethics to truth. The first is the one marked by Pythagorism, which lays out the behavior required to make the transition from impure to pure, from the contingent to the eternal.[61] A subject may establish itself as the subject of truth only if it is able to purify itself and become the container of a truth that will be revealed to it. The other route is the one running close to *parrhesia*, which views truth as a practice with no objective guarantees, sustained solely by the courage of saying what one believes to be true: a courage that requires ceaseless monitoring of one's own judgment. In the *First Alcibiades* meditation is spoken of as care of the soul, but the latter pursues knowledge from the perspective of a dualistic ontology, the distinction between body and soul. Thus everything in the realm of experiment, examination, and verification disappears from Socratism in order to seek the ontological foundation of humankind along a metaphysical path.

Plato's *Laches* seems to open up a perspective that is different from the soul's contemplation of eternity. This is the perspective from which the "aesthetics of existence" took its start, which confronts political power through the instrument of *parrhesia*. Here, courage plays a central role. It is a matter of combating fear, in the sense of managing it simply with the exercise of one's own virtue. The figure of Socrates presented in this dialog is a composite of the traits distinguishing the life of the *parrhesiastes*: the courage to stand up, alone, against power; the risky exposure of the citizen in front of the Assembly; the care of the self that becomes exhortation of others to an extremely rigorous discipline. This was the same rigorous discipline later adopted by the Cynics, for example, whose very flesh was ingrained with the imprint of an ethos. Now, Socrates is all these things rolled together. Unlike in the *First Alcibiades* in the *Apol-*

ogy, in *Laches* he is a *parrhesiastes* not only because of the speeches that he gives but also because of the way of life that he leads. Here we have the Socratic "aesthetics of existence": the attempt to transform one's life into the space of visibility for truth, through gestures, actions, and choices. Unlike the wise Stoic, he makes himself open to a constant restlessness, to that movement of relentless self-questioning that he cannot renounce, on penalty of death. He submits his life to a "touchstone," to a continuous test, with no guarantees of success. It is an exercise in the art of distinction, the art that makes it possible to discern what good or evil things we have done. Socrates becomes a master of *parrhesia* in *Laches* not so much because he is wise but because there is no contradiction between his discourse and his *bios*. "Care of the self," *parrhesia*, the capacity to differentiate between good and evil, and courage are all intimately connected elements that Foucault sees placed on the horizontal plane of a praxis that in addition to being an ethics can simultaneously become a politics.

Foucault continually returns to the alternative represented by the *First Alcibiades* on the one hand, and *Laches* on the other. The *First Alcibiades* establishes the power of the psyche as an ontological reality distinct from the body, correlative with a mode of knowledge of self that takes the form of the contemplation of a suprasensible reality. Living in truth, according to this vision, means conducting the soul toward the mode that is proper to it: to participation in the divine. In other words, this is a path of metaphysical subjectivity, of the discourse that reveals to human beings their essence and what they must do to conform with it. Ethics, in this perspective, dictates the rules of conduct that human beings must follow to rejoin the ontological foundation that corresponds to them. However, another interpretation of *logon didonai*, of "giving an account" of oneself, is possible— and this is the way in *Laches*. It is the way of the aesthetics of existence, in the sense of an art of living that one chooses as an exemplary life, to immortalize oneself in the only way possible in leaving traces of oneself in the memory. In other words, we become subjects, we "subjectivize" ourselves, directly and exclusively through the actions we perform and the words we pronounce. This is the praxis that we will have to give an account of all through life. This is something that Foucault repeats with frequency: establishment of the *bios*, not of the psyche, truth as questioning and exercise of discernment, not contemplation. From the perspective of *Laches*, to live in truth means taking the risk of telling people that courage is needed to give oneself a certain form. The ethical problem of truth does not address the issue of the conditions under which an utterance can be recognized as true.

As much as Foucault drags us into an opposition that can at times seem forced, the message he is sending us is clear. We do not become subjects only by making ourselves receptors of a truth that comes from outside. Subjectification does not arise solely in subjecting ourselves to a power that "saves" by eradicating the negative in us once and for all. We can also become and remain subjects through a continuous athletics of the judgment, through constant discernment that ponders all over again, each and every time, what is good and what is evil. Foucault is telling us that with Socrates, Western culture was faced with two possibilities: one that relates the truth of ethics to the other world and one that is built around an "other life," in the sense of a real life that can be different from what it is. With *Laches*, in short, the subject starts down a subterranean current that would be tied ethically to the truth—not to seek and attain the true world beyond the world, but to reflect on what must be in relation to the possible forms of life of the individual and of the city.

Power in itself is not evil. Political evil does not depend simply on a lust for power that is unable to curb itself. Nor does it derive purely from an alienating structure and from a corrupt system. The possibility of the evil of domination is also linked to the way we constitute ourselves as subjects, to how a subject responds to, maintains, accepts, or reacts to relations of power. This, then, is what is at stake in Foucault's investigations between the folds of the tradition: to reveal a passage, a narrow one, to be sure, that is always in danger of being closed, leading us to the place of a possible disruption—the disruption of the dispositifs that set up a vicious circle along with power. As we know, Foucault's way is not the construction of a collective subject that reestablishes political good in history. But neither is it the path of the negative utopia or the "inoperative community."[62] Nor can it be traced back to the pursuit of an identity that is plural and nomadic with a vengeance. Rather, it is the way of a possible "ethical revolution," the singular revolution of a *bios* that manages to become an ethos, and of an ethos that can make itself into a praxis—the practice of a constant exercise of freedom. In many respects, then, the texts of Foucault's last courses lead to a sort of "anarchic constitution" of the self, in the literal sense of the term: a self that, while remaining the actor of its own responsibility, still relates to itself, to others, and to the city with the least amount of dependency possible. No different from Nietzsche's Dionysus-Zarathustra, whose courage consists in finding the difficult balance of self-government, the anarchic subject of *parrhesia* also responds to how it manages to give itself form—because becoming subjects does not mean only shielding ourselves from the pressures and orders that arrive from the outside. It also signifies, in accord once again with Nietzsche, knowing how to bring conflict and division inside the self and how to withstand them. In this sense, as Foucault so often repeated, either the revolution will be ethical or it will never be.

Parrhesia Put to the Test: Practices of Dissidence Between Eastern and Western Europe

Socrates in Prague

In the lecture on Socrates that Foucault gave on February 22, 1984, he focused on the book by Jan Patočka called *Plato and Europe*, strongly recommending it to his students. In his opinion, it was the only text "among modern books of the history of philosophy, at any rate, to give a very important place to the notion of *epimeleia* [care, attention]."[1] Indeed, the idea of "care of the self," as "care for the soul," is identified by the Czech philosopher as being the root of Western metaphysics, and consequently as guiding the course of European rationality. As Foucault explains, although it is true that Patočka still adheres to a concept of soul that is tied to a dualistic conception of the human—which we would like to leave behind—the importance of the Czech philosopher's work, in his judgment, remains unassailable.

Foucault's remarks are somewhat misleading. The difference between the uses that the two authors make of the concept of *epimeleia* is more complicated, and at the same time less drastic, than we are led to believe. This is especially the case because, as I will argue, Patočka's notion of the soul does not revive some sort of metaphysical dualism at all; rather, it provides an opportunity for rethinking the ethical subject within the framework of a phenomenological theory, defined by the author himself as an "asubjective phenomenology" whose connection with Husserlian transcendentalism has been severed.[2] "Care for the soul" as Patočka intends it, in its capacity to broaden into praxis and dissidence, is in the first place a philosophical practice, freeing individuals from the idea of being in a political relationship in which they always occupy the negative pole and will always do so. Patočka's appeal to the Lifeworld (*Lebenswelt*)—with its contradictory demands—becomes the tool for opposing evil, an evil that speaks the abstract and bureaucratic language of political power.

I certainly do not intend to reconstruct the philosophical biography of the Czech thinker. I would rather shed light on the resonances that I see between the philosophical perspectives of Foucault and Patočka. What I want to bring to the fore is the theoretically virtuous circularity that gets established between "care of the self" and *parrhesia* as they are reformulated by Foucault and the practice of dissidence as it was understood by Patočka and the intellectuals close to him. Not many people have remarked on the importance that Foucauldian philosophy had for some dissident philosophers, and on the impact that "dissidence" had on the thinking of Foucault. Very few have grasped the crucial importance of this interweaving and the possibilities it opens up for a *sui generis* recognition of the pathologies of power—above all, of the role that subjectivity plays in sustaining or rejecting these pathologies. This is not simply a question of a shared terminology arising out of a confluence of their works, or their choice of coinciding texts and themes. Rather, I believe that we can trace out a shared, core set of problems that are elaborated and modified over time, partly because of the mutual influence these thinkers had on each other. I am convinced that Foucault, on the one hand, and Patočka and Václav Havel, on the other, were all driven by the same question. This question is what I will attempt to give voice to, allowing it to lead us deeper into another area in the maze connecting evil with power.

The web of relations between Foucault and what is referred to as "dissidence" has yet to be investigated, even from the simple perspective of intellectual history. Of course, revisiting the philosophical-political thought of the "dissidents" is in some respects easier today than it was in the past. The climate of the Cold War imposed a polarization that made it more difficult to judge any positions that were not lined up unilaterally on one side or the other of the two poles. Often labeled as liberal and anticommunist, often identified with a sort of humanistic, existential Christianity, the thought of Eastern European intellectuals and its critical capacity has been hugely neglected. It was not easy for the Western European intellectuals—

particularly for the French, who at the time were engaged in deconstructing humanistic rationalism and its associated morality—to understand and accept the sometimes ingenuous use that the philosophers of Eastern Europe often sought to make of Husserl's phenomenology and the concept of "Lifeworld." For many intellectuals in Central Eastern Europe, phenomenology was a method of radical inquiry through which the concept of *Lebenswelt* gained an enormous polemical capacity in confronting official culture and thought.[3] Certainly, there were careful readers, especially in France, who did not simplify and who grasped the profound and anything-but-contingent implications of these ethics and philosophy.[4] However, once the Gulag effect, so to speak, had passed, thought on dissidence was mostly dismissed as being overly tied to particular historical circumstances. Opening up a space for seeing it with new eyes, then, is a worthwhile endeavor, by placing it in a context that does not simply label it as an outdated condemnation of real socialism, but rather frames its theoretical and critical strategy in terms of a discourse about the present.

Michel Foucault contributed to opening up this interpretative perspective: at the end of the 1970s he had already grasped the theoretical opportunities it offered for an ontology of the present and for an analysis from inside and "from below" of the everyday mode in which subjects internalize, strengthen, or weaken relationships of power.

As his courses at the Collège de France testify, Foucault was paying more and more attention to what was happening in the countries of Central Eastern Europe, particularly in Poland and Czechoslovakia. We also know that his works were smuggled into Prague and disseminated around intellectual circles.[5] Foucault's study of the microphysics of power and his investigation into power-knowledge relations were applied to the structures of what the intellectuals of Eastern Europe, in Havel's footsteps, began to call "post-totalitarianism" or "decadent totalitarianism." Even though the *samizdats* differed between each other, with very distant ideological and theoretical backgrounds, many of them were directly inspired by Foucault's latest works to emphasize the importance of subjective strategies for changing the course of things, and more generally to emphasize the impact of the ethical dimension in political life. These intellectual circles gathered together all those who later took a stand in supporting Charter 77, the first genuine political movement to arise from the time of the Prague Spring. Regardless of their different origins—from lovers of rock to theologians—everyone considered it their duty to oppose the regime's "institutionalized lie" and to initiate a series of behaviors and practices that answered to the notion of "living in truth." Everyone in Prague, as well as in Brno and Bratislava, knew about these illegal meetings. They were known as occasions for a restricted number of researchers, scholars, and opponents of the regime to meet and discuss particular philosophical arguments together. The police might raid at any moment, and when they did, the reading materials were sequestered, the foreign students were taken back to the border, and the dissidents were arrested. Some European intellectuals, especially from France—Jacques Derrida and Jean-Pierre Vernant to name the most well-known—supported the clandestine groups with funding and by providing banned books, but also by frequently participating personally in the discussions. It was out of these circumstances that the names of certain authors who were deemed "crucial" for political struggle began to emerge. Among these, at the top of the list, was that of Michel Foucault. When he became aware of the strong resonance that his texts were having with the seminars and the *samizdats*, Foucault expressed his desire to attend. After several failed attempts, the trip was finally organized; however, at the time he was expected in Prague in the spring of 1984, Foucault was already very ill and no longer able to travel.

The interest that fueled the French philosopher was certainly political in nature: the intellectual activity of Czechoslovakia was an overt challenge to the regime, and its "unorganized" and "scattered" methods of opposition could not fail to interest him. It was a sort of fabric of resistances, woven by what Foucault would call "counter-conducts," aimed less at taking the place of power than at upsetting the rules of the power play deployed by the regime. Without espousing conclusions that in my opinion are too unilateral and blunt—according to which Foucault changed his stance on power purely as a result of the influence that Eastern European dissidence had on him—the resonance is surprising.[6] The general assumption that they shared was precisely a rejection of the idea that power is always rooted in an objectivizable, external reality, that it is always a power monopolized by "others" in a place that is not our own—the power of "other institutions," "other groups," "other classes," the power of a foreign sphere that has nothing to do with our own ways of life. As we know, this is an approach that Foucault always sought to avoid—extremely successfully in his final works.

If there is one thing that really united those who revolved around the Charter 77 opposition movement, it is the conviction that in order for political action to be effective, it can derive only from an ethics. That is to say, political action must be the side effect of an ethos—a position and a conduct—rooted firmly in the habits of the individual's *Lebenswelt*. They formulated their political critique in philosophical terms, according to which domination, the Gulag, and oppression in general are not the effect of some demonic essence of Communist power, but rather the result of gestures and daily actions that reinforce each other and ensure the functioning of the regime. The first objective of the "Chartists" was to tear down the image of a rocklike, anonymous state mechanism that left innocent subjects with the sole option of enduring it. In itself, power is neither guilty nor innocent. For this reason, the search for a "good power"—constructed in order to counter a "bad power"—is both naïve and politically ineffective. The critique of the dissidents can thus be described as aimed at dismantling the myth of passive obedience and unmasking the subjective "desires" of "depersonalization."[7] This is the source of Patočka's criticisms, and later Havel's, against the ideological justifications with which we allow the mark of conformism to be imprinted on us, in both the East and the West. If it is true that the political pathologies of the contemporary world are the result of a hyper-rationalism turned to nihilism, the appeal to universalistic, normative theories does not suffice to counteract its consequences. When subjectivity remains unchanged, all that happens is an overturning of those who monopolize political action, without changing the real structure of the exercise of power. A much more useful approach is to probe into the microphysical dynamic of the collision between individuals—their lifeworld—and the bureaucratic legality of the system claiming to be neutral and anonymous.

Now, we may recall that already in the 1977–78 course "Security, Territory, Population," speaking about the insurrection of subjugated disciplines—the resurgence "from below" of "discredited" forms of knowledge—Foucault mentions the relevance of what is taking place in Central Eastern Europe. He did so again in the 1983 lectures and, as we have said, in those of 1984. It is clear that the French thinker disliked using the terms "dissent" and "dissidence," words that for him were still too connotative of a rigid political schema, preferring instead the noun "counter-conducts."[8] But there is no doubt that Foucault had in mind the emblematic life of Jan Patočka as an exemplary case of counter-conduct, rooted in the "care of the self." And it is very likely that the acts of resistance as well as the thought of a few "dissidents" accompanied the last phase of Foucault's philosophy.

In short, for Foucault and others, Eastern European dissidence can be modeled as a rare example in history in which philosophy was actualized into resistance against an omnipervasive power, almost as if thought had succeeded in giving life to a movement that was able to produce political change by communicating the contagion from individual to individual. Evidently, in this circularity *in action* between historical experience, ethos, and philosophy, the French philosopher was able to substantiate the mechanisms whereby a subject becomes and remains the transmission belt for the dynamics of domination. At the same time, he had the possibility to verify how a form of resistance to power relations that had turned into domination could take shape, based on daily gestures that are not necessarily heroic and extraordinary; how a subject can constitute itself as a force field, as the locus that feeds back against and counteracts the systemic pressures of a political evil that has become "normal"—because those who did not chose the path of exile, such as Patočka and Havel, with whom Foucault had the most intense intellectual exchange, were personally experiencing the liberating force of an ethical choice. As we will discuss from various angles, for these authors the only possibility for blocking the propagation of the normality of evil is through the special relationship that the self entertains with itself, with its own life and death, and by making itself a witness before others of its own truth. This is the same cluster of ideas that became central in Foucault's last works. It should also be said that for Patočka and his students,[9] Foucault was among the few Western thinkers who had grasped the theoretical and polemical capacity of the "subject of responsibility" and, in probing it, had identified clues regarding how a dissident subjectivity is organized.

Beyond their contrasting styles and undeniably significant theoretical differences, what unites the thought of Foucault and thought on dissent is the complication of the relationship between subject, evil, and power, the awareness that a hypothetical opposition to the excesses and abuses of power can no longer be conceived on the basis of the model of a collective subject of good that will replace the great perpetrator of evil.

The Double Movement of the Heretical Soul (Patočka)

Jan Patočka's writings on Socrates cannot fail to bring to mind Foucault's reading of Socratic *parrhesia*. The life story of the Prague philosopher itself is a demonstration of how a philosophical appeal to a particular ethical conduct may go beyond the bounds of a purely hermeneutic exercise. By accepting Havel's proposal to become the spokesman of Charter 77,[10] Patočka's own life became a testimony to the veracity of his words: "To be relevant, a philosophical thought, whatever it may be, must take a position on the front line."[11] When he officially became an opponent of the regime, Patočka was followed, spied on, and arrested by the political police. After enduring very long and grueling interrogations, the last one for more than ten hours, he died of a brain hemorrhage on Sunday, March 13, 1977. Though there is no doubt about the political significance of his end, one question still remains to be answered: What philosophical meaning should we assign to it? What does the "care for the soul" that Patočka talks about have to do with the question of evil?

In his 1973 book *Plato and Europe*,[12] the text used and cited by Foucault, he begins with Husserl's diagnosis from the *Crisis of European Sciences and Transcendental Phenomenology* and Heidegger's investigation into technology, focusing, however, on a specific issue. The reason the twentieth century marked the collapse of European culture is because Europe strayed from its authentic and original discovery: the soul and its care. Invented by the Greek philosophers, considered both mortal and immortal, in either case the soul "must be cared for."[13] Indeed, this is the only way for mortals to become immortal. Immortality is not presented by Greek philosophy as inherent in the essence of the soul; immortality is not one of its intrinsic qualities. Rather, the soul is an energy, an activity, a movement triggered by a specific relation of the psyche with a way of being that it perceives as permanent and eternal. For this reason Patočka views the soul as what allows us to overcome the simple dualism of the mythical world, the dualism between the everyday and the divine. Here in the text on Plato a distinction emerges that recurs throughout all his works: the difference between the "forces of the day" and the "forces of the night." The *"daily"* is the familiar world where people live all the time, the land that welcomes them, allowing them to firmly take root in it. It is the positive, the good, the substrate on which they stand. It is what in *Le monde naturel et le mouvement de l'existence humaine* corresponds to the "first movement of existence," the one that accepts us into the world and makes us feel part of the world.[14] In the pre-philosophical world, what in the *Heretical Essays* roughly coincides with the "prehistorical" or better with the "ante-historical," these forces of the day, of rootedness and being at home, are opposed by the forces of the night—"the nocturnal"—the forces of a "counter-reality," of the stranger, fear, and "dark, indescribable evil."[15] The conflict between the two forces, understood as the relation between two distant, opposing worlds, is the problem of the mythical world. However, this mythical perception always occurs over again in the individual history of each person. Indeed, everybody senses the contrast between a welcoming, reassuring force and one that disturbs and uproots. This is the movement of existence: a disturbance that shakes us out of the reassurance offered by the forces of the day, exposing us to the truth that reveals the precariousness of our lives.

Philosophy is nothing but the attempt to process the despair that comes from the "damnation" of death.[16] Thus Heraclitus is presented by Patočka as someone who departs from where the tragic experience of Oedipus had arrived, seeking to keep the two parts together—day and night—through the logos. Pre-Socratic philosophy therefore discovers the "care of the soul" as the exclusive possibility for humans to question everything. It was the Platonic teachings that later brought this practice dedicated to "a new forming of the self" to the apex of its expressive possibilities.[17] In the 1973 text, Patočka gives a detailed analysis of Plato's dialogs to arrive at a summary of what for him are the three basic features of the Socratic invention. The soul is *courageous*—it exposes itself to the questioning process. It is *disciplined*—it subordinates all the matters of life to the battle of thought. And it is *just*—it does what it feels that it must do. It sets its own criterion for how to conduct itself. In short, it endows itself with its own style, in the knowledge that ordinary life, the everyday life of the city, usually follows the criterion of *doxa* (opinion/appearance): "Care of the soul then, discovers *both*: δόξα as well as the unitary idea. It discovers the irreconcilable as well as the permanent, the passing as well as the precise—both discoveries are equally fundamental."[18] Taking care of the soul means not putting an end to the movement, in other words, knowing how to keep oneself at the height of the discovery of duality and co-belonging.

"The project of the soul that is self-forming" cannot fail to have a political impact. For Patočka, in it is rooted the "idea of politics," that of a shared existence conceived on the basis of justice that would remain the regulating principle for all later conceptions of community. Despite destructions and catastrophes, the heart of the European heritage—namely, the care of the soul that is practiced in duality—survived for almost two thousand years. It was only in the twentieth century that Europe turned completely against this legacy, leading to the triumph of concern for everyday life, for the domination of the world, and for the exclusive affirmation of force and power.

Certainly, the language of Patočka, still so heavily marked by the terms of old European humanism, if not by classical metaphysics, together with the lack of differentiation between Socrates and Plato, forms a strong impediment to understanding what I think is the philosophically heretical intention of this work on the Greek philosopher—that is, to relaunch the concept of soul as a bulwark against nihilism, but also, paradoxically, as a barrier to all forms of substantialization of thought, whether Christian or subjectivist. The "heretical" intention that supports Patočka's concept of soul had already been made evident in some of his writings from the mid-1950s revolving around the concept of "negative Platonism," coming forcefully to the surface again in his last work, *Heretical Essays in the Philosophy of History*, written during the years of disillusionment and "normalization."[19] What we have here, once again, is the fundamental caesura consisting in the birth of philosophy and Greek politics, and in the emergence of the question of truth and freedom—in a word, the origin of the soul, viewed more than ever in these passages not as a substance or foundation but as a praxis or a continuous practice.[20]

At the time Patočka was writing, very little, if anything, of this tension underlying the process of questioning existence seemed to remain. The technological civilization was showing itself to be very similar in some ways to the prehistorical period.[21] In keeping with Heidegger, Patočka views most of the path that modern reason took as a progressive, growing rejection of the movement toward the truth that corresponds to "care for the soul," to turn instead toward a life shut down and crushed into the exploitation of entities. In his eyes, the present seems to have returned to where history originated: in the chaining of life to its self-consumption, in the unidimensionality of work, understood as a fundamental mode of the banal passing of time.[22] Hence, from care for the soul we pass to care for security.

What appears in many respects as yet another installment of twentieth-century *Kulturkritik* acquires the force of a powerful, original thought in the final pages of the *Heretical Essays*, entitled "Wars of the Twentieth Century and the Twentieth Century as War."[23] What he seeks is to show how the demonic character of the twentieth century is much more complicated than how it has often been presented. At first glance, the twentieth century appears in the final essay as a relapse into the demonic,[24] into the spiral of destructiveness triggered by the power of nothingness and meaninglessness: "That century is an epoch of the night, of war, and of death."[25] Millions of victims sacrificed along with the destruction of places and memories seem to have brought humanity to the culmination of ruin. It was almost as if that demon who cares about nothing and "negates everything" had achieved its final, ultimate manifestation. As World War I (the "decisive event in the history of the twentieth century") brought to light, the technical transformation of the world, "the transformation of the world into a laboratory for releasing reserves of energy accumulated over billions of years,"[26] was achieved almost exclusively through the unleashing of war. The allusion to Heidegger's *Gestell* is obvious. But, equally clearly, the emotional tone of Patočka's analysis is completely different from the diagnoses of the German philosopher.

In fact, explains Patočka, what we have here is not simply the advent of the "realm of darkness." The wars for conquering and dividing up Europe were aimed at making the European continent into a gigantic energetic complex available to the "realm of the day." Thus "the forces of the day," the forces that claim to work for progress and to seek peace, "for four years sent millions of humans into hellfire, and the front line is the place which for four years hypnotized all the activity of the industrial age."[27] It was in the name of life that the forces of the day pushed the soldiers to the front. It was the "demonic of the day" that made war appear as the antidote to war and that leveraged death for its own purposes, "us[ing] in the service of the day what belonged to the night and to eternity." The demon of the day "poses as the all in all" but in reality drains dry even what lies beyond its limits.[28] And when the world wars ended, only a few of the fires of combat had been put out, because the war continued. It did so through terror, the fear of violence and death, and also simply through the threat of a more miserable life. The forces of the day convinced people to fight for them. In this way they accumulated more and more power and with it a tremendous capacity for manipulation and extortion.

What did the bloody wars of the twentieth century and the ideologies that inspired them teach us? What "secret" of the age is Patočka revealing to us? That a distorted relationship between life and death reached its apex of perversion in the twentieth century; more than anything, it is because the putting to death was organized—and continues to be organized—in the name of peace, under whose banner life is preserved. The "eschatology of peace," which champions the proclamation of a better tomorrow, was the watchword by which "we died by the millions," making it possible to transform mass death into an unpleasant, temporary—but necessary—interlude in the grand design for life's continuity. "From the perspective of the day," life is everything for individuals. It is the absolute value, and for them, the only one that matters. But for the "forces of the day," for the power and force that accumulate life and energy, on the contrary, the life of the individual—and even less, the death of the individual—does not exist.[29] The forces of the day certainly act as if the end did not exist. They plan the death of the individual with total detachment, like a simple compilation of tables and statistics, or the barely perceptible movement of plots on a graph. Consequently, although helped by death, day and life dominate uncontested in the will to war and destruction. We will never be able to free ourselves from war until we remove ourselves from the hegemony of triumph exercised by the day and by life.

Jan Patočka's final message resounds unequivocally: the undisputed, grand old lady of the century was not death but life, which monopolizes and captures both individuals and collectivities. The "powers of the day" thus lose their primordial innocence, to become the vehicles of a power that manifests as an event of evil. Like Foucault, who in his 1976 lectures collected under the title *"Society Must Be Defended,"* focused on the tangled web formed by biopower, disciplinary power, and sovereign power—the tissue of domination that unleashes death in the name of life—Patočka also dramatically points his finger at the absolutization and maximization of life as a powerful instrument of death.[30] What he is trying to describe here is a new sphere of ideology, something that not only inheres in so-called totalitarian visions of the world, but also threatens liberal democracies from within. Like Soviet communism, they promise a lasting peace and a life liberated from need. The typical action of the "forces of the day" is in fact to saturate the problem with meaning, with the pretense of solving it.

When observed from an ontological perspective, Patočka seems to conclude, these forces certainly did not run only through the twentieth century; however, only in the twentieth century were they able to fully implement the separation between death and life in such a way as to make life the absolute other of death. In the *Heretical Essays*, the mutual alterity of life and death receives one of its most powerful critiques. In Patočka's reckoning it precipitated nineteenth-century European history into the interminable event of evil, from the Great War to the Gulags, that sealed the complicity between the orgiastic, the demonic, and the elementariness of life. The reason for this in the first place is that the accumulation of energy and force—the objective of the forces of the day that seek to expand and multiply—has to find opportunities for discharging itself. War is the most effective tool for rapidly releasing this accumulated potency.[31] In the second place, if life is the supreme value according to the simple fact that it is life, and if there is consequently nothing that merits its sacrifice, it opens the door to an endless process of devaluation. It is reduced to a life without value, one that has no reason to offer any resistance to the hold that power has on it. Thus, precisely because it has negated its nocturnal side—its inextricable bond with death—life is submerged by violence and death. Having been denied, death returns, but in the form of devastation.

Hence, if humanity seems to have reached the culmination of ruin, if the wars of the twentieth century are a cypher for the total loss of meaning, how is nihilism to be dealt with, without it being transformed into a new dogma? Without winding up, that is, in a celebration of pure, simple meaninglessness? This is the true philosophical problem in Patočka's work. An appeal peeks out from between the lines in all the *Heretical Essays*: to return to a different relationship between life and death, made possible "today" by the testimony of those who, having been appalled by their experiences of conflict, have grasped its deeper meaning; with the possibility that from inside that horror—or perhaps thanks to that horror—one might reemerge having gained something positive. Even as the forces of the day push soldiers to the front, the close-up experience of death saps those very forces of their power.[32] None of these forces has any power on the life of the individual anymore: "In face of that [of death], all the ideas of socialism, of progress, of democratic spontaneity, of independence and freedom appear impoverished."[33] They make sense only if they integrate the memory of the great discovery (lived, not intellectual) that the night cannot be eliminated from the day, only if they do not deny recognition of the impossibility of eliminating death from life—the very same death that appears as a mere nonexistence from the absolutizing standpoint of the day. For Patočka, stumbling into death, orienting our conduct on the basis of the bond that death maintains with life, means changing the content of all the signifiers of existence.

Fundamentally, Patočka is saying that the relationship between life and death occurs in only two modes, which are incompatible with each other. The first is the one adopted by all the wars of the twentieth century, which continues to be active not only in post-totalitarian regimes but surreptitiously in Western liberal democracies as well. According to this way of thinking, death and the dead are nothing but a tribute to be paid for the affirmation of life, the price paid for the conformism of whoever accepts the stabilization of life. It is the bill presented to us by the forces of the day to which, in reality, we all feel bound—because these forces are ultimately created and made powerful by our bonds, our needs, by everything that roots life into a system of guarantees and protections that has been rid of all threats. In the eyes of the people who have been to the front, however, a second perception is revealed. Only in this sense can one say that the sacrifice of the victims has had a value: it served to liberate from the objectivizing power of the forces of the day. To give an "absolute meaning" to the power of these dead does not mean sacralizing their "sacrifice" or believing that this is ethical conduct par excellence. Rather, it means recognizing that these dead, by virtue of being dead, cannot and should not be justified in the name of something else. "To die for" socialism and communism, "to die for" a race or democracy are nothing but masks that life exploits to increase its own power. Now, on the other hand, if death is taken as constitutive of our individual lives, even the "meaning of the world" may be reconsidered. It is therefore the awareness of death that strips the claims of the day of the urgency that grows strong by feeding on our fear.

Patočka's view, closer to that of Heraclitus than to those of Plato or Christianity, is that people who have recognized the "superiority of the night" are privy to another way of connecting life and death. They know that death is not the "nothing" that the forces of the day would have us believe it is, and this knowledge gives them a capacity to deconstruct all the narratives and all the calculations that maximize life. The experience of the front can only be gained individually, but it acquires meaning solely by being shared and communicated. This is the foundation of the "solidarity of the shaken," the starting point from which to begin anew in reconceiving politics and community. It is the solidarity between people who have seen all certainties shaken up and who can no longer go back to viewing them as something obvious. It is a solidarity that transcends all senses of belonging, that does not allow itself to be identified with any "class," profession, nationality, or culture. It is the community of those who were able to understand what is at stake in life and in death, and therefore in history, and who are able to understand that history is this conflict of bare life, shackled by terror, with "*life at the peak*" not planning the everydayness of future days, but clearly seeing that everydayness, life, and peace itself have an ending of their own. Only someone who is able to grasp this and is capable of conversion, in a sort of *metanoia*, is "a spiritual person."[34]

I do not think that Jacques Derrida got it completely right in his book *The Gift of Death*.[35] To sacrifice oneself does not only have a deeply religious meaning in Patočka. Another legacy can be gathered from his words, which certainly do bear traces of a Christian sensibility. Sacrifice, as a limit idea of an ethical conduct, can be understood as a radical gesture that, by taking back ownership of the possibility of one's own death, renews the meaning of one's life and removes it, as far as this lies within its power, from the unidimensionality of objectified identities. Derrida was instead convinced that Patočka's ethics are ultimately rooted in his faith in a supreme being and that therefore the "political promise" deriving from them rests on ideas of responsibility and mystery that are also essentially Christian. Of course, this is a heretical Christianity, Derrida makes clear, but one still based on the ineffability of the divine. From Derrida's perspective, Patočka's political philosophy responds to evil, but it entrusts the possibility of resisting it to the idea of a *mysterium tremendo* that in the end yields to "the logic of a messianic eschatology." Is this really what Patočka had in mind? Or did Patočka's language end up confusing even an acute reader like Derrida?[36]

When Patočka talks about a place and time of change, when he talks about the subject of responsibility, when he talks about a salvation of history, what is he thinking about? Perhaps a revolution of the spirit, in the sense of a final salvation that originates from a revival of Christian Europe? I believe, instead, that salvation does not occur for Patočka except in the paradoxical awareness of its impossibility.[37] There is no salvation, in the sense of a final eschatology. We might think, rather, about how to avoid disaster, passing through the narrow door of a change in our way of being subjects, in how we ask ourselves questions. There is a *metanoia* at play, but an individual one, which has no other time or place except in the attitude of the self toward itself. This is a subject that "lives in truth" simply from the fact that he or she is aware that care for death is inseparable from care for life. And if a way out of the collapse of European history is imaginable by recalling the past, it is not the religious past but rather the philosophical past that we must refer to—in particular, to the "care of the soul" that shapes Patočka's thought from the outset as negative Platonism.

It was in a series of writings from the mid-1950s, published as "Negative Platonism,"[38] that the topic of *epimeleia* had its beginnings. These pieces, which were published only posthumously, are viewed by some critics as being central to Patočka's philosophy, since they cast a retrospective light on his entire theoretical development.[39] These essays are said to contain irrefutable evidence of how the Czech philosopher distanced himself at the very outset from any attempt at integral humanism as a possible escape from nihilism. In these writings, more clearly than in his book on *Plato and Europe*, and less dramatically than in the *Heretical Essays in the Philosophy of History*, it is already clear that the soul is not to be construed metaphysically. "Care for the soul" refers to the movement of distancing ourselves from what we have been led into. As he would emphasize in the 1973 book, the soul is the place of "philosophizing," if by philosophizing we mean the action of a life that goes outside itself and returns to itself. Philosophy would not therefore be understood by Socrates as the guide for a soul on the road toward eternal truth. Rather, philosophy is the praxis of questioning that triggers the thought process. This perspective has no other objective except to preclude life being identified with one of the simple opinions arising out of the circumstances. Patočka's Socrates is therefore the heretic who shakes the very foundations of Greek society; he is the merciless critic of all those who presume to be able to deduce absolute norms from *doxa*. "Negative Platonism," in short, is something completely different from the metaphysical Platonism on which the edifice of Western philosophy was erected. Patočka's approach is certainly indebted to Nietzsche and Heidegger. Although they reject Plato's writing in toto, Patočka instead, not unlike Arendt and Foucault, saves and makes the most of the dialogs out of which insights for an independent "Socratic moment" can be drawn. The Heideggerian "step backwards from the metaphysical" cannot, according to Patočka, pass around Socrates, whence his desire to recover him in a non-Platonic or even anti-Platonic key. In his opinion, to portray Socrates as someone who has no certainties, who knows that he does not know, served Plato as his antithesis in order to better state the positivity of his theory of truth and justice. For Plato, in short, Socrates would be the example of uncertainty that must be overcome.

Not so, for the Czech philosopher. The philosophy of Socrates is a "negative philosophy," not only because it refuses to assume any positive content of truth, but because it appropriates negativity as a condition for being able to be free—in order to be capable, that is, of a distance, a shift, an overcoming of all objectifications. It means continually freeing oneself and others from all bonds—the bonds imposed by tradition, by the schemata of others and our own—and from our possessions. It means being able to "leap into a space in which nothing concrete provides [human life] with support."[40] To establish a distance from the objects of the world allows us to see them, for the first time, in the context of the whole, from the perspective of life but also from that of death. In this sense and only in this sense, for Socrates truth, clarity, and freedom are one and the same thing. The greatness of Socrates lies in having kept himself transcendent to his given reality without ever arriving at a place that would put an end to the movement of transcendence. This is Socratic freedom according to Patočka. Unlike positive Platonism, which takes the view that one can take the upward path until reaching the realm of ideas, negative Platonism never expects to go beyond concrete, historical experience. It affirms the value of the act of transcendence, but without hypostatizing an end or an ending to the movement.

On these lines, the "negative" experience of freedom is the experience of transcendence, which is different from the experience of passivity. Socrates gave it the name of learned ignorance, but Plato explains it by resorting to a transcendental system and being: the doctrine of the two worlds of ideas and appearances. Alongside Socratic freedom, Patočka juxtaposes the concept of *chorismos*, serving as in Heidegger to indicate a separation, but not between two realms coordinated or linked by something third that would embrace them both. *Chorismos* is separateness in itself. Or better yet, it denotes the very movement of separating: "The mystery of the *chorismos* is like the experience of freedom, and experience of a distance with respect to real things, of a meaning independent of the objective and the sensory."[41]

We therefore observe an undeniable continuity between these writings on Socrates and the essays written in the mid-1970s in which the image of the dissenting intellectual takes shape. "The spiritual person," he writes in these years, "is precisely someone who exposes himself or herself to the negative."[42] It is someone who lives in rootlessness, someone who has the sense of a totality that translates into the awareness that the objects of our present perception are not the whole. Because of this, instead of being something objective, the idea of totality is the dispositif of "a disobjectifying power." For this reason, it cannot be transformed into a doctrine of truth, or into a doctrine of the good: "Our capacity for truth depends on our capacity to distance ourselves, to free ourselves from the grasp of objects. The call to truth is the call to freedom."[43] Patočka's Socrates, seen through the lens of Heideggerian phenomenology, thus interweaves freedom and truth. As for Heidegger, truth is "allowing beings to be," but it is also, above all, a movement of life that constitutes itself as ethos: the ethical freedom that in the first place allows the given normativity to be challenged and allows us to detach ourselves from the ingenuousness of convictions that are handed down to us.[44]

To put it in other terms, then, the soul is a path of subjectification, similar to the care of self as *parrhesia* that appears in Foucault's last works. It is a path that in the first instance consists of a process of questioning: a continuous questioning of the subject about itself and about its conditions, about its being having become what it has become, and why reality takes shape the way it does. Patočka does not abandon the term "soul," one that comes with heavy connotative baggage, but he uses it mostly in the Greek sense of a specific ability and skill. It is a sign that stands for the action of transcending, in the sense of a continual deferral.[45] Becoming ethical subjects thus means being able to perceive a difference, the difference between life as it presents itself to us and life in its co-belonging with death; and being able to make this tension a "non-ecstatic" and "non-orgiastic" antidote to the power of the everyday. That is why Patočka is able to state in the *Heretical Essays* that "care for the soul" is indistinguishable from "care for death." In other words, the soul is the factual *a priori* of any choice: it is our original freedom, because it is the perception of and constant tension between two possibilities.

The meanings of the words used by metaphysics thus undergo a radical deconstruction in Patočka's thought. Or at least, that is how I see it. The soul, I like to think, is not a separate substance from the body; it is not what survives the body and can aspire to eternal life. It is what in the subject offers constant resistance. It is the movement that distances it from the force of things, from the authority of politics, from the threat of violence, from the pressure of the desire for life. In a word, it is the power to resist another power.

Shifting the "Front Line":
The Revolutionary Power of an Ethos

As Patočka observed in his last writings, for a philosophical thought to be meaningful it must take a position "at the front line," because the fight of power against freedom also expresses itself in a fight against philosophy. "The front line" is the analogy that he frequently uses to give a sense to the experience of the dissidents, even when the "front"—as in the last decades of the philosopher's life—shifted and pitted itself against a regime that superseded the totalitarian harshness of its beginnings. We may recall how he ended his essay "Wars of the Twentieth Century and the Twentieth Century as War": the means that the dictatorship had used to impose a state of war had lost their extreme character of terror and mobilization. The trials, the destructions of entire groups, and the prison camps had been gradually abandoned. However, another war had begun, a war that now revealed its entire peaceful, "daytime" face, due to a propaganda of lies that by appealing to the will to live and to possess was creating cynical demoralization.[46]

Appeals to the "spiritual person," to "sacrifice," to "philosophy," to "care for the soul," to the "community of shaken" that Patočka launched were taken up by many intellectuals who gravitated around Charter 77. In the eyes of the dissidents, Patočka represented the indisputable Socratic example of a "life in truth": someone who, to remain faithful to its own philosophical daemon, had made a gift of his own death. However, they were well aware that Patočka's warning was not an invitation to heroic and spectacular acts. They were quite clear on the fact that what truly trips up the mechanism of oppression is an action composed of individual acts, which, precisely by virtue of their inconspicuous and nonpolitical nature, constitute the true cause of scandal for the regime. Before dying, with his "tiny practices" shared daily with the Chartists, Patočka demonstrated his loyalty toward what is "unavailable": the loyalty that he derived from an awareness of "the presence of the night in the day." Simply put, he held firm to the irreducibility of his life to the actions and norms of the system, thus demonstrating the public importance of thought—the profound link between "philosophical praxis" and dissent.

Philosophical thought, for Patočka, has nothing to do with the accumulation of knowledge that assures the subject of its self-sufficiency. Rather, as we have said, it is a mode of existence that calls for a radical undertaking, that of relentlessly questioning the affirmative power of what exists. Those who seek truth—Patočka would never tire of repeating—are obliged to allow everything disturbing, irreconcilable, enigmatic, nocturnal to grow inside them: everything opposed to the "order of the day," to the unquestioning acceptance of the power of the moment. This is because those who "live in search of truth" must assume "death in life," by committing themselves to never betraying the truth of the Heraclitean *polemos* as the inseparable union of life and death.[47] Resistance to the forces of the day, to life conceived as a body that persists and as a project that has been pacified and brought to completion, finds its deconstructive strength in the outlook of the night. The awareness of conflict, as a trait that is common to all things, frees us from the arrogance of a contingency that denies precisely its contingent nature. The basis of our freedom is founded in "primordial contingency," the freedom to unchain ourselves from "secondary contingencies" that demand obedience, docility, and subordination, to satisfy the immense, organic body of humanity.

Nevertheless, unlike in Heidegger, "being-for-death" in Patočka does not serve the subject to gravitate around its own authenticity, but to dedicate it, if this proves necessary, to the breaking of the vicious circle of the *protego ergo obligo* (I protect, therefore I obligate). Up to this point, the ontology of finitude does not have a cognitive value, but rather primarily an ethical and political meaning. What the positive powers (*potenze*) of reality want—from technology to totalitarianism—is precisely the negation of the night, of the non-evident, the subordination of possibility to reality.[48] This is why dissident philosophers believe that what they do is "go to the front"; this is why philosophical thought, as the only real opportunity available to everyone to counteract the normality of evil, is by definition "a politics of dissent." Thus, in my opinion, it is not far-fetched to view the experience of dissidence that revolved around Charter 77 as an attempt to transpose and "experiment with" the ethico-political value that Patočka's philosophy expressed. Consequently, insofar as we are force fields marked by life and death, examining the depth of the dissidence and conflict that we ourselves are makes it possible to reveal unexpected possibilities of power.

Jan Patočka is certainly not the only thinker to draw attention to the distinguishing trait in the struggle against political evil that resides in the link between philosophy, choices in ways of living, and sacrifice.[49] He may remind us of another "legendary" figure of dissent, Czeslaw Milosz, who had already made forceful claims regarding the specific character of the Central Eastern European "philosophical way."[50] In *Une autre Europe*, written during his exile in Paris and published in 1964, the obsolescence of ancient conceptual categories is made evident by key experiences in the form of tragic life choices, told through the sacrifices made by the people of Eastern Europe.[51] It is not a new idea of the state, or of the political apparatus, that can become the driving force. If there is hope, it lies in a conduct of life that one decides to adhere to daily. This ethical choice is what Milosz, too, defined as "the philosophical way": breaking down the mechanisms through which power reproduces itself by focusing on the concrete and the everyday.

Certainly, unlike the totalitarian climate that the great Lithuanian writer had fought against, the one that Patočka and Havel grappled with was a climate of "half war," which has its own peculiar ways of objectivizing and destroying people, turning them into raw material at the disposal of force. Resistance is no longer punishable by immediate execution, but the penalty is to rot in jail, in isolation, with "life plans and possibilities wasted."[52] The observations of the two Czech thinkers pertain, in fact, to the last stage of "real socialism," when it is certainly possible for dissidents to open up a chink in the vicious cycle of fear. More so than before, then, the urgent topic of thought becomes the dynamics of the normality of evil, in its dual meaning. First of all, this is in the sense that power now works with "normal" instruments aimed at the establishment of norms, both implicit and explicit, and it no longer appeals to a continuous state of exception. Second, what is at play is not so much the behavior dictated by an enthusiastic adherence to the premises of the ideology-truth, as it is the everyday life of survival in the so-called existential lie: a conduct consisting of a set of external acts that do not necessarily need to correspond to the faith in the mystifications of the system, but that contribute to maintaining the system no less than the interiorization of the ideological faith and the violent, repressive mechanisms do. In a sense, the goal remains unchanged: to bring all aspects of life into conformity with the normativity of political power.

The best account of daily life during real socialism,[53] one of the most illuminating first-person accounts of the dynamic of the normality of evil, can be found in the short masterpiece entitled *The Power of the Powerless* by Václav Havel.[54] The text, circulated almost two years after the drafting of Charter 77, had an explosive effect. Read almost exclusively as a political manifesto, the book was too quickly forgotten by the West under the mistaken impression that it pertained exclusively to Eastern Europe, with the superficial judgment that it was a moralizing work. In reality, I believe that behind the intentionally simple, almost banal language lies hidden one of the most effective microphysical analyses of the relationship between evil and power—an investigation that has much to teach us on the dynamics between subjectification and domination, and that proves to be all the more convincing because "classical totalitarianism" was in the process of normalizing itself, so to speak, into a sort of "social auto-totality."

The intellectuals of the West have to clear their heads of the classical image of tyrannical power, suggests Havel at the beginning of his text, according to which a small group of people seize power by force and exercise it over the majority by crushing them. Tyranny of this sort is structurally unstable. The Soviet bloc achieved unprecedented resiliency by using instead a pervasive network of tools of persuasion and individual involvement. More than others, the countries of real socialism were able to create a system of tyranny without tyrants, servitude without masters, and herds without shepherds. However, the *Power of the Powerless* does not assume the system as an *a priori*: it neither presupposes it nor hypostatizes it. It seeks instead to show how a network of relationships consolidates itself starting *from the bottom*, from one compromise to the next, in order to make itself into a system. There are not many texts like this one that are able to probe the everyday mechanisms through which power becomes impersonal and anonymous, so as to reveal how subjects themselves become agents of automatism for that domination, without following any philosophical-political theories. The malice of the system, its lack of freedom and its destructiveness, is based on an intricate web woven by constraints that are tolerated and accepted because they are considered obvious and unchangeable. These constraints are perceived as necessary, partly because life becomes more tranquil thanks to the inertia and passivity. To live in relative well-being, it is advantageous to partake in the "system identity" so as to become "cosupporters" of the "automatism" of the whole. On these lines, the new political situation can be defined by Havel as a "social auto-totality": a regime representing the historical encounter between the legacy of the past and consumer civilization. Havel's little book therefore contains much more than reflection on the regimes in Central and Eastern Europe. It offers an analysis of the very mechanics of the exchange of power during the phase when it is being shaped into its "biopolitical" form.[55]

Why did a greengrocer in Prague display the sign "Workers of the world unite" in his shop window along with the onions? asks Havel. Certainly not because he truly believes in the unification of workers from around the world, or because he had reflected on the significance of this possible unification. He did so—and did so like clockwork every year—because his gesture, like a thousand other "innocent" concessions to the regime, was required by the norms, and complying with them ensured a more protected life. The greengrocer displayed it because everyone else was doing it. And they all did it to get along in life and to get along "in harmony with society." In reality, what he should have written in the sign was: "I can be depended on, I behave exactly in the manner expected of me." In other words, I am meek and obedient, so I have the right to a good life. However, continues Havel, if the greengrocer were ordered to display the slogan "I am afraid of losing the benefits I've gained and that is why I am unquestioningly obedient," he would refuse to do it. In the ideology of late socialism, there is no need for believers, but there is a need for conformists who repeat the official rituals. This is the only way the regime can consolidate itself: through the use of "shared humiliation." Indeed, it is in the nature of the new post-totalitarian system, says Havel, to involve every person in the power structure, not so much as a way of constructing its cast-iron identity but because through cynical compliance it can cooperate in the attitude of "anything goes." This conformist participation is at the same time what allows everyone, from "the greengrocer [. . .] to the highest functionary," to conceal from themselves the "low foundations" on which their high proclamations are erected. Easy adaptation to the official language gives them the opportunity for transfiguring their own "fallen existence."

The ideological rhetoric is what allows them to disguise their daily shame. To appeal to the value of universal solidarity between workers allows them to mask—both to those above them and to those below them—their docility, the petty reasons for their compliance, the squalid reasons behind the choices made by power: "[Ideology] offers human beings the illusion of an identity, of dignity [. . .] it enables people to deceive their conscience and conceal their true position and their inglorious *modus vivendi*, both from the world and from themselves[. . . .] The primary excusatory function of ideology, therefore, is to provide people, both as victims and pillars of the post-totalitarian system, with the illusion that the system is in harmony with the human order and the order of the universe."[56] Ideology is the great excuse, now almost purely verbal, behind which the subjects, the victims but at the same time the supporters of the system, may continue to believe that they are subordinating themselves to something disinterested and "higher than his or her own personal survival."[57] This is a form of active legitimation that starts off as a communal bond and, thanks to social proclamations and pre-established formulas, reinforces the well-established recursive character of the vicious circle of power.

Even though Havel's interpretation of the phenomenon of totalitarianism follows Arendt's, he also certainly continues in the wake of studies on ideology by Eastern European thinkers. Beyond the analysis provided by his teacher Patočka, I also think about Milosz's magnificent contribution, *The Captive Mind*.[58] In this masterpiece of 1953, the Lithuanian writer narrates how thought capitulates under the blows of Communist dialectics. With the unsparing lucidity of someone trying to soothe a burning wound—the choice of exile—he tries to show how a mind struggles to resist the fascination of the doctrine and, at the same time, to explain how intellectuals adhere to the logic of the system (what Milosz called the *Murti-Bing*). Ideology, the "Doctrine," the "System," the *"Murti-Bing"*— all basically synonymous—successfully establish themselves through the illusion of total knowledge and incontestable, necessary, and inevitable power, because they are imposed directly by history. Thought and language, uncertain and relational methods, are reduced to automatic, modular processes. This is the perfect blend, he reveals to us, that prevented even a single tear from being shed for the murdered victim. Every weakness of the heart was countered by an instance of absolute purity, disembodied and imperative, in a strange combination of rationalistic determinism and collective magic. Milosz's book is thus an incredible description of the stages that a mind passes through to arrive at its own desertification. It is the narrative of how a mind is gradually uprooted from the perception of the real, from emotions, and from common sense. Although initially the dynamics of societal reorganization conducted in the name of the fight between old and new face significant resistance, in the end they carry everyone along to the crucial conversion. During the journey toward the capitulation of the self, however, a cruel battle is staged between the old and the new, the past and the present. It is a battle fought, therefore, between the angel and the devil, but their respective identities have become hazy. The old angel could be the new devil, and vice versa. Consider, for example, the inner conflict experienced by Roubachov in Arthur Koestler's *Darkness at Noon*.[59] The war is long and difficult and the "system" does not win all the battles. Redistributing the roles between Good and Evil takes time and sacrifice. The "system" reaches full stasis only when the language, rotund and coherent, has lost all links with flesh-and-blood human beings.[60] Hence, conversion is accomplished slowly, one compromise at a time, one new word at a time, until finally individuals come to completely identify with their role. Virtuous believers are immunized from any doubt, are freed from anxiety, and have become pure, too. Their conscience no longer has any scruples or regrets, and they now proceed shielded against the corrupting power of dismay and pity. "Purity is the devil," Milosz used to say, also obsessed by Dostoevsky and an imagination studded with gnostic metaphors.[61] Not unsurprisingly, he was convinced that in addition to the prophecy announcing the Bolshevik revolution, *Demons* also contained the secret behind the nihilistic evil of Europe.

But if the "ideology of the believer" was a Manichean universe divided between good and evil, and if from this dualism was derived the Ten Commandments of revolutionary virtues—from spying to ruthlessness—then the ideology of the last stage of real socialism is instead better definable as an "ideology of 'as if'." This is the definition Miroslav Kusy gave it in an essay that adds an intelligent voice to the conversation initiated by *The Power of the Powerless*.[62] The new ideology does not aim at creating purity and orthodoxy, but at filling in the abyss between the real and the supposed ideal by providing a convex mirror that invites everybody to see in it what they are expected to see. The transvaluation of the negative into the positive does not play out in training the mind to accept specific ideas as much as it does through ritual, through the repeated recitation of a script. The new ideology is language training more than anything else: price increases are called "adjustments in the relations between prices," while scarcity of goods is called "rationalization of consumption," and so forth. Above all, we might say, it is an integral language that seeks to saturate every empty space by naming practically every single thing, so that the negative can never make it into words. Certainly it is an agent of unconditional consent, but it no longer insinuates itself deep into the recesses of the psyche. As a rule, one should behave "as if" one were living under fully realized socialism, even if everybody knows that the reality is a clamorous historical failure—and silently, everybody knows that they know. In other words, unlike in the past, schizophrenia is permitted. Though one must recite the political mantra against passivity, absenteeism, and lack of principles, in reality managing to get by through various forms of wheeling and dealing is allowed; though one must ideologically praise socialism, one can silently languish in political apathy. All this is at the cost of a hyperformalization of all expressions of existence, because there is no more trust in the spontaneous manifestations of the political and ideological consciousness. However, the system cannot renounce the "doctrine of socialism" and continues to apply it in the most utilitarian way possible. The ideology serves as a transmission belt within the system. Everybody behaves as if they truly still believed in the reality of socialism, as if there were a tacit agreement between the members of the pact. In reality, the agreement is constantly breached, both by those who have power—by taking the content of the "as if" literally when it serves them—and by the "powerless"—who, when they work up their courage, have no remorse in exposing the emptiness of the "as if." However, so long as none of the parties take it to an extreme, the game goes on. The language of "actually realized socialism" continues to be spoken. As soon as the norm of repeatability is violated, sanctions immediately spring into place. Or rather, when the agreement is violated out of sight, the regime tolerates it, but if the breach takes place in public, the regime must show itself to be capable of suppression when people take themselves out of the game. "Living a lie"—the expression used most often by the dissidents to refer to post-totalitarianism—indicates all these practices.

All this implies that the life "as if" allows—and perhaps even demands—a certain cynical detachment.[63] Ideology is still an agent of integration and totalization, but consent can be reduced to passive assent.

"Living a lie" thus becomes physiological: the purpose of its functioning is simply to ensure that facts can be integrated into the "ritual." Unlike Orwell's Oceania, this is not the big lie, then, that directs the lives of individuals, transcending them. Rather, these lives are working together, all together, to progressively consolidate the web of power that deprives them of their expressive possibilities—because even though it is true that there are different hierarchical positions, it is equally indisputable that the exclusive purpose of the system is not to maintain the dominant group. It aims for global self-perpetuation, what Havel called "the system's general automatism." Nevertheless, the "System is not the subject." Each person, individually, by accepting the rules of the game, allows the game to continue. Without the greengrocer's obedience, the office worker's obedience would be in question; without the conformism of the office worker, the teacher's would be at risk, and so on, in an endless, mutually dependent network. Each person suggests that the other repeat something because each believes that the other has the same expectation. In this way, through actions considered to be innocent, each contributes to constructing the desolate landscape of everyday life—because the greengrocer's sign as well as the teacher's slogans and the office worker's habits remind everyone where they are living, what is expected of them, and what they must do if they do not want to be isolated. They remind everyone what to avoid so as to not "alienate themselves from society," to violate the rules of the game, and to jeopardize their tranquil life. For Havel, the easy absolution that everyone grants themselves is in reality a deception, because each person's conformism forces the other to accept the powers that be. They are all obedient victims of the system, but by acting this way, they are at the same time guilty subjects. The moment they adapt to circumstances, they collaborate in perpetuating them: "They do what is done, what is to be done, what must be done, but at the same time—by that very token—they confirm that it must be done in fact."[64] To comply with a requirement means continuing to perpetuate it. Thus, in essence, "each helps the other to be obedient." This indifference toward everything and everyone is the great power through which, in Havel's view, the normality of evil operates and the collective inertia cements the bases of an enormous power that continues to solidify itself thanks to docility and distraction.

In the post-totalitarian world, evil no longer produces the mass of corpses of those who are considered "in excess," because each individual has found his or her own comfortable position in the systematic demoralization. In the "social auto-totality," "position in the power hierarchy determines the degree of responsibility and guilt, but it gives no one unlimited responsibility and guilt, nor does it completely absolve anyone."[65] The legal system itself contributes to making the system's automatism run more smoothly; by citing compliance with the regulations, everything seems to unfold in the name of correctness. The "base" exercise of power wraps itself "in the noble apparel of the letter of the law; it creates the pleasing illusion that justice is done." In the end, everybody has an excuse: they have all complied with the law. If, then, the system cannot get by without the law, a possible counterstrategy would be to force it to adhere to the letter of the law. Rather than an act of conforming with the law, applying "the letter of the law"[66] can in some cases be a way to reveal the merely ritual and oppressive character of the legal system.[67]

Everything in Havel seems in the end to refer to a fundamental, original conflict: the conflict between what he calls the "aims of life" and the "aims of the system." This contrast is based on an assumption that is never clearly expressed by the author, and that he largely derives from Patočka: the difference between individual life and life in the generic sense, between the instinct of a life to make itself into a subject, into a *bios*, and the tendency of life to preserve itself, or rather, to enhance itself into a "great organic body of humanity." It is a conflict that presents itself, in Havel as in Patočka, as the struggle between the impetus for freedom and the impetus to integrate oneself into a system, so that the system can take over the management of life: "Thus the conflict between the aims of life and the aims of the system is not a conflict between two socially defined and separate communities; and only a very generalized view [. . .] permits us to divide society into the rulers and the ruled. In the post-totalitarian system, this line runs de facto through each person."[68] For this reason, we might add, Milosz's dualism must be called into question. Fundamentally, it suggests a vision of the world in which Evil (the Party and its Knowledge) took captive a society of innocent citizens and potential thinkers who, if only they had been free, would certainly have not abdicated their conscience. Havel almost appears to have discovered in the end that it is precisely this residual Manicheanism that prevents us from uncovering the true place where the battle is waged, thereby preventing us from fighting it: because the battle takes place in the very heart of the subject, it is on this front, first and foremost, that we must take a stand. Havel never tires of repeating that "living a lie" is not reducible to a domination that some people impose on others; rather, it is something that enmeshes all of us and that we all help to create. This is not due to some diabolical, hidden desire; nor is it the fault of a hyper-rational aberration, which the supporters of a catastrophic "Dialectic of Enlightenment" are too quick to accept. It is simply because in each of us there is a part that resonates with, or rather desires, such a system. This is the part that blocks the free and risky action of the self—the action of what Havel defines as our "better self"—in favor of objectivizing conformity: "In everyone there is some longing for humanity's rightful dignity, for moral integrity, for free expression of being and a sense of transcendence over the world of existence. Yet, at the same time [. . .] [i]n everyone there is some willingness to merge with the anonymous crowd and to flow comfortably along with it down the river of pseudolife."[69]

"Living in Truth" and the Opposition to Kitsch

As in the case of Patočka, Havel's language undoubtedly runs the risk of imprinting his work with the dialectic between authentic and inauthentic, especially when it uses a concept as provocative and apparently naïve as that of "living in truth." Milan Kundera, who maintained a polemical stance against Havel starting from the years of the Prague Spring, did not hesitate to make him the target of a fierce critique and radical questioning.[70] His masterpiece, *The Unbearable Lightness of Being*, which by no coincidence opens and closes with the name of Nietzsche, could be read as a long polemic with Havel that complicates the ethical position of dissent.[71] When is it possible to distinguish between "living a lie" and "living in truth," especially at the elementary level of daily life? Tomas, one of the protagonists of the novel, as we will recall, is trapped at the center of a web woven by other people's expectations. He has to decide whether to retract what he had written in an article on Oedipus, or whether to confirm what he had stated and consequently accept being fired from the hospital where he works as a surgeon. This choice is made even more difficult by the fact that to a certain extent it was the publishers of the magazine who edited his article in such a way as to make it appear in clear opposition to the regime. He thus finds himself placed in the role of a "tragic victim"—a role that he did not choose—who is forced to deal with two ways that people look at him, both of which obfuscate the meaning of any decision he might make. On the one hand, there is the condescending smile of those who are used to making compromises with power, who would like to be able to welcome him into their ranks; on the other hand, from the heights of moral superiority, there is the scornful smile of the "scrupulously honest." Tomas is suddenly aware that everyone wants him to sign the retraction: the former because his capitulation and cowardice would legitimize their behavior as normal, restoring their lost honor; the latter, because they do not want to give up the view that their courage is an exclusive privilege. This is why they actually nurture a secret love for cowards. The protagonist feels at the mercy of a public that he did not choose and that in any case would compromise the authenticity of his "dissent." In the end, when Tomas does not recant and loses his job, he owes his decision more to a desire to not disappoint the expectations of the "moral heroes" than to a wish to break the rules of the game. Given the ease with which information is transmitted in "occupied" Prague, he does find the prospect of being spoken of as a coward unacceptable. But he has no intention of treating his action as exemplary. As a result of his failure to retract his statement, when he finds himself face to face with "professional dissidents" who ask him to sign a petition against the regime, Tomas pulls back. Once again the gaze of others—whether the editor of the underground magazine, or his abandoned son in whose eyes he could redeem himself—reduces him to a role: it pins him, like a chess player who has run out of winning moves, to that single article on Oedipus, to that "single, primitive 'no!' in the face of the regime."[72] His son praises the contents of his father's essay, reading it as a sublime rejection of any compromise, as salvaging the profound meaning of the difference between good and evil. Tomas pulls back and refuses to subject himself to the imperious injunction "thou shalt sign." He does not accept the notion that signing corresponds to choosing good, only partly because he no longer understands the meaning of the ancient, eternal distinction between good and evil. He also says no because in the moment of choosing he perceives the full effect of the curse that is cast on every decision by the fate of living only once.[73] The fact that "human life occurs only once" pins us to guilt and responsibility: the consequences of our acts can never be redeemed. This time for Tomas the scenario really is tragic: because what is being challenged is the very principle of freedom. Evil would have its way in any case, whether he signed the petition (Tereza had already been followed and threatened by the police, and if Tomas signed it the consequences for her could be fatal) or not. In the end, his cloying attachment to Tereza, a deep and real bond as it turns out, wins the battle. The idea that something could happen to her is intolerable to him, even if he knows that this is not his freedom. The free act of saying no to power and dissolving the bonds—the lightness and giddiness of freedom that would ensue from being alone—is blocked by a relationship that, although heavy and painful, structures his life. In this case, too, where does the border lie between "living in truth" and "living a lie"?

The circularity between truth, freedom, and dissidence traces a line that is a great deal finer and more tortuous than the one the dissidents who "heroically" remained in their homeland believed they could draw. The tangle between life and power is so tightly wound that it is very often unresolvable—so much so that it is almost always confusing to us. First of all, this is because as Kundera believes, implicitly in agreement with Havel on this point, power is a magic "circle," a protective orbit around which we perceive a vacuum. In this regard, in *The Book of Laughter and Forgetting*,[74] his first work written in exile, he describes the image, introduced by the laughing Devil and Angels, of young people dancing in a circle under the eyes of the military in front of a nuclear power plant. Their actions express the presumption of describing on the ground "a magical circle uniting them like a ring," chained together by a sense of shared innocence—an innocence that they seek to throw in the policemen's faces through their lighthearted, childlike dancing.[75] The image stages a sharp, eloquent contrast: on the one hand the "false" unity of the police, imposed and in ranks, and on the other the "true" union of the young people in the circle; on the one hand the sullen activity of lying in wait and command, and on the other the arabesques of joyful play. The opposition only obscures the ease, however, with which one can pass from the sincerity of innocence to the enthusiasm of the hunt for any "false moves."[76] Even when we break rank or leave the circle of political power, even when we break out of the rings and rows in which politics and society compel us to live, power continues to circulate—and almost never innocently. A domineering and coercive collective structure is not the only means through which power is exercised. Even if we extricate ourselves from its most visible grip, power follows us on every plane, all the way to the inevitable barrier created by the gaze of others: the public gaze, which can transform relationships between individuals into relations of surveillance and spying, but also the gazes of the people near to us and our loved ones. Thus, for Sabina—Tomas's friend and "free" lover—"living in truth," lying neither to ourselves nor to others, means simply "living away from the public eye."[77]

For Kundera as for Foucault, much more so than for Havel, prior to any other assessment, power relations are relationships between bodies, and they are therefore inevitable. However, they do not take shape simply as a vectorial composition between different forces. They ignite psychological dynamics that, once triggered, remain largely constant, governing intimate situations as much as they do political events. In Lacanian terms, many of Kundera's characters experience power relations in the same way as the encircling of the individual by the mother, as if these relations prolonged that first, foundational power relation. True, obedience to power is diffused through constraints and fear, but also by a subjugation that is spontaneous, so to speak, driven by an ambivalent and dizzying force, almost as if it were "the insuperable longing to fall."[78] This is what can push us toward the magic circle and its attractive force. It can count on a subject with a troubled identity, who, traversed by opposing vectors that it does not want to acknowledge, is frequently the obstacle to its own liberation. Many of Kundera's characters thus remain locked into relations that create pain and suffering.

As we have said, Kundera's microphysics bring the polemic against Havel and its supposed belief in authenticity well beyond the perimeter of political relations, to have an impact on intimate relationships. Moreover, as if prefiguring a kind of genealogy of power, he pushes on to name the very root of domination. The relationship between human beings and animals is indeed central to many of his works. It returns constantly, almost as if to remind us that the evil of oppression of humans over humans will be inevitable until it is eradicated from its true source. With the argumentative freedom that only literature allows, Kundera's philosophical and political hypothesis resounds in a way that is both elementary and effective: the domination of humans over animals is the *a priori* of all domination. So much so that the narrative of Genesis should be told differently: God did not create man to make him lord of the animal kingdom; rather, man invented God to justify and sanctify the dominion that he had usurped for himself "over the cow and the horse."[79] The right to kill animals, Kundera notes accordingly, has been one of the few assumptions that humanity

has always agreed on. In it is rooted, for example, the Cartesian prejudice that the animal is an "animated machine," according to which a dog's
cries of pain are nothing but the grating of a poorly functioning mechanism. Now, says Kundera provocatively, only in the relationship between
humankind and animals can the true ethical character of a subject be put
to the test. "Mankind's true moral test, its fundamental test (which lies
deeply buried from view), consists of its attitude towards those who are
at its mercy: animals."[80] If the interpersonal bond is always conditioned
by relations of conventionalities and power, if our mutual benevolence is
stained by the suspicion of self-interest, the true absence of wickedness can
be measured only in behaviors toward those who do not hold any power
or represent any force.

Nietzsche, under whose aegis the novel closes, is evoked to give consistency to the image of a locus "somewhere outside of power." The scene
is well known. In 1889 the German philosopher was staying in Turin; he
left his hotel and embraced a horse. This gesture has always been seen as
the beginning of Nietzsche's madness. Kundera interprets it rather as an
expression of the pain that the philosopher had to endure in imagining humanity's redemption from its folly of power. At the time, Nietzsche "had
removed himself from the world of people." He sees a horse being beaten,
and under the eyes of the coachman with whip in hand, he puts his arms
around the animal and bursts into tears. His tears have a profound philosophical meaning. It is a plea of apology to animals made in the name of
all humanity for the contempt and domination that Descartes had formal-
ized so well in degrading the animal to a machine. In Kundera's view, only
the Nietzschean utopia, so to speak, can respond to Havel's appeal to the
true "power of the powerless." The possibility of moral innocence arises, it
would seem, in the possibility of being able to listen not only to humans,
but also to the suffering animal. It calls up the stage when humanity was
not yet the "lord and master of nature" and the animals knew nothing of
the consequences that would befall them once the earthly paradise was
abandoned.

Very rarely, however, has humanity passed the test described by the
writer. Indeed, our relations with animals have very often served as testing grounds for domination. Kundera reminds us that in Czechoslovakia
shortly before the outbreak of harsh repressive measures and waves of ar-
rests by the party after the Prague Spring, an aggressive campaign was

launched against dogs, depicted by the propaganda as the harbingers of various diseases dangerous to society. There is an unforgettable scene in *Farewell Waltz*,[81] in which a pensioner's hunt for the "last dog" is transformed into the event that convinces Jakub of how right he is to leave the country, leading him to a series of thoughts that could easily be part of a wider reflection on the normality of evil. Jakub is not particularly troubled by people who beat dogs intentionally or even, perhaps, with pleasure—in this case, the old men protected by uniforms who zealously wield poles and use violence against stray animals. Perhaps they are spurred by wickedness, but more probably by a desire for order and, at the same time, according to Jakub-Kundera, a desire for death. It is the same desire that transforms the human world into an inorganic realm in which everything is amenable to a norm and where everything can operate and function in accordance with the specified rhythm. In fact, if life is a perpetual revival of disorder, the desire for order is the virtuous pretext by which human beings' hatred for the concrete lives of others justifies their crimes.[82] Jakub has already known all this for a long time: he knows, we might say, that for the death drive to operate on a large scale it must be elevated to a political universal and act in the name of goodness and life. This is the only way that its hoped-for capacity can be reached. But what he clearly perceives for the first time is the real reason this wounds and disturbs him: the real reason he is about to leave his country is the demonstration of another truth, a truth that is opposite but at the same time complementary to this one. The old men with the poles are "part of the game," so to speak. They have always existed in history, and those who hate disorder and use poles to create order will always exist; they are the eternal jailers and perennial persecutors. What upsets him, though, is a person like Ruzena, like so many others: a pretty girl who happens to be on the scene and who, at the beginning, participates as a mere spectator. But once catalyzed by the dynamics of the hunt, she uses this opportunity to redeem the insignificance of her own life and immediately falls into line with the new norm. No longer is she satisfied to simply watch without stopping the beating, or to turn her gaze elsewhere. No, Ruzena immediately takes the side of the persecutors. Or at the very least, she mimics their behavior. Jakub, whose concern is to hide a dog that he had rescued by chance, grasps all the horror implicit in the situation. For him, what is unbearable is the idea that "onlookers are ready to restrain the victim during an execution."

Although at one time the soul of the crowd identified with the misery of those who were persecuted, today, he concludes, it identifies itself with the miserable, gray face of the executioners: "He felt the animal's warm body under his hand, and he realized that the blond young woman had come to announce to him, as a secret sign, that he would never be liked in this country and that she, the people's messenger, would always be ready to hold him down so as to offer him up to the men threatening him with poles with wire loops."[83] Perhaps this is why Jakub is not assailed by feelings of guilt when he realizes that he did nothing to prevent Ruzena from swallowing a pill that may very well have contained poison. And thus, between passers-by who become executioners, murderers who do not want to kill (Jakub himself), and the guilty who feel no guilt, Kundera's writing celebrates the death of Raskolnikov, and with him, once again, the eclipse of the Dostoevsky paradigm and its hegemony.

At first Jakub likens himself to the protagonist of *Crime and Punishment*, because the murder he committed was also pointless and disinterested,[84] but in the end he has to acknowledge that his intention to commit crimes is far removed from the propensity for crime of Dostoevsky's hero: "So I am a murderer out of high-mindedness, he said to himself, and the thought seemed ridiculous and sad." Raskolnikov had killed out of a desire for knowledge, in order to test himself when confronted with the killing of an old woman looked on as useless and harmful. Through the experiment of killing the contemptible old woman, he aimed above all at understanding the meaning of murder and the possibility of killing without feeling any emotions. The purpose of his crime, in a nutshell, was to look into that abyss of human freedom that can lead people to the ultimate act: to do evil for evil's sake. True, she was a despicable creature, but she was still willed by God. While he hacked the old lady to death, he had the clear perception—which was exactly what fueled the experiment—that he was transgressing the supreme law, because he was sacrificing a human being on the altar of existential experimentation. Jakub, for his part, had no need of any such evidence. For some time now he had lived in a world where there was no more sacredness in human lives, lives whose obliteration was not perceived as a sacrifice, and certainly not as an absurd sacrifice made to cruelty. This was the time of honest perpetrators, "now brazenly innocent, now sadly craven."[85] Raskolnikov served his sentence for his crime by being tormented with guilt. He finally collapsed under the weight of his act because he was overwhelmed by a sense of tragedy. As much as Jakub tried to imagine that the nurse really could have died because of his voluntary negligence, he felt nothing, and he marveled at the indifference and lightness that he felt in the face of this crime. He could not help but wonder, however, whether precisely this lightness and indifference were not more terrifying than all the turmoil that Dostoevsky's hero had experienced.

Perhaps even Kundera, so strongly opposed to any rhetoric of moral conscience, is thus suggesting an answer to the problem of the origin of evil—the question of where it introduces itself into relations between human beings. We cannot stop at the opposition between "living in truth" and "living a lie," which in his opinion is confused and can be eluded. The origin and contemporary character of evil must be sought in the disappearance of a sense of the tragic, that is to say, in the ease with which we dull the perception of the negative in order to adapt, without creating any friction, to whatever norm of life has currently achieved hegemony. This is what stands behind his memorable indictment of kitsch in *The Unbearable Lightness of Being*, pages that contrary to the author's intentions became an emblem of dissident philosophy as well as the emblem of a certain type of "impolitical" critique of communism.[86] In reality, Kundera's critique is a more profound, radical discussion. It takes its aim not only at communism, but at all "the European faiths, religious and political," all the visions that start from the assumption that the world is just and being is good. Kitsch, ultimately, is nothing but "a categorical agreement with being."[87] Because the word has been so overused in popular speech, the Czech writer reminds us, we have forgotten its original ontological meaning: "Kitsch is the absolute denial of shit, in both the literal and figurative senses of the word." Kitsch is the movement that eliminates from the visual field everything in human existence that might appear as essentially unacceptable. It is the "empire of the positive," we might say: a discourse in which the only images and thoughts allowed to circulate are ones that banish doubt, bewilderment, and anxiety. This is the essence of Sabina's nightmare: a universe reduced purely to the dimension of kitsch. The ugliness of real socialism is not what disgusts her. What disturbs her far more is rather the beauty mask that the regime feels the need to impose; not alarm at the pain that communism causes, but at the smile that it manages to induce. Everybody has to be seen smiling to prove their devout contentment; or rather, everyone must try to be "in proper agreement," not simply with communism but with being as such.

As a categorical agreement with being, for Kundera, kitsch has as many names as there are answers purporting to resolve the question of being. Kitsch can be Catholic, Protestant, or Jewish; Fascist, Communist, or democratic; national or international; feminist or chauvinist. In actuality, it is no different from the attitude that never puts life as such and its meanings into question: when a specific norm of life prevails, it is adopted as the only existing possibility. What the norm has excluded in order to assert itself, what it has overshadowed or constrained, has no importance. The only thing of importance is that being be. The unwritten motto (of the May Day parades and all the other Communist marches, and all other marches) was not "Long live Communism" but rather, writes Kundera, "Long live life!" The great power of political movements is measured by the capacity that they have to appropriate that tautology, especially their capacity to proclaim it to others with conviction: "Often I think: tragedy has deserted us; and that may be the true punishment."[88] There is no doubt for Kundera that when we lost our perception of the tragic, ushering in the triumph of the positive—the world of kitsch—at the same time we regressed to an elementary dualism. If we are required by the symbolic order in which we live to expel the negative, if everything is done to anesthetize the sense of tragedy, then the return to an interpretation of human conflicts in terms of an elemental struggle between good and evil is inevitable. Ultimately, this is where the strength of real socialism lies.

Now, in spite of his desire to distance himself from a dialectic between authentic and inauthentic—the naïve opposition that, in his opinion, nurtures the moral pride of the "professional dissidents"—his condemnation of kitsch is a firm stance in favor of a space for dissent. When asked why he is in conflict with the power of his country, his answer is because he defended, and continues to defend, the novel and its spirit.[89] To defend the novel, for him, means taking a stance in supporting a concrete existence that has not been expunged of its diverse, discordant possibilities, standing up for a narrative in which the truth is not the exclusive possession of any of the characters but only the inextricable movement that brings them together and separates them. In other words, to remain faithful to writing a novel means for him to oppose the categorical agreement with being, to open oneself up to a way of life that creates friction with the real, to make space for a gap through which the tragic can continue to make itself perceptible to us.

But is a "life in truth" that Havel thematizes, following in Patočka's footsteps, really so different from Kundera's condemnation of kitsch? Is it not also a way, admittedly somewhat naïve, of describing a form of life that seeks to create friction with the unquestioned norm of life? What if it is not, as Kundera polemically assumed, just a label of authenticity to be stuck on a role, even in the case of the dissident? We could try to think of it as an "aesthetics of existence," in Foucault's sense, namely, as the choice of an ethos that opposes the "categorical agreement with being." The only thing it presupposes is the free act of refusing to participate in the game, the decision to not respect its rules. As we have already pointed out, for Havel "living in truth" certainly cannot mean restoring a presumed legality against an illegality; in itself, the law is meaningless. But neither should living in truth be taken as denoting a codified disagreement, whose practice one knows beforehand. "In truth" may include "any means by which a person or a group revolts against manipulation," from striking workers to rock concerts.[90] Precisely because every expression of freedom, in the sense of an action that was not planned and predetermined, is in itself a political threat, any profanation of the rituals with which the regime draws its own magic circle—from abstention to a publicly announced break—is potentially subversive. It is subversive because it disrupts the trajectories along which the system applies its pressures. This is what lies behind Havel's clearly stated opposition to an idea of "dissidence" as a profession, which he rejects as vigorously as he denies the efficacy of a traditional vision of political opposition. First of all, as we have said, this is because in reality there is no polarization of power relations that would allow us to clearly locate the opposing positions. And also, the need of each person to resist the pressures of "auto-totality" does not come from an *a priori* image of political change, but from the concrete intentions of individuals and from their desire to not be dominated. The aim of an opposition to revolutionize the system through violent action makes no sense, not "because the idea seems too radical, but on the contrary, because it does not seem radical enough."[91] In the first instance, then, "living in truth" means the possibility "for anyone" to embed change inside a deeper layer than governmental or technological changes to the system. It is a point of departure, starting from the factual and *from below*, for the movement of an individual life that begins to express its own desire for change. To make this happen, individuals must emancipate themselves from their own compromise with post-totalitarianism, by first of all refusing to reproduce the system's mechanisms inside themselves. What Havel called the "existential revolution" is, in reality, the movement of withdrawal and disidentification from the hegemonic norm of life: the free act, as he puts it, that is alone capable of breaking the vicious circle of objective guilt.[92]

What we need if we are to break the normality of evil, then, is an "existential revolution." Havel refers to Heidegger's diagnosis on the epoch of planetary technology, and he shares the German philosopher's judgment on the general crisis of the West and democracy. However, he firmly rejects the fatalistic conclusion. With the desire to subvert the meaning of all historical theodicies, he challenges the resigned tone in which we are told that "only a God can save us now" from the evil of nihilism.[93] Salvation will not come from history or from the system. If there is to be salvation from power, from a power that becomes domination, it will arrive only from ethics, from choosing an ethos as a form of life and a style of thought. Havel's way of conceiving dissidence acts only indirectly on the structure of power. It does not organize parties and it does not consolidate the multitudes. Nevertheless, a "life in truth" is not restricted to the existential and ethical spheres; it can be made *immediately* political. The conceivability of "another life," no different from Kundera's perception of the tragic, opens up the space for an indirect pressure on power, because the expressive dimension of a "life in freedom" will inevitably force the system to react, making it constantly alternate its response between forced tolerance and repression.[94]

What if one day the greengrocer stopped displaying the sign with the slogan? What if he started refusing to vote and saying what he thought at party meetings? Maybe he would be transferred to a manual labor job and see his hopes for spending his vacation in Bulgaria and sending his kids to college go up in smoke. He would probably be persecuted by all the people who administer punishments and who make it their business to ensure that the "automatism" of the system continues. However, his actions would not be merely an individual offense. Far more seriously, he would break the rules of the game: he would disrupt the game as such. Crying out that the emperor is naked, precisely "because the emperor is in fact naked," the greengrocer would break through the stone façade that seeks to encircle the entire life of individuals and society. Through that narrow opening in the curtain, he would demonstrate to all that the nakedness of the emperor can be seen and touched. Escaping from the rules of the game, interrupting the inertia of everyday life, may in certain contexts prove to be extremely dangerous actions. The fact that they are able to become examples proves that they have the power to communicate the contagion—a contagion with potentially subversive effects. This is why intellectuals in Prague never tire of repeating that true dissidence is nothing but thought. Far from being a purely speculative activity, "living in truth" is a vigorous "exercise of the judgment" that reflects on the conditions of existence: it is the adoption of an ethos that withholds its consent to the "categorical agreement with being" and that, for this reason, remains silent when required to shout "Long live life!"

Poor Devils Who "Worship" Life: Us

In bringing our journey to a close, I would like to briefly comment on a well-known text, *The Drowned and the Saved*, published by Primo Levi a year before his death.[1] One of the greatest books of the twentieth century, it holds in its pages a full-fledged philosophical inquiry into the normality of evil. Its message, although seemingly more placid than the one conveyed by the account of his experience in Auschwitz, is perhaps more disquieting.

Almost forty years later, then, the author seems to have honed the definitive answer to the frantic question he posed as the title of his first masterpiece: *If this is a man*.[2] By returning to the question after such a long hiatus, he seems to have arrived, lucid and remorseless, at a final judgment. Now, the prisoner who is reduced to waste matter is a man, but so are those responsible for reducing him to that condition. And these are completely ordinary people, who acted out of the same interests and passions that we find in any power relationship, and that we will always find. This is Levi's realistic, bitter warning. Had these harsh words of his not been written by someone who had personally lived through the experience, they would have been even more shocking. *The Drowned and the Saved* does not simply confront the paradox of bearing witness—the obstacles of the memory and the transformation of shame into guilt. I believe that this remarkable text, justly read and reread, staged and performed both in Italy and abroad, contains the most sober, but perhaps also the most effective, refutation of all demonological conceptions of power—that of Nazi power, certainly, but primarily of power in general. It provides a damning, microphysical investigation into how, in certain circumstances, the thousand threads of the desire for life and the many faces of consent to authority provoked by the desire for life bind themselves together and become tightened to the point of fusing into total domination of man over man. As far as our inquiry is concerned, it offers one of the clearest, most powerful confirmations of the unilateralism and inadequacy of the Dostoevsky paradigm.

Thus, by ideally opposing Levi to Dostoevsky and what the Russian writer represents, we can conclude that the Muselmann—what resulted from the degradation of the camp—was not solely and not predominantly the product of the abyssal freedom of a subject who had taken the place of God; nor was he the object on which the perverse *jouissance* of the death impulse had been discharged. He became what he became through a dense but ordinary weave of intentions, actions, and objectives whose weft proved fatal. We never find a definition of what power is or a definition of the essence of evil in Levi's writings. For him, too, evil and power are not substances; rather, they are shifting dynamics whose trajectories intersect one another, partially due to the fierce determination to survive.

Not surprisingly, Levi has been compared to Elias Canetti.[3] The assumption behind Canetti's *Crowds and Power* lies in the conviction that "the situation of survival is the central situation of power."[4] Whether he is analyzing "closed crowds" or "open crowds," "baiting crowds" or "flight crowds," "revolutionary crowds" or "resisting crowds," ultimately Canetti is trying to understand the reasons behind the behaviors of the crowd in the concentration camps—the "closed crowd" within which the individual returns to a state of almost absolute isolation.[5] Now, although he draws his material from a chronologically differentiated social phenomenology, he asks an obsessive, recurring question that forms the basis of his political anthropology: What intense, inextricable passion moves power, that of someone in a crowd, and that of someone who faces the crowd? It is a difficult question to answer when looking at everyday experiences. We need to examine situations that suspend the habits of civilization, the barriers that protect us from a face-to-face impact with death. Although the rich tableau of *Crowds and Power* portrays a highly articulated variety of crowd formations, it does trace out a constant in the life of power. If conventions mask the sense of joy that the living feel when faced with the dead, this is not the case in war or under some extreme circumstances when the pleasure of those who manage to stay alive can even be expressed as a virtue.[6] Whoever wins in battle and thus survives the enemy feels his strength growing, until, after putting himself repeatedly to the test, "he will win the thing most precious to a fighter, a sense of *invulnerability*."[7] As Canetti admirably explains, it is as if the body of the survivor grew in strength and power, suffused with all the enemies he has killed, incorporating them one by one until he has the feeling of absolute omnipotence.[8] The passion of staying alive in the place of others, of confronting the dead, is such an intense one that it can become insatiable, driving those who are addicted to it to continuously satisfy their urge. The man who has acquired a taste for power and survival wants to *accumulate* them, and for this reason he will seek out any occasion for increasing them, stretching the limits of an existence that in the normal course of affairs would prohibit this sort of behavior with the most severe punishments.[9] If an individual alone cannot kill as many people as his passion for survival dictates, he may make use of executioners whom he binds to himself by manipulating them, to use them as tools in his delirious ascent toward extermination. In Canetti's view, power is measured by the number of dead. The deep root of power resides in the desire of the One to survive the many: to be able to literally stand on top of everything and above everyone, to remain alive and standing on a boundless expanse of corpses. The secret of power lies precisely in the craving to survive large numbers of the dead, because ultimately, the true will of the powerful is to be the only one left alive, and as long as there are people, he will never feel safe.[10]

But no matter how brilliantly the connection between power and survival is described, the imposing schema drawn by *Crowds and Power* ends up depicting only the extreme view of the scene, as in the many "visions" that have converged in the Dostoevsky paradigm. In other words, once again he describes the grandiose figure of those who hold power and distribute death, leaving in the shadow the actions of all those who have contributed to making their greatness grow: exactly the focus of Levi's apparently stripped-down account. Unlike Canetti's reconstruction, Levi's is not a "phenomenology of the powerful." Rather, if we were to assign it a place in an ideal history of thought on the relationship between evil and power, it would rank as one of the most convincing refutations of all dualistic theories, even at the painful, disturbing price of discovering that the status of victim does not in itself confer a certificate of innocence.

This is something we have seen repeatedly: when the deconstructive intent takes aim at a conception of evil that identifies it with the power of nothingness, the possibility of separating the space of power into two opposite poles inevitably fades away. We found confirmation of this in Nietzsche's genealogy and in the political philosophy of dissent; in Arendt's taunts regarding the banality of evil, and in Foucault's challenge of *parrhesia*. We tracked down some precedents through a "non-simple" reading of Freud and psychoanalysis, and the philosophy of Heidegger and Levinas. Whenever the "Dostoevskian" status of evil is put into question, the dichotomous image becomes more complicated: drawing hard-and-fast boundaries between "absolute demons" and "defenseless victims" becomes difficult. And when dualism—both political and moral—is abandoned, it is subjectivity that calls out to be investigated: not only and not so much because it is the bearer of wicked dispositions, but because it very often serves as the involuntary support of domination. Ultimately, this is also what Levi courageously sought to answer, exposing himself to the risk of discovering the trigger of that evil, as he says, in himself.

Almost everything in his writing contradicts Dostoevsky's vision. Levi—he confesses with some embarrassment—never really warmed to the great Russian writer.[11] His work, *The Drowned and the Saved*, can truly be read, then, as a "countertext" to *Demons* and the Legend of the Grand Inquisitor. It refutes the Manichean conception of power that opens up an abysmal gap between the feverish will for power of the wicked and the Old Man versus the indistinct passivity of the masses. Dualism is certainly a reassuring refuge, Levi tells us. This is why it has become the most popular key for explaining and understanding power. Our desire to distinguish clearly between friend and foe is all the more powerful the more we need to protect ourselves from a complexity that confuses us. In fact, as we have observed on several occasions, nothing simplifies reality better than the act of automatically separating good from evil. It would be nice, says Levi, to be able to "emulate Christ's gesture on Judgment Day: here the righteous, over there the reprobates," here the innocent, the oppressed, and the destroyed, over there the perpetrators. But if our desire for simplification is understandable and justifiable, he warns us, simplification is not. We must have the courage of "a less turbid spirit" than what *Demons* depicts in the halls of power: we must keep our gaze fixed on the normality and the banality of people who are always caught up in a dense web of relationships.[12]

For these reasons, Levi has no hesitation in making the concentration camp—the place that we are most prone to interpret in dualistic

terms—the laboratory of his analysis. It is true that the structure of the totalitarian regime, which the concentration camp reproduces on a smaller,
more intensive scale, makes it almost impossible to control from below.
However, no matter how much even the harshest political reality aspires to
totality, apart from the extermination camp, it can never completely eradicate freedom; some form of reaction always remains possible. It seems almost completely absent only in the camps, where almost all forms of revolt
were quashed. By what criterion, then, are we to judge people's different
behaviors? How and on what basis can we distinguish between the circles
of that particular hell? And, most importantly, why judge at all, if this is
ultimately an exceptional situation whose characteristics are certainly not
applicable to our everyday life? This is precisely Levi's challenge: to keep
a firm grip on the uniqueness of the situation while at the same time creating bridges with ordinary reality, with the normal relations of human
beings in society, "with our reality." So even though his message is never
ambiguous—there are victims and persecutors, and no wider judgment
must ever lump them together; hanging the SS officers and other functionaries is necessary and remains so—this cannot be the last word on the
topic. The quality of this tension is precisely what makes Levi's last confrontation with Auschwitz perhaps the most precious, but also the most
"scandalous" treatise on the normality of evil.

To fully understand the dynamics in the connection between evil
and power, we must more closely examine the area that separates the perpetrators of the persecutions from the victims who were made absolutely
innocent by instantaneous death: "Only a schematic rhetoric can claim
that that space is empty: it never is." Levi is insistent on this point: as in
all relations of power, and even more so in the concentration camp, if we
want to really understand, we cannot stop at the two blocs of victims and
persecutors. In the picture that the writer paints, hazier tones predomi-
nate: "It is a gray zone, poorly defined, where the two camps of masters
and servants both diverge and converge. This gray zone possesses an incredibly complicated internal structure." Disturbingly, "The hybrid class
of the prisoner-functionary constitutes its armature and at the same time
its most disquieting feature."[13] Contrary to what we would like to hope,
he continues, the more methodically harsh the oppression—the more demonic it is in its design—the more extensively ordinary people are willing
to collaborate.

Even among camp prisoners, whose every individual will and desire should have been extinguished, there spread a form of conflict that was not solely the pure and simple struggle for survival. It was something more than a simple attempt to stay alive. The same multiplicity of motives that always compels us to accept the powerful, and by accepting them, make them grow, also exists in a camp barracks. In the deprived world of the prisoners we find, for example, the "vying for prestige [. . .] a seemingly irrepressible need in our civilization": the desire of those who find themselves on the bottom rungs of the social ladder to throw off their humiliation and contempt and cast it on the newcomers, inventing a new, lower-ranking category on which to discharge the burden of the offenses received from above. That is why, Levi tells us, in places where we would expect to find solidarity in misfortune, it is unlikely that we will. Indeed, the *Zugang*—the newcomer—was greeted in the camp with all the prisoners' accumulated hostility, because he had the smell on him of a life that was still too intact, and therefore threatening to them. Certainly, the enemy was the Nazis, "but the hoped for allies [. . .] were not there."[14] In contrast to how some hagiographic postwar literature would have it, the camp did not sanctify the victims; it degraded them. It corrupted them, through psychological and physical violence, to the point of making them identical to the images that the guards had of them.

The gray zone, present in every human society, from the totalitarian regime to "a big industrial factory," is the armature on which power props itself up. It is marked, first of all, by the inevitable rise of the climbers, which the circle of the powerful is forced to accept and sometimes encourages. And the more total the domination, the more it attracts "the human type who is greedy for power." The "middle ring" coincides in the first place with "the hybrid class of the prisoner-functionary": numerous, poorly defined types. They represent an "average, unselected sample of humanity."[15] Certainly, many of the chiefs of the labor squads—the *Kapos*—were chosen directly by the commanding officers or their delegates. They were common criminals whose new, unexpected career offered them an alternative to detention; they were political prisoners who were exhausted, and sometimes even Jews who saw the role as the only way to escape the "final solution." It is ridiculous, Levi insists, to expect of them the behavior "of saints and stoic philosophers," because in the vast majority of cases their behavior was rigidly preordained: they were reduced to animals in the space of a few days or a few weeks.[16]

However, Levi does not refrain from judging, and he delivers his verdict on "the many" who "spontaneously" aspired to power. The number of sadists was small, but the frustrated were numerous: these are people who outside the camp and outside the totalitarian society would have been blocked from social elevation owing to their lack of merit. And many of them had been contaminated by their oppressors. These people, he explains, were willing to collaborate for several reasons: mistaken judgment, ideological seduction, servile imitation of the victor, short-sighted desire for any advantage, cowardice, and certainly in some cases, lucid calculation aimed at eluding the imposed orders. Everybody, however, took an active part in weaving the fabric of the gray zone, which, perhaps more than any other place, reveals to us one of the secrets of "voluntary servitude." If these people abounded in the camps, then they also abound outside that enclosed space, and they always will. We will never understand the enormous power of evil if we restrict our gaze to the SS, wishing concentration camps away with the facile indignation of "Never again!" Our need and ability to judge falters when faced with the *Sonderkommandos*, the Special Squads. These are the men who worked the ovens, "the miserable manual laborers of the slaughter," the only ones who—in contrast to the grotesque defense of the Nazis who were dragged into court—were legitimately able to invoke *Befehlnotstand* ("the state of compulsion following an order"). In reality, not even the rigid either-or with which these people were faced— immediate obedience or instant death—can quell Levi's obsessive question: "Why did they accept that task? Why didn't they rebel? Why didn't they prefer death?" And again: Why, unlike those who rebelled and about whom we know nothing, did they prefer "a few more weeks of life (what a life) to immediate death"?[17]

The answer is, because the members of the gray zone, as much as they differ from each other, all share one common trait: the desire to preserve their privilege, which in the camp meant staying alive as long as possible. It was a privilege, the writer immediately adds, that was overrated and poorly calculated, one that yielded very little and in many cases involved nothing but extra work. Above all, it was a privilege that was destined in most cases to end very soon, but not before having administered an additional dose of suffering to others. But they were greedy—we were greedy—for life, for more and more life. In this case, too, Levi duly manages to be broad-minded, even if it requires toughness and courage. Without ever giving in to the temptation of simplifying, Levi's writing proceeds along concentric circles toward a core of truth that is difficult to pin down but can nevertheless be articulated: from Eichmann to the *Sonderkommandos* (that "band of half-consciences. Whether high or low it is difficult to say"), *everybody* collaborated with the evil that feeds off unsuspecting signatures ("because a signature costs little") and shrugs of the shoulders (because "If I did not do it, someone else worse than I would").[18] In short, evil "feeds on itself—*out of a desire for servitude and smallness of soul*," out of our ambiguity and blind reverence for authority.[19] And even if a regime establishes itself through terror, it can only consolidate itself through compliance. These are the most effective "vectors and instruments of the system's guilt" that we insist on not wanting to see or hear. What brought human beings to recognize themselves in the Muselmann is in reality an elementary, primary passion, the most common of all: the obstinacy of continuing to live at any cost, even in small doses and only for a short time. This is the root of power—what leads us to desire ever larger doses of it. It is an obstinacy that would not be so willful, concludes Levi, if it were not accompanied by the denial of reality and the dream of omnipotence, "forgetting that we are all in the ghetto, that the ghetto is walled in, that outside the ghetto reign the lords of death, and that close by the train is waiting."[20]

With the profound, moving simplicity that only literary prose is capable of, in just a few, concise passages Levi delivers this "truth" about the connection between evil and power that twentieth-century philosophy was never able to capture. The only thought that came close to this "truth," in my opinion, is the one revolving around the paradigm of the "normality of evil," of the "mediocre demons." The reason for thinking in oppositions leading all thought on evil and on the evil of power astray is that its dynamic is ruled by an original, fundamental dichotomy that is often thoughtlessly assumed by common wisdom as well: *the dichotomy that separates life from death, making life the absolute other of death, and vice versa.* Although the Dostoevsky paradigm posited the absolutization of death as a condition for the event of evil, it failed to think through the consequences of the absolutization of life.[21]

In spite of the place from which Levi speaks to us, he disengages himself in the most straightforward way from the idea of evil as the power of nothingness, as the "desire for evil for the sake of evil"—"the discovery" of those who, as we said in the first part of this book, sought to overcome the limits of Kant's radical evil. Even if *The Drowned and the Saved* deliberately refrains from making any philosophical claims, it obviously echoes the reasons that we have looked for in passages from Nietzsche, Levinas, Arendt, Foucault, the Prague philosophers of dissent—in all the places that seem to cast doubt on the undisputed equation between evil and the will to death, or in other words, between evil and that disastrous instance of the subject (whether singular or collective) that impels it to destroy for the sake of destruction. This equation, as we have seen, is firmly adhered to by those who sought to oppose it to another, equally powerful identity between good and life, as well as those who wielded it as a cognitive weapon to arrive at an understanding of the abyss.

The point is not that absolute demons do not exist. This is not what I have sought to argue. The Dostoevsky paradigm and the paradigm of the normality of evil are not mutually exclusive. Their complementarity is often required to explain the "event of evil." Stavrogins of various kinds certainly do exist, as do Grand Inquisitors. But if their actions give rise to political contexts of total domination, it is not because their will to nothingness awakens and disinhibits the drive to destruction that lies dormant in the many. What happens much more frequently is that the absolutization of death succeeds because it is able to perfectly integrate itself with the opposite tendency to absolutize life.

Ultimately, Levi's subdued conclusions seem to confirm this. We are so hungry for life and hence so "dazzled by power" that we forget our essential truth: that death is part of life. In order to gain a few more instants, to increase the feeling of our power and the length of our life for even a single moment, to make us recognizable from the reality in which we are immersed and be saved by it, there is almost nothing we will not come to terms with. The secret of power, then, can be explained, prosaically, by looking at the desire whose root we all share and from which it is unlikely that we will be able to free ourselves: the desire to maximize life—which in the modern age has become the supreme value.

. . .

As a matter of fact, we have already heard a story about human beings who do not abuse their abyssal freedom, in the Legend of the Grand Inquisitor. They even give up the most precious gift they have, the capacity to choose between good and evil, in order to pursue their glum happiness, made of bread and other childish wants; but above all to unburden themselves of the anguish with which this poisoned gift fills them. Certainly, the scene recounted by Ivan in the *Brothers Karamazov* is distorted by its dualistic, topological simplification. Moreover, the multitude is never homogeneous: it is composed of a variety that remains unexpressed by Dostoevsky, portrayed instead by Levi in the gray zone. However, the "biopolitical pact"—obedience and submission in exchange for protection and well-being—on which pastoral power is based is clearly brought into focus in its elementary logic by both writers.

But how does this pact work today? One thing is for sure: although the absolutization of life as the value of a collective entity—an ethnicity, people, or race—has seen a decline, it has been replaced by the imperative to maximize the life of the individual, in social self-affirmation and especially in optimizing the biological quality of the individual body. What promises and expectations are being levered, then, to produce the docility and consent that, as we have seen, represent some of the most effective vectors of political evil? Our problem is no longer what Foucault labored over in the late 1970s, explaining how biopower—the power that in the modern age took charge of the biological life of the population and its improvement—was able to easily transform itself into total domination over death. As he himself pointed out at the beginning of the 1980s, although the regimes between the two world wars focused on the life of the collective body, promoting its health, biopolitics in liberal and democratic societies in the West are different. The societal functionings in which we find ourselves immersed exert control over our lives and direct our behaviors and styles of conduct, but they do so not by limiting or impeding our movements, or by imposing prohibitions and regulations. It is true, as many post-Foucauldians note, that pastoral power perpetuates itself. But places from which it radiates that are clearly identifiable no longer exist. Instead, what we are witnessing is the fragmentation and multiplication of powers that claim the right to regulate our lives. Without imposing transcendental regulations or norms, they manage and promote the protection of life by endorsing the performance of what are presumed to be "normal" and "physiological" human behaviors and by incentivizing processes that are supposed to lead to well-being.

Having entrusted birth, death, and disease to the power and knowledge of the life sciences, these appear to us increasingly as something we can control. In the final analysis, the critics of neoliberal biopolitics are right when they say that an imagination imbued with the idea of optimizing life is fundamental to the mutual reinforcement between new medical and biotechnological sciences on the one hand, and the demands of capital accumulation on the other.[22] It is true that the logic of "human capital"—which requires subjects to think and act as entrepreneurs of themselves and of their own corporeality—takes the biological life of people as something in which to invest, as a vehicle to increase profit.[23] But is this viewpoint adequate for grasping the deep, perhaps even metaphysical, roots of an imagination saturated by positivity that elevates the staying power, duration, and fitness of our biological lives to the supreme value? Simply removing the demand for profit may not be sufficient to give individuals back their joyful, independent life power. No matter how useful and innovative many of the diagnoses on the new forms of interaction between life and power are—from "post-Foucauldian," biopolitical approaches to eulogies of Deleuzian potentiality aimed at probing the "field of immanence" of power relations—they neglect the question regarding the sphere of "immaterial mediations." They seem to imply that any reference to the symbolic context means appealing to a spirit beyond the sensible reality. However, as we have said in the course of our inquiry, a symbolic order is a whole—situated in a given time and space—composed of images, of meanings received and transmitted, of perceptions that are introjected and projected onto others. It is a historical and concrete *a priori* of stratifications of meaning, both individual and collective, that acts on all the players involved without their necessarily being aware of it, inducing them to share its system of presuppositions.[24] It is a set of norms that, though not forcing anyone to comply with them, prompts people to reproduce its assumptions and content. And even if normativity is no longer expressed today through prohibitions, by restricting the field of possibilities it does continue to forcefully impose itself by conveying its initial assumptions through myriad imperatives according to which life is inherently positive. You need to live, you absolutely need to live. You need to live at your best, enhancing and actualizing to the utmost all the potential that you have been given. In response to these implicit injunctions, our core values become our faith and hope in a life without limitations, in which nothing is left unexpressed.

There is no question that today the interdependence of life and power has become a ubiquitous vortex: on the one hand, in hypermodern societies we *all* potentially come into contact with the hold that power exercises; and on the other, our whole life, even our bodily and biological life, takes on political importance. This is not just a matter of *conservatio vitae*, but rather an irresistible stimulus to behave in conformity for the sake of possibilities to enhance and prolong our lives. There is no doubt that modern Western democracies have given us countless opportunities for self-realization. This is not a matter of disputing the results of "civilization," culture, or the sciences; nor is it about impugning all policies for care and protection. Rather, the point is to question the side effects that the illusion of immortality creates in the relationship between subjectivity and power—because there is no doubt that the more opportunities a life has to enhance its self-affirmation and prolong its duration, the more it lends itself to being determined by others. The more we expose our lives to the light and hold of power, the fewer spaces elude its control.

We internalize imperatives that dictate "what ought to be," and we adapt seamlessly to the norms, so much so that, as the culture critics complain, our lives now seem programmed to become prey to the petty seductions of consumerism and the society of the spectacle. But to continue blaming anonymous and deceptive power, which entices us only to better oppress us, or which tempts us only to better exploit us, means once again resorting to the excuses offered by the dualistic vision. In other words, no power today threatens us or blackmails us with violence, and the magic of the hidden manipulators is openly displayed before the eyes of anyone who cares to look. If the new normativity for the optimization of life has managed to prevail along with new forms of acquiescence and indifference, this is because we not only accept it, we seek to implement it at any cost.

Ours is a never-ending quest that, like it or not, reinforces the various powers on which it depends. The reason it has proved to be so ingrained is because it responds to the desire rooted in our deepest passions, the one Levi writes about that is so easily overindulged and abused. It is the desire to be and to persist, which today is finally expressed as the pure desire to stay alive—to have more and more life before us that must be constantly improved. And obviously, the more we want to live and feel powerful and alive, the more we depend on the complicated network of powers and recognitions that assure us that we are.

In a certain paradoxical sense, our present times seem to demonstrate that Kant was right after all in his characterization of radical evil as excessive self-affirmation—were it not for the fact that, today, reason has no need to reverse the incentive of the maxims or to lie in order to disguise the transgression. Our contemporary "You must" demands exactly the sort of self-affirmation that the "moral law" was meant to prevent. The new imperative in the West exhorts us to maximize our own life—first and foremost our biological life. We might almost rephrase the categorical imperative as: "Make improving your life the absolute, universal law of your conduct."

Hence, absorbed by the peremptoriness of an infinite project (maximizing life can only be an endless commitment), we have neither the time nor the space to gain any distance from ourselves, to perceive and judge the often painful reality that "is out there."[25]

.   .   .

I like to think of the last lectures Michel Foucault gave before his death as an invitation to imagine a break in the circuit running between desire for life, normativity, power, and evil. Faced with our growing willingness to return to the matrix of power, the course held at the Collège de France during the months of February and March 1984 entitled "The Courage of Truth,"[25] also dedicated to the theme of *parrhesia*, could thus be viewed as Foucault's proposal for a radical practice of withdrawal and disidentification.

The Stoics, the Skeptics, and the Cynics—the subject of the course—on par with Socrates (the Socrates who is least like Plato), also made *parrhesia* into a form of resistance against the normativity that power seeks to impose. Analyzed in a selective and certainly unilateral fashion, the philosophy of the Cynics serves Foucault to talk about the choice of a specific ethos as a method for distancing oneself from the identities imposed by one's context. The Cynic makes his *bios* into an *alethurgia*, a *direct* manifestation of the truth, not an abstract or transcendent truth, not a truth that can be inferred or predicated, but a truth as bearing witness to the self. The *bios kunikos*—the "dog's life"—is a constant provocation to common sense. The Cynic perennially brings the nomos into question in order to give a voice back to nature. The wretched, nomadic "life in truth" that he leads is an example of freedom, because it engages in an interminable practice of virtualizing all identifications. The *parrhesia* of the Cynics is therefore a sort of "radicalized Socraticism" according to which having the courage to openly state the truth to the powerful is no longer enough. Instead, we must challenge the totality of conventions and the recognitions of power with our existence and our bodies. The Cynic must abide by this choice to the extreme, to the point of paradox, until becoming indifferent to adversity, misfortune, poverty, and disregard. The life of the Cynic is a "scandalous" one, because unlike the Stoic who practices *praemeditatio malorum*, he does not limit himself to imagining all possible evils. He lives in what most people consider to be bad: deprivation, exile, and poverty. The condition of his freedom consists in not being afraid of losing anything: not goods or recognition, not signs of power or wealth.[26]

There is no doubt that the message transmitted by Foucault in his last few lectures is primarily a provocation. It is obvious that rediscovering Cynicism does not mean simply rehabilitating a particular, slightly forgotten figure of ancient philosophy. Rather, it means being able to describe or even just imagine a possible alternative path in the relationship between subjectivity, truth, ethics, and power.[27] For this reason, the Cynics' reference to "animality" is understood by Foucault as a choice to live in a certain way that only a subject can make. Far from suggesting a bodily life that is impersonal and wild, beyond good and evil, the animal way of life—what Diogenes pursues, for example—it is the decision embarked on by an ethical subjectivity, which transforms someone's life into a polemical attitude, into a permanent practice of the discriminating judgment. The adoption of a critical ethos is therefore a tool that can interrupt the repeatability by which power reproduces itself. It would seem that after questioning himself for years on the relationship between subjects and power, Foucault concluded that it was not possible to force it by getting outside the process that individuates a life so as to lose oneself in the incessant movement of the innocence of becoming. Foucault's challenge, wrapped up in his interest in "care of the self" and *parrhesia*, thus lies in suggesting a possibility for "otherwise" becoming subjects, for thinking of ways of subjectification that minimize the terrains for dependence and abuse of power.[28] Indeed, for the *bios kunikos*, evil is everything that traps us in the identifications of the nomos and does not allow critique. As Foucault never tires of repeating in these lectures as well, "where there is obedience, there cannot be *parrhesia*."[29] But the inverse is also true: where there is no *parrhesia*, domination can expand without encountering any resistance. Perhaps the "revolutionary truth" of the Cynics that lies at the heart of Michel Foucault is that the world can never change—it will never become different from how it is—unless individuals change their way of becoming and remaining subjects.

The Cynic is there to remind us that a power exercised on a subject is also always a power accepted by that subject—like the greengrocer in Prague, for that matter, who one day stops displaying the sign in his store window. Bringing the ancient ethos of the Cynics to our attention, therefore, is not a mere exercise in antiquarian history; nor is Foucault reintroducing a model that is presumed to have worked in the past. He brings to evidence a counterfactual that makes the breaking of a vicious circle conceivable: *the circularity between the need that the subject has for power, and the need that power has for the subject's need.* Power—the various powers—play with our desire for life; they take advantage of our demand to be "saved," so to speak, to be compensated for our obedience with the signs and names that make us feel more and more alive.

.   .   .

What collective effect could be set in motion if the suspicion began to spread that we do not seek "salvation"? That we are not interested in the illusory promise to enhance or prolong the "duration" of our lives, dangled before us by big or small powers? That we are willing to withdraw ourselves from protection, even at the risk of possibly continuing to remain comfortably in ourselves? In short, what if, as an experiment of the imagination, in response to the Cynics' provocation, we also tried to summon up the untimely force of ancient wisdom?

As a first step, of course, we should bet on the fact that the judgment of reality still lies in our hands. In the final analysis, this is what everybody has wagered on who has sought to oppose evil as an excess of power. We, too, are compelled to believe, without too many epistemological cautions, that we are capable of distinguishing between what is real and what is told to us in falsehood. This is not so much to gain true knowledge of ourselves and the world but to be able to make the parrhesiastic game—the act of responding in first person and with our body, with our form of ethical life—the truth that we utter. Certainly, we have no wish for exile or political adversities, and we have no intention of living without a home or family, or coupling in the public square as Diogenes did.

Nevertheless, let us pause for a moment on the most well-known anecdote that has been handed down to us on the life of the Cynics.

Alexander, the king of Macedonia, is in search of the now world-famous Diogenes, because if he were not Alexander the Great, he would like to live the life of the Cynic philosopher. The king therefore sets out to find him, so that he can meet him in person. When he finally finds Diogenes on the beach, sunbathing in the nude, legend has it that Alexander asked him the fateful question of the powerful: "What can I do for you? Tell me your wishes. I am willing to do anything for you." Just think how stunned the Macedonian king must have been at Diogenes' incredible response: "All I want from you is to move, because you're blocking the sun!" Imagine the absolute sense of freedom that we, too, would have felt in his place for having acted at least once in the knowledge that our life and our death are part and parcel of each other.

Notes

Additional notes provided by the translator are in square brackets.

CHAPTER 1: THE DOSTOEVSKY PARADIGM

1. Fyodor Dostoevsky, *Demons: A Novel in Three Parts*, trans. and annotated by Richard Pevear and Larissa Volokhonsky (New York: Random House, Vintage Classics, 1995), p. 43.

2. See W. Schubart, *Dostoyevsky und Nietzsche. Symbolik ihres Lebens* (Lucerne: Vita Nova, 1939); for an overview on the subject, and a comprehensive history of the philosophical reception, S. Givone, *Dostoevskij e la filosofia* (Rome-Bari: Editori Laterza, 2007, orig. pub. 1984), remains fundamental.

3. Fyodor Dostoevsky, *Notes from Underground*, trans. Richard Pevear and Larissa Volokhonsky (New York: Knopf, 1993, orig. pub. 1864). It is common opinion among Dostoevsky critics, starting with Lev Shestov, that with *Notes from Underground* the writer enters the period when he is no longer just a "great psychologist" "but a philosopher, a philosopher of the tragedy of the human spirit" (L. Šestov, *La filosofia della tragedia. Dostoevskij e Nietzsche*, ed. E. Lo Gatto, Naples: Edizioni scientifiche italiane, 1950, orig. pub. 1903). [Quote translated from the Italian. An English version is available in L. Shestov, *Dostoevsky, Tolstoy, and Nietzsche*, trans. Bernard Martin, *Tolstoy & Nietzsche*, and Spencer Roberts, *Dostoevsky & Nietzsche* (Athens: Ohio University Press, 1969).] This is the same view expressed by Nicolas Berdyaev in *La concezione di Dostoevskij* (Turin: Einaudi, 2002, orig. pub. 1923), foreword by Sergio Givone. [English version: *Dostoievsky: An Interpretation*, trans. Donald Attwater (London: Sheed & Ward, 1934, orig. pub. 1923); quote translated from the Italian.] On the philosophical significance of *Demons*, see also Sergius Hessen (Sergei Gessen), *Die Tragödie des Guten in "Brüder Karamasoff": Versuch einer Darstellung der Ethik Dostojewkis*, in German (Bonn: F. Cohen, 1929).

4. See S. Givone, *Dostoevskij e la filosofia*, pp. 101ff.

5. L. Šestov, *La filosofia della tragedia*; L. Pareyson, *Dostoevskij. Filosofia, romanzo ed esperienza religiosa* (Turin: Einaudi, 1993), a collection of essays and handouts for teaching that Pareyson dedicated to the Russian writer starting from the late 1960s.

6. G. Lukács, *Dostoevskij*, ed. M. Comet (Milan: SE, 2000), p. 32. This is the Italian edition of the text by G. Lukács, established by J. C. Nyìri, *Dostojewski*.

Notizen und Entwürfe, taken from his notes, Akadémai Kiadò, 1985 (his personal papers held in the Budapest archives were reorganized at the hands of his students A. Heller and F. Fehér). These are the notes written by Lukács in the 1920s, probably contemporary with *The Theory of the Novel* of 1916 (English edition: trans. Anna Bostock, MIT Press, 1971), on what was meant to be a book entirely dedicated to Dostoevsky. Although in the 1950s Lukács repudiated the writings of his youth, his belief that the Russian writer and his "anti-hero" Stavrogin marked a turning point in the history of the West never faded.

7. Berdyaev, *La concezione di Dostoevskij*, p. 23; translated from the Italian edition.

8. I'm referring to André Glucksmann's *Dostoevskij à Manhattan* [Dostoevsky in Manhattan] (Paris: Robert Laffont, 2002).

9. See Roberta De Monticelli, *Esercizi di pensiero per apprendisti filosofi* (Turin: Bollati Boringhieri, 2006), pp. 89ff.

10. See L. Shestov, *La filosofia della tragedia*.

11. Immanuel Kant, *Religion Within the Limits of Reason Alone*, trans. with an introduction and notes by Theodore M. Greene and Hoyt H. Hudson (New York: Harper Torchbooks, 1960, orig. pub. 1793).

12. See Paul Ricoeur, *Finitude and Guilt* (Chicago: Regnery, 1965, orig. pub. 1960), and especially *The Symbolism of Evil* (New York: Beacon, 1967). By Ricoeur see also *Evil: A Challenge to Philosophy and Theology* (London: Continuum, 2007, orig. pub. 1986).

13. On this point see K. Flasch, *Agostino d'Ippona: Introduzione all'opera filosofica* (Bologna: il Mulino, 1983).

14. On evil as *privatio boni*, see especially *On Free Choice of the Will*, 3, 13, 36; and *Confessions*, 7, 12, 18. For all, see the quotation from Augustine, *Confessions*, ed. Henry Chadwick (Oxford: Oxford University Press, 1991), book VII, 12, 18: "Therefore, either corruption does not harm, which cannot be the case, or (which is wholly certain) all things that are corrupted suffer privation of some good. If they were to exist and to be immune from corruption, they would be superior because they would be permanently incorruptible. What could be more absurd than to say that by losing all good, things are made better? So then, if they are deprived of all good, they will be nothing at all. Therefore as long as they exist, they are good. Accordingly, whatever things exist are good, and the evil into whose origins I was inquiring is not a substance, for if it were a substance, it would be good. Either it would be an incorruptible substance, a great good indeed, or a corruptible substance, which could be corrupted only if it were good. Hence I saw and it was made clear to me that you made all things good, and there are absolutely no substances which you did not make." On Augustine and the question of evil, see G. R. Evans, *Augustine on Evil* (Cambridge: Cambridge University Press, 1982), and the now classic R. Jolivet, *Le problème du mal d'après Saint Augustin* (Paris: Gabriel Beauchesne et fils, 1936); H. Häring, *Die Macht des Bösen: Das Erbe Augustins* (Zürich: Gütersloher Verlagshaus Mohn, 1976).

15. The passages in Augustine's *On the Nature of Good* are entirely clear in this regard. Available at http://www.ccel.org/ccel/schaff/npnf104.toc.html (accessed January 14, 2013).

16. On evil as *aversio* or a turning away of the human will—an inversion that deviates from the superior toward the inferior—see Augustine, *City of God*, XII, 1–9. On this topic see Rüdiger Safranski, *Das Böse oder Das Drama der Freiheit* [Evil or the drama of freedom] (Munich: Hanser, 1997).

17. The modern exploration of the idea of evil deserves a discussion of its own. Not surprisingly, the crucial episode that starts with Leibniz and theodicy and ends in the early writings of Kant, by way of the Enlightenment critiques from Bayle to Voltaire, has occupied many philosophical histories of the idea of evil. For the problem of evil in the modern era, see for example E. Borne, *Le problème du mal* (Paris: Puf, 1973); A. Sculler, W. Von Rahden (eds.), *Die andere Kraft. Zur Renaissance des Bösen* (Berlin: Akademie Verlag, 1993); C. Colpe, W. Schmidt-Beggemann (eds.), *Das Böse. Eine historische Phänomenologie des Unerklärlichen* (Frankfurt am Main: Suhrkamp, 1993); C. Crignon (ed.), *Le mal* (Paris: Flammarion, 2000); Rüdiger Safranski, *Das Böse oder Das Drama der Freiheit* (Munich: Hanser, 1997); F. Besset, *Il était une fois le mal. La fracture onto-logique* (Paris: L'Harmattan, 2002); Susan Neiman, *Evil in Modern Thought: An Alternative History of Philosophy* (Princeton: Princeton University Press, 2002). Unfortunately, I learned about the important book by Adi Ophir, *The Order of Evils: Toward an Ontology of Morals* (New York: Zone Books, 2005), only after finishing my work. Although Ophir develops his ideas along different paths, his work reaches conclusions that are very consonant with my own.

18. Richard J. Bernstein, *Radical Evil: A Philosophical Interrogation* (Cambridge: Polity Press, 2002), especially pp. 14–42. For more on the moral perspective of thought on evil ushered in by Kantian philosophy, see the essays in M. P. Lara (ed.), *Ripensare il male. Prospettive contemporanee* (Rome: Meltemi, 2003), especially the articles by Richard J. Bernstein, H. E. Allison, G. Leyva, M. Cooke, and A. Ferrara.

19. We may recall what Goethe wrote to Herder, on June 7, 1793, in this regard: "After requiring a long life to purify his philosophical cloak of all sorts of prejudices that besmirched it, Kant has now ignominiously smeared it with the shameful stain of radical evil, so that Christians might be tempted to kiss its hem." (Goethe, *Werke*, IV, 10, p. 75, translated from the Italian.)

20. Kant, *Religion Within the Limits of Reason Alone*, p. 30.

21. Ibid., p. 32.

22. Ibid., p. 31. See also p. 32: "Hence the distinction between a good man and one who is evil cannot lie in the difference between the incentives [. . .] but rather [. . .] [in] which of the two incentives he makes the condition of the other."

23. Ibid., p. 32.

24. Ibid., p. 41.

25. See Pranteda, *Il legno storto: I significati del male in Kant* (Florence: Olschki, 2002).

26. Kant, *Religion*, pp. 38 and 36.

27. Ibid., p. 28.

28. Ibid., p. 31 (italics added).

29. Ibid., p. 31.

30. Ibid., p. 32 (italics added).

31. F. W. J. Schelling, "Philosophischen Untersuchungen über das Wesen der menschlichen Freiheit und die damit zusammenhängenden Gegenstände," in *Sämmtliche Werke*, vol. 7, ed. K. F. A. Schelling (Stuttgart and Augsburg, 1860, orig. pub. 1809), pp. 333–416; English edition *Philosophical Investigations into the Essence of Human Freedom*, trans. and introduction by Jeff Love and Johannes Schmidt (Albany: State University of New York Press, 2006), pp. 1–80.

32. Schelling, *Philosophical Investigations*, p. 23. Rudiger Safranski, for example, is of this opinion in *Das Böse*.

33. See for example X. Tilliette, *L'absolu et la philosophie: Essais sur Schelling* (Paris: Puf, 1987); and L. Pareyson, *Ontologia della libertà: Il male e la sofferenza* (Turin: Einaudi, 1995). But also Jean-Luc Nancy, *The Experience of Freedom* (Stanford: Stanford University Press, 1993, orig. pub. 1988); Safranski, *Das Böse*; C. Ciancio, *Libertà e dono dell'essere* (Genoa: Marietti, 2009); H.-J. Friedrich, *Der Ungrund der Freiheit im Denken von Böhme, Schelling und Heidegger* (Stuttgart: Frommann-Holzboog, 2009).

34. On this topic see in particular Schelling, *Philosophical Investigations on the Essence of Freedom*, pp. 80ff.

35. See Martin Heidegger, *Schelling's Treatise on the Essence of Human Freedom*, trans. Joan Stambaugh (Athens: Ohio University Press, 1986, orig. pub. 1936).

36. Schelling, *Philosophical Investigations*, p. 26.

37. Ibid., where this union-distinction is made explicit through the analogy of the relationship between gravity and light in nature (pp. 26–27; 25). The ever dark ground is the foundation for the light that exists. Spinoza's notion of *causa sui* is criticized for being abstract and thus hindering a proper conception of God's ground as something that is within God himself.

38. Ibid., p. 31.

39. Ibid., pp. 38–40.

40. Ibid., pp. 31–33.

41. Ibid., p. 32.

42. Ibid., p. 41.

43. Ibid., p. 55.

44. Ibid., p. 34.

45. Ibid., p. 35.

46. See Heidegger, *Schelling*.

47. This is also discussed in Slavoj Žižek, *The Indivisible Remainder: An Essay*

on Schelling and Related Matters (London and New York: Verso, 1996), in which he states, interpreting Schelling through Lacan, that for the German philosopher evil is not the particular as such, but its perverse unity with the universal: "[S]uch a presumption to believe that my words and deeds are directly words and deeds of the big Other (Nation, Culture, State, God), a presumption which 'inverts' the proper relationship between the Particular and the Universal: when I proclaim myself the immediate 'functionary of Humanity' (or Nation or Culture), I thereby effectively accomplish the exact opposite of what I claim to be doing—that is, I degrade the Universal dimension to which I refer (Humanity, Nation, State) to my own particularity" (pp. 36ff.).

48. Schelling, *Philosophical Investigations*, p. 54.

49. Ibid., p. 42.

50. For Peter Citati "every single aspect of *Demons* embodies the image of perfection" (*Il male assoluto: Nel cuore del romanzo dell'Ottocento* [Milan: Mondadori, 2000], p. 323). According to Citati, in this work Dostoevsky masterfully maintains a light and almost ironic approach to a problem that had always obsessed him: the vast reality of evil.

51. Regarding the term *nihilism*, its occurrences, and its changes in meaning in philosophical discourse, see for example D. Arendt (ed.), *Nihilismus. Die Anfänge von Jacobi bis Nietzsche* (Köln: Hegner, 1970); F. Volpi, *Il nichilismo* (Rome-Bari: Laterza, 2004).

52. One of the first works to put the term into circulation with this meaning was Ivan S. Turgenev's *Fathers and Children* (1861), trans. Constance Garnett (New York: P. F. Collier & Son, 1917), toward which Dostoevsky was consistently antagonistic. Among the intellectuals who spread the term and the concept of nihilism in Russia, we must remember Nicholas A. Dobrolyubov, a proponent of democratic and progressive radicalism; and Dimitri P. Pisare, who was extremely critical of all forms of anthropologism and moralism. But the biggest name to be mentioned is that of Nicholay G. Chernyshevsky, who in 1863 wrote the novel *What Is to Be Done?* in which he promoted a sort of materialistic utopianism. The book was immensely influential and became one of the key manifestos of Russian nihilism.

53. For a "snapshot" summary of the cultural situation in Russia, see I. Egorov, *Aus den Mysterium des russischen nihilismus. Aufzeichnungen eines ehemaligen Nihilisten* (Leipzig and Berlin: Friedrich, 1885); T. G. Masaryk, *La Russia e l'Europa: Studi sulle correnti spirituali in Russia*, ed. E. Lo Gatto (Bologna: Boni, 1971, orig. pub. 1913). See Franco Venturi, *The Roots of Revolution: A History of the Populist and Socialist Movements in 19th Century Russia*, trans. Francis Haskell (New York: Knopf, 1960, orig. pub. 1952).

54. The murder of the student perpetrated by Nechayev seems to have been what attracted Dostoevsky's attention to the ideas of Nechayev and his circle.

55. For more on Nechayev's pamphlet and the controversy surrounding its authorship, see M. Confino, *Il catechismo del rivoluzionario. Bakunin e l'affare Nečaev*

(Milan: Adelphi, 1976, orig. pub. 1973); M. A. Bakunin, *Michel Bakounine et ses relations avec Sergej Nečaev, 1870–1872, écrits et matériaux, introduzione e note di Arthur Lehning* (Leiden: Brill, 1971).

56. The letter of October 9, 1870, explains why the epigraph chosen for the novel is a passage from the Gospel of Luke describing how Christ allowed the demons to leave the body of a man from Gerasenes to go into a herd of swine instead. Once the demons had entered the bodies of the pigs, the animals threw themselves from a hill into a lake, where they drowned. "Exactly the same has happened with us in Russia," writes Dostoevsky in the letter. "The devils went out of the Russian and entered into a herd of swine—into the Nechayevs, Serno-Solovioviches, etc. These are drowned and will be drowned, and the healed man, from whom the devils had been cast out, is sitting at the feet of Jesus." An English translation of the letter can be found in *Dostoevsky: Letters and Reminiscences*, trans. S. S. Koteliansky and J. Middleton Murry (London: Chatto & Windus, 1923), p. 92. The full passage from the Gospel of Luke is in Luke 8: 26–39.

57. Dostoevsky, *Demons*, p. 258.

58. Ibid., p. 258.

59. Ibid., p. 259.

60. Ibid., p. 259.

61. Ibid., p. 259.

62. Ibid., p. 260.

63. Ibid., p. 260.

64. Ibid., pp. 384–385.

65. Notably, Möller van den Bruck, who wrote the introduction to Dostoevsky's *Sämtliche Werke* and co-edited this German edition with Dmitry Merezhkovsky. Möller van den Bruck claimed that he drew on *A Writer's Diary* as his source for the criticism of the West as well as for the phrase "conservative revolution." In actuality, Möller looked less to Dostoevsky and more to Merezhkovsky's "Russian Renaissance," which emphasized the political conservatism of the great Russian writer. For an overview of the political interpretations of Dostoevsky, see the useful work by Roberto Valle, *Dostoevskij politico e i suoi interpreti: L'esodo dall'Occidente* (Rome: Archivio Guido Izzi, 1990). For more on how this political judgment took root in Russia as early as the late nineteenth century, see the debate between Soviet writers in G. Kraiski (ed.), *Rivoluzione e letteratura: Il dibattito al 1 Convegno degli scrittori sovietici* (Bari: Laterza, 1967), especially the introduction by Vittorio Strada. See also the introduction by Vittorio Strada to V. Rozanov, *La leggenda del Grande Inquisitore* (Genoa: Marietti, 1989, orig. pub. 1894); as well as Strada's *L'etica del terrore: Da Fëdor Dostoevskij a Thomas Mann* (Rome: Liberal, 2008).

66. For more on pluralism in Dostoevsky, see Mikhail Bakhtin, *Problems of Dostoevsky's Poetics*, trans. and ed. by Caryl Emerson (Minneapolis: University of Minnesota, 1984, orig. pub. 1963).

67. Albert Camus, *The Rebel* (New York: Alfred K. Knopf, 1984, orig. pub. 1951), in which, in opposition to Sartre, he discusses "logical crime" as an outcome of the "age of ideologies," when the absurd no longer dwells solely in the heart of man, but also asserts itself in history. In Camus, Dostoevsky's vision takes on a much broader scope than mere conservatism, becoming one of the most insightful explanations of nihilism. According to this view, Dostoevsky's aim was not to consecrate history, as critics like Berdyaev would have it. Rather, with *Demons* and *The Brothers Karamazov*, the Russian writer demonstrably captured the essence of our age: the replacement of the foundational role of the Cartesian *cogito* with the principle of revolt, now expressed as "I rebel, therefore we are." But already in the *Myth of Sisyphus* (1942), an entire chapter was devoted to Kirillov, whose role was to represent the protest of modern man against a world that no longer provides any answers.

68. See Sigmund Freud, "Dostoevsky and Patricide (1927)," in *Writings on Art and Literature* (Stanford: Stanford University Press, 1997), pp. 234–255, in which he states that after being imprisoned, Dostoevsky switched from a Fourier-style socialism to a set of genuinely reactionary beliefs.

69. Dostoevsky, *Demons*, p. 261.

70. Fyodor Dostoevsky, *The Notebooks for The Possessed*, trans. Victor Terras, ed. Edward Wasiolek (Chicago: University of Chicago Press, 1968).

71. Dostoevsky, *Demons*, p. 400.

72. Bakhtin, *Problems of Dostoevsky's Poetics*, p. 96.

73. Berdyaev, *Dostoievsky: An Interpretation*, pp. 102ff. In that period of the nineteenth century, says Berdyaev, people like Verkhovensky, Kirillov, and Stavrogin were nonexistent. Individuals of their kind would appear only later, in the twentieth century. For the Russian philosopher, Dostoevsky was "too apocalyptic" to fall under the political category of conservative or reactionary. Berdyaev does not believe at all that one can return to the past through the revolution of the spirit. Dostoevsky's hostility, he says, is not that of ancient man but rather that of the apocalyptic man: "A revolution of the spirit opposes a spirit of revolution. Dostoevsky was very much the apocalyptic man and the usual standards of revolutionary and counter-revolutionary cannot be applied to him. For him revolution was as near as may be to reaction" (p. 136). To Berdyaev's mind, the struggle between revolution and counterrevolution is too superficial (p. 135).

74. Fyodor Dostoevsky, *The Notebooks for The Possessed*.

75. See P. Evdokimov, *Dostoïevsky et le problème du mal* (Lyon: Éditions du Livre Français, 1942).

76. Berdyaev, *La concezione di Dostoevskij*, p. 30; translated from the Italian edition.

77. Dostoevsky, *Notes from Underground*, where we find the famous passage: "Oh, tell me, who first announced, who was the first to proclaim that man does dirty only because he doesn't know his real interests; and that were he to be en-

lightened, were his eyes to be opened to his real, normal interests, man would immediately stop doing dirty, would immediately become good and noble[. . . .] Oh the babe! oh, the pure, innocent child! and when was it, to begin with, in all these thousands of years, that man acted solely for his own profit? [. . .] And what if it so happens that *on occasion* man's profit not only may but precisely must consist in sometimes wishing what is bad for himself, and not what is profitable?" (pp. 20–21).

78. Bakhtin, *Problems of Dostoevsky's Poetics*, p. 96.

79. For Rozanov and Ivanov it symbolizes his flouting of the Russian people's soul, his betrayal of the fatherland; see V. Rozanov, *La leggenda del Grande Inquisitore*; V. Ivanov, *Dostoevskij. Tragedia, mito, mistica* (Bologna: il Mulino, 1994, orig. pub. 1932).

80. As Sergio Givone maintains in *Dostoevskij e la filosofia*. As a matter of fact, Kierkegaard's notion of the demonic has extraordinary similarities with Dostoevsky's character. See Søren Kierkegaard, *The Concept of Anxiety*, trans. Reider Thomte and Albert B. Anderson (Princeton: Princeton University Press, 1980), especially section 2: "Anxiety About the Good (the Demonic)" (pp. 118–154).

81. Dostoevsky, *Demons*, p. 45.

82. A similar scene takes place in which the governor asks Stavrogin to account for his maniacal gesture. Stravrogin approaches him, pretending that he wants to reveal a secret, and then bites the governor's ear so hard that the old man almost has a heart attack.

83. Dostoevsky, *Demons*, p. 205.

84. This is Sergio Givone's view in *Dostoevskij e la filosofia*.

85. It has been noted several times in the critical literature that the character who really grasps Stavrogin's "dualism" is his unfortunate wife Marya Timofevna. In a memorable scene she insists on not wanting to recognize him and accuses a "usurper" of seeking to take his place.

86. Ibid., p. 675.

87. Fyodor Dostoevsky, *The Brothers Karamazov (1878–1880)*, trans. Constance Garnett, ed. Ralph Matlaw (New York: Norton Critical Editions, 1976), p. 87.

88. Dostoevsky, *Brothers Karamazov*, p. 272. More than a hundred years of interpretations have focused on this episode, from Rozanov to Merezhkovsky, from Shestov to Lukács, from Bakhtin to Camus, from Pareyson to Sloterdijk.

89. Camus, *The Rebel*.

90. Dostoevsky, *Demons*, p. 676.

91. Regarding Stavrogin's indifference, as the greatest of evils in Dostoevsky's multiform phenomenology, see the fine essay by R. De Monticelli, "Al di là del bene e del male? Leggendo Dostoevskij," in his previously cited *Esercizi di pensiero*, pp. 89ff.

92. Dostoevsky, *Demons*, p. 618.

93. Ibid., p. 618.

94. This is the view of Evdokimov in *Dostoïevsky et le problème du mal*.

95. Dostoevsky, *Demons*, pp. 385–386.

96. Ibid., p. 371.

97. On this topic, see the incisive pages by Remo Bodei on "La colonizzazione delle coscienze" in his *Destini personali. L'età della colonizzazione delle coscienze* (Milan: Feltrinelli, 2002), pp. 189ff.

98. Dostoevsky, *Brothers Karamazov*, p. 726.

99. Ibid., p. 736.

100. G. W. F. Hegel, *Faith & Knowledge*, trans. H. S. Harris (Albany: SUNY Press, 1977, orig. pub. 1802).

101. I cannot dwell here on the great passages in the works of Hegel that more directly address the question of evil. One of the most significant for the discussion on the concept of evil is certainly chapter VI of the *Phenomenology of Mind*, which concerns the dissolution of the moral conception of the world, entitled "Evil and the Forgiveness of It." G. W. F. Hegel, *The Phenomenology of Mind*, vol. II, trans. J. B. Baillie (New York: Macmillan, 1910, orig. pub. 1807), pp. 679ff. This quote is from §669, p. 407.

102. Georg Wilhelm Friedrich Hegel, *Philosophy of History*, trans. John Sibree (New York: F. Collier & Son, 1902), p. 60.

103. Dostoevsky, *Brothers Karamazov*, pp. 730–731.

104. Ibid., p. 731.

105. Ibid.

106. Ibid., p. 590.

107. Dostoevsky, *Demons*, p. 115.

108. Ibid., pp. 236ff.

109. Ibid., pp. 237–238.

110. See V. Vitiello, *Cristianesimo e nichilismo. Dostoevskij-Heidegger* (Brescia: Morcelliana, 2005).

111. All these quotations are from Dostoevsky, *Demons*, pp. 617–618.

112. Dostoevsky, *Brothers Karamazov*, p. 701.

113. See also the densely packed pages that Evdokimov devotes to these passages in *Dostoïevsky et le problème du mal*. He pushes Dostoevsky's interpretation of evil in an exclusively theological and metaphysical direction, however.

114. On the impossibility of reducing Dostoevsky's work to a prophecy about the failure of the revolutionary cycle that started with the 1789 French Revolution, see R. Valle, *Dostoevskij politico e i suoi interpreti*.

115. Carl Schmitt's position in his "Dialog on Power" (available in Italian as *Dialogo sul potere*, Genoa: il melangolo, 1994) might appear Dostoevskian at first sight: he shows that when the source of power was no longer identified with the cosmos, and later with God, this event marked the identity of evil and power—the same power that Christianity had gone so far as to justify as God's will, at least in the hegemonic Pauline tradition.

116. For this topic, see the important observations by Agnes Heller, *General Ethics* (Hoboken: Wiley, 1988).

CHAPTER 2: INSTINCTS, DRIVES, AND THEIR VICISSITUDES

1. Lev Shestov, "Dostoevsky and Nietzsche: The Philosophy of Tragedy," trans. Spencer Roberts, in *Dostoevsky, Toslstoy and Nietzsche*, ed. Bernard Martin (Athens: Ohio University Press, 1969). The quote from Nietzsche appears in Friedrich Nietzsche, *Werke*, VIII (Leipzig, 1901), p. 158. On the relationship between Dostoevsky and Nietzsche, see the beautiful work by Dmitri Nikulin, *The Gods and Demons of Dostoevsky and Nietzsche*, as yet unpublished. My deep thanks to the author for allowing me to read the manuscript.

2. See Fyodor Dostoevsky, *Notes from Underground* (1864), trans. Richard Pevear and Larissa Volokhonsky (New York: Knopf, 1993).

3. Friedrich Nietzsche, *Frammenti postumi*, 1885–1887, ed. Sossio Giametta (Milan: Adelphi, 1975), chapter 5, p. 71. This is volume 8 of the complete works: *Opere complete*, ed. Giorgio Colli and Mazzino Montinari (Milan: Adelphi, 1964–2001). [The English version used for quotes is *The Will to Power*, trans. Walter Kaufmann and R. J. Hollingdale (New York: Random House, 1967); however, when there are discrepancies, they are modified to reflect the Italian version.] See the famous passages entitled "European nihilism" (pp. 9ff.), in which, among other things, we read on p. 10: "But among the forces cultivated by morality was truthfulness: this eventually turned against morality, discovered its teleology, its partial perspective—and now the recognition of this inveterate mendaciousness that one despairs of shedding becomes a stimulant."

4. Friedrich Nietzsche, *On the Genealogy of Morals* (1887), trans. Walter Kaufmann, in *Basic Writings* (New York: Random House, Modern Library, 1968), pp. 439–599. This citation, p. 452.

5. Friedrich Nietzsche, "Ecce Homo" (1888), trans. Walter Kaufmann, in *Basic Writings*, pp. 657–800. These citations come from pp. 722–724.

6. The phrase appears in Nietzsche's "Ecce Homo," p. 739, clearly alluding to his *Human, All-Too-Human*, trans. R. J. Hollingdale (Cambridge: Cambridge University Press, 1986, orig. pub. 1878).

7. Friedrich Nietzsche, "Twilight of the Idols, or How to Philosophize with a Hammer" (1889), trans. R. J. Hollingdale, in *Twilight of the Idols and The Anti-Christ* (London: Penguin Books, 1968), p. 117: "higher swindle." See also "Ecce Homo," p. 744: *Human, All-Too-Human*, "this monument of rigorous self-discipline with which I put a sudden end to all my infections with 'higher swindle', 'idealism', 'beautiful feelings', and other effeminacies." Calling his philosophy a psychology was a provocative gesture of reframing the metaphysical question par excellence. In the first instance, it is obvious that for Nietzsche good and evil are not metaphysical entities, but attitudes and temperaments of "subjec-

tive types." If so, the heir to the question of good and evil, from which a new morality is to be derived, must be psychology. It is a psychological investigation that, before any other statement of content, begins with suspicion toward the judgments made by philosophers on the value of life—judgments that speak about the speakers and not about the thing itself. Behind the philosophical wisdom that declares earthly life has no value, he advises us, we have to learn to hear the voices of the old, the decadent, the tired, and the defeated.

8. Nietzsche, "Ecce Homo," p. 787.

9. Nietzsche, "Beyond Good and Evil" (1886), in *Basic Writings*, p. 221.

10. Ibid., p. 221. On the relationship between Nietzsche and British thought, through the reconstruction of the relationship between Nietzsche, Spencer, and Mill, see M. C. Fornari, *La morale evolutiva del gregge* (Pisa: Edizioni ETS, 2006).

11. On this topic, see the fragments 296–300 from Spring–Fall 1887 in *Will to Power*, trans. Walter Kaufmann and R. J. Hollingdale (New York: Random House, Vintage Books, 1968), pp. 166–169. These quotes are from pp. 172 and 168.

12. Nietzsche, *Will to Power*, p. 151. [Translation slightly modified to reflect the Italian version.]

13. Nietzsche, "Beyond Good and Evil," p. 220.

14. To dwell on the idea of nature in Nietzsche would take us too far astray. However, it is a key question that in my view has recently regained a central place in Nietzsche studies. On this topic see, for example, B. Stiegler, *Nietzsche et la biologie* (Paris: Puf, 2001); G. Moore, *Nietzsche, Biology and Metaphor* (Cambridge: Cambridge University Press, 2002); and V. Lemm, *Nietzsche's Animal Philosophy: Culture, Politics, and the Animality of the Human Being* (New York: Fordham University Press, 2009).

15. Nietzsche, "Ecce Homo," p. 712. On the same page we read: "What mankind has so far considered seriously have not even been realities but mere imaginings—more strictly speaking, *lies* prompted by the bad instincts of sick natures that were harmful in the most profound sense—all these concepts, 'God', 'soul', 'virtue', 'sin', 'beyond', 'truth', 'eternal life'.—But the greatness of human nature, its 'divinity', was sought in them.—All the problems of politics, of social organization, and of education have been falsified through and through because one mistook the most harmful men for great men—because one learned to despise 'little' things, which means the basic concerns of life itself."

16. See the timeless essay by Michel Foucault, "Nietzsche, Genealogy, History (1971)," in Donald F. Bouchard (ed.), *Language, Counter-Memory, Practice: Selected Essays and Interviews*, trans. Donald F. Bouchard and Sherry Simon (Ithaca: Cornell University Press, 1977), pp. 139–164.

17. Nietzsche, *Genealogy of Morals*, p. 462. See pp. 463–464, where we read: "[In the various languages] I found they all led back to the *same conceptual transformation*—that everywhere 'noble', 'aristocratic' in the social sense, is the basic concept from which 'good' in the sense of 'with a privileged soul' necessarily

developed: a development which always runs parallel with that other in which 'common', 'plebeian', 'low' are finally transformed into the concept 'bad'."

18. Nietzsche, *Will to Power*, p. 187.

19. Ibid. [Translation slightly modified to reflect the Italian version.]

20. Ibid. [Translation slightly modified to reflect the Italian version.]

21. Nietzsche, "Beyond Good and Evil," p. 320.

22. Nietzsche, *Will to Power*, p. 187.

23. Ibid. In this order of succession, the "Christian type" is the intermediary form between the second and the third types, "now with the former, now with the latter predominating."

24. Gilles Deleuze, *Nietzsche and Philosophy* (1962), trans. Michael Hardt (New York: Columbia University Press, 2006).

25. Nietzsche, *Genealogy of Morals*, p. 472.

26. Nietzsche, "Thus Spake Zarathustra (1883–1885)," trans. Walter Kaufmann, in *The Portable Nietzsche* (New York: Viking Press, 1954), pp. 103–439. I refer in particular to "Beyond Good and Evil," *On the Genealogy of Morals*, and the posthumous fragments collected in *Will to Power*; that is, to the passages that introduce and develop the notion of *Wille zur Macht*.

27. What I am referring to, in very broad terms and in an inevitably vague way, are interpretations that simplify Nietzsche's thought along "libertarian" lines in order to save him from fascist readings. These interpretations take their inspiration from Georges Bataille's brilliant reading; see his *On Nietzsche* (London: Continuum, 2008, orig. pub. 1945), and see also Maurice Blanchot's interesting afterword to the Italian edition: "Su Nietzsche" (Milan: SE, 1994, orig. pub. 1945). For an overview of the Nietzschean "left," see Jan Rehmann, *Postmoderner Links-Nietzscheanismus. Deleuze & Foucault. Eine Dekonstruktion* (Hamburg: Argument-Verlag, 2004).

28. Nietzsche, *Genealogy of Morals*, pp. 532ff.

29. Ibid., pp. 531 and 503.

30. See Nietzsche, "Beyond Good and Evil," p. 502.

31. All citations appear on page 532 of *Genealogy of Morals*, where we read: "This man of the future, who will redeem us not only from the hitherto reigning ideal but also from that which was bound to grow out of it, the great nausea, the will to nothingness, nihilism; this bell-stroke of noon and of the great decision that liberates the will again and restores its goal to the earth and his hope to man; this Antichrist and antinihilist; this victor over God and nothingness—he must come one day."

32. See Gilles Deleuze, *Nietzsche and Philosophy*, trans. Janis Tomlison (New York: Columbia University Press, 1983), p. 24.

33. Dostoevsky, *Demons*, p. 590.

34. See also R. Dionigi, *Il doppio cervello di Nietzsche* (Macerata: Quodlibet, 2000, orig. pub. 1982).

35. Nietzsche, *Genealogy of Morals*, p. 501.

36. Friedrich Nietzsche, *On the Advantage and Disadvantage of History for Life* (1874), trans. Peter Preuss (Indianapolis: Hackett, 1980), p. 14.

37. Nietzsche, *Genealogy of Morals*, p. 488.

38. Ibid., pp. 490–492.

39. Nietzsche, "Beyond Good and Evil," p. 234.

40. Ibid., p. 375: "What Europe owes to the Jews? Many things, good and bad, and above all one thing that is both of the best and of the worst: the grand style in morality, the terribleness and majesty of infinite demands, infinite meanings, the whole romanticism and sublimity of moral questionabilities—and hence precisely the most attractive, captious, and choicest part of those plays of color and seductions to life."

41. Nietzsche, *Genealogy of Morals*, pp. 493–532.

42. Ibid., pp. 520ff.

43. Ibid., p. 520.

44. Ibid.

45. Ibid., p. 521.

46. Ibid.

47. Ibid., p. 528.

48. Nietzsche, *Will to Power*, pp. 192–193.

49. Ibid., p. 192 (italics added).

50. Ibid., p. 193. [Translation slightly modified to reflect the Italian version.]

51. Nietzsche, "Beyond Good and Evil," p. 200.

52. Jean-Luc Nancy, "Considerazioni sul male," in F. Rella (ed.), *Il Male. Scritture sul male e sul dolore* (Bologna: Edizioni Pendragon, 2001), pp. 101–108.

53. Jacques Lacan, *The Seminar of Jacques Lacan. Book VII. The Ethics of Psychoanalysis 1959–1960*, ed. Jacques-Alain Miller, trans. Dennis Porter (New York: Norton, 1992), p. 185.

54. For an overview of the collective imagination of a generation that reoriented its thought from the deep trauma of the First World War, see for example P. Fussell, *La grande guerra e la memoria moderna* (Bologna: il Mulino, 1984); S. Audoin-Rouzeau, A. Becker, C. Ingrao, H. Rousso, *La violence de guerre. 1914–1945: Approches comparées des deux conflits mondiaux*, Éd. complexe, Paris IHTP (Brussels and Paris: CNRS, 2002). For one of the most lucid and timely analyses of the exemplarity of the First World War, see Ernst Jünger, "Der Kampf als inneres Erlebnis," in his *Sämtliche Werke, Essays*, vol. 7 (Stuttgart: Klett-Cotta, 1980), pp. 11–103.

55. Sigmund Freud, "Thoughts for the Times on War and Death" (1915), in the *Public Domain Edition of Freud's Complete Works*, ed. Ivan Smith (online version, copyright 2000, 2007, 2010, 2011), pp. 3065–3092; http://www.gildedgreen.com/freud/freud.html.

56. Freud, "Thoughts for the Times on War and Death," p. 3073.

57. Freud, "Beyond the Pleasure Principle" (1920), *Complete Works*, pp. 3713–3762; Freud himself had anticipated the criticisms of his essay, defending himself

from the objection that it must have been written in the wake of personal grief. In fact, in January 1920, his close, generous friend Anton von Freund and his favorite daughter, Sophie, died within days of each other.

58. Freud, "Beyond the Pleasure Principle," p. 3738.

59. Ibid., p. 3760.

60. Let us recall that *Vermischung* is not only between the two instincts of life and death: it seems, rather, to be an ambivalence that is implicit in each of the individual drives. Just as Eros is essential to the rise of civilization, even though it can also be disruptive and become destructive, in the same way, death instincts can be creative. Human activity is a channeling of aggression, but when the latter can no longer be expressed in a creative way toward the outside, it can turn into destructiveness.

61. Freud, "Group Psychology and the Analysis of the Ego (1921)," in *Complete Works*, pp. 3763–3834.

62. Freud, "Civilization and Its Discontents" (1929), in *Complete Works*, pp. 4462–4532.

63. Ibid., p. 4503.

64. Ibid.

65. Ibid., p. 4505.

66. Ibid., p. 4510.

67. "The Devil would be the best way out as an excuse for God; in that way he would be playing the same part as an agent of economic discharge as the Jew does in the world of the Aryan ideal." Ibid., p. 4510.

68. Ibid., p. 4512.

69. Rüdiger Safranski, *Das Böse oder Das Drama der Freiheit* [Evil or the drama of freedom] (Frankfurt: Fischer, 1997). Italian version *Il male: Ovvero il dramma della libertà* (Milan: Longanesi, 2006, orig. pub. 1997), pp. 220ff. On the death drive as a hermeneutical key to the history of civilization, see M. Plon, H. Rey-Flaud (eds.), *La pulsion de mort entre psychanalyse et philosophie* (Paris: Édition Erès, 2004), especially the essay by B. Sichère, "Nous sommes déjà très suffisamment une civilisation de la haine," pp. 127–148.

70. See the entry on *Pulsion de mort* by J. Laplanche and J.-B. Pontalis in their *Vocabulaire de la psychanalyse* (Paris: Puf, 1967).

71. "The Ethic of Honesty" is the title of a chapter of the timeless book by Philip Rieff, *Freud, the Mind of the Moralist*, 3rd ed. (Chicago: University of Chicago Press, 1979, orig. pub. 1959), pp. 300–328. On this topic see also the pages dedicated to Freud in Richard J. Bernstein, *Radical Evil: A Philosophical Interrogation* (Cambridge: Polity Press, 2002).

72. Freud, "Instincts and Their Vicissitudes" (1915), in *Complete Works*, pp. 2955–2974.

73. Ibid., p. 2971.

74. The title of the chapter in Gilles Deleuze, *Coldness and Cruelty* (New York: Zone Books, 1989, orig. pub. 1967), pp. 111–121.

75. All of Georges Bataille's work could be reinterpreted in the light of the liberating force of evil. In addition to his literary works, starting with *Blue of Noon* (1935), trans. Harry Matthews (London: Penguin), see especially *On Nietzsche* (1945); *The Accursed Share, Volume 1: Consumption* (1949), trans. Robert Hurley (New York: Zone Books, 1991); *Erotism: Death and Sensuality* (1957), trans. Mary Dalwood (San Francisco: City Lights, 1986); *Literature and Evil*, trans. Alastair Hamilton (London: Marion Boyars, 1985, orig. pub. 1957).

76. Even if defining them as post-Bataille might seem forced, many works by these two authors seem to confirm and extend the reflection on evil begun by Georges Bataille. See, respectively, Jean Baudrillard, *The Transparency of Evil: Essays on Extreme Phenomena* (1990) (Verson: London, 2009); *The Intelligence of Evil: or, The Lucidity Pact* (2004) (New York: London, Bloomsbury Academic, 2005); and by Jean-Pierre Dupuy, see his *Petite métaphysique des tsunamis* (Paris: Seuil, 2005); and *Avons-nous oublié le mal?* (Paris: Bayard, 2002). Taking a very similar direction, there are the works by Michel Maffesoli, *La part du diable. Précis de subversion postmoderne* (Paris: Flammarion, 2002), and Bernard Sichère, *Histoires du mal* (Paris: Grasset, 1995).

77. Bataille, *Literature and Evil*, Preface, ix.

78. Ibid., p. 156.

79. Ibid., p. 102.

80. Despite their ambivalent, changing attitude toward him, we can say that André Breton and Paul Eluard were the ones who brought the most significant literary attention to the "*divin marquis.*" For an annotated bibliography and exhaustive information on the different stances taken toward Sade's work, from the Surrealists to authors in the 1970s in France, I refer to V. Barba (ed.), *Interpretazioni di Sade* (Rome: Savelli, 1979).

81. Pierre Klossowski, *Sade My Neighbor*, trans. Alphonso Lingis (Evanston, IL: Northwestern University Press, 1991, orig. pub. 1947); Maurice Blanchot, *Lautréamont and Sade* (1949), trans. Stuart Kendall and Michelle Kendall (Stanford: Stanford University Press, 2004); Jean Paulhan, *Le marquis de Sade et sa complice: Ou les revanches de la pudeur* (Paris: Lilac, 1951).

82. Bataille, *Literature and Evil*, p. 107.

83. Ibid., p. 110.

84. Bataille, *Literature and Evil*, p. 120.

85. It was Lacan, at the beginning of the 1960s, who took on the relationship between the question of evil in Sade and the Kantian categorical imperative. See Jacques Lacan, *The Seminar. Book VII. The Ethics of Psychoanalysis*.

86. Deleuze, *Coldness and Cruelty* (New York: Zone Books, 1989, orig. pub. 1967). The citation in this paragraph comes from pp. 26–27. Deleuze's position with regard to the Freudian death drive changed its tone dramatically in Gilles Deleuze and Felix Guattari, *Anti-Oedipus. Capitalism and Schizophrenia*, vol. 1, trans. Eugene Holland (New York: Routledge, 1999, orig. pub. 1972); and in *A Thousand*

Plateaus: Capitalism and Schizophrenia, trans. Brian Massumi (Minneapolis and London: University of Minnesota Press, 1987, orig. pub. 1980), in which, along with Guattari, he believes that it can occupy a minor role compared to the affirmative positivity of the good libido, the driving force for the "body without organs."

87. Lacan, *The Seminar: Book VII*, p. 201.

88. See especially the sections on "The splendor of Antigone" and "Antigone between two deaths."

89. See Slovoj Žižek, *Did Somebody Say Totalitarianism? Five Interventions in the (Mis)Use of the Notion* (London and New York: Verso, 2001); and *For They Know Not What They Do: Enjoyment as a Political Factor* (London, New York: Verso, 2008, orig. pub. 2000).

90. Erich Fromm, *Anatomy of Human Destructiveness* (New York: Holt, Rinehart & Winston, 1973).

91. André Green, "Pourquoi le mal?" in J.-B. Pontalis (ed.), *Le mal* (Paris: Gallimard, 1988). By Green see also *Life Narcissism, Death Narcissism*, trans. Andrew Weller (London: Free Association Books, 2001, orig. pub. 1983); and *The Work of the Negative* (London: Free Association Books, 1999, orig. pub. 1993). See also the always topical work by Norman O. Brown, *Life Against Death: The Psychoanalytical Meaning of History* (London: Routledge and Kegan Paul, 1959).

92. Through Freud's "scandalous discovery," the extreme political pathologies of the twentieth century would be read as a passage to the act of an original fantasy: to break down the differentiated nature of things so as to return to the original perfection in which differences and distinctions are unknown. These are all attempts, Dostoevsky would have said, on the part of human beings who want to become God and, thanks to His omnipotence, to dismantle the world, with its specificities and limitations, so as to remake it from the start. However, not being able to create, they are doomed to destroy. As Cornelius Castoriadis writes in *The Imaginary Institution of Society*, trans. Kathleen Blamey (Cambridge: MIT Press, 1988, orig. pub. 1975), p. 298, this is an objective that, if pursued "directly," without any mediation, puts us before a "monster of unifying madness" that seeks to eradicate all differences and recapture the stage of primary unity without any mediation. This, in its turn, leads just as much to individual forms of evil, subjective pathologies, as it does to collective forms of evil, a sort of "clinical psychosis of political totalitarianism." With regard to the fury toward the undifferentiated, we might recall the function that mimetic desire plays in René Girard's theory. See for example René Girard, *Violence and the Sacred*, trans. Patrick Gregory (Baltimore and London: Johns Hopkins University Press, 1977, orig. pub. 1972); and *The Scapegoat*, trans. Yvonne Freccero (Baltimore and London: Johns Hopkins University Press, 1986, orig. pub. 1982).

93. On this topic, see Peter Sloterdijk, *Rage and Time: A Psychopolitical Investigation* (New York: Columbia University Press, 2010, orig. pub. 2006).

CHAPTER 3: ONTOLOGICAL EVIL AND THE TRANSCENDENCE OF EVIL

1. As far as I know, there are basically two texts that explicitly address the Heideggerian concept of evil: C. Wodzinki, *Heidegger i problem zla* (Warschau: Slowo/Obraz Terytoria, 1994); and B. Irlenborn, *Der Ingrimm des Aufruhrs. Heidegger und das Problem des Bösen* (Vienna: Passagen Verlag, 2000). There is an essay by M. S. Frings, "Is There Room for Evil in Heidegger's Thought or Not?" *Philosophy Today*, 32, 1988: 79–92, but it limits its study to *Being and Time*. The question of evil is also addressed in J.-M. Salanskis, *Heidegger, le mal et la science* (Paris: Klincksieck, 2009), although not as the main subject.

2. Martin Heidegger, *Introduction to Metaphysics*, trans. Gregory Fried and Richard Polt (New Haven: Yale University Press, 2000, orig. pub. 1935).

3. Martin Heidegger, "Letter on Humanism," trans. Frank Capuzzi, in *Pathmarks* (Cambridge: Cambridge University Press, 1998), pp. 239–276.

4. Martin Heidegger, "Language in the Poem: A Discussion on Georg Trakl's Poetic Work," *On the Way to Language*, trans. Peter Hertz (New York: Harper & Row, 1971, orig. pub. 1953), pp. 159–198.

5. Martin Heidegger, *Contributions to Philosophy (Of the Event)*, trans. Richard Rojcewicz and Daniela Vallega-Nue (Bloomington: Indiana University Press, 2012).

6. The importance of this step in the fundamental work *Contributions to Philosophy* is discussed by Reiner Schürmann in *Broken Hegemonies*, trans. Reginald Lilly (Bloomington: Indiana University Press, 2003); especially in the second part of volume 2, entitled "The Diremption: On Double Binds Without a Common Noun (Heidegger)," pp. 511–632.

7. This is one of the three dialogs written by Heidegger during the spring of 1945 and published in 1995 by Ingrid Schüssler with the title *Feldweg Gespräche*, volume 77 of the complete edition of the works of Heidegger (Frankfurt am Main: Vittorio Klostermann, 1995, referred to as *GA, Gesamtausgabe*). English version: *Country Path Conversations*, trans. Bret W. Davis (Bloomington: Indiana University Press, 2010). The third dialog is pp. 132–160.

8. See the letters written to his wife in March 1945, in which he describes his emotional and philosophical state at that time. See Martin Heidegger, "Mein Liebes Seelchen!" *Briefe Martin Heidegger an seine Frau Elfriede (1915–1970)*, ed. Gertrud Heidegger (Munich: DVA, 2005).

9. See Heidegger's *Contributions to Philosophy*, p. 44: "If an undeveloped spiritualism lies dormant someplace, then that place is the Russian people."

10. Fyodor Dostoevsky, *Sämtliche Werke*, ed. Möller van den Bruck and Dimitri Merezhkovsky, published between 1906 and 1923, by Piper (Munich). For more on Gadamer's observations, see Sergio Givone, *Dostoevskij e la filosofia* (Rome-Bari: Laterza, 2007), p. 27.

11. Heidegger was a careful reader of Nicolas Berdyaev and in particular *The*

Origin of Russian Communism (1938), trans. R. M. French (Ann Arbor: University of Michigan Press, 1960). For Heidegger, even communism has to do with *Ereignis*. Russia is certainly a land of deep spirituality and also of a spirituality that had managed better than others to grasp the ontological scope of fully realized nihilism, and would continue to do so. In 1958 in Aix-en-Provence he confided to Jean Beaufret: "I have good reason to believe that Russia will perhaps one day be the country where what I wanted to say in *Sein und Zeit* will be really understood" (information reported by Jean Beaufret in an interview with Frédérique de Tovarnicki in the latter's *À la rencontre de Heidegger. Souvenirs d'un messager de la Forêt-Noire*, Paris: Gallimard, 1993).

12. I prefer to translate *das Bösartige* as "malice" rather than as "that which is malicious." As will be clear from the text, malice refers to a subjective meaning of the notion of evil that is openly contested by Heidegger.

13. Martin Heidegger, *Being and Time*, trans. John MacQuarrie and Edward Robinson (New York: Harper & Row, 1962, orig. pub. 1927), §58.

14. Martin Heidegger, E. Blochmann, *Briefwechsel 1919–1969*, ed. J. W. Storck (Marbach am Neckar: Deutsche Schillergesellschaft, 1989), pp. 31–33; cited in English in Rüdiger Safranski, *Martin Heidegger: Between Good and Evil*, trans. Ewald Oser (Cambridge: Harvard University Press, 1998), p. 181.

15. Martin Heidegger, "What Is Metaphysics?" in *Basic Writings*, trans. David F. Krell (New York: Harper & Row, 1977, orig. pub. 1929), pp. 89–110.

16. Heidegger, "What Is Metaphysics?" p. 97.

17. Heidegger, *Contributions to Philosophy*, p. 80.

18. Ibid., p. 103.

19. Ibid.

20. Ibid. Evil in this context has to do with the "darkening of the world," which implies "a disempowering of the spirit, its dissolution, diminution, suppression, and misinterpretation." Heidegger then claims that Europe is in a vise grip between Russia and America, which, from a metaphysical point of view—that is, as regards their characterization of the world and their relationship to the spirit—are equivalent. The disempowering of the European spirit comes from Europe itself: "Dasein began to slide into a world that lacked that depth from which the essential always comes and returns from human beings [. . .]. The prevailing dimension became that of extension and number [. . .]. All this was further exacerbated both in America and in Russia until the unlimited carelessness about the ever-identical and indifferent, to the point that this pure quantitative turned into a kind of quality. In these countries, mediocrity, indifference, are no longer something unimportant or miserably empty, but represent the dominance and the intrusiveness of things that in attacking every value, every spirituality able to compete with the world, destroy it and portray it as a lie. *This is the onslaught of what we call the demonic [in the sense of the destructively evil]. There are many omens of the arising of this demonism, in unison with the growing perplexity and un-*

certainty of Europe against it and within itself. One such omen is the disempowering of the spirit in the sense of its misinterpretation." *Introduction to Metaphysics*, trans. Gregory Fried and Richard Polt (New Haven: Yale University Press, 2000), pp. 47–49 (italics added).

21. Heidegger, *Schelling's Treatise on the Essence of Human Freedom*, trans. Joan Stambaugh (Athens: Ohio University Press, 1984, orig. pub. 1936), p. 97.

22. Ibid., p. 103.

23. Ibid., pp. 110, 142.

24. Ibid., pp. 142, 143.

25. Ibid., p. 143 (italics added).

26. Ibid., pp. 144–145.

27. On the possibilities for a different thought on evil than the reading of this text provides, when it privileges the approach of a "tragic" interpretation, see Reiner Schürmann's masterful reading in "The Diremption," in his *Broken Hegemonies*.

28. Schürmann, *Broken Hegemonies*, pp. 527 and 533 quoting Heidegger, *Beiträge zur Philosophie (Vom Ereignis)* (Frankfurt am Main: Vittorio Klostermann, 1989), p. 251.

29. Schürmann, *Broken Hegemonies*, pp. 605ff.; quote is on p. 610.

30. Heidegger, "Evening Conversation: In a Prisoner of War Camp in Russia, Between a Younger and an Older Man," in *Country Path Conversations*, pp. 132–160, this quote on p. 133 (slightly modified translation of the original German text in *GA 77*, p. 207).

31. Ibid., p. 134; translation slightly modified. The original text reads: "Das Wesen des Bösen ist der Ingrimm des Aufruhrs, der nie ganz ausbricht, und der, wenn er ausbricht, sich noch verstellt und in seinem versteckten Drohen oft ist, als sei er nicht" (*GA 77*, p. 207).

32. See Irlenborn, *Der Ingrimm des Aufruhrs*.

33. Heidegger, "Evening Conversation," p. 135.

34. Heidegger, *GA 77*, p. 241 (italics added).

35. Heidegger, "Evening Conversation," p. 135.

36. Ibid., p. 136.

37. Ibid., pp. 137–138.

38. Ibid., p. 138.

39. Ibid., pp. 142, 140, 139.

40. Ibid., p. 136.

41. Ibid., p. 139 (italics added).

42. Ibid., pp. 140ff.

43. Ibid., p. 141.

44. Heidegger, *Contributions to Philosophy*, pp. 277–284; but see also the section on "Da-sein and the People," p. 224.

45. For all these points see Schürmann's "The Diremption," in *Broken Hegemonies*, pp. 511–632.

46. Heidegger, *Contributions to Philosophy*, p. 210.

47. Heidegger, "Evening Conversation," pp. 146 and 140.

48. Heidegger, "Evening Conversation," pp. 134, 147, and 148.

49. Ibid., pp. 154–155.

50. Ibid., p. 153.

51. Heidegger, "Evening Conversation," p. 154. The Younger Man states that "Subjectivity has its essence in that the human—the individual, groups, and the realms of humanity—rises up to base himself and to assert himself as the ground and measure of what is actual. With this rebellious uprising into subjectivity emerges the uprising into work as that form of achieving by means of which the devastation of the earth is everywhere prepared for and ultimately established as unconditional." The Old Man responds, "The national thus remains definitive when nations unite in agreement on the international." To which the Younger Man concludes, "The national and the international are the selfsame. The international, if it were to genuinely come about, would be what the mountain range is in relation to the individual mountains."

52. Ibid., p. 157.

53. Jacob Taubes, "From the Adverb 'Nothing' to the Substantive 'Nothing': Deliberations on Heidegger's Question Concerning Nothing," in *From Cult to Culture: Fragments Toward a Critique of Historical Reason*, ed. Charlotte Elisheva Fonrobert (Stanford: Stanford University Press, 2010), pp. 124–136.

54. See Rudolf Carnap, "Überwindung der Metaphysik durch Logische Analyse der Sprache," *Erkenntnis*, 2, 1932. Reprinted in English as "The Elimination of Metaphysics Through Logical Analysis of Language," in *Logical Positivism*, ed. Alfred Jules Ayer (New York: Free Press, 1959), pp. 60–81.

55. The thinker who must be mentioned in this regard is Luigi Pareyson. See especially *Ontologia della libertà: Il male e la sofferenza* (Turin: Einaudi, 1995), excerpts of which are available in English as "Ontology of Freedom" in Luigi Pareyson, *Existence, Interpretation, Freedom: Selected Writings*, ed. Paolo Diego Bubbio (Aurora, CO: Davies Group, 2009), pp. 217–260.

56. Luigi Pareyson's teaching in Turin left an enormous intellectual legacy that has been transmitted along different lines of thought. Some of his inheritors include Gianni Vattimo, Sergio Givone, Claudio Ciancio, Joseph Riconda, Ugo Perone, and Federico Vercellone.

57. Karl Barth, "God and Nothingness," in *Church Dogmatics III.3 The Doctrine of Creation* (London: Continuum, 2010; orig. T&T Clark), pp. 1–78.

58. Paul Ricoeur, *Evil: A Challenge to Philosophy and Theology* (1986) (London: Continuum, 2007).

59. See for example the book by Hans Jonas, *The Gnostic Religion* (Boston: Beacon Press, 1958).

60. I refer, of course, to Max Horkheimer and Theodor W. Adorno, *Dialectic of Enlightenment: Philosophical Fragments*, trans. Edmund Jephcott (Stanford:

Stanford University Press, 2002, orig. pub. 1944). On the topic of progressive immanentism, see Eric Voegelin, "The political religions" (1938), in his "Modernity Without Restraint," Manfred Henningsen (ed.), *The Collected Works of Eric Voegelin*, vol. 5 (Columbia: University of Missouri Press, 2000), pp. 19–74; W. Gurian, "Totalitarianism as Political Religion," in C. J. Friedrich (ed.), *Totalitarianism in Perspectives: Three Views* (New York: Praeger, 1969); R. Aron, "The Future of Secular Religions" (1944), in his *The Dawn of Universal History*, trans. Barbara Bray (Basic Books, 2002). This theory of progressive immanentism and secular religions has a strong bond with critical readings of the Russian philosophy of Dostoevsky.

61. Ernst Jünger's "Totale Mobilmachung" first appeared in the journal *Kriegund Krieger*, edited by Jünger (Berlin: Junker und Dünnhaupt, 1930). An English version is available in *The Heidegger Controversy: A Critical Reader*, trans. Joel Golb and Richard Woli (Cambridge: MIT Press, 1991), pp. 119–139.

62. On the hermeneutic circle that gets set up between philosophy, totalitarianism, and evil around the middle of the last century, see Simona Forti, *Il totalitarismo* (Rome-Bari: Laterza, 2005), pp. 67–114, and the collection of essays *La filosofia di fronte all'estremo. Totalitarismo e riflessione filosofica*, ed. Simona Forti (Turin: Einaudi, 2004).

63. The work I am referring to by Hans Jonas is *The Imperative of Responsibility: In Search of an Ethics for the Technological Age* (Chicago and London: University of Chicago Press, 1984, orig. pub. 1979), which can also be read as a response formulated many years later to the question of nihilism that he first posed in his work on gnosticism.

64. Emmanuel Levinas, "Reflections on the Philosophy of Hitlerism (1934)," trans. Seán Hand, *Critical Inquiry*, 17(1), Autumn 1990: 62–71.

65. In 1939 Levinas was called to arms, and having been taken prisoner, he remained in a concentration camp for most of the war.

66. For a specific discussion on the link between evil and ontology in Levinas's thought, see especially C. Chalier, *La persévérance du mal* (Paris: Cerf, 1987); and F. Nodari, *Il male radicale tra Kant e Lévinas* (Florence: Giuntina, 2008).

67. Emmanuel Lévinas, "De l'évasion," *Recherches Philosophiques*, 5, 1935–1936. English version: *On Escape/De l'évasion*, trans. Bettina G. Bergo (Stanford: Stanford University Press, 2003).

68. Emmanuel Levinas, *Existence and Existents* (1947), trans. Alphonso Lingis (The Hague and Boston: Martinus Nijhoff, 1978).

69. Emmanuel Levinas, *Totality and Infinity: An Essay on Exteriority*, trans. Alphonso Lingis (Pittsburgh: Duquesne University Press, 1969, orig. pub. 1961).

70. Emmanuel Levinas, *Otherwise Than Being or Beyond Essence* (1974), trans. Alphonso Lingis (Dordrecht and Boston: Kluwer Academic, 1978).

71. We might recall the opening statement of his great book *Totality and Infinity*: "Everyone will readily agree that it is of the highest importance to know whether we are not duped by morality" (Preface, p. 21).

72. Emmanuel Levinas, "Useless Suffering" (1982), in *Entre Nous: On Think-ing-of-the-Other*, trans. Michael B. Smith and Barbara Harshav (New York: Co-lumbia University Press, 1983), pp. 91–102.

73. On how Jewishness assumes a religious value in Levinas but also speaks for the universal human condition, see the essays "Reflections on the Philosophy of Hitlerism"; *On Evasion*; "L'actualité de Maÿmonide" (1935) in *Traces*, V, 1982, pp. 97–100; and "L'essence spirituelle de l'antisémitisme" (1938) in *Traces*, V, 1982, pp. 109–111.

74. Levinas, "Useless Suffering," pp. 92–93.

75. Emmanuel Levinas, "Transcendance et Mal" was published in French in *Le Nouveau Commerce*, 41, 1978: 55–75; an English version appears as chapter 11 of *Collected Philosophical Papers*, trans. Alphonso Lingis (Dordrecht: Martinus Ni-jhoff, 1987), pp. 175–186.

76. Philippe Nemo, *Job and the Excess of Evil* (1977), trans. Michael Kigel (Pittsburgh: Duquesne University Press, 1998).

77. Levinas, "Transcendence and Evil," p. 178.

78. Ibid., pp. 179–180.

79. Ibid., p. 180.

80. On this topic, see Jean-François Lyotard, *The Differend: Phrases in Dispute*, trans. Georges Van Den Abbeele (Minneapolis: University of Minnesota Press, 1988); and *Lessons on the Analytic of the Sublime: Kant's Critique of Judgment*, §§ 23–29, trans. Elizabeth Rottenberg (Stanford: Stanford University Press, 1994, orig. pub. 1991).

81. Levinas, "Transcendence and Evil," p. 180.

82. Ibid., p. 181.

83. Ibid., p. 183.

84. Ibid., p. 185.

85. Ibid., p. 158.

86. Ibid., p. 182 (italics added).

87. Ibid., p. 185.

88. I agree with Simon Critchley's idea that Levinasian ethics had not yet be-come a theory of the subject in *Totality and Infinity*, as they did in *Otherwise Than Being*. See Simon Critchley, *Infinitely Demanding: Ethics of Commitment, Politics of Resistance* (London: Verso, 2008).

89. Alain Badiou, *Ethics: An Essay on the Understanding of Evil*, trans. Peter Hallward (London: Verso, 2001, orig. pub. 1993).

90. This argument is continued, so to speak, in the book by Alain Badiou en-titled *The Century*, trans. Alberto Toscano (London: Polity Press, 2007, orig. pub. 2005). In this work, twentieth-century consciousness is presented as divided in two. To one side we have those who accept the horror of the real as necessary to "break the history of the world in two," who submit to the necessity of destruction for the creation of the new. On the other side stand those who believe that if the

real is marked by horror it is better to resign oneself to it and give up. For the author, the latter prefer to shield themselves from the horror to take refuge in moderation and the critique of "grand narratives" (p. 31). For a continuation of debate started by Badiou's book, see for example Alain Badiou, *Circonstances, 3. Portées du mot "juif"* (Paris: Lignes, 2005); Slavoj Žižek, *In Defense of Lost Causes* (London: Verso, 2008); and Alain Badiou and Alain Finkielkraut, *L'explication. Conversation avec Aude Lancelin* (Fécamp: Lignes, 2010).

91. Levinas, "Useless Suffering," p. 241, note 7.

92. Levinas, "Useless Suffering," p. 97.

93. On the concept of "excess" in relation to the crimes perpetrated by the Nazis against the Jews, see Philippe Lacoue-Labarthe and Jean-Luc Nancy, "The Nazi Myth," trans. Brian Holmes, *Critical Inquiry*, 16(2), Winter 1990: 291–312.

94. The reference is to Theodor Adorno's dictum that "To write poetry after Auschwitz is barbaric" (from his 1949 essay, "Cultural Criticism and Society," reprinted as the first essay in *Prisms*, trans. Samuel and Sherry Weber, Cambridge: MIT Press, 1983, p. 34). On this topic, see once again Badiou, *The Century*.

CHAPTER 4: THANATOPOLITICS AND ABSOLUTE VICTIMS

1. I follow Michel Foucault's lexicon here, which makes no qualitative terminological distinction between biopolitics and biopower.

2. Primo Levi, *If This Is a Man*, trans. Stuart Woolf (New York: Orion Press, 1959), p. 103.

3. Ibid., p. 103.

4. Annette Wieviorka, *The Era of the Witness*, trans. Jared Stark (New York: Cornell University Press, 2006, orig. pub. 1998).

5. For an intelligent summary of discussion on the topic in history circles, see for example J.-M. Chaumont, *La concurrence des victimes. Génocide, identité, reconnaissance* (Paris: La Découverte, 1997); Enzo Traverso, *El pasado, instrucciones de uso. Historia, memoria, política* (Madrid: Marcial Pons, 2007); Esther Benbassa, *Suffering as Identity: The Jewish Paradigm*, trans. G. M. Goshgarian (London: Verso, 2010, orig. pub. 2007).

6. Giorgio Agamben, *Homo Sacer: Sovereign Power and Bare Life*, trans. Daniel Heller-Roazen (Stanford: Stanford University Press, 1998); and *Remnants of Auschwitz: The Witness and the Archive*, trans. Daniel Heller-Roazen (Brooklyn: Zone Books, 1999). Written in the same period from a closely allied perspective, see the work of A. Brossat, *L'épreuve du désastre. Le XXe siècle et les camps* (Paris: Albin Michel, 1996). See also Penelope Deutscher, "The Inversion of Exceptionality: Foucault, Agamben, and 'Reproductive Rights'," in *South Atlantic Quarterly*, 107(1), 2007: 55–70; Alessia Ricciardi, "From Decreation to Bare Life: Weil, Agamben, and the Impolitical," in *Diacritics*, 39(2) 2009: 75–93; Samuel Weber, "Bare Life and Life in General," in *Grey Room*, 46, Winter 2012: 6–25.

7. See the lecture texts of the seminars that Derrida held at the École des hautes études en sciences sociales between 2001 and 2002, published as *The Beast and the Sovereign, Volume I*, trans. Geoffrey Bennington (Chicago and London: University of Chicago Press, 2009); the reference is on pp. 316ff. For Derrida a distinction of this type cannot even be traced to the writings of Aristotle—the philosophical locus where Arendt, Foucault, and Agamben believe they can identify the separation between life in the biological sense and life in a human-political sense. According to the French philosopher, the Aristotelian *zoon politikon* and the allied *zoon logon echon*, far from being an oversight that led the Greek philosopher to a purely terminological confusion between *zoe* and *bios*, instead demonstrates the fact that not only does modernity have a biopolitical core, but so does Western politics as a whole. That is to say, politics has always captured and worked on *zoe* in the belief that it can transform it. On the difference between *zoe* and *bios* in a broad philosophical and political perspective, see Pier Paolo Portinaro, *Breviario di politica* (Brescia: Morcelliana, 2009), pp. 11–22.

8. In particular, Derrida, *The Beast and the Sovereign*.

9. Roberto Esposito, *Bios: Biopolitics and Philosophy*, trans. Timothy Campbell (Minneapolis: University of Minnesota Press, 2008), which reconstructs, among other things, the main phases of the thought on biopolitics as well as providing full bibliographic references; see also by Esposito *Third Person: Politics of Life and Philosophy of the Impersonal*, trans. Zakiya Hanafi (London: Polity, 2012). For a mapping of the disciplinary areas pertaining to biopolitics, see the work of C. Geyer (ed.), *Biopolitik. Die Positionen* (Frankfurt am Main: Suhrkamp Verlag, 2001); T. Lemke, *Biopolitik zur Einführung* (Hamburg: Junius Verlag, 2007); A. Moreau, *Le biosiècle: Bioéconomie, biopolitique, biocentrisme* (Paris: L'Harmattan, 2009); Laura Bazzicalupo, *Biopolitica. Una mappa concettuale* (Rome: Carocci, 2010).

10. As far as Michel Foucault is concerned, the works most relevant to biopower are *The Will to Knowledge: The History of Sexuality, Volume 1*, trans. Robert Hurley (New York: Random House, 1978, orig. pub. 1976), especially pp. 115–132; *"Society Must Be Defended": Lectures at the Collège de France (1975–1976)*, trans. David Macey (New York: Picador, 2003), pp. 239–264; *Security, Territory, Population: Lectures at the Collège de France (1977–1978)*, trans. Graham Burchell (New York: Picador, 2007); *The Birth of Biopolitics: Lectures at the Collège de France (1978–1979)*, trans. Graham Burchell (New York: Palgrave Macmillan, 2008). As far as Hannah Arendt is concerned, the themes of the birth of the social and the triumph of the *animal laborans* are to be found especially in *The Human Condition* (Chicago and London: University of Chicago Press, 1998, orig. pub. 1958); and in "Introduction *into* Politics" which appears in Hannah Arendt, *The Promise of Politics*, ed. Jerome Kohn (New York: Schocken Books, 2005), pp. 93–200; on the death camps, see Hannah Arendt, *The Origins of Totalitarianism* (New York: Harcourt, 1976, orig. pub. 1951); and the essays collected in *Essays in Understanding 1930–1954: Formation, Exile, and Totalitarianism*, ed. Jerome Kohn (New York:

Shocken Books, 1994). Works on Arendt and the problem of the social question relevant to our discussion include Seyla Benhabib's *The Reluctant Modernism of Hannah Arendt* (Thousand Oaks: Sage, 1996); and Hannah Fenichel Pitkin, *The Attack of the Blob: Hannah Arendt's Concept of the Social* (Chicago: University of Chicago Press, 1998).

11. Foucault, *The Will to Knowledge*, p. 143.

12. On this topic, see Fina Birulés, *Una herencia sin testamento: Hannah Arendt* (Barcelona: Herder Editorial, 2007), especially the chapter "Un crecimento no natural de lo natural," pp. 107–127; Antonella Moscati, "'Biopolitica' e singolarità in Hannah Arendt," *Aut aut*, 328, 2005: 99–118. For a comparison between Arendt and Foucault on biopolitics, see Kathrin Braun, "Biopolitics and Temporality in Arendt and Foucault," *Time and Society*, 16(1), 2007: 5–21; Andre Duarte, "Hannah Arendt, Biopolitics and the Problem of Violence: From *Animal Laborans* to *Homo Sacer*," in Dan Stone and Richard H. King (eds.), *Hannah Arendt and the Uses of History: Imperialism, Race and Genocide* (London: Berghahn Books, 2007); Claire Blencowe, "Foucault's and Arendt's 'Insider View' of Biopolitics: A Critique of Agamben," *History of the Human Sciences*, 23(5), 2010: 113–130.

13. In the phenomenological articulation of human activities contained in *The Human Condition*, labor is synonymous with the human-nature metabolism, the sustenance of *zoe*. It is the dimension of necessity that characterizes the sphere of the needs of human life. Much could be said about this freedom-necessity distinction, which somehow remains tied to a mind-body dualism, making the body the substrate of the biological animal, linked to needs, and the mind the place of possible freedom. This dualism can be explained, in my view, by the trauma of what she considered to be a genuine ontological crime that took place in Auschwitz. On what and how the theme of birth somehow manages to undermine the rigidity of this dualism, see Miguel Vatter, "Natality and Biopolitics in Hannah Arendt," *Revista de Ciencia Política*, 26(2), 2006: 137–160.

14. "Introduction *into* Politics," published in English in *The Promise of Politics*, pp. 93–200, are fragments, for the most part written in 1955, out of which *The Human Condition* is supposed to have emerged, but some of its passages speak more directly and effectively than the finished work.

15. Arendt, *The Promise of Politics*, pp. 144–145.

16. In the text *Security, Territory, Population*, Foucault shows how the population, with its demographic regularities, epidemics, and so forth, opens the way to the new art of governing that would otherwise have remained blocked between family and sovereignty: "With the household and father on the one hand, and the state and sovereignty on the other, the art of government could not find its own dimension" (p. 103). See the article by Antonella Moscati, "'Biopolitica' e singolarità in Hannah Arendt," *Aut aut*, 328, 2005: 99–118. See also Amy Allen, "Power, Subjectivity, and Agency: Between Arendt and Foucault," in *International Journal of Philosophical Studies*, 10(2), 2002: 131–149. For a general overview of the

biopolitical turn, see the chapter "A Genealogy of Politics: From Its Invention to the Biopolitical Turn," in Chiara Bottici, *Imaginal Politics: Images Beyond Imagination and the Imaginary* (New York: Columbia University Press, 2014).

17. As Giorgio Agamben expresses it in *Homo Sacer*, pp. 45ff.

18. Michel Foucault, "Pouvoir et savoir," interview with Shiguehiko Hasumi, in Foucault, *Dits et écrits, II* (Paris: Gallimard, 2001), pp. 399–414. [These quotes are translated from the Italian.] In this interview Foucault says that what fueled his research into power was the trauma of an excess of power that his generation was forced to confront. "Fascism and Stalinism," he argues, "posed the problem of an excess of power [. . .] not only of the state apparatuses, the party, the bureaucracy (in short, the places intended to host and preserve the essence of power), but of individuals over each other." He adds: "It was from the end of Stalinism onwards that the question of power began to impose itself in all its starkness." He recalls: "There was the need to think about this problem of power, but in the absence of conceptual tools for its thought[. . . .] Many others have set themselves the problem of the excesses of power starting from Stalinism. All those, for example, who starting from a Marxist point of view have examined the so-called phenomenon of bureaucratization of the party. My way of posing the same problem is different. I don't attempt to see what kind of aberration is produced in the apparatus of the state that has led to this excess of power. On the contrary, I try to see how an inflation of power circulates in everyday life, in relations between the sexes, in the family, between the sick and medical science." In other interviews during the same years, also included in *Dits et écrits, II*, Foucault argues that as early as 1956 it was clear to him that "the two black beasts" (fascism and Stalinism) were not at all historical interludes, but rather epoch-making events.

19. On the history and uses of the concept, the reader is referred to my book *Il totalitarismo* (Rome-Bari: Laterza, 2005).

20. Although coming from a different perspective, the observations in Adriana Cavarero's *Horrorism: Naming Contemporary Violence* (New York: Columbia University Press, 2010) are crucial in this regard.

21. Arendt, *The Origins of Totalitarianism*, p. 459.

22. Hannah Arendt, Karl Jaspers, *Correspondence 1926–1969*, trans. Robert and Rita Kimber (New York: Harcourt Brace, 1992; letter from Arendt to Jaspers dated December 17, 1946, italics added), p. 69.

23. See Cavarero, *Horrorism*. For Hannah Arendt, *horror* is not expressed in reaction to the atrocity of factual circumstances, insists Cavarero, but rather to an attack on the ontological structure of reality itself.

24. See Hannah Arendt, "A Reply to Eric Voegelin" (1953), in *Essays in Understanding, 1930–1954: Formation, Exile, and Totalitarianism*, ed. Jerome Kohn (New York: Shocken Books, 1994), pp. 401–408.

25. Hannah Arendt, "The Image of Hell" (1946), pp. 197–205; and the following essays also appearing in *Essays in Understanding, 1930–1954*: "Social Science

Techniques and the Study of Concentration Camps" (1950, pp. 232–247), "Mankind and Terror" (1953, pp. 297–306), "On the Nature of Totalitarianism: An Essay in Understanding" (1954, pp. 328–360).

26. Hannah Arendt, "Karl Marx and the Tradition of Western Political Thought (1953)," *Social Research*, 69(2), Summer 2002: 273–319.

27. On the modern revolution that elevated life to a supreme good, resulting in another, crucial revolution through which Christianity overturned the ancient relationship between humankind and the world, see the final pages of *The Human Condition*. They are to be read together with those on the *animal laborans* and the writings on Marx, together with chapters on racism and in particular on Darwinism in *The Origins of Totalitarianism*.

28. Arendt, "Mankind and Terror," p. 304.

29. In "On the Nature of Totalitarianism" of 1954, Arendt describes the series of steps leading to "bare life" even more effectively than in *The Origins of Totalitarianism*.

30. On this topic, see the intelligent remarks by Davide Tarizzo in *La vita. Un'invenzione recente* (Rome-Bari: Laterza, 2010).

31. Gilles Deleuze, *Foucault* (London: Continuum, 1999, orig. pub. 1986).

32. Foucault, *"Society Must Be Defended,"* p. 249.

33. Ibid., p. 254.

34. Ibid., p. 258.

35. Ibid., p. 255.

36. Ibid., p. 256.

37. Ibid., p. 259.

38. Ibid., p. 260 (italics added).

39. Ibid., p. 261.

40. "Whenever you have these socialisms, these forms of socialism, or these moments of socialism that stress the problem of the struggle, you therefore have racism" (Foucault, *"Society Must Be Defended,"* p. 262).

41. Michel Foucault, "How Is Power Exercised?" trans. Leslie Sawyer, part of "The Subject and Power," *Critical Inquiry*, 8(4), 1982: 777–795, this quote p. 789. "Is this to say that one must seek the character proper to power relations in the violence which must have been its primitive form, its permanent secret, and its last resource, that which in the final analysis appears as its real nature when it is forced to throw aside its mask and to show itself as it really is?"

42. See James W. Bernauer, *Michel Foucault's Force of Flight: Toward an Ethics for Thought* (Atlantic Highlands, NJ, and London: Humanities Press International, 1990); and also by Bernauer, "Spirit and Flesh: Toward a Post-Shoah, Post-Modern Incarnational Ethic," in J. Bemporad, J. T. Pawlikowski, and J. Sievers (eds.), *Good and Evil After Auschwitz: Ethical Implications for Today* (Hoboken: KTAV, 2000).

43. George Orwell, *1984* (London: Signet Classic, 1950, orig. pub. 1949); Winston's final torture (the "personalized" violence that takes place in the novel once

the threshold to Room 101 has been crossed) foreshadows the final stage of human destitution, not only for Winston Smith but for all the future victims. On this topic, see for example Claude Lefort, "Le corps interposé: 1984 de Orwell" (1984), in his *Écrire à l'épreuve du politique* (Paris: Calmann-Lévy, 1989), pp. 15–36. For a recent discussion on *1984* from the point of view of political philosophy, see a previous work of mine, Simona Forti, "Scene di paranoia in Oceania. Per una rilettura di *Nineteen Eighty-Four*," in S. Strong, M. Revelli (eds.), *Paranoia e politica* (Turin: Bollati Boringhieri, 2007).

44. See Wolfgang Sofsky, *Traktat über die Gewalt* [Essay on violence] (Fischer Taschenbuch Verlag, 2005, orig. pub. 1996). See also the Italian collection of essays by Wolfgang Sofsky, *Il paradiso della crudeltà. Dodici saggi sul lato oscuro dell'uomo* (Turin: Einaudi, 2001).

45. See Claudia Card, *The Atrocity Paradigm: A Theory of Evil* (Oxford: Oxford University Press, 2002). By the same author, see *Genocide's Aftermath: Responsibility and Repair* (Malden: Blackwell, 2007).

46. Out of the vast literature on genocides, the works that are pertinent to our inquiry include J. Sémelin, *Purificare e distruggere. Usi politici dei massacri e dei genocidi* (Turin: Einaudi, 2007, orig. pub. 2005); Michael Mann, *The Dark Side of Democracy: Explaining Ethnic Cleansing* (Cambridge: Cambridge University Press, 2005); Georges Bensoussan, *Europe. Une passione génocidaire* (Paris: Mille et une nuits, 2006); Wolfgang Sofsky, *The Order of Terror: The Concentration Camp* (Princeton: Princeton University Press, 1999, orig. pub. 1993); Enzo Traverso, *The Origins of Nazi Violence*, trans. Janet Lloyd (New York and London: New Press, 2003, orig. pub. 2002). The most important pioneering works in the comparative study of genocides are Léon Poliakov, *Harvest of Hate: The Nazi Program for the Destruction of the Jews of Europe*, revised ed. (New York: Schocken Books, 1979, orig. pub. 1951); George L. Mosse, *Toward the Final Solution: A History of European Racism* (New York: Howard Fertig, 1978); Norman Cohn, *Warrant for Genocide: The Myth of the Jewish World Conspiracy and the Protocols of the Elders of Zion*, 2nd ed. (Junction, OR: Serif, 2006); Helen Fein, *Accounting for Genocide: Victims and Survivors of the Holocaust—National Responses and Jewish Victimization During the Holocaust* (New York: Free Press, 1979); and especially Leo Kuper, *Genocide: Its Political Use in the Twentieth Century* (New Haven: Yale University Press, 1981); Yves Ternon, *L'État criminel: Les génocides au XXIème siècle* (Paris: Seuil, 1995). We now have the indispensable collection edited by Donald Bloxham and A. Dirk Moses, *The Oxford Handbook of Genocide Studies* (Oxford: Oxford University Press, 2010), which provides extended studies on the different genocides, and for the first time gives an account of the many disciplines that make up "genocide studies."

47. In reality, as we know, the stratagem of portraying others as animals was not restricted to modern genocide. The first exterminations, which took place in the New World, provided the original script for the twentieth century to copy.

The highly civilized Spaniards of the sixteenth century exterminated the Indios, often convinced that they were "half-men (homunculi), in whom you will barely find the vestiges of humanity." This is how the sophisticated translator of Aristotle, Juan Ginés De Sepúlveda, expressed himself in *Democrates Alter: Or, on the Just Causes for War Against the Indians*, from *Boletín de la Real Academia de la Historia*, XXI, October 1892. Originally translated for *Introduction to Contemporary Civilization in the West* (New York: Columbia University Press, 1946, 1954, 1961). Available at http://www.columbia.edu/acis/ets/CCREAD/sepulved.htm (accessed November 8, 2013).

48. The citations come from book 9 of the Benjamin Jowett translation of Plato's *Republic*, available at Internet Classics Archive by Daniel C. Stevenson, Web Atomics, http://classics.mit.edu/Plato/republic.mb.txt (accessed November 11, 2013). See Mario Vegetti, "Paranoia nella tirannide antica," in Simona Forti and Marco Revelli (eds.), *Paranoia e politica*, pp. 43–57. The works on tyranny by D. Lanza, *Il tiranno e il suo pubblico* (Turin: Einaudi, 1977) and by G. Giorgini, *La città e il tiranno* (Milan: Giuffrè, 1993) remain essential reading.

49. See A. Brossat, *Le corps de l'ennemi. Hyperviolence et démocratie* (Paris: La fabrique, 1998). From a different but equally useful perspective, see G. De Luna, *Il corpo del nemico ucciso. Violenza e morte nella guerra contemporanea* (Turin: Einaudi, 2006).

50. See Robert Jay Lifton, *The Nazi Doctors: Medical Killing and the Psychology of Genocide* (London: Macmillan, 1986); R. N. Proctor, *Racial Hygiene: Medicine Under the Nazis* (Cambridge: Cambridge University Press, 1988); also, by the same author, *The Nazi War on Cancer* (Princeton: Princeton University Press, 1999); P. Weindling, *Health, Race and German Politics Between National Unification and Nazism: 1870–1945* (Cambridge: Cambridge University Press, 1989); for all genocides, see Y. F. Khong, *Analogies at War: Korea, Munich, Dien Bien Phu, and the Vietnam Decisions of 1965* (Princeton: Princeton University Press, 1982), and R. A. Koenigsberg, *Hitler's Ideology: Embodied Metaphor, Fantasy, and History* (Charlotte: Information Age, 2007). The linguist George Lakoff and his theory of embodied mind are important for these interpretations. See especially George Lakoff and Mark Johnson, *Metaphors We Live By* (Chicago: University of Chicago Press, 1980).

51. A quotation from an important manual by Rudolf Ramm, used by the faculty of medicine at the University of Berlin, cited by Robert Jay Lifton, *The Nazi Doctors*, p. 30.

52. R. N. Proctor, *Racial Hygiene*, pp. 225ff. See also the work by E. Schwab, *Hitler's Mind: A Plunge into Madness* (New York: Praeger, 1992), with a chapter entitled "The Pasteur-Koch Complex," arguing that the two scientists provided the model around which Hitler's paranoid emotional system took form.

53. Cited by Lifton, *The Nazi Doctors*, pp. 27ff.

54. Étienne Balibar also makes this point, especially in the chapter "Class

Racism" in Étienne Balibar and Immanuel Wallerstein, *Race, Nation, Class: Ambiguous Identities*, 2nd ed. (London: Verso, 2011, orig. pub. 1988), pp. 204–216.

55. See the work by Koenigsberg, *Hitler's Ideology*, cited above.

56. Based on Roberto Esposito, *Immunitas: The Protection and Negation of Life*, trans. Zakiya Hanafi (Cambridge: Polity, 2011).

57. See Roberto Esposito, *Bios. Biopolitica e filosofia* (Turin: Einaudi, 2004); especially the chapter "Tanatopolitica (il ciclo del genos)," pp. 115–157, this quote translated from the Italian on p. 140; English edition *Bios: Biopolitics and Philosophy* (Minneapolis: University of Minnesota Press, 2008), especially the chapter "Thanatopolitics (The Cycle of *Genos*)."

58. See Heinrich Himmler, *Geheimreden 1933 bis 1945: Und anderen Ansprechen*, ed. B. F. Smith and F. Peterson, with an introduction by J. C. Fest (Berlin: Propylaen, 1974). The quotes are taken from the Nizkor project translation at http://www.nizkor.org/hweb/people/h/himmler-heinrich/posen/oct-04 -43/ (accessed November 12, 2013).

59. See the perennially relevant work by Mary Douglas, *Purity and Danger: An Analysis of Concepts of Pollution and Taboo* (London: Taylor & Francis, 2002, orig. pub. 1966).

60. The English version is *Race and State*, trans. Ruth Hein, vol. 2, *The Collected Works of Eric Voegelin* (Baton Rouge: Louisiana State University, 1997). The original German text is *Rasse und Staat* (Tübingen: J. C. B. Mohr, 1933). See also volume 3 of the *Collected Works*, *The History of the Race Idea from Ray to Carus* [*Die Rassenidee in der Geistesgeschichte von Ray bis Carus*] (Berlin: Junker und Dünnhaupt, 1933], which was also quickly withdrawn from circulation. On the significance of *Race and State*, its influence, and the criticisms it has received, see the essay by P.-A. Taguieff, "Eric Voegelin, 1933: Un philosophe face à l'idée de race et au racisme," which appears before the French translation: *Race et État* (Paris: Vrin, 2007), pp. 7–88.

61. Specifically starting from Ernst Renan's *Histoire générale et système comparé des langues sémitiques* (Paris: L'Imprimerie Impériale, 1855).

62. Cited by R. Schäfer, "Zur Geschichte des Wortes 'zersetzen'," *Zeitschrift für Deutsche Wortforschung*, 18, 1962: 40–80. [Translated from the Italian.] See also A. Bein, *Der Jüdische Parasit*, "Vierteljahrshefte für Zeitgeschichte," ed. H. Rothfels and T. Eschenburg (1965), pp. 121–149. Although written from a different perspective, see S. Jansen, *Schädlinge Geschichte eines wissenschaftlichen und politischen Konstrukt, Campus* (Frankfurt am Main, 2003).

63. On this topic, see the still strikingly beautiful book by Joshua Trachtenberg, *The Devil and the Jews: The Medieval Conception of the Jew and Its Relation to Modern Antisemitism*, 2nd ed. (Philadelphia: Jewish Publication Society of America, 2002, orig. pub. 1943).

64. For more on this dual schema that structured fear toward the Jews, see the still essential work by Léon Poliakov, *The History of Antisemitism. Vol. 4: Suicidal*

Europe (1870–1933), trans. George Klin (Philadelphia: University of Pennsylvania Press, 2003, orig. pub. 1955).

65. On this topic, see Michele Battini, *Il socialismo degli imbecilli. Propaganda, falsificazione, persecuzione degli ebrei* (Turin: Bollati Boringhieri, 2010).

66. On this dichotomy and its continuation into Nazi antisemitism, see among others Enzo Traverso, *The Origins of Nazi Violence*, trans. Janet Lloyd (New York and London: New Press, 2003, orig. pub. 2002).

67. A very important essay in this regard was Heinrich von Treitschke's "Ein Wort über unser Judentum," *Preussischen Jahrbüchern*, vol. 44–45, 1880–1881, in which he legitimized the opposition between Jewish society and German community as a supreme scientific truth. See the edition by W. Boehlich, *Der Berliner Antisemitismusstreit* (Frankfurt am Main: Insel-Verlag, 1965): arrogant and power-hungry, "the Jews are our evil" (p. 20). [Translated from the Italian.]

68. Otto Weininger, *Sex and Character: A Survey of Principles* (New York: Putnam, 1906, orig. pub. 1903, now Cornell University Library Digital Collections).

69. See, respectively, Ferdinand Tönnies, *Community and Civil Society*, trans. Margaret Hollis (Cambridge: Cambridge University Press, 2001, orig. pub. 1887); Georg Simmel, *The Philosophy of Money* (Oxon: Routledge Classics, 2011, orig. pub. 1900); Werner Sombart, *The Jews and Modern Capitalism* (New Brunswick, NJ: Transaction, 2009, orig. pub. 1911).

70. See Alphonse Toussenel, *Les Juifs rois de l'époque: Histoire de la féodalité financière* (Paris: Librairie de l'École Sociétaire, 1845), but also his famous *L'Esprit des bêtes [mammifères de France]* (Paris: J. Hetzel, 1868); Édouard Drumont, *La France Juive. Essai d'histoire contemporaine* (Paris: Flammarion, 1886). For an overview, see Pierre-André Taguieff, *La couleur et le sang. Doctrines racistes à la française* (Paris: Mille et une nuits, 1998).

71. See Wilhelm Marr, *Der Weg zum Siege des Germanenthums über das Judenthum: Vom nicht-konfessionellen Standpunkt aus betrachtet* (Berlin: Hentze, 1880).

72. See Eugen Karl Dühring, *Die Judenfrage als Racen-, Sitten-, und Culturfrage* (Karlsruhe and Leipzig: H. Reuther, 1881); available in English as *The Jewish Question: A Racial Moral and Cultural Question with a World-Historical Answer* (Brighton: Nineteen Eighty-Four Press, 1997).

73. See Theodor Fritsch, *Handbuch der Judenfrage* (Hamburg: Hermann Beyer Verlag, 1887). It went through reprints repeatedly toward the end of the century and throughout the years of the Third Reich.

74. Paul de Lagarde, *Juden und Indogermanen, eine Testing nach dem Leben* (Göttingen: Dieterich, 1887).

75. Paul de Lagarde, *Deutsche Schriften, Letzte Gesamtausgabe* (Göttingen: Dieterich, 1886), p. 330.

76. Otto Spengler, *Der Untergang des Abendlandes* (Munich: Beck, 1923); English edition, *The Decline of the West*, trans. Charles Francis Atkinson (New York: Knopf, 1926).

77. Ibid., pp. 951–962.

78. The image of the Jewish parasite is profoundly rooted in the lowest social classes as well, thanks to a popular literature that expressed the same ideas, combining them with nationalist romanticism and a cheap racial mythology. A significant example of this is the book by Artur Dinter, *Die Sünde wider das Blut. Ein Zeitroman* (Leipzig: Wolferlag, 1918). Its author, who narrates the trials and tribulations of a young Aryan whose blood has been corrupted by his first Jewish wife, provides a compendium of all the commonplaces that accompany the parasite idea. Both in this work and in others, such as *Der Kampf um die Geistlehre* (Leipzig: Matthes und Thost Verlag, 1921), in which his literary talents are combined with his philosophical pretensions, all the ancient images of the Jew—the moneylender, the exploiter, the international conspirator, and especially the devil—are welded together into the figure of the parasite. This is the same explosive mixture of mythology, political paranoia, demonology, and biology that was put into circulation, with great success, by *The Protocols of the Elders of Zion*.

79. Eberhard Jäckel, *Hitler's World View: A Blueprint for Power*, trans. Herbert Arnold (Cambridge: Harvard University Press, 1981), pp. 58–59.

80. See Adolf Hitler, *Mein Kampf* (München: Lehmanns Fachbuchhandlung Verlag, 1938), pp. 188–194. The quotes in English are from the Ralph Manheim translation (Boston: Houghton Mifflin, 1998).

81. Ibid., p. 305.

82. Ibid., pp. 310ff.

83. Ibid.

84. Ibid., p. 327.

85. Ibid., pp. 286–287.

86. Ibid., pp. 325–326.

87. Alfred Rosenberg, *The Myth of the Twentieth Century: An Evaluation of the Spiritual-Intellectual Confrontations of Our Age* (Ostara, 1930), www.ostarapublications.com. For more on Rosenberg, see his *Blut und Ehre* (Munich: Hoheneichen Verlag, 1934), and *Gestalten der Ideas* (Munich: Hoheneichen Verlag, 1936). In the same perspective, the official positions of the NSDAP are developed by E. Krieck, *Völkisch-politische Anthropologie* (Leipzig: Armanen-Verlag, 1936). On the Aryan myth as it appears in this pre-Nazi and Nazi literature, see the indispensable Leon Polyakov, *The Aryan Myth: A History of Racist and Nationalist Ideas in Europe* (Barnes and Noble, 1996).

88. Rosenberg, *The Myth of the Twentieth Century*, p. 280.

89. "Absolutes Without Limits" is translated literally from the German edition, as quoted in Jean-Luc Nancy and Philippe Lacoue-Labarthe, "The Nazi Myth," trans. Brian Holmes, *Critical Inquiry*, 16(2), Winter 1990: 291–312, p. 305; the English version of Rosenberg has "bloodless absolutes," p. 2.

90. Ibid., pp. 6–14. Jean-Luc Nancy and Philippe Lacoue-Labarthe are among

the few philosophers who recognize the importance of this nonbiologistic version of Nazi racism, which is less concerned with genetic and naturalistic control than in reproducing Hellas in a copy that finally creates the truth of the original. Lacoue-Labarthe and Nancy rightly point out that this obsession for embodying a type is connected with Germany's obsession regarding its lack of political identity, a theme that runs through many of the works of its contemporary thinkers. Philippe Lacoue-Labarthe, *Heidegger, Art, and Politics: The Fiction of the Political*, trans. Chris Turner (Oxford: Blackwell, 1990, orig. pub. 1987); Jean-Luc Nancy, Philippe Lacoue-Labarthe, "The Nazi Myth," trans. Brian Holmes, *Critical Inquiry*, 16(2), Winter 1990: 291–312.

91. Rosenberg, *The Myth of the Twentieth Century*, p. 271.

92. Ibid., p. 279. For that matter *Mein Kampf* (1925–28) states: "National Socialism is [seen] as the formation and realization of its own image, *weltanschauunlich*" (p. 680); it is the creation of a world according to which the idea of the creator of form is precisely the Aryan. "The *weltanschauunlich* struggle is not just any enterprise of domination: it is a world formation[. . . .] The Aryan will have to be much more than a world subjected and exploited by Aryans: it will have to be a world that has become Aryan. The *Weltanschauung* must incarnate itself absolutely; it therefore requires a total overturning of the entire public life according to its points of view, of its *Anschauungen*" (p. 506).

93. Ibid., p. 279.

94. For more on this type of "idealistic" racism, which Rosenberg spearheaded, see my article "The Biopolitics of Souls: Racism, Nazism and Plato," *Political Theory*, 34(1), 2006: 9–32.

95. See Voegelin, *Rasse und Staat*, pp. 30ff. [Quote translated from the Italian.]

96. Norman Cohn offers a similar interpretation in *Europe's Inner Demons: The Demonization of Christians in Medieval Christiandom* (Chicago: University of Chicago Press, 2001, orig. pub. 1973). It provides a sort of genealogy of Manicheanism as a way of conceiving the world, from witch hunting to antisemitism. Cohn lists some crucial characteristics of this mentality, which always views disorder as a sign of negativity. The first, essential characteristic is the need to master the disturbing and the uncertain. This is connected to the demand for absolute control over the totality of the real, which is divided into a vision of the end and the end of history, the project of a future state in which disorder will be completely eliminated. Despite all the planning, there is always some detail that escapes the universal schema. This is the existence of evil—an active force that can be easily located in a group who is made responsible for the remaining disorder. To wipe out disorder, this group must be wiped out.

97. Rosenberg, *The Myth of the Twentieth Century*, p. 280.

98. The reference is to Oskar Schmitz and his *Der Jude. Judentum und Deutschtum* (Berlin, 1926), pp. 17–33.

99. Rosenberg, *The Myth of the Twentieth Century*, p. 280.

100. Ibid., p. 280; "Das ist die spezifische höchst gefährliche Form der Jüdischen Weltverneinung" (p. 460, German edition).

101. Ibid., p. 280.

102. Ibid., p. 280.

103. Rosenberg relies on his reading of Arno Schickedanz, *Sozialparasitismus im Völkerleben* (Leipzig: Lotus-Verlag, 1927), which says that Judaism is the diametric opposite of a perennial race ("Ideal einer konstanten Rasse").

104. Rosenberg, *The Myth of the Twentieth Century*, p. 281ff. On Nietzsche, see pp. 364ff.

105. For example, the weighty tome by Kurt Hildebrandt, *Platon. Der Kampf des Geistes um die Macht* (Berlin: Bondi, 1933; Italian version Turin: Einaudi, 1947). There were many writings between 1932 and 1934 that combined Plato's philosophy with the National Socialist movement. I will limit myself to citing the ones most widely read and circulated: J. Bannes, *Hitler und Platon* (Berlin and Leipzig: de Gruyter, 1933), and *Hitlers Kampf und Platons Staat* (Berlin and Leipzig: de Gruyter, 1933); A. Gabler, *Platon und Der Führer* (Berlin and Leipzig: de Gruyter, 1934). In Italy, this tradition was mainly followed by Julius Evola, *Sintesi di dottrina della razza* (Milan: Hoepli, 1938), and *Il mito del sangue* (Milan: Hoepli, 1942). Evola also viewed the body as a phenomenalization of the soul—of the soul of the race, not the individual soul. For Evola, too, the supreme value for each ethnic group was the perfect form of its bodily appearance and its "spiritual" form, which had to correspond to each other. F. Freda reintroduces this critical perspective in *Platone. Lo Stato secondo giustizia* (Padua: Edizioni di Ar, 1996); and *I lupi azzurri* (Padua: Edizioni di Ar, 2001).

106. His most famous work, entitled *The Racial Elements of European History*, which circulated in an abridged version called the *Volksgünther*, became a sort of breviary owned by every self-respecting German household. See H. K. F. Günther, *Rassenkunde des deutschen Volkes* (Munich: Lehmanns Fachbuchhandlung Verlag, 1922); English version: *The Racial Elements of European History*, trans. G. C. Wheeler (London: Methuen, 1927). The classification of the European population into races, following the popular wisdom of the time, is not very original. It was influenced by the taxonomy of Houston Stewart Chamberlain, in his *Die Grundlagen des 19. Jahrhunderts* (Munich: Bruckmann, 1899); English version: *The Foundations of the Nineteenth Century*, trans. John Lees (London: John Lane, Bodley Head, 1911). The main races are divided into the Nordic, the Western, the Eastern, the Dinaric, the Baltic, and the Phalic, all combinations of corresponding bodily and mental traits. According to Evola, it was Günther more than anyone else who was responsible for reshaping the idea of "races of the spirit" into a sound doctrinal theory. Indeed, he was one of the most popular authors during Nazism. During the 1920s he wrote many treatises on the races, in addition to *The Racial Elements of European History*, which was reprinted sixteen times, with more than one hundred thousand copies in circulation. See

Hans K. F. Günther, *Rassenkunde Europas* (Munich: Lehmanns Fachbuchhandlung Verlag, 1928); and his *Rassenkunde des Jüdischen Volk* (Munich: Lehmanns Fachbuchhandlung Verlag, 1929). When the National Socialist movement was on the threshold of seizing power, Günther's work was already integral to the ideology of the movement. He taught social anthropology at the University of Jena, where in 1930 Hitler came to attend to his inaugural lecture. His work had an extended influence on numerous magazines and associations, and in 1935 he assumed the chair of political anthropology at the University of Berlin. On the role of Günther in "the philosophy of national socialism," see Eric Voegelin, *Race and State*. As regards his role in the history of eugenics, see Paul Weindling, *Health, Race and German Politics Between National Unification (1870–1945)* (Cambridge: Cambridge University Press, 1989).

107. See Hans K. F. Günther, *Platon als Hüter des Lebens* (Munich: Lehmanns Verlag, 1928), pp. 3–29. [All quotes are translated from the Italian.]

108. See the above and Hans K. F. Günther, *Humanitas* (Munich: Lehmanns Verlag, 1937). These two books also went through numerous reprints. Darwin is barely mentioned, and the modern *auctoritates* for these texts—Vacher de Lapouge, Ammon, Galton, and Gobineau—are adapted to a peculiar "eugenic" need that is presented as being entirely derived from Plato.

109. H. K. F. Günther, *Platon als Hüter der Verfassung des Lebens*, pp. 3–29.

110. Günther, *Platon als Hüter des Lebens*, p. 70 (italics added).

111. Ibid., p. 88.

112. Ibid., pp. 40ff.

113. Ibid., p. 56.

114. See Ludwig F. Clauss, *Rasse und Seele, eine Introduction in den Sinn der leiblichen Gestalt* (Munich: Lehmanns Fachbuchhandlung Verlag, 1933).

115. Ibid., pp. 55ff. [All quotations from Clauss are translated from the Italian.]

116. Ibid., pp. 70–80.

117. The fifth chapter is called "Der Erlösungsmensch. Die Vorderasiatische Rasse"; see Clauss, *Rasse und Seele*, pp. 146–171.

118. Ibid., pp. 160ff.

119. Ibid., p. 170.

120. Ibid., pp. 171 and 180. The Jewish aspiration for spirit never sets its sights on high. The reason is "because in this type, the spirit is not something that flows freely from the inside outwards, so as to conceive the world as something to be adapted and bent to their law," as befits the Nordic type. For the Middle Eastern type, the spirit comes from the outside, and must follow a schema predetermined from on high. This is also what their religion commands. If "in the beginning was the Word," and the word is the letter, then the letter is something immovable and unchangeable: "Man's duty is therefore to ingest the book, to be penetrated by its commandments to the point that they permeate, immobilize, and congeal everything internal." The Jew is the doctor of the Law, the executor of dogma. The

Spirit understood as dogma, then, is nothing but life petrified, immobilized, and "frozen." A dead word. In short, a spirit hostile to life.

121. Günther, *Humanitas*, pp. 10ff. [All citations from this work are translated from the Italian.]

122. Ibid., p. 24.

123. On p. 22 of the same work, see "When the idea of *humanitas* was united, in Rome, with the Stoic conception of the world, what came out of it was the ideal of the inflexible sage who remained celibate in order to preserve his seriousness and severity, an ideal that in the Middle Ages and in the modern age contributed to the extinction of many vital and valorous hereditary energies."

124. Ibid., p. 30.

125. Ibid., p. 30.

126. Ibid., p. 30.

127. See p. 18 of the same work. But even if the bodies are simply copies of the larger natural world, inside of which life degrades from its maximum power to total powerlessness, as the theorists of biologistic racism put forward, the objective does not change.

128. See Adriana Cavarero, *Horrorism: Naming Contemporary Violence* (New York: Columbia University Press, 2008, orig. pub. 2006).

129. The role that Jacques Derrida accords compassion toward the suffering of animals is more complex; see Jacques Derrida, *The Animal That Therefore I Am*, trans. David Wills (New York: Fordham University Press, 2008, orig. pub. 2006). Equally complex is the idea put forward by Bonnie Honig, *Antigone, Interrupted* (Cambridge: Cambridge University Press, 2013).

CHAPTER 5: THE LEGEND OF THE GRAND INQUISITOR REINTERPRETED FROM BELOW

1. Fyodor Dostoevsky, *The Brothers Karamazov* (1878–1880), trans. Richard Pevear and Larissa Voloknonsky (New York: Farrar, Straus and Giroux, 2002), pp. 248, 250.

2. The legend of the Grand Inquisitor has been interpreted by plenty of readers as a prophecy of the disasters to come in the twentieth century. For all these points, see Peter Sloterdijk, *Critique of Cynical Reason* (1983), trans. Michael Eldred (Minneapolis: University of Minnesota Press, 1987), especially part two, chapter 7, "The Grand Inquisitor, or: The Christian Statesman as Jesus Hunter and the Birth of the Institutional Doctrine out of the Spirit of Cynicism."

3. Dostoevsky, *The Brothers Karamazov*, p. 257.

4. Ibid., p. 257.

5. Ibid., pp. 253, 251.

6. Among the most well-known interpretations along these lines is Paul Evdokimov, *Dostoïevsky et le Problème du mal* (Lyon: Éditions du Livre Français, 1942),

who believes that, as a discursive strategy, the theodicy of the Grand Inquisitor is in reality a satanodicy.

7. Dostoevsky, *Demons*, p. 255.

8. Ibid., p. 259.

9. Ibid., pp. 259, 252.

10. Ibid., pp. 251–260.

11. Ibid., pp. 259, 251.

12. Ibid., pp. 252, 254.

13. Ibid., p. 258.

14. On this, in particular, and on the political use of the "sad passions" in general, see the timeless pages of Remo Bodei, *Geometria delle passioni. Paura, speranza, felicità: Filosofia e uso politico* (Milan: Feltrinelli, 1991), pp. 82ff.

15. Raul Hilberg, *The Destruction of the European Jews* (London: W. H. Allen, 1961).

16. The bibliography on this topic, as we know, is immense. For our purposes, we cannot fail to mention at least the works of Christopher R. Browning, *Ordinary Men: Reserve Police Battalion 101 and the Final Solution in Poland* (New York: HarperCollins, 1998, orig. pub. 1992); and Saul Friedländer, *Nazi Germany and the Jews*, 2 vols. (New York: HarperCollins, 1998/2007). For a systematic approach that makes the point about this paradigm shift by listing the various types of "normal perpetrators," see Michael Mann, *The Dark Side of Democracy: Explaining Ethnic Cleansing* (Cambridge: Cambridge University Press, 2009).

17. See Theodor W. Adorno, Else Frenkel-Brunswik, Daniel Levinson, and Nevitt Sanford, *The Authoritarian Personality* (New York: Norton, 1993, orig. pub. 1950).

18. On August 14, 1971, the experiment began in the Stanford prison that would make the name of its designer, Philip Zimbardo, world-famous. From among the many volunteers who came forward, twenty-four students were selected for the experiment, all of whom were declared to be socially well integrated, with normal intelligence, and a "completely normal personality." They were divided and assigned randomly to the role of guards or inmates and locked up in a fake prison in the basement of the Stanford University Department of Psychology. The guards, who took turns covering the three daily shifts, had the task of controlling the inmates' lives to the greatest possible extent. Although physical violence was prohibited, in less than a week—the study was planned to run two weeks—the rate of brutality, humiliation, and oppression grew to the point that the experiment had to be discontinued. The observation that disturbed Zimbardo and the other researchers on that occasion was the ease with which their starting hypothesis was confirmed: in other words, the speed with which "aberrant and antisocial" behavior was produced under prison conditions (or in "total situations") in such a way that sadistic behavior could be induced in individuals who had no original propensity to sadism. Zimbardo, submerged in a sea of controversy and feelings of guilt,

would not give a detailed summary of the conclusions generated by the experiment until thirty years later. Philip G. Zimbardo, Craig Haney, and Curtis Banks, "Interpersonal Dynamics in a Simulated Prison," *International Journal of Criminology and Penology*, 1, 1973: 69–97; Philip G. Zimbardo, *Quiet Rage: The Stanford Prison Study Video* (Stanford: Stanford University Press, 1989); Craig Haney and Philip G. Zimbardo, "The Past and the Future of U.S. Prison Policy: Twenty-five Years After the Stanford Prison Experiment," *American Psychologist*, 53, 1998: 709–727; Philip G. Zimbardo, Christine Maslach, and Craig Haney, "Reflections on the Stanford Prison Experiment: Genesis, Transformations, Consequences," in Thomas Blass (ed.), *Obedience to Authority: Current Perspectives on the Milgram Paradigm* (London: Erlbaum, 2000), pp. 193–238; and the most recent, highly popular book by Philip G. Zimbardo, *The Lucifer Effect: Understanding How Good People Turn Evil* (New York: Random House, 2007), in which the researcher analyzes the Abu Ghraib incident through the lens of the conclusions he refined on the basis of the 1971 experiment.

In 1974, the first results of the other great laboratory experiment designed to investigate "blind obedience to authority," carried out by Stanley Milgram, were published. In this case as well, volunteers were recruited who were absolutely normal and unaware of the experiment's purpose. The scene it set up became unforgettable: people sat in front of fake devices and were instructed by "fake instructors," invested by a "fake scientific authority," to inflict a series of fake electrical shocks on a pretend victim, whose role was portrayed by an actor. This victim responded to the electric shocks with an expertly modulated series of "vocal feedback": grunts and groans with increasing intensity, to cries of pain and calls for help until falling into silence. Two-thirds of the subjects were so obedient to the scientific authority, which advocated for continuing the experiment, that they ended up administering the maximum voltage. The motivations that Milgram put forward to explain to himself and to the scientific community such a high degree of obedience were articulately argued, but we can sum them up with the thesis that deference to authority is the result of social learning—more specifically, a behavioral tendency to comply with the instructions of those who are in a higher hierarchical position. See Stanley Milgram, *Obedience to Authority: An Experimental View* (New York: HarperCollins, 1974).

19. Hannah Arendt, *Eichmann in Jerusalem: A Report on the Banality of Evil* (New York: Penguin Classics, 2006, orig. pub. 1963).

20. On this topic, see the recent essay by Richard J. Bernstein, "Are Arendt's Reflections on Evil Still Relevant?" in Seyla Benhabib (ed.), *Politics in Dark Times: Encounters with Hannah Arendt* (Cambridge: Cambridge University Press, 2010), pp. 293–304. Also relevant are the articles in the same book by Susan Neiman, "Banality Reconsidered," pp. 305–315; and Seyla Benhabib, "International Law and Human Plurality in the Shadow of Totalitarianism: Hannah Arendt and Raphael Lemkin," pp. 219–246. Finally, see the interesting article by Judith Butler,

"Hannah Arendt's Challenge to Adolf Eichmann," in *The Guardian*, August 29, 2011, which, in my opinion, gives undue emphasis to Arendt's defense of Kant, however.

21. On the Lacanian and Deleuzian interpretation of Sade in regard to the relation between evil and power, see the section "Beyond Morality and Beyond Pleasure: In the Footsteps of Nietzsche and Freud" in Chapter Two of this book.

22. See Michel Onfray, *Le Songe d'Eichmann* (Paris: Galilee, 2008).

23. Ibid., p. 126. On the voice of conscience and how it has served as an excuse, similar observations can be found in her diaries of the early 1950s; see Hannah Arendt, *Quaderni e diari 1950–1973* (Vicenza: Neri Pozza, 2007, orig. pub. 2002), notebook 8, January 1952, p. 165.

24. Hannah Arendt, "Some Questions of Moral Philosophy," in *Responsibility and Judgment*, ed. Jerome Kohn (New York: Schocken Books, 2003), pp. 49–146. The essay, edited by Jerome Kohn, brings together the manuscripts of the four lectures given in 1965 at the New School for the course entitled "Some Questions of Moral Philosophy," and the lecture notes for the seventeen sessions of the 1966 Chicago course called "Basic Moral Propositions," which differ from the lectures only on a few points. These variations are reported by the editor in the endnotes.

25. Arendt, "Some Questions of Moral Philosophy," pp. 53–54.

26. Arendt, "Personal Responsibility Under Dictatorship (1964)," in *Responsibility and Judgment*, pp. 17–48, quotation on p. 24.

27. Arendt always fluctuated between a valuation in line with the German philosophical tradition, from Kant to Heidegger, according to which biological life is the animal substrate devoid of meaning, and the consideration that the driving force of singularization is already enclosed within the bodily individualization of each person, the instant we come into the world. On this topic see also M. Vatter, "Natality and Biopolitics in Hannah Arendt," *Revista de Ciencia Política*, 26(2), 2006: 137–160; Peg Birmingham, *Hannah Arendt and Human Rights: The Predicament of Common Responsibility* (Bloomington: Indiana University Press, 2006). The feminist perspective on this topic is important. See for example Bonnie Honig (ed.), *Feminist Interpretations of Hannah Arendt* (University Park: Pennsylvania State University Press, 1995); Mary Dietz, *Turning Operations: Feminism, Arendt, Politics* (New York: Routledge, 2002); and Linda Zerilli, *Feminism and the Abyss of Freedom* (Chicago: University of Chicago Press, 2005).

28. Immanuel Kant, *Critique of Pure Reason*, trans. and ed. Paul Guyer and Allen W. Wood (Cambridge: Cambridge University Press, 1998, orig. pub. 1781), p. 684.

29. Immanuel Kant, *Lectures on Ethics (1775–1781)* (Cambridge: Cambridge University Press, 1997), 27: 283, p. 76.

30. Arendt, "Some Questions of Moral Philosophy," pp. 107ff.

31. Ibid., pp. 277–278, note 9 to p. 72.

32. Arendt, "Personal Responsibility Under Dictatorship," p. 48.

33. Arendt, "Some Questions of Moral Philosophy," pp. 120–121.

34. On this see also Hannah Arendt, *The Life of the Mind* (New York: Harcourt, 1978), especially pp. 129ff.

35. Arendt, "Some Questions of Moral Philosophy," p. 66.

36. Ibid., p. 107.

37. This does not mean, Arendt explains, that the Christian religion has failed to produce authentic examples of the ethical life. "Men" like Jesus of Nazareth and St. Francis, who pursued "good" in a thoroughly "creative" way, certainly not in a docile or passive manner, are a demonstration of this. Totally uninterested in power over others, their goodness flowed out from an excess of energy, from a generous self-denial, from a sort of Nietzschean "virtue that gives." Already in *The Human Condition*, the figure of Jesus is contrasted with Christian doctrine.

38. See Hannah Arendt, *Lectures on Kant's Political Philosophy*, ed. Ronald Beiner (Chicago and London: University of Chicago Press, 1992, orig. pub. 1982).

39. I have discussed the question of judgment in Hannah Arendt at length in another book, along with the role that it plays in the imagination, in common sense, and in the "enlarged mentality." Interested readers are referred to Simona Forti, *Hannah Arendt tra filosofia e politica* (Milan: Bruno Mondadori, 2006), pp. 350ff.

40. Arendt, *The Life of the Mind*, pp. 190, 192.

41. Arendt, "Some Questions of Moral Philosophy," p. 122.

42. Ibid., p. 122.

43. Ibid., pp. 95ff.

44. "To ask someone who lacks a capacity to think to acknowledge their guilt is utterly nonsensical": Hannah Arendt, *Denktagebuch. 1950–1973* (Munich: Piper, 2002). [Translated from the Italian edition *Quaderni e diari 1950–1973*, XX, p. 842.]

45. Arendt, "Some Questions of Moral Philosophy," pp. 100–101.

46. For example, as in many interpretations in the wake of that by Jean-François Lyotard in his *Lectures d'enfance* (Paris: Galilée, 1991).

47. H. Arendt, *Quaderni e diari 1950–1973*, pp. 842–844.

48. See the earlier section "In the name of life: Arendt and Foucault," in Chapter Four.

49. It would be interesting to juxtapose the perspective that opens up from Arendt's thought with Deleuze's search for "a new image of thought." Indeed, Deleuze attempts to conceive of being as difference, in the face of a tradition that has constantly assumed that "difference is evil." This is where the controversy arose regarding the fact that the model of traditional thought is founded on conformity and conformism. For this reason thought should not be complacent, but rather creative and critical. From the viewpoint of this new image of thought, evil will no longer be error, but senselessness, or the inability to pose problems. See Gilles Deleuze, *Difference and Repetition*, trans. Paul Patton (London: Continuum, 2004, orig. pub. 1968), pp. 164ff.

CHAPTER 6: A DIFFERENT GENEALOGY

1. On this topic, see Hannah Arendt, *Lectures on Kant's Political Philosophy*, ed. Ronald Beiner (Chicago and London: University of Chicago Press, 1992, orig. pub. 1982).

2. "Introduction *into* Politics" is the English translation of a collection of articles from her papers edited by Ursula Ludz and published with the title *Was ist Politik? Fragmente aus dem Nachlaß* (Munich and Zurich: Piper, 1993). It contains a series of fragments written by Arendt that were meant to be fleshed out into a book for the German publisher Piper, which never saw the light. It appears in Hannah Arendt, *The Promise of Politics*, ed. Jerome Kohn (New York: Schocken Books, 2005), pp. 93–200.

3. Paul Ricoeur, *The Symbolism of Evil*, trans. Emerson Buchanan (Boston: Beacon Press, 1969), pp. 257–259.

4. See Hannah Arendt, *Denktagebuch 1950–1973*, July 1955 (Munich: Piper Verlag, 2002); Italian translation *Quaderni e Diari 1950–1973* (Vicenza: Neri Pozza, 2007), pp. 455–456.

5. Augustine, *City of God*, book 13, chapter 14 (New York: Bantam Doubleday Dell, 1958), pp. 278–279.

6. On the problem of disobedience as the original human action, see G. Briguglia, "Si stetissent primi parentes. Elementi di un modello politico tra filosofia ed esegesi," *Archives d'histoire doctrinale et littéraire du Moyen-Âge*, 73, 2006: 43–62; and the thoughtful essay by E. Coccia, "'Inobedientia'. Il peccato di Adamo e l'antropologia giudaico-cristiana," *Filosofia politica*, 22(1), 2008: 21–36.

7. Augustine, *City of God*, book 14, chapter 1, p. 295 (italics added).

8. Thomas Aquinas, *Quaestio disputed de malo* (QQ. 4–5).

9. See E. Coccia, "'Inobedientia'. Il peccato di Adamo e l'antropologia giudaico-cristiana."

10. Clearly, from a historiographical perspective, this assertion needs to be more nuanced. In the history of political thought, for example, the right of resistance to tyrannical power would seem at first sight to refute this series of equations. However, as much as disobedience became a form of behavior that was, if not quite virtuous, at least encouraged, the fact remains that it was allowed because it responded to a primary obedience to the law that the tyrant had transgressed. So the equation between transgression and evil remains, even if in this case the transgression is perpetrated by a prince or a sovereign who makes himself into a tyrant.

11. Augustine, *City of God*, Philipp Schaff edition, part 2, book 19, chapter 16, p. 411.

12. Briguglia, "Si stetissent primi parentes."

13. Augustine, *City of God*, p. 411. The passages from Genesis that Augustine is referring to are Genesis 1:21–31, especially 26: "And God said, Let us make man in our image, after our likeness: and let them have dominion over the fish of the sea,

and over the fowl of the air, and over the cattle, and over all the earth, and over every creeping thing that creepeth upon the earth" (King James version).

14. As regards the relationship between evil and Divine omnipotence, see the useful summary by James A. Keller, *Problems of Evil and the Power of God* (Aldershot: Ashgate, 2007).

15. See Peter Sloterdijk, *Über die Verbesserung der Guten Nachricht. Nietzsche fünftes Evangelium* (Frankfurt am Main: Suhrkamp Verlag, 2001).

16. Friedrich Nietzsche, *Frammenti postumi*, 1887–1888, ed. Sossio Giametta (Milan: Adelphi, 1971), 5 (265); English version: *The Will to Power*, trans. Walter Kaufmann and R. J. Hollingdale (New York: Random House, 1967), p. 166.

17. Nietzsche, *Will to Power*, pp. 129–130.

18. See Gilles Deleuze, *Nietzsche and Philosophy*, trans. Michael Hardt (New York: Columbia University Press, 2006, orig. pub. 1962); Michel Foucault, "Nietzsche, Genealogy, History (1971)," in Donald F. Bouchard (ed.), *Language, Counter-Memory, Practice: Selected Essays and Interviews*, trans. Donald F. Bouchard and Sherry Simon (Ithaca: Cornell University Press, 1977), pp. 139–164.

19. Nietzsche, *Will to Power*, pp. 465, 462.

20. See *Will to Power*, p. 120, where we read: "Democracy is Christianity made natural: a kind of 'return to nature' after on account of its extreme antinaturalness it could be overcome by the opposite values. Consequence: the aristocratic ideal henceforth loses its naturalness." See also pp. 145–146.

21. Nietzsche, "Thus Spake Zarathustra" (1883–1885), trans. Walter Kaufmann, in *The Portable Nietzsche* (New York: Viking Press, 1954), pp. 103–439. These quotes, pp. 129 and 281.

22. Nietzsche, *The Free Spirit*, p. 244; and *Beyond Good and Evil*, p. 306, in *Basic Writings*, trans. Walter Kaufmann (New York: Modern Library, Random House, 2000).

23. For an exhaustive comparison between Nietzsche and Tocqueville, see the book by B. Krulic, *Nietzsche penseur de la hiérarchie. Pour une lecture "tocquevillienne" de Nietzsche* (Paris: L'Harmattan, 2002).

24. Some of the most explicit passages, like this one, can be found in Nietzsche, *Beyond Good and Evil*, in *Basic Writings*, pp. 366–367.

25. Ibid., p. 367. With regard to Nietzsche's legacy in strictly political thought, see the monumental, exhaustive collection of essays edited by H. V. Siemens and V. Roodt, *Nietzsche, Power and Politics: Rethinking Nietzsche's Legacy for Political Thought* (Berlin and New York: Walter de Gruyter, 2008).

26. See Nietzsche's inaugural lecture given in Basel in 1869, "Homer and Classical Philology," trans. J. M. Kennedy, in vol. 6 of *The Complete Works of Friedrich Nietzsche*, ed. Oscar Levy (Edinburgh and London: T. N. Foulis, 1909), pp. 145–170. But see also "Homer's Contest" by Nietzsche in vol. 2 of *The Complete Works of Friedrich Nietzsche* (Edinburgh and London: T. N. Foulis, 1911). On the persistence of this agonistic paradigm, which Nietzsche carries through to his last

works, together with the leonine image and the image of the young boy, see the excellent article by Rossella Fabbrichesi, "Agone nietzscheano," in her *Ermeneutica e grecità* (Pisa: ETS, 2009), pp. 49–90.

27. Friedrich Nietzsche, *On the Genealogy of Morals* (1887), trans. Walter Kaufmann, in *Basic Writings* (New York: Modern Library, Random House, 2000), pp. 439–599. These quotes, pp. 476 and 472.

28. Ibid., p. 475. On the ethical meaning of *agon* see A. K. Jensen, "Anti-Politicality and Agon in Nietzsche's Philology," in H. V. Siemens and V. Roodt (eds.), *Nietzsche, Power and Politics*, pp. 319–347; see also S. Novello, *Albert Camus as Political Thinker: Nihilisms and the Politics of Contempt* (New York: Palgrave Macmillan, 2010), especially pp. 109ff.

29. Nietzsche, *Genealogy of Morals*, p. 477. This is the famous passage mentioning the "blond beast" that has provided fodder for many uses and abuses of interpretation.

30. This meaning of good remains unchanged in Nietzsche's writings until the end. See Friedrich Nietzsche, "The Anti-Christ," in *Twilight of the Idols and the Anti-Christ* (London: Penguin Books, 1968), pp. 123–199.

31. Nietzsche, *Genealogy of Morals*, p. 475.

32. The journey of the antipolitical goes through various stages, culminating in the "democratic age," when the herds have internalized the relationship of obedience to such an extent that they believe themselves incapable of doing without a herdsman. In a less astonishing, speculative key compared to *On the Genealogy of Morals*, but in some ways more systematically, in fragments composed between 1887 and 1888, Nietzsche traces out an evolutionary framework for this "dialectic of impotence" by which the passive forces gain political power. In this connection we read: "Datum: the oppressed, the lowly, the great masses of slaves and semi-slaves *desire power*. First step: they make themselves free—they ransom themselves, in imagination at first, they recognize one another, they prevail. Second step: they enter in to battle, they demand recognition, equal rights, 'justice'. Third step: they demand privileges (—they draw the representatives of power over to their side). Fourth step: they demand exclusive power, and they get it—In Christianity, three elements must be distinguished: (a) the oppressed of all kinds, (b) the mediocre of all kinds, (c) the discontented and sick of all kinds. With the first element Christianity fights against the political nobility and its ideal; with the second element, against the exceptional and the privileged (spiritually, physically—) of all kinds; with the third element, against the natural instinct of the healthy and happy. When a victory is won, the second element steps into the foreground; for then Christianity has persuaded the healthy and happy to its side (as warriors in its cause), likewise the powerful (as interested parties on account of the conquest of the mob)—and now it is the herd instinct, the mediocre nature which is of value from any point of view, which gets its supreme sanction through Christianity. This mediocre nature at last grows so conscious of itself (—acquires courage for itself—) that it arrogates even *political* power to itself" (Nietzsche, *Will to Power*, p. 126).

33. Nietzsche, *Genealogy of Morals*, primarily in §16, pp. 488ff.

34. See the sections dedicated to Nietzsche in the second chapter of this book.

35. Nietzsche, *Genealogy of Morals*, p. 522.

36. Nietzsche, *Zarathustra*, p. 597.

37. Ibid., p. 564.

38. Ibid., pp. 576 and 468.

39. Nietzsche, *Will to Power*, p. 160.

40. All this is set out with great lucidity and concision in Nietzsche's *Will to Power*, pp. 123–124.

41. Nietzsche, *Genealogy of Morals*, pp. 468–469.

42. Ibid., p. 469, some italics added.

43. Ibid., p. 553.

44. Nietzsche, *Will to Power*, pp. 160–162.

45. Nietzsche, *Beyond Good and Evil*, p. 403.

46. Starting with the *Gay Science*, for example, Nietzsche never tires of repeating the dissatisfaction and discomfort expressed in aphorism 377 of this work. The title is unequivocal, "We Who Are Homeless," and there is nothing ambiguous about its content: "Among Europeans today there is no lack of those who are entitled to call themselves homeless in a distinctive and honorable sense[. . . .] We children of the future, how could we be at home in this today? [. . .] We 'conserve' nothing; neither do we want to return to any past periods; we are not by any means 'liberal'; we do not work for 'progress'[. . . .] We are no humanitarians; we should never dare to permit ourselves to speak of our 'love of humanity'; our kind is not actor enough for that. Or not Saint-Simonist enough, not French enough[. . . .] But on the other hand we are not nearly 'German' enough [. . .] to advocate nationalism and race hatred and to be able to take pleasure in the national scabies of the heart and blood poisoning that now leads the nations of Europe to delimit and barricade themselves against each other as if it were a matter of quarantine[. . . .] We who are homeless are too manifold and mixed racially and in our descent, being 'modern men', and consequently do not feel tempted to participate in the mendacious racial self-admiration and racial indecency that parades in Germany today[. . . .] We are, in one word— and let this be our word of honor—good Europeans." *Gay Science*, trans. Walter Kaufmann (New York: Vintage Books, Random House, 1974, orig. pub. 1882), pp. 339–340.

47. On Nietzsche and Darwinism, see J. Richardson, *Nietzsche's New Darwinism* (Oxford: Oxford University Press, 2004). In general, on Nietzsche's stances with respect to the life sciences, see B. Stiegler, *Nietzsche et la biologie* (Paris: Puf, 2001); G. Moore, *Nietzsche, Biology and Metaphor* (Cambridge: Cambridge University Press, 2002); and V. Lemm, *Nietzsche's Animal Philosophy: Culture, Politics, and the Animality of the Human Being* (New York: Fordham University Press, 2009).

48. Nietzsche, *Will to Power*, p. 344. See also the edition of his posthumous

notes *Frammenti postumi*, 1885–1887, ed. Sossio Giametta (Milan: Adelphi, 1975), pp. 77–78.

49. Nietzsche, *Will to Power*, p. 346.

50. Ibid., p. 384. See also p. 256.

51. Ibid., p. 153.

52. Nietzsche, *Genealogy of Morals*, pp. 556ff.

53. Nietzsche, *Beyond Good and Evil*, p. 394.

54. Deleuze, *Nietzsche and Philosophy*, p. 120.

55. Nietzsche, *Will to Power*, p. 460.

56. Ibid., pp. 191–192.

57. Ibid., p. 479.

58. Ibid., p. 470.

59. Ibid., p. 492, which reads: "Domination of the passions, not their weakening or extirpation!—The greater the dominating power of a will, the more freedom may the passions be allowed."

60. Friedrich Nietzsche, "Ecce Homo" (1888), trans. Walter Kaufmann, in *Basic Writings* (New York: Modern Library, Random House), pp. 657–800. This quote, p. 679.

61. Nietzsche, *Will to Power*, p. 193.

62. Ibid., p. 384.

63. Giorgio Colli, Introductory note to Friedrich Nietzsche, *Ecce Homo. Come si diventa ciò che si è* (1888) (Milan: Adelphi, 1981), pp. x–xv; translated from the Italian.

CHAPTER 7: STRATEGIES OF OBEDIENCE AND THE ETHOS OF FREEDOM

1. Michel Foucault, "Le retour de la morale," interview with Gilles Barbedette and André Scala, May 29, 1984, and published in *Les Nouvelles littéraires*, June 28 and July 5, 1984, 2937: 36–41; English version in *Politics, Philosophy, Culture: Interviews and Other Writings, 1977–1984*, ed. Lawrence D. Kritzman, trans. Thomas Levin and Isabelle Lorenz (New York: Routledge, 1988), pp. 242–254.

2. Foucault, "The Return of Morality," pp. 250–251. Also highly significant in this regard is the text of another interview, given to Rux Martin on October 25, 1982, when Foucault was holding seminars in the United States at the University of Vermont. In the transcription we read: "Nietzsche was a revelation to me. I felt that there was someone quite different from what I had been taught. I read him with a great passion and broke with my life, left my job in the asylum, left France: I had the feeling I had been trapped. Through Nietzsche, I had become a stranger to all that." In *Technologies of the Self: A Seminar with Michel Foucault*, ed. Luther H. Martin, Huck Gutman, and Patrick H. Hutton (Amherst: University of Massachusetts Press, 1988), pp. 9–15. This quote is on p. 13.

3. The reference is to the well-known essay by Jürgen Habermas, "The Entry

into Postmodernity: Nietzsche as a Turning Point [*Drehscheibe*, 'turntable'']," in *The Philosophical Discourse of Modernity: Twelve Lectures*, trans. Frederick G. Lawrence (Cambridge: MIT Press, 1998, orig. pub. 1985), pp. 83–105. Some of the most well-known critiques on these lines are José Guilherme Merquior's *Foucault* (Berkeley and Los Angeles: University of California Press, 1985); and Luc Ferry and Alain Renaut, *French Philosophy of the Sixties: An Essay on Antihumanism*, trans. Mary H. S. Cattani (Amherst: University of Massachusetts Press, 1990, orig. pub. 1985). According to these theories, which make a much less cogent case than Habermas's essay, Foucault is little more than an anarchic, anti-logocentric, and consequently irrationalist repeater of Nietzsche. On the relationship between Nietzsche and Foucault, but taking a completely different direction, see A. Kremer-Marietti, *Michel Foucault: Archéologie et généalogie* (Paris: Librairie générale française, 1985); D. Janicaud, "Rationalité, puissance et pouvoir," in his *Foucault Philosophe* (Paris: Seuil, 1989), according to which Foucault reduced Nietzsche's concept of *Macht* (force, power, potency) to the sole idea of power; John Rajchman, *Michel Foucault: The Freedom of Philosophy* (New York: Columbia University Press, 1985); Jon Simons, *Foucault and the Political* (London: Routledge, 1995); Hubert Dreyfus and Paul Rabinow, *Beyond Structuralism and Hermeneutics* (Chicago: University of Chicago Press, 1983). See also Michael Mahon, *Foucault's Nietzschean Genealogy: Truth, Power, and the Subject* (Albany: State University of New York Press, 1992). And, of course, Gilles Deleuze, *Foucault* (London: Continuum, 1999, orig. pub. 1986).

4. See Michel Foucault, "'Nietzsche, Freud, Marx' (1964)," English trans. in *Aesthetics, Method, and Epistemology*, James D. Faubion (ed.), *Essential Works of Foucault, 1954–1984*, vol. 2, trans. Robert Hurley and others (New York: New Press, 1998), pp. 269–278. For many critics, Foucault's 1971 essay on Nietzsche is seen as the sign of his turning point, the transition from his "archeological" phase to his "genealogical" one. As we know, Foucault, along with Deleuze, was the editor of the French edition of Nietzsche's works for the publisher Gallimard.

5. On Foucault's critique of the legal theory of sovereignty, see for example *The Will to Knowledge: The History of Sexuality, Volume 1*, trans. Robert Hurley (New York: Random House, 1978, orig. pub. 1976), in particular pp. 115–132; "*Society Must Be Defended*" (1975–1976), trans. David Macey (New York: Picador, 2003), especially pp. 23–64.

6. Michel Foucault, "The Ethic of Care for the Self as a Practice of Freedom" (interview with Helmut Becker, Raúl Fornet Betancourt, and Alfredo Gomez Müller, January 20, 1984), trans. J. D. Gauthier, *Philosophy Social Criticism*, 12, 1987: 112–131.

7. Judith Butler, *The Psychic Life of Power* (Stanford: Stanford University Press, 1997).

8. See the section "In the Name of Life: Arendt and Foucault" in Chapter Four.

9. Foucault, "The Ethic of the Care of Self," p. 129.

10. Michel Foucault, "The Subject and Power," *Critical Inquiry*, 8(4), Summer 1982: 777–795; this quote, p. 790.

11. Foucault, "The Ethic of the Care of Self," p. 123.

12. There are a few clear-cut discontinuities that stand out against the continuous "microphysics" background: the change from the archaeological to the genealogical approach, and from the focus on disciplines of knowledge to the investigation of biopower. Sovereignty, disciplinary power, biopower: the passages that express how subjects, knowledge, and power interact with each other, all marked by specific indicators, are many. The debt Foucault owes to Heidegger's "epocality" is evident in this cross-sectional scanning of the epochs, traversed by an underlying continuity. For a comparison of the philosophy of Heidegger and that of Foucault, see Alan Milchman and Alan Rosenberg (eds.), *Foucault and Heidegger: Critical Encounters* (Minneapolis: University of Minnesota Press, 2003).

13. Michel Foucault, *Security, Territory, Population: Lectures at the Collège de France (1977–1978)*, trans. Graham Burchell (New York: Picador, 2007).

14. Ibid., p. 108. This text can be analyzed from many other perspectives, including the relationship between sovereignty, the society of discipline, and the management of government, or the transition from the concept of people to the idea of population. The reading that I will give these lectures is necessarily reductive and selective.

15. Foucault, *Security, Territory, Population*, pp. 115ff.

16. Ibid., p. 122.

17. Ibid., pp. 126ff., 128.

18. Ibid., p. 173. On this interplay between the economy of salvation and pastoral power from a theological point of view, see Giorgio Agamben, *The Kingdom and the Glory: For a Theological Genealogy of Economy and Government*, trans. Lorenzo Chiesa and Matteo Mandarini (Stanford: Stanford University Press, 2007), p. 201.

19. In reality, some passages in Foucault's work seem to cover the same ground as secularization theories, even if Foucault refuses to present his analysis as if it had been drawn from the "theorem of secularization." See the meticulous account that Philippe Büttgen gives of this in his essay on "Théologie politique et pouvoir pastoral," *Annales HSS*, 62(5), Sept.–Oct. 2007: 1129–1154. For Foucault, in the West, church and state were two separate realities. The crucial junction in the relationship between religion and politics does not lie in the interplay between church and state. For him the heart of the link between the religious tradition and Western politics is to be found precisely in the relationship between the pastorate and the government—especially in the constants that can be found in the function of two figures that, not unsurprisingly, in many European languages have one and the same name: the minister. In particular see Foucault, *Security, Territory, Population*, pp. 192ff.

20. Ibid., p. 148 (italics added).

21. See also a paper that he gave at a conference held at the University of

Tokyo, shortly after the course of 1978 ended. The conference paper appears in English with the title "Sexuality and Power" in Michel Foucault, *Religion and Culture*, ed. Jeremy R. Carrette, trans. Richard A. Lynch (New York: Routledge, 1999), pp. 115–130.

22. Foucault, *Security, Territory, Population*, pp. 230ff.

23. Ibid., pp. 230ff. Foucault is even clearer on this opposition in the speech he gave for the Tanner Lectures on Human Values, later published as "*Omnes et singulatim*: Toward a Criticism of Political Reason," in Sterling M. McMurrin (ed.), *The Tanner Lectures on Human Values* (Salt Lake City: University of Utah Press, 1981).

24. On this concept see also Michel Foucault, "*Omnes et singulatim*," pp. 237ff.

25. Foucault's reference for verifying the accuracy of *apatheia* and *impassibilitas* as identical concepts is Augustine, *City of God*, book 14, chapter 9.

26. Foucault, "*Omnes et singulatim*," p. 239.

27. Foucault, *Security, Territory, Population*, p. 231.

28. Ibid., pp. 231, 234.

29. In the previous chapter we closely examined the passages in Nietzsche that appear to have "guided" Foucault's reading.

30. On this topic see D. Fassin and D. Memmi, "Le gouvernement de la vie, mode d'emplois," in *Le gouvernement des corps*, ed. D. Fassin and D. Memmi (Paris: Éd. de l'Ehess, 2004), pp. 9–33; see also B. Andrieu, "La fin de la biopolitique chez Michel Foucault," *Le Portique* (online, 2004), pp. 13–14.

31. See M. Senellart, "La pratique de la direction de conscience," in F. Gros, C. Lévy (eds.), *Foucault et la philosophie antique* (Paris: Editions Kimé, 2003) (conference proceedings June 21–23, 2003, held at Paris XII), pp. 153–174.

32. Michel Foucault, *The Hermeneutics of the Subject: Lectures at the Collège de France, 1981–1982,* trans. Graham Burchell (New York: Palgrave Macmillan, 2005, orig. pub. 2001).

33. See Frédéric Gros, "Situation du cours," in François Ewald et al. (eds.), *L'hérmeneutique du sujet: Cours au Collège de France, 1981–1982* (Paris: Gallimard-Le Seuil, 2001), pp. 489–526; and also by Frédéric Gros, "La parrhêsia chez Foucault (1982–1984)," in *Foucault. Le courage de la vérité* (Paris: Puf, 2002), pp. 155–166.

34. The transcript of the 1979–80 course was published in the original language in 2012: Michel Foucault, *Du Gouvernement des vivants. Cours au Collège de France (1979–1980)* (Paris: Gallimard-Seuil, 2012). A detailed analysis of the lectures can be found in Jean-Michel Landry's "Confession, Obedience, and Subjectivity: Michel Foucault's Unpublished Lectures *On the Government of the Living*" in *Telos*, 146, Spring 2009: 11–123. In order to understand how Foucault's research during these years focused on the need to comprehend why the power of the government of men requires acts of truth beyond that of obedience, the lectures he gave at the Université Catholique de Louvain in 1981 are important. They have been collected as *Mal faire, dire vrai. Fonction de l'aveau en justice*, ed. Fabienne

Brion and Bernard E. Harcourt (Louvain: Presses Universitaires de Louvain/University of Chicago Press, 2012).

35. Michel Foucault, *Technologies of Self: A Seminar with Michel Foucault*, ed. Luther H. Martin, Huck Gutman, and Patrick H. Hutton (Amherst: University of Massachusetts Press, 1988).

36. Michel Foucault, "The Battle for Chastity," in *Politics, Philosophy, Culture: Interviews and Other Writings, 1977–1984*, ed. Lawrence D. Kritzman, trans. Thomas Levin and Isabelle Lorenz (New York: Routledge, 1988), pp. 227–241.

37. Foucault, *Security, Territory, Population*. The works of Tertullian that are especially important for him are *De Anima*, *De Baptismo*, and *De Poenitentia*. For Tertullian's role in establishing the Christian concept of original sin, Foucault refers to M. Spanneut, *Le stoïcisme des Peres de l'Église. De Clément de Rome à Clément d'Alexandrie* (Paris: Seuil, 1957). With regard to the transition from paganism to Christianity, the essential work for Foucault is by Peter Brown, *The Making of Late Antiquity* (Cambridge: Harvard University Press, 1978). See Frédéric Gros, Carlos Levy (eds.), *Foucault et la philosophie antique* (Paris: Kime, 2003).

38. In addition to the course of 1980, for more on this topic see also the essay by Foucault entitled "Technologies of the Self," in *Technologies of the Self*, pp. 16–49.

39. The notes in Foucault's essay refer to *The Works of John Cassian*, trans. Edgar C. S. Gibson, in *A Select Library of Nicene and Post-Nicene Fathers of the Christian Church, Second Series*, ed. Philip Schaff, vol. II (Buffalo: Christian Literature, 1894).

40. See the lectures "On the Government of the Living" of March 19 and 26, 1980, currently available only in the original French edition (*Du Gouvernement des vivants. Cours au Collège de France [1979–1980]*, Paris: Seuil, 2012). Starting at this point, Foucault began to use a whole series of concepts analyzed by Pierre Hadot in his essay on "Ancient Spiritual Exercises and 'Christian Philosophy' (1981)" available in English in *Philosophy as a Way of Life*, trans. Michael Chase (Oxford: Blackwell, 1995), pp. 126–144.

41. See Johannes Cassianus, *Conlatio abbatis Moysi secunda. De Discretione* [Conference with Abbot Moses. On discretion]; Foucault's interpretation is based largely on this text, extending to the other *Conferences* as well. The English version, edited by Philip Schaff, can be viewed online at http://en.wikisource.org/wiki/Nicene_and_Post-Nicene_Fathers:_Series_II/Volume_XI/John_Cassian (accessed August 5, 2013).

42. On this point see also Foucault, *Technologies of the Self*, pp. 46ff.

43. Foucault, "The Battle for Chastity," p. 240.

44. Cassian, *Conferences of John Cassian*, part 1, conference 2, chapter 10.

45. Michel Foucault, *Technologies of the Self*.

46. In spiritual literature, Foucault reminds us, this practice receives the name of *exagoreusis*: this is the continual "verbalization" or record of one's thoughts that takes place as part of the relationship of total obedience to the master, a relationship based on giving up one's own will and one's own self; see Foucault, "The Battle for Chastity."

47. Foucault, *Security, Territory, Population*, pp. 234ff.

48. The famous passage reads as follows: "But within modern and contemporary philosophy there is another type of question, of critical questioning whose birth we see precisely in the question of *Aufklärung* or in Kant's text on the Revolution. This other critical tradition does not pose the question of the conditions of possibility of a true knowledge; it asks the question: What is present reality? What is the field of possible experiences? Here it is not a question of the analytic of truth but involves what could be called an ontology of the present, of present reality, an ontology of modernity, an ontology of ourselves. It seems to me that the philosophical choice confronting us today is the following. We have to opt either for a critical philosophy of truth in general, or for a critical thought which takes the form of an ontology of ourselves, of present reality. It is this latter form of philosophy which, from Hegel to the Frankfurt School, passing through Nietzsche, Max Weber and so on, has founded a form of reflection to which, of course, I link myself insofar as I can." From *The Government of Self and Others: Lectures at the Collège de France 1982–1983*, trans. Graham Burchell (New York: Palgrave Macmillan, 2010), pp. 20–21. See Michel Foucault, "What Is Enlightenment?" (Qu'est-ce que les Lumières?), in Paul Rabinow (ed.), *The Foucault Reader* (New York: Pantheon Books, 1984, orig. pub. 1983), pp. 32–50.

49. Foucault, "What Is Enlightenment?" p. 42. On this topic, see the important essay by M. Vatter, "El acontecimento de la libertad en Foucault," *Constituciòn y resistencia. Ensayos de teoria democràtica*, ed. Universidad Diego Portales (Santiago, 2011). The essay by Richard J. Bernstein, "Foucault: Critique as Philosophical Ethos," has retained all its power and relevance. Republished in *Critique and Power: Recasting the Foucault/Habermas Debate*, ed. Michael Kelly (Cambridge: MIT Press, 1994), pp. 211–241. On the problem of freedom in Foucault, see also R. E. Flathman, *Freedom and Its Conditions: Discipline, Autonomy and Resistance* (New York: Routledge, 2003); J. Revel, *Expériences de la pensée: Michel Foucault* (Paris: Bordos, 2005); T. May, "Freedom: Foucault's Conception of Freedom," in D. Taylor (ed.), *Michel Foucault: Key Concepts* (Durham: Acumen, 2011).

50. In the lecture on February 17, 1982, as part of the course "The Hermeneutics of the Subject," Foucault criticizes the rhetoric of the "return to the self," to the authenticity of the self, noting almost a sort of impossibility of filling these ethical appeals with any sort of content. However, he continues, precisely the creation of such an ethics is "an urgent, fundamental, and politically indispensable task, if it is true after all that there is no first or final point of resistance to political power other than in the relationship one has to oneself" (p. 252).

51. Frédéric Gros, "À propos de l'herméneutique du sujet," in G. Le Blanc and J. Terrel (eds.), *Foucault au Collège de France. Un itinéraire* (Bordeaux: Presses universitaires de Bordeaux, 2003), pp. 149–163.

52. See the lectures on Plato's *First Alcibiades*, which in the eyes of Foucault was the first great philosophical discussion of "care of the self." As in many other

cases, Plato remains an ambiguous figure: although he lexically opens up a perspective (in this case, the *epimeleia*), at the same time he conceptually leads it back to the perspective that will prevail in the metaphysical tradition (in this case, the *gnothi seauton*). Although influenced by the work of Pierre Hadot, "Ancient Spiritual Exercises and 'Christian Philosophy'" (1981), Foucault had a different vision from that of the French Classicist, who did not see this ambivalence or this bifurcation. For Hadot, in fact, Plato's work remained faithful to a "traditional" conception of the "Know yourself." See also Pierre Hadot, "La figure du Sage dans l'Antiquité Greco-latine," in *Les Sagesses du Monde*, ed. G. Gadoffre (Paris: Editions universitaires, 1991), pp. 9–26.

53. Foucault, *The Hermeneutics of the Subject*, pp. 180ff.

54. Ibid., p. 184.

55. Ibid., p. 185 (italics added).

56. Ibid., p. 480.

57. As for example in Michel Foucault, *The Use of Pleasure: The History of Sexuality II* (New York: Random House, 1985, orig. pub. 1984), p. 8.

58. Michel Foucault, *Fearless Speech* (Los Angeles: Semiotext(e), 2001), transcripts of the six lectures Foucault gave on *parrhesia* in Berkeley in 1983; pp. 19–20.

59. Michel Foucault, *The Government of Self and Others: Lectures at the Collège de France 1982–1983*, trans. Graham Burchell (New York: Palgrave Macmillan, 2010).

60. Michel Foucault, *The Courage of the Truth. (The Government of Self and Others II) Lectures at the Collège de France 1983–1984*, trans. Graham Burchell (New York: Palgrave Macmillan, 2011).

61. Regarding this bifurcation of ethics, see the entire 1984 course, *The Courage of Truth*, pp. 57ff.

62. The reference is to the philosophical proposal of Jean-Luc Nancy, *The Inoperative community* (Minneapolis and Oxford: University of Minnesota Press, 1991, orig. pub. 1986).

CHAPTER 8: *PARRHESIA* PUT TO THE TEST

1. See the lecture of February 22, 1984, in which Foucault speaks about *Plato and Europe* by Jan Patočka, in *The Courage of the Truth. (The Government of Self and Others II) Lectures at the Collège de France 1983–1984*, trans. Graham Burchell (New York: Palgrave Macmillan, 2011), p. 127.

2. Patočka formulates the idea of "asubjective phenomenology" in his *Papiers phenomenologiques*, ed. E. Abrams (Grenoble: Millon, 1995). For this concept in English see *Jan Patočka: Philosophy and Selected Writings*, ed. Erazim Kohák (Chicago and London: University of Chicago Press, 1989), which also contains a complete bibliography of his works in French, German, and English as well as Czech.

3. See Paul Ricoeur, "Jan Patočka et le nihilisme," *Esprit* 166, 1990: 30–37, now in *Lectures 1. Autour du politique* (Paris: Seuil, 1991), pp. 84–91.

4. I am thinking, for example, of the importance that Claude Lefort's interpretation of Aleksandr Solzhenitsyn's *The Gulag Archipelago, 1918–1956: An Experiment in Literary Investigation* (New York: Harper & Row, 1973) had on intellectual debate in France. See his *Un homme en trop. Essai sur "L'archipel du goulag"* (Paris: Seuil, 1976).

5. In this regard, we are fortunate to have the personal observations provided by Jeannette Colombel, "Michel Foucault et la dissidence tchécoslovaque," in Alain Brossat (ed.), *Michel Foucault. Le jeux de la vérité et du pouvoir: Études transeuropéennes* (Nancy: Presses Universitaires de Nancy, 1994), pp. 163–166. In the same collection of essays, see the article by Á. Szakolczai, "Foucault passe à l'Est: Liens et interactions," pp. 101–110.

6. This is the theory that Á. Szakolczai presents in "Foucault passe à l'Est," pp. 105ff.

7. For example Vaclav Belohradsky, *Il mondo della vita: Un problema politico. L'eredità europea nel dissenso e in Charta '77* (Milan: Jaca Book, 1981), pp. 20ff.

8. Michel Foucault, *Security, Territory, Population: Lectures at the Collège de France (1977–1978)*, trans. Graham Burchell (New York: Picador, 2007), p. 200. In the same course, in which he talks about the revolt of subjugated knowledges, Foucault had already used the term "counter-conduct" in place of the overly determined "dissent." In that context, in which he tries to explain what the possible counter-conducts and practices of disobedience are, he clearly refers to the historical experience of the Eastern bloc. In this regard he writes: "In fact, maybe the word 'dissidence' is exactly suited for these forms of resistance that concern, set their sights on, and have as their objective and adversary a power that assumes the task of conducting men in their life and daily existence. The word would be justified for two reasons, both of them historical. The first is that in fact the word 'dissidence' has often been employed to designate religious movements of resistance to pastoral organization. Second, its current application could in fact justify its use since, after all, what we [call] 'dissidence' in the East and the Soviet Union, really does designate a complex form of resistance and refusal, which involves a political refusal, of course, but in a society where political authority, that is, the political party, responsible for defining both the country's characteristic form of economy and structures of sovereignty, is at the same time responsible for conducting individuals in their daily life through a game of generalized obedience that takes the form of terror, since terror is not when some command and strike fear into others. There is terror when those who command tremble with fear themselves, since they know that the general system of obedience envelops them just as much as those over whom they exercise their power. We could speak, moreover, of the pastoralization of power in the Soviet Union. Certainly there is bureaucratization of the Party. There is also pastoralization of the Party, and dissidence, the

political struggles that we put together under the name of dissidence, certainly have an essential, fundamental dimension that is refusal of this form of being conducted[. . . .] The whole pastoral practice of salvation is challenged[. . . .] 'We do not want this pastoral system of obedience. We do not want this truth. We do not want to be held in this system of observation and endless examination that continually judges us, tells us what we are in the core of ourselves, healthy or sick, mad or not mad, and so on'. So we can say [that] this word dissidence really does cover a struggle against those pastoral effects I talked about last week. And it is precisely because the word dissidence is too localized today in this kind of phenomena that it cannot be used without drawback[. . . .] So let's give up this word, and what I will propose to you is the doubtless badly constructed word 'counter-conduct'— the latter having the sole advantage of allowing reference to the active sense of the word 'conduct'[. . . .] And then maybe this word 'counter-conduct'enables us to avoid a certain substantification allowed by the word 'dissidence'" (pp. 267–268).

9. For a reconstruction of the intellectual environment of Patočka's teachings, see A. Laignel-Lavastine, *Esprits d'Europe. Autour de Czeslaw Milosz, Jan Patočka, Istvan Bibo. Essai sur les intellectuels indépendants à la d'Europe central au XXe siècle* (Paris: Gallimard, 2005); and by the same author, *Jan Patočka: L'esprit de la dissidence* (Paris: Michalon, 1998).

10. See Havel's memory regarding Patočka's choice: Václav Havel, *Interrogatorio a distanza: Conversazione con Karel Hvizdala* (Milan: Garzanti, 1990, orig. pub. 1986).

11. "Entretien avec Jan Patočka (1967)," in E. Tassin and M. Richir (eds.), *Jan Patočka: Philosophie, phénoménologie, politique* (Grenoble: Millon, 1992), p. 31. On this topic see Paul Ricœur, "Jan Patočka, le philosophe-résistant" (1977), in *Liberté religieuse et défense des droits de l'homme. Hommage à Jan Patočka* (Paris: Centre d'Études Istina, 1977), pp. 128–131, republished in Paul Ricoeur, *Lectures 1. Autour du politique* (Paris: Seuil, 1991), pp. 69–73. With regard to Patočka's philosophical journey and his distancing from Husserl, see Jan Patočka, *Surcivilisation et son conflict interne*, which dates from the mid-fifties, now in his *Liberté et sacrifice. Écrits politiques* (Grenoble: Millon, 1990), pp. 99–177. On the concept of asubjective philosophy in Patočka, see Paul Ricoeur, "Preface aux *Essais heretiques*" (1981), in Ricoeur's *Lectures 1*, pp. 74–83; R. Barbaras, *Le Mouvement de l'existence: Etudes sur la phenomenologie de Jan Patočka* (Chatou: Éditions de la Transparence, 2007); and R. Barbaras, "Phenomenology and Henology," in I. Chvatik, E. Abrams (eds.), *Jan Patočka and the Heritage of Phenomenology: Mallory Papers* (London and New York: Springer, Dordrecht-Heidelberg, 2011), pp. 99–110; R. Barbaras, *L'ouverture du monde: Lecture de Jan Patočka* (Chatou: Éd. de la Transparence, 2011). Perhaps even more important than his relationship with Heidegger was the philosophical bond he had with Eugen Fink. See Eugen Fink and Jan Patočka, *Briefe und Dokumente. 1933–1977*, (ed.) M. Heinz, B. Nessler (Prague, Freiburg, Munich: Orbis Phaenomenologicus, 1999).

12. Jan Patočka, *Plato and Europe*, trans. Petr Lom (Stanford: Stanford University Press, 2002, orig. pub. 1973).

13. Patočka, *Plato and Europe*, p. 80.

14. See Jan Patočka, *Le monde naturel et le mouvement de l'existence humaine* (Dordrecht: Kluwer, 1989, orig. pub. 1964); however, it already appears in his previous work *Le monde naturel comme problème philosophique* (The Hague: Nijhoff, 1976, orig. pub. 1936).

15. Patočka, *Plato and Europe*, p. 44.

16. Ibid., pp. 35, 36, 47.

17. Ibid., p. 95.

18. Ibid., p. 93.

19. Jan Patočka, *Heretical Essays in the Philosophy of History* (Chicago: Open Court, 1996). On this, see Paul Ricoeur, "Jan Patočka et le nihilisme," *Esprit*, 166, 1990: 30–37; also available in Ricoeur's *Lectures 1.*, pp. 84–91.

20. See especially the essays by Patočka in *Heretical Essays in the Philosophy of History*, "Does History Have a Meaning?" pp. 53–78; and "The Beginning of History," pp. 27–52.

21. Patočka, "Is Technological Civilization Decadent, and Why?" in *Heretical Essays*, pp. 95–118.

22. Patočka, "Does History Have a Meaning?"

23. Patočka, "Wars of the Twentieth Century and the Twentieth Century as War," in *Heretical Essays*, pp. 119–138.

24. See also Patočka's essay, "Is Technological Civilization Decadent, and Why?"

25. Patočka, "Wars of the Twentieth Century," p. 120.

26. Ibid., p. 124.

27. Ibid., p. 125.

28. Ibid., p. 127.

29. Patočka, "Wars of the Twentieth Century," pp. 129ff.

30. Michel Foucault, "Society Must Be Defended." In *Lectures at the Collège de France 1975–76*, trans. David Macey (New York: Picador, 2003).

31. See M. Crepon, "'La guerre continue' (la reprise de Patočka)," in his *Vivre avec. La pensée de la mort et la mémoire des guerres* (Paris: Hermann Éditeurs, 2008), pp. 91–112.

32. In this regard, Patočka turns to the observations of Ernst Jünger, "Der Kampf als inneres Erlebnis" (1922), in his *Sämtliche Werke, Essays*, vol. 7 (Stuttgart: Klett-Cotta, 1980), pp. 11–103.

33. Patočka, "Wars of the Twentieth Century," pp. 130ff.

34. Ibid., pp. 134–135.

35. Jacques Derrida, *The Gift of Death* (Chicago and London: University of Chicago Press, 1995, orig. pub. 1992), which examines the essay by Patočka, "Is Technological Civilization Decadent, and Why?"; quote on p. 28.

36. In this connection see the discussion of the relationship between Patočka

and Derrida in Edward F. Findlay, *Caring for the Soul in a Postmodern Age: Politics and Phenomenology in the Thought of Jan Patočka* (Albany: State University of New York Press, 2002).

37. See especially Patočka's essay "The Beginning of History."

38. See Jan Patočka, *Pé e o duši. Sv. 2. Negativní platonismus*, ed. I. Chvatik and P. Kouba (Prague: Archivni Soubor, 1987). The English translation, from which I cite, is Jan Patočka, "Negative Platonism: Reflections Concerning the Rise, the Scope, and the Demise of Metaphysics and Whether Philosophy Can Survive It," in Erazim Kohák (ed.), *Jan Patočka: Philosophy and Selected Writings* (Chicago: University of Chicago Press, 1989), pp. 175–206.

39. See the important articles on "negative Platonism" by E. Evink and "The Relevance of Patočka's 'Negative Platonism'," in I. Chvatik and E. Abrams (eds.), *Jan Patočka and the Heritage of Phenomenology*, pp. 57–70; T. Ullmann, "Negative Platonism and the Appearance-Problem," in the same book, pp. 71–86. See also Edward F. Findlay, *Caring for the Soul*, and with very similar positions, the later book by P. S. Merlier, *Patočka. Le soin de l'âme et l'Europe* (Paris: L'Harmattan, 2009).

40. Patočka, "Negative Platonism," pp. 180ff.

41. Ibid., p. 198.

42. Jan Patočka, "L'homme spirituel et l'intellectuel"(1975), in *Liberté et sacrifice. Ecrits politiques* (Grenoble: Millon, 1990), pp. 243–257. [This quote translated from the French, p. 247: "L'homme spiritual, au contraire, s'expose precisement au negative; sa vie est une vie a decouvert."] English version: "The Spiritual Person and the Intellectual," in *Living in Problematicity*, ed. Eric Manton, trans. Eric Manton and E. Kohak (Prague: OIKOYMENH, 2005), pp. 51–69.

43. Patočka, "L'homme spirituel et l'intellectuel," p. 246.

44. For this reason, following Derrida, we can say that "care for the soul" in Patočka combines the Platonic meaning of learning to die, the *melete thanatou* of the *Phaedo*, and Heidegger's concept of *Sorge*. In short, the idea of "care for the soul" derives directly from the Platonic dialogs, but it is read through Heidegger's critique of metaphysics. See Patočka, *Heretical Essays*.

45. Ricoeur is right to stress that the Aristotelian concept of the soul as self-motion is grafted into Patočka's conception of the soul. See his "Preface to the French Edition" (1981) of Jan Patočka's *Heretical Essays in the Philosophy of History* (Chicago: Open Court, 1996), pp. vi–xvi.

46. Patočka, *Heretical Essays*, p. 133.

47. The theory that is set out fully in *Heretical Essays* was already formulated in several other writings of his. See especially the essays in *Liberté et sacrifice*, "Équilibre et amplitude dans la vie" (1939), pp. 27–39; "L'homme spirituel et l'intellectuel" (1975), pp. 243–257.

48. See Patočka, "L'homme spirituel et l'intellectuel," pp. 243–257.

49. Perhaps this connection can help us better understand the meaning of

Levinas's philosophy as well, the other great landmark for Western European thinkers.

50. Czeslaw Milosz, a Lithuanian like Emmanuel Levinas, was the winner of the 1980 Nobel Prize for literature. In 1951 he was in Paris as the cultural attaché and decided to seek political asylum. In 1953 the first edition of his masterpiece was published: *La pensée captive. Essai sur les logocraties populaires* (Paris: Gallimard, 1953); English translation: *The Captive Mind* (New York: Vintage, 1990).

51. Czeslaw Milosz, *Une autre Europe* (Paris: Gallimard, 1964).

52. Patočka, "Wars of the Twentieth Century," p. 134.

53. This is Slavoj Žižek's opinion in *Did Somebody Say Totalitarianism? Five Interventions in the (Mis)Use of a Notion* (London: Verso, 2001).

54. Václav Havel, *The Power of the Powerless: Citizens Against the State in Central-Eastern Europe*, ed. John Keane, trans. Paul Wilson (London: Hutchinson, 1985). Appearing in the form of *samizdat* at the end of 1978, it was translated into French and Italian in 1979 and into English in 1985. On the intellectual biography of Havel see, for example, J. Keane, *Václav Havel: A Political Tragedy in Six Acts* (New York: Basic Books, 1999); and J. Picq, *Václav Havel: Force des sans-pouvoir* (Paris: Michalon, 2000).

55. See the remarks by Steven Lukes in his "Introduction" to Václav Havel, *The Power of the Powerless: Citizens Against the State in Central-Eastern Europe*, ed. John Keane (London: Hutchison, 1985), pp. 1–9.

56. Ibid., p. 14.

57. Ibid., p. 25.

58. Czeslaw Milosz, *The Captive Mind* (New York: Vintage, 1990, orig. pub. 1953).

59. Arthur Koestler, *Darkness at Noon* (New York: Scribner, 2006, orig. pub. 1940).

60. In this regard Victor Klemperer's book *The Language of the Third Reich. LTI: Lingua Tertii Imperii* (London and New York: Bloomsbury Academic, 2006, orig. pub. 1947) is illuminating.

61. During a discussion with Herbert Marcuse; see Czeslaw Milosz, *Visions from San Francisco Bay* (New York: McGraw-Hill, 1983).

62. See Miroslav Kusy, "Chartism and 'Real Socialism'," in Václav Havel, *The Power of the Powerless*, pp. 97–114.

63. This is the view of Slavoj Žižek, *Did Somebody Say Totalitarianism?*

64. Havel, *The Power of the Powerless*, pp. 18–19.

65. Ibid., p. 19.

66. Ibid., pp. 44ff.

67. Ibid., p. 47.

68. Ibid., p. 20.

69. Ibid., p. 20.

70. See the discussion that began with Milan Kundera, "Il destino ceco," *listy*

7–8, 1968; Václav Havel, "Le illusioni di Kundera," *Host do domu*, 15, 1968–1969; and Milan Kundera, "Le illusioni di Havel," *Host do domu*, 15, 1968–1969. See M.-O. Thirouin, M. Bayer-Weinmann (eds.), *Désaccords parfaits: La réception paradoxale de l'oeuvre de Milan Kundera* (Grenoble: Ellug, 2009).

71. Kundera's polemical treatment of Havel surfaces, although less explicitly, in many of his works written before and during his stay in France.

72. Kundera, *The Unbearable Lightness of Being* (1984), trans. Michael Henry Heim (New York: HarperCollins, 1999), p. 217.

73. This perspective explains the brilliant attack of the novel made in reference to Nietzsche's 'eternal return', interpreted as what pins us to the guilt of our own pasts. For Kundera, the 'eternal return' refers to the perspective from which things appear, devoid of the attenuating circumstance of their fleetingness. See Milan Kundera, *The Unbearable Lightness of Being*, pp. 222ff.

74. Milan Kundera, *The Book of Laughter and Forgetting* (New York: HarperCollins, 1999, orig. pub. 1978).

75. Ibid., pp. 88ff.

76. See ibid., pp. 232ff.

77. Kundera, *The Unbearable Lightness of Being*, p. 112.

78. Tereza's relationship with her mother in *The Unbearable Lightness of Being* and the relationship between the mother and the son in *Life Is Elsewhere* (trans. Aaron Asher, New York: HarperCollins, 2000, p. 61) are emblematic of this point.

79. These are the arguments that we read in *The Unbearable Lightness of Being*, chapter 7, entitled "Karenin's Smile," pp. 279ff. This quote is on p. 286.

80. Ibid., p. 289.

81. Milan Kundera, *Farewell Waltz*, trans. Aaron Asher (New York: HarperCollins, 1998, orig. pub. 1973).

82. Ibid., pp. 108–109.

83. Ibid., pp. 109–110.

84. Ibid., pp. 255–257.

85. Ibid., p. 256.

86. See all of Kundera's essays in which he criticizes the "position" of the dissident as a bearer of authenticity. Of interest in this regard is his *The Curtain: An Essay in Seven Parts*, trans. Linda Asher (New York: HarperCollins, 2008, orig. pub. 2005), especially the fourth part, entitled "What Is a Novelist?" pp. 85ff.

87. Kundera, *The Unbearable Lightness of Being*, p. 248.

88. Milan Kundera, *The Curtain*, p. 111.

89. Milan Kundera, *The Art of the Novel*, trans. Linda Asher (New York: Grove Press, 1988, orig. pub. 1986). On the particular form of subversion that Kundera's works represent, see F. Ricard, *Le dernier après-midi d'Agnès: Essai sur l'oeuvre de Milan Kundera* (Paris: Gallimard, 2003).

90. Havel, *Power of the Powerless*, p. 23.

91. Ibid., p. 43.

92. For this theory about Havel, see Slavoj Žižek, *Did Somebody Say Totalitarianism?*

93. On p. 55 of *Power of the Powerless* Havel refers explicitly to the interview with Heidegger in *Der Spiegel* of May 13, 1976 ("Nur noch ein Gott kann uns helfen"); translated into English as "Only a God Can Save Us," by Lisa Harries and Joachim Neugroschel, in *Martin Heidegger and National Socialism: Questions and Answers*, ed. Gunther Neske and Emil Kettering (St. Paul: Paragon House, 1990), pp. 41–66.

94. As Havel intends a "life in truth," it must at the same time be a "life in freedom."

CHAPTER 9: POOR DEVILS WHO "WORSHIP" LIFE

1. Primo Levi, *The Drowned and the Saved*, trans. Raymond Rosenthal (New York: Vintage International, 1989).

2. Primo Levi, *If This Is a Man*, trans. Stuart Woolf (New York: Orion Press, 1959, orig. pub. 1947).

3. The names of the two Jewish writers are often brought together, especially in literary criticism; see for example Frances Bartowski, *Travelers, Immigrants, Inmates: Essays in Estrangement* (Minneapolis: University of Minnesota Press, 1995); Ilan Stavans (ed.), *The Oxford Book of Jewish Stories* (New York: Oxford University Press, 1998); Ilan Stavans (ed.), *The Schocken Book of Modern Sephardic Literature* (New York: Schocken Books, 2005). As regards a wider, philosophical perspective, see Sergio Parussa, "The Shame of the Survivor," *Journal of Modern Jewish Studies*, 7(1), 2008: 91–106.

4. Elias Canetti, *Crowds and Power*, trans. Victor Gollancz (New York: Farrar, Straus and Giroux, 1984, orig. pub. 1960). The quote is from Elias Canetti, *The Conscience of Words* (New York: Farrar, Straus and Giroux, 1984, orig. pub. 1972), p. 16.

5. Because, let us recall, if the formation of crowds is put into motion by the desire to overcome fear—fear of contact, hierarchies, and differences—the limit of its own growth is almost always found in power. The return of both hierarchies and differences is therefore inevitable, especially the individual's return to isolation.

6. On this, see especially Canetti, *The Conscience of Words*, pp. 14ff.

7. Ibid., p. 17.

8. On this in particular, Canetti, *Crowds and Power*, pp. 228ff.

9. Canetti, *The Conscience of Words*, p. 20.

10. The same compulsion that for Canetti lies at the heart of the destructiveness of the mass exterminations of his time can also be seen in paranoid delusions, in the infamous delusion of Daniel Paul Schreber, for example, or in the still rudimentary dynamics of tribal chiefs—as if everywhere we look we will find the dynamic that causes a *Führer* to gather around himself crowds of people, who become smaller and more irrelevant the closer they get to him, until the scene is set

in which a great man kills and absorbs everyone else, remaining so alone and powerful that he survives for all eternity.

11. Primo Levi, *The Voice of Memory: Interviews 1961–1987*, trans. Robert Gordon (Cambridge: Polity, 2000), pp. 101, 146. In the interview with Giorgio Segrè, published in the same text, Levi acknowledges his proximity to Arendt's theory on the banality of evil (p. 270).

12. Levi, *The Drowned and the Saved*, pp. 37, 40.

13. Ibid., pp. 40, 42.

14. Ibid., pp. 40, 38.

15. Ibid., pp. 47, 49.

16. Ibid.

17. Ibid., pp. 58–59.

18. Ibid., p. 68.

19. Ibid., p. 86.

20. Ibid., p. 69.

21. Anyone who has read Reiner Schürmann's essential work *Broken Hegemonies*, trans. Reginald Lilly (Bloomington: Indiana University Press, 2003, orig. pub. 1996), will clearly perceive the background I am working from.

22. On this topic, see especially Nikolas Rose, *The Politics of Life Itself: Biomedicine, Power, and Subjectivity in the Twenty-First Century* (Princeton and Oxford: Princeton University Press, 2007); Melinda Cooper, *Life as Surplus: Biotechnology and Capitalism in the Neoliberal Era* (Seattle and London: University of Washington Press, 2008).

23. See Michel Foucault, *The Birth of Biopolitics: Lectures at the Collège de France (1978–1979)*, trans. Graham Burchell (New York: Palgrave Macmillan, 2008).

24. On this, see Pierre Bourdieu, *Masculine Domination* (Stanford: Stanford University Press, 2001, orig. pub. 1998).

25. Michel Foucault, *The Courage of the Truth. (The Government of Self and Others II) Lectures at the Collège de France 1983–1984*, trans. Graham Burchell (New York: Palgrave Macmillan, 2011).

26. See ibid., pp. 231ff.

27. In this regard, Foucault mentions Paul Tillich's *The Courage to Be* (New Haven: Yale University Press, 2000, orig. pub. 1952), which establishes the difference between *Kynismus* and *Zinismus*, a distinction that can be found in many texts on the topic, such as in Peter Sloterdijk, *Critique of Cynical Reason* (Minneapolis: University of Minnesota Press, 1988, orig. pub. 1983).

28. Foucault points out that animality plays an entirely different role in Cynicism from what it traditionally covers in philosophy. The animality of the Cynics is not the corporeality identified with evil in contrast to which the soul assumes its character of good.

29. Foucault, *The Courage of Truth*, p. 336.

Index of Names

Cultural Memory | in the Present

Ban Wang, *Illuminations from the Past: Trauma, Memory, and History in Modern China*

James Phillips, *Heidegger's* Volk: *Between National Socialism and Poetry*

Frank Ankersmit, *Sublime Historical Experience*

István Rév, *Retroactive Justice: Prehistory of Post-Communism*

Paola Marrati, *Genesis and Trace: Derrida Reading Husserl and Heidegger*

Krzysztof Ziarek, *The Force of Art*

Marie-José Mondzain, *Image, Icon, Economy: The Byzantine Origins of the Contemporary Imaginary*

Cecilia Sjöholm, *The Antigone Complex: Ethics and the Invention of Feminine Desire*

Jacques Derrida and Elisabeth Roudinesco, *For What Tomorrow . . . : A Dialogue*

Elisabeth Weber, *Questioning Judaism: Interviews by Elisabeth Weber*

Jacques Derrida and Catherine Malabou, *Counterpath: Traveling with Jacques Derrida*

Martin Seel, *Aesthetics of Appearing*

Nanette Salomon, *Shifting Priorities: Gender and Genre in Seventeenth-Century Dutch Painting*

Jacob Taubes, *The Political Theology of Paul*

Jean-Luc Marion, *The Crossing of the Visible*

Eric Michaud, *The Cult of Art in Nazi Germany*

Anne Freadman, *The Machinery of Talk: Charles Peirce and the Sign Hypothesis*

Stanley Cavell, *Emerson's Transcendental Etudes*

Stuart McLean, *The Event and Its Terrors: Ireland, Famine, Modernity*

Beate Rössler, ed., *Privacies: Philosophical Evaluations*

Bernard Faure, *Double Exposure: Cutting Across Buddhist and Western Discourses*

Alessia Ricciardi, *The Ends of Mourning: Psychoanalysis, Literature, Film*

Alain Badiou, *Saint Paul: The Foundation of Universalism*

Gil Anidjar, *The Jew, the Arab: A History of the Enemy*

Jonathan Culler and Kevin Lamb, eds., *Just Being Difficult? Academic Writing in the Public Arena*

Jean-Luc Nancy, *A Finite Thinking*, edited by Simon Sparks

Theodor W. Adorno, *Can One Live after Auschwitz? A Philosophical Reader*, edited by Rolf Tiedemann

Elissa Marder, *Dead Time: Temporal Disorders in the Wake of Modernity (Baudelaire and Flaubert)*

Reinhart Koselleck, *The Practice of Conceptual History: Timing History, Spacing Concepts*

Niklas Luhmann, *The Reality of the Mass Media*

Hubert Damisch, *A Theory of /Cloud/: Toward a History of Painting*

Jean-Luc Nancy, *The Speculative Remark: (One of Hegel's bon mots)*

Jean-François Lyotard, *Soundproof Room: Malraux's Anti-Aesthetics*

Jan Patočka, *Plato and Europe*

Hubert Damisch, *Skyline: The Narcissistic City*

Isabel Hoving, *In Praise of New Travelers: Reading Caribbean Migrant Women Writers*

Richard Rand, ed., *Futures: Of Jacques Derrida*

William Rasch, *Niklas Luhmann's Modernity: The Paradoxes of Differentiation*

Jacques Derrida and Anne Dufourmantelle, *Of Hospitality*

Jean-François Lyotard, *The Confession of Augustine*

Kaja Silverman, *World Spectators*

Samuel Weber, *Institution and Interpretation: Expanded Edition*

Jeffrey S. Librett, *The Rhetoric of Cultural Dialogue: Jews and Germans in the Epoch of Emancipation*

Ulrich Baer, *Remnants of Song: Trauma and the Experience of Modernity in Charles Baudelaire and Paul Celan*

Samuel C. Wheeler III, *Deconstruction as Analytic Philosophy*

David S. Ferris, *Silent Urns: Romanticism, Hellenism, Modernity*

Rodolphe Gasché, *Of Minimal Things: Studies on the Notion of Relation*

Sarah Winter, *Freud and the Institution of Psychoanalytic Knowledge*

Samuel Weber, *The Legend of Freud: Expanded Edition*

Aris Fioretos, ed., *The Solid Letter: Readings of Friedrich Hölderlin*

J. Hillis Miller / Manuel Asensi, *Black Holes / J. Hillis Miller; or, Boustrophedonic Reading*

Miryam Sas, *Fault Lines: Cultural Memory and Japanese Surrealism*

Peter Schwenger, *Fantasm and Fiction: On Textual Envisioning*

Didier Maleuvre, *Museum Memories: History, Technology, Art*

Jacques Derrida, *Monolingualism of the Other; or, The Prosthesis of Origin*

Andrew Baruch Wachtel, *Making a Nation, Breaking a Nation: Literature and Cultural Politics in Yugoslavia*

Niklas Luhmann, *Love as Passion: The Codification of Intimacy*

Mieke Bal, ed., *The Practice of Cultural Analysis: Exposing Interdisciplinary Interpretation*

Jacques Derrida and Gianni Vattimo, eds., *Religion*